The US vs China

Manchester University Press

Geopolitical Economy

Geopolitical Economy promotes fresh inter- and multi-disciplinary perspectives on the most pressing new realities of the twenty-first century: the multipolar world and the renewed economic centrality of states in it. From a range of disciplines, works in the series account for these new realities historically. They explore the problems and contradictions, domestic and international, of capitalism. They reconstruct the struggles of classes and nations, and state actions in response to them, which have shaped capitalism, and track the growth of the public and de-commodified spheres these dialectical interactions have given rise to. Finally, they map the new terrain on which political forces must now act to orient national and international economies in equitable and ecological, cultural and creative directions.

The US vs China

Asia's new Cold War?

Jude Woodward

Manchester University Press

The right of Jude Woodward to be identified as the author of this work has been asserted by her in accordance with the Copyright, Designs and Patents Act 1988.

Published by Manchester University Press
Altrincham Street, Manchester M1 7JA

www.manchesteruniversitypress.co.uk

British Library Cataloguing-in-Publication Data
A catalogue record for this book is available from the British Library

ISBN   978 1 5261 2199 8   hardback

ISBN   978 1 7849 9342 9   paperback

First published 2017

Typeset in Gill Sans by
Servis Filmsetting Ltd, Stockport, Cheshire
Printed in Great Britain by
CPI Group (UK) Ltd, Croydon CR0 4YY

Contents

Figures

Maps

All the maps that appear in this book were created by James David Smith, who retains the copyright on their use in any other context.

Tables

Acknowledgements

There are many to whom I am indebted in one way or another in the writing of this book and I apologise for anyone missed.

The greatest contribution of anyone was Redmond O'Neill, to whom this book is dedicated, even though he didn't know that I would write it. But over more than three decades we discussed all the fundamental issues covered in it – and many more. These discussions, and the reading and reasoning that flowed from them, formed my views and way of thinking more than anything else in my life. His critical and agile mind – as well as his sense of fun and love of life – made an impression on all who met him, and I was privileged to know him so well and share so much with him.

I owe particular thanks to John Ross, senior fellow at the Chongyang Institute for Financial Studies at Renmin University, Beijing, whose work on the Chinese economy provided the backbone for the economic material in this book, especially in Chapters 1 and 2, and who originated the figures and tables.

I am also hugely grateful to Keith Bennett who, often over a good Chinese meal, has been a source of ideas, facts and critiques that were invaluable to the process of writing this book. Keith read the manuscript in exemplary detail and pointed out many weaknesses, which I have tried to correct.

I would like to particularly thank my editor, Radhika Desai, who subjected every page of the manuscript to rigorous criticism, challenged every argument, pointed out many extraneous and unnecessary diversions and altogether made this a much better book than it was when I started out. It was sometimes painful, but in the end entirely worthwhile. I would also thank Alan Freeman, who had faith in this book, relentlessly pursued helping me find a publisher, and, with Radhika, spent generous amounts of time helping to refine my original proposal and thereby the content of this book.

There are many people who have contributed to my thinking on the subject of this book. I have had many discussions on developments in world politics and the economy with Barry Gray, Michael Burke, and other friends and colleagues, which are reflected in these pages. These others particularly include Kate Hudson, general secretary of CND, with whom I have not only discussed these issues over years, but whose love, friendship and support helped in many other ways.

I am extremely grateful to James Smith who produced all the maps that appear in this book. And to everyone at Manchester University Press who helped me through the editing and publishing process.

I strongly believe that it is necessary to spend time in China to understand how Chinese people and their government see the world and to appreciate how strongly this contrasts with how China is seen in the West. My links with China originated when I was in Ken Livingstone's London's Mayor's Office, to which I owe the opportunity to get to know China. Working on London's Chinese New Year led to my first trip to China to arrange cultural exchanges. As a result of that I had responsibility for setting up and organising the London promotional offices in Beijing and Shanghai. In 2008 I oversaw the Beijing Olympic torch relay in London, where I learned from Fu Ying, ambassador to London at that time, how China saw the Olympics as an opportunity to present the treasures and depth of Chinese culture to the world – in the way that China had received Shakespeare, Sherlock Holmes and Hollywood from the West, but without the 'unfair treaties' and colonial occupations. And also during the torch relay I received an object lesson in the capacity of powerful lobbies to whip up such extreme hostility to China that it completely obscured what China was trying to say.

The links I made through this period led to my time teaching at Shanghai Jiao Tong University and lecturing elsewhere in China after 2008. In this context I must thank my friends, Liu Tongbo and Zhao Bingbing, neither of whom have any responsibility for the contents of this book, but the many discussions I had with each of them taught me so much about China, how it sees itself and the rest of the world.

To conclude, I want to thank my friend Helen Shaw for her wisdom and affection. And the doctors at Guy's Hospital – thank you NHS – for their care when I fell ill and needed major surgery during the writing of this book.

Last but not least my thanks to my family: to the family that made me – my mum, brother, Patrick, and sister, Laura, and much-missed dad; and my own little family. Particularly love and thanks to my husband, Rod Robertson, especially for putting up with my bad temper when the writing wasn't going so well! But mainly to him and my darling stepdaughters Katy and Mary for the love, laughs and good times together that make any endeavour possible.

Abbreviations

A2/AD – Area Access/Access Denial (military capability)
ACFTA – ASEAN-China Free Trade Area
ADB – Asian Development Bank
ADIZ – Air Defence Identification Zone
AIIB – Asian Infrastructure Investment Bank
APEC summit – Asia-Pacific Economic Cooperation summit
APT – ASEAN Plus Three (China, Japan and South Korea)
ASEAN – Association of Southeast Asian Nations
BCIM – Bangladesh, China, India, Myanmar
BCP – Burmese Communist Party
BJP – Bharatiya Janata Party
BRIC/BRICs – Brazil, Russia, India, China
BRICS – Brazil, Russia, India, China, South Africa
CELAC – Community of Latin American and Caribbean States
CFR – Council on Foreign Relations
CIA – Central Intelligence Agency
CPC – Communist Party of China
CPEC – China-Pakistan Economic Corridor
CPKI – Committee for the Preparation of Korean Independence
CPPCC – Chinese People's Political Consultative Conference
CRS – Congressional Research Service
CSTO – Collective Security Treaty Organisation
DPJ – Democratic Party of Japan
DPP – Democratic Progressive Party (Taiwan)
DPRK – Democratic People's Republic of Korea
ECFA – Economic Cooperation Framework Agreement (China-Taiwan)
EEZ – Exclusive Economic Zone
FDI – foreign direct investment
GATT – General Agreements on Tariffs and Trade
GDP – gross domestic product
GFCF – gross fixed capital formation
GMD – Guomindang (Kuomintang)

IMF – International Monetary Fund
IMF WEO – International Monetary Fund World Economic Outlook
IPP – intellectual property protection
ISDS – Investor-State Dispute Settlement
ISIS – Islamic State of Iraq and Syria
JETRO – Japan External Trade Organization
LDP – Liberal Democratic Party (of Japan)
MLPA – Movement for the Liberation of Angola
MNDAA – Myanmar National Democratic Alliance Army
NATO – North Atlantic Treaty Alliance
NED – National Endowment for Democracy
NLD – National League for Democracy (Myanmar)
NLF – National Liberation Front (Vietnam)
NPC – National Peoples' Congress (China)
NPT – Nuclear Non-Proliferation Treaty
OECD – Organisation for Economic Cooperation and Development
OPEC – Organization of the Petroleum Exporting Countries
PLA – People's Liberation Army
PPPs – purchasing power parities
PRC – People's Republic of China
RAAF – Royal Australian Air Force
RCEP – Regional Comprehensive Economic Partnership
RMB – renminbi (currency of PRC)
ROC – Republic of China (Province of Taiwan)
ROK – Republic of Korea
SCO – Shanghai Cooperation Organisation
SEATO – Southeast Asia Treaty Organization
SIPRI – Stockholm International Peace Research Institute
TAR – Tibet Autonomous Region
THAAD – Terminal High Altitude Area Defence
TPP – Trans-Pacific Partnership
UAE – United Arab Emirates
UMNO – United Malays' National Organisation
UNCLOS – United Nations Convention on the Law of the Sea
UNGA – United Nations' General Assembly
UNITA – National Union for the Total Independence of Angola
USSR – Union of Soviet Socialist Republics
VCP – Vietnam Communist Party
WHO – World Health Organization
WMDs – weapons of mass destruction
WTO – World Trade Organization

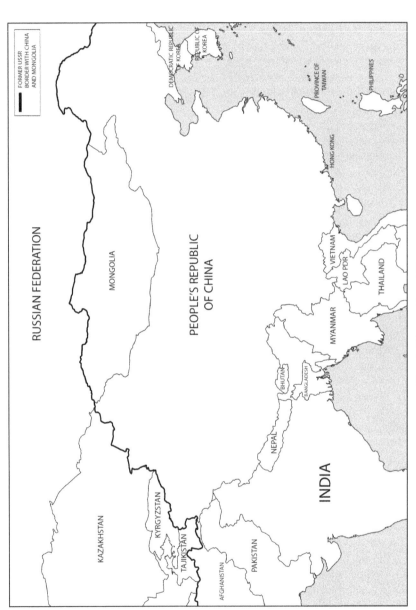

FORMER USSR
BORDER WITH CHINA
AND MONGOLIA

RUSSIAN FEDERATION

MONGOLIA

KAZAKHSTAN

KYRGYZSTAN

TAJIKISTAN

AFGHANISTAN

PAKISTAN

NEPAL

BHUTAN

BANGLADESH

INDIA

PEOPLE'S REPUBLIC
OF CHINA

MYANMAR

LAO PDR

VIETNAM

THAILAND

HONG KONG

PROVINCE OF
TAIWAN

PHILIPPINES

DEMOCRATIC REPUBLIC
OF KOREA

REPUBLIC OF
KOREA

Map 1 *China and its neighbours*

Introduction: America's Pacific century?

The US has engaged upon a mighty attempt to carry through an axial strategic reorientation of its foreign policy to confront the challenges presented by the rise of China. This has meant trying to wrench the focus of US foreign policy 180 degrees from the 'transatlantic' priorities of the twentieth century to launch instead 'America's Pacific century' (see Map 1). Donald Trump's presidency has meant some changes in tactics – threatening a trade war and ramping up US demands on its allies to up their arms spending – but in its fundamentals his policy is essentially a continuation of that launched under President Barack Obama in 2010 to 'pivot' US foreign policy to focus on China. Although Obama claimed benign motives for this shift, in fact, as this book demonstrates, its real aim was to contain and constrain China through policies echoing those of the Cold War against the USSR. Trump has deepened this orientation.

The mechanisms of this US policy turn – examined in detail in this book – have been military, diplomatic and economic. On the military front the majority of US naval resources were shifted from the Atlantic to the Pacific, its bases expanded in size and number and its allies, particularly Japan, encouraged to rearm. Diplomatically it meant an offensive to reinvigorate its Pacific alliances and persuade its friends and allies to resist China's economic overtures and 'good neighbour' diplomacy. Obama's key economic initiative was the controversial Trans-Pacific Partnership (TPP), a proposed US–Japan-led 'free trade' bloc offering preferential access to the US market as an alternative to trade with China. While Trump immediately abandoned this particular initiative, the essence of the policy – to put an economic squeeze on China – has continued. On the election stump Trump repeatedly accused China of currency manipulation, cheating on trade, stealing jobs and threatened to impose a 45 per cent tax on Chinese imports.

Within days of his election, Trump sharpened the US stance on China by accepting a congratulatory phone call from president Tsai of Taiwan, thereby, in terms of protocol, treating her as equal to a 'head of state' rather than a 'provincial governor' in line with Taiwan's international status as a 'province of China'.[1] This was followed by a series of hardline anti-China appointments to Trump's core team. These included rabid China hawk, Peter Navarro, whose books include: *Crouching tiger – what China's militarism means for the world*; *Death by China – confronting the dragon, a global call to action*; and *The coming China wars: where they will be fought and how they can be won*.[2] Dan DiMicco, another key Trump trade advisor and former steel executive, was known for arguing that China is to blame for the US's industrial woes and that it had been waging a two-decade-long trade war with the US.[3] Others in the Trump administration's new inner circle included Alexander Gray, who previously worked for Republican congressman Randy Forbes, an outspoken China critic, and Mike Pillsbury, author of *The hundred year marathon*, which argues that China is gearing up for world domination.[4] Rex Tillerson, Trump's secretary of state, used his confirmation hearings to suggest that the US might install a naval blockade in the South China Sea to bar China from its islands in the Spratlys – a step that would clearly risk armed confrontation. Trump's team immediately announced a major naval build-up in East Asia, including proposals to base a second aircraft carrier in the South China Sea, deploy more destroyers and submarines and expand or add new bases in Japan and Australia, and flagged the possibility of installing 'air force long-range strike assets' in South Korea.[5]

In short, the Trump–Pence administration continued in an even stronger form the policies of confrontation with China inaugurated by Obama. Any concerns that this could prove risky or counterproductive in dealing with China were dismissed with the argument that this new 'peace through strength' approach would put real muscle behind US policy in the region that had been lacking under Obama.

However, while Trump deployed a more pugnacious tone on China, his policy confronted the same constraints and problems as those, which, in the end, limited Obama's success against China. Trump claimed he could overcome such checks through more bullish steps than Obama was prepared for, but that would mean embarking on a trade war with China in a situation where China's economy has been more rapidly growing and dynamic than the US. It would mean taking steps that risk escalation to armed confrontation with China, an outcome that neither US elites nor the mass of its population are currently prepared for. A more aggressive policy towards China is undoubtedly more dangerous for the world, but for any US administration to actually prove more successful than Obama would mean surmounting the multiple obstacles to such an outcome that are outlined in this book.

Obama's Pacific turn

The origins of the US turn to confrontation with China, intensified by Trump and launched by Obama, were clearly set out in a landmark article published in autumn 2011 by then US secretary of state Hillary Clinton entitled 'America's Pacific century', outlining the US's new global strategic priorities.[6] The US stood at a 'pivot point', she said, which critically demanded a fundamental reorientation of US foreign policy. Asia had become 'the key driver of world politics', and therefore to 'sustain our leadership, secure our interests, and advance our values' it was vital that the US make 'similar investments as a Pacific power' to its 'post-World War II commitment to building a comprehensive and lasting transatlantic network of institutions and relationships'. Alongside this, while for the previous decade US attention and resources had been absorbed by the Middle East, Iraq and Afghanistan, the US now had to be 'smart' in reprioritising the allocation of its resources to the Asia-Pacific region. This policy became known as the US 'pivot to Asia'.

Reminding the world that the US 'is both an Atlantic and a Pacific power', Clinton announced this turn was one of 'the most important tasks of American statecraft over the next decade', sitting at the heart of its 'overall global effort to secure and sustain America's global leadership'. And at the centre of this were relations with China, which Clinton described as among 'the most challenging ... the United States has ever had to manage'. With this policy shift, the US was declaring that 'the US would not sit aside as China ... established itself as regional leader'.[7]

While China had always been on the US's crowded radar, it had never before been the determining question in US long-term strategies. US engagement with China had begun in the nineteenth century when, after the defeat of the Qing dynasty in the Opium Wars, it extracted extraterritorial privileges for US merchants in the 1844 Treaty of Wangxia, which the Chinese dubbed one of the 'unfair treaties'. In the early twentieth century the US, alongside the European powers, vied with Russia and Japan for influence in China. After the overthrow of the Qing dynasty it sought favour with rising nationalist forces by supporting the Guomindang (GMD) in its attempt to fend off the rise of Mao's communists. After 1945, as civil war resumed, the Truman administration was split between those who wanted to throw US weight behind the GMD and those who believed it was already a lost cause. It backed the GMD, but had little effect on the outcome and US political circles debated 'who lost China' long after the communist victory in 1949.

The US refused to recognise the government of the People's Republic of China (PRC) and a year later, when the US was de facto at war with China on the Korean peninsula, its policy-makers debated extending the war to China itself. In the Cold War decades that followed, as discussed in Chapter 5, American administrations were happy to 'triangulate' the tense relations between China and the USSR amid the widening Sino-Soviet split, initially allying with Moscow to contain China and, from 1972, decisively locking China into its global strategies against the USSR.[8] In the tumult of the events of 1989 the US hoped that the 'fall of communism' might extend to Beijing, but instead the protests in Tiananmen Square were crushed. But although the Bush administration imposed sanctions most were subsequently lifted by the Clinton administration in the face of a powerful business lobby in favour of trade with China.[9] But through all these ups and downs, at no point in this chequered history could it be claimed that the US considered China its number-one, global strategic problem.[10]

The twenty-first-century rise of China, coupled with the US's own accelerating relative decline, changed this decisively. How to respond to the 'China challenge' moved to the heart of US foreign policy concerns.

China's economic rise

China's unflagging economic advance – with growth averaging over 10 per cent per annum for three decades to 2011 – saw it overtake Germany in 2007, and then Japan in 2010 to become the world's second largest economy. It became the world's largest exporter and second largest importer in 2009, and surpassed the US as the world's largest trading nation in 2013. In 2013 it also displaced the US as the world's largest industrial producer. In a switch that took place at incomparable speed, according to data

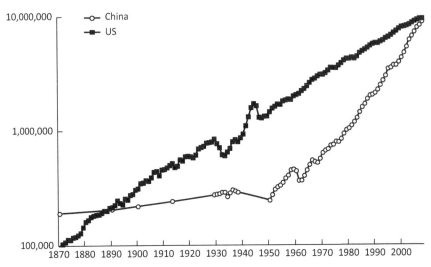

Figure I.I *China and US GDP in the long run*
Source: *Maddison, World Population, GDP and Per Capita GDP. I-2008 AD*
© *John Ross*

from the United Nation (UN), China's total industrial production went from 61 per cent of the US level in 2007 to 125 per cent by 2013.[11] Considering manufacturing alone – that is, excluding mining, electricity generation and gas and water supply – the gap is even wider. In 2007 China's manufacturing output was 62 per cent of the US level, by 2013 it was 135 per cent – $2.7 trillion compared to $2 trillion in the US. No other country's industrial production even approaches China's – in 2013 China's industrial output was 335 per cent of Japan's and 389 per cent of Germany's.

The long-term trends in the growth of the Chinese and US economies are presented in Figure 1.1, which shows how China's economy has been steadily gaining on the US since the 1980s.

On the basis of these trends, even before the international financial crisis, China's gross domestic product (GDP) would have overtaken the US within a couple of decades, but following 2008 and the further slowing of growth in the US and the West, this accelerated. Between 2007 and 2015 the Chinese economy more than tripled in size, while the US economy grew by only about 20 per cent.[12] As a result World Bank estimates suggest China's economy actually overtook that of the US in 2014 in terms of purchasing power parities (PPP).[13] China does not accept the PPP measure, but it would require a dramatic turnaround for its GDP not to overtake the US's, even in market prices, within the next decade (see Figure 1.2).[14]

Of course, even if PPP estimates were accurate and the Chinese economy is already larger than the US economy, this would not mean that China had the same fundamental economic strength as the US. In 2014 China's GDP per capita ($12,880) was still less than a quarter that of the US ($54,597).[15] If expected growth rates were maintained in both economies it would be at least 2050 before China catches up on this measure. Moreover, the US enjoys other advantages, at least for the time being: the

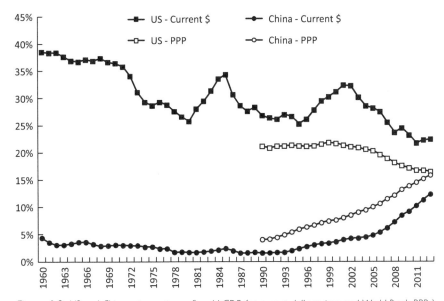

Figure 1.2 *US and China – percentage of world GDP (at current dollar prices and World Bank PPPs)*
Source: *Calculated from World Bank World Development Indicators*
© John Ross

dollar remains the world's leading currency; the US has far more advanced infrastructure and technology; and it is home to many of the world's largest corporations – the 2016 Forbes Global 2000 lists 39 US companies in the top 100 largest companies compared to China's 15.[16] Nonetheless the dynamic growth of the Chinese economy is already a challenge to US global economic supremacy.

A US-led unipolar world is already challenged

While the Chinese economy is not large or advanced enough to offer a comprehensive economic alternative to relations the major advanced economies have with the US, it already makes a significant difference in less developed regions of Asia or Latin America and a decisive difference in even less developed regions such as sub-Saharan Africa. This has already begun to radically change economic choices for developing countries.

The result was rather neatly summarised by South African Trade Minister Rob Davies during a 2010 trade mission to China; he told the *Financial Times* that China's expanding presence in Africa 'can only be a good thing' because it means that 'We don't have to sign on the dotted line whatever is shoved under our noses any longer … We now have alternatives and that's to our benefit.'[17] The significance of this for the US is hard to overestimate.

The relative decline of the US economy meant that it has less capacity to use economic leverage alone to bind countries across the developing world to its strategic priorities. For example, in the first 15 years of this century Latin America saw pro-US neoliberal governments replaced by governments that refused to toe the US line on foreign and regional policy. At the UN they overwhelmingly opposed the 2003 war against Iraq, blocked support for the assault on Syria in 2013, voted to recognise a Palestinian state in the West Bank and Gaza and abstained on or voted against condemning Russian absorption of the Crimea in 2014. While the right was able to reclaim the offensive electorally from 2015, primarily as a result of economic problems linked to the fall in global commodity prices, South America is far from returning to a state of supine subordination to the US. And with fewer regional acolytes willing to give it cover and act as proxies, the US's ability to intervene has remained limited.

The Pax Americana begins to buckle

While John F. Kennedy famously protested that the Pax Americana was 'not ... enforced on the world by American weapons of war', in fact the iron fist in the US velvet glove has long been the largest war machine ever assembled in human history.[18] But indeed it was the size of the US economy, the role of the US dollar and its de facto and de jure domination of the post-1945 financial institutions agreed at Bretton Woods that were the chief instruments of US power. This was *backed* by military capacity not imposed by it.

But while the US had emerged from the Second World War as 'incomparably the greatest single nation in the world' with vast global political and economic aspirations to 'apply its directing power to the inordinately complex and unpredictable realities' of the post-war world, it was never actually great enough for the scale of its ambitions.[19] Very rapidly its attempts to apply its strength, while refusing to see the limits of its capabilities, began to demonstrate fundamental weaknesses (see Table 1.1). By the mid-1970s the US's capacity to deliver economic advantage to the whole world had begun to visibly decline as its domestic expenditure – on the Vietnam War and buying domestic peace – outstripped GDP growth. Slowing growth and declining competiveness were increasingly reflected in growing trade and budget deficits. From 1986 it became a net importer

Table 1.1   *US GDP as percentage of world GDP*

	1990 international Geary-Khamis dollars[1]	World Bank $ PPPs[2]	World Bank Current $ Exchange Rates[2]
1870	8.90%	–	–
1900	15.80%	–	–
1913	18.90%	–	–
1940	20.60%	–	–
1951	27.70%	–	–
1960	24.30%	–	38.60%
1980	21.10%	22.50%	25.10%
2008	18.60%	19.80%	23.20%
2012	–	18.30%	21.90%

1. *Calculated from Maddison World Population, GDP and Per Capita GDP*
2. *Calculated from World Bank World Development Indicators*
© John Ross

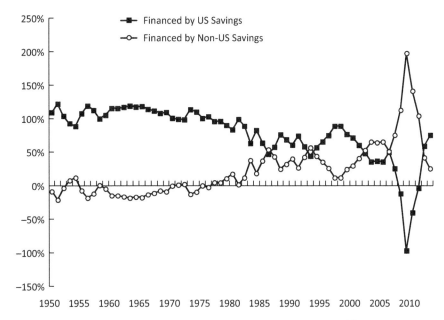

Figure 1.3 *US financing of net fixed investment (percentage of GDP)*

Source: *Calculated from Bureau of Economic Analysis NIPA Tables 1.5.5 & 5.1*
© *John Ross*

of capital (see Figure 1.3) However, as the US increasingly needed to suck in resources to maintain a level of military and other expenditures that were outstripping its savings, the dollar's role as reserve currency ensured that cash flowed in, through persuading allies such as Japan and the Organization of the Petroleum Exporting Countries (OPEC) members to buy up US Treasury debt.[20] While this could not halt the US's relative economic decline it ensured an extension of US leadership.

The fall of the USSR in 1989–91 seemed to promise a new lease of life for this US leadership and for the neoliberal prescriptions of the 'Washington consensus' implemented by the International Monetary Fund (IMF) and the World Bank. But in reality the US economy remained in the doldrums and what it could offer the rest of the world was already insufficient to buy compliance with US strategic objectives in some areas, particularly in parts of the Middle East, hence the US's increasingly frequent resort to military force from the 1990s. But force is a costly option with often unstable results, as the quagmires born of US interventions in Iraq and Libya have shown.

While the relationship of forces today remains in the US's favour, especially if its European partners and Japan are added into the global equation, it is no longer simply paramount and even its most sycophantic supporters question how long the US can remain the unchallenged leader of the capitalist world. Even its closest allies have begun to hedge against that eventuality, as when the UK signed up to China's Asian Infrastructure Investment Bank (AIIB).[21] China's GDP definitively overtaking the US will be a further milestone on a road that inevitably arrives at the end of US global pre-eminence, a fact of which the US is deeply aware.

Putting an economic squeeze on China

China had been moving up the US agenda for a decade, but its arrival at the centre of attention coincided with the election of Obama in autumn 2008. Bush's presidency had been focused on the 'war on terror'; the wars in Iraq and Afghanistan and their ramifications claimed the resources and attention of US army personnel, security advisors, diplomatic staff and foreign policy experts. However, already in 2006 the Quadrennial Defence Review had noted that 'China has the greatest potential to compete militarily with the United States and field disruptive military technologies that could over time offset traditional US military advantages'.[22]

In 2008 as the financial crisis sent the US economy reeling and at the same time China's balance of trade in goods surplus with the US hit an historic high of $268 billion, the issue became unavoidable.[23] On the 2008 presidential campaign trail, the Alliance of American Manufacturers, steelworkers unions and others lobbied that China should be designated a 'currency manipulator', allegedly keeping the renminbi (RMB) exchange rate artificially low. If formally adopted by Congress this designation opens the door to punitive tariffs on imports. Obama, like Trump in 2016, played to the gallery, promising that he would tell the Chinese: 'you guys keep on manipulating your currency, we are going to start shutting off access to some of our markets'.[24]

But under Obama nothing came of it. On the one hand, China allowed the exchange rate of the RMB to appreciate by around 4 per cent a year between 2005 and 2012. But chiefly, there was no stomach for a trade war with China, which would hurt US exports to China at least as much as China's to the US and the resulting price rises would be unpopular. Protectionist policies, of the type Trump promised, that wall off the US from cheap Chinese commodities would not aid uncompetitive American companies; the space vacated would be rapidly occupied by cheap imports from Mexico, Vietnam and elsewhere.

However, while no comprehensive punitive measures were implemented, a whole series of piecemeal steps had been taken against China over the previous two decades. The arms embargo imposed after Tiananmen Square in 1989 continues to restrict a whole range of high-technology exports to China, ranging from computer components to farm equipment. Despite a vocal American business lobby calling for an easing of this ban – for example, a 2010 American Chamber of Commerce report estimated that lifting it could deliver $64 billion in otherwise 'lost sales' to China by 2019 – it is still in place.[25] Similarly the 1988 Exon-Florio Amendment, which allows the blocking of sensitive foreign investments on 'security considerations', has been used to veto takeovers and acquisitions by Chinese companies. The major Chinese telecommunications company Huawei was blocked from acquiring US network company 3Com Corporation in 2008 and its bid for a contract with Sprint Nextel to install telecommunications infrastructure was similarly ruled out in 2010.

While such measures can impede Chinese manufacturing in scaling up technologically, they cannot stop it altogether. Rising Chinese investment in research and development (R&D) alongside mergers and acquisitions of high-technology companies elsewhere is moving China up the technology ladder quite rapidly.[26] Other US attempts to curb competition from China were similarly ineffective. The 2012 imposition of

30 per cent tariffs on Chinese solar companies for alleged 'dumping' did hurt but it pro-voked tit-for-tat measures against US polysilicons used in solar panels.

Indeed, it is hard to envisage any economic sanctions that the US could have realisti-cally imposed that would have halted Chinese growth or slowed it to levels satisfactory, and unthreatening, to the US.

Persuading China to change economic course

With punitive measures having limited impact, the US tried to persuade China to pursue a range of neoliberal policies – privatisation, deregulation, ending or reducing state and state-aided investment and so on – which would open the Chinese economy up to both US commodities and capital while slowing its growth. Such tactics had succeeded with Yeltsin's Russia where 'shock therapy' led to catastrophic destruction of the Russian economy and thus its potential to act as a global counterweight to the US.[27]

But China has no equivalent of Yeltsin – a leader willing to comply with the West's demands – and so US economic policy interventions against China have been confined to an assault from think tanks, the economic and financial media, Western business schools and economics departments arguing China should urgently deepen market 'reform' through privatisations and deregulation. As China's previous stellar rates of growth of 10 per cent or more slowed to a merely remarkable 6–7 per cent from 2014, this lobby suggested that the entire post-1978 Chinese economic model had run its course and must be abandoned.[28] These interventions, while they had little impact on the actual policies of the Chinese government, did skew the parallel discussions in Chinese academic institutions and the media. This is one reason why Xi Jinping has railed against subordination to 'Western values' in Chinese universities and think tanks, and promoted research institutes that are explicitly independent of the West – 'think tanks with Chinese characteristics'.[29]

Contrary to stereotypes in the West, there is considerable debate in China on con-troversial questions, including economic policy. In this context, one Western argument that gained traction is that the Chinese economy is critically unbalanced by its high rate of investment compared to its relatively low household consumption. Particularly after the $586 billion stimulus in response to the 2008 crisis, it was claimed that this imbal-ance was choking the development of the internal market, leaving growth dependent upon exports and vulnerable to protectionist tariff wars.

This was the argument of the 2012 World Bank report entitled *China 2030, building a modern, harmonious and creative society*.[30] The report was commissioned by the PRC's Ministry of Finance to canvass opinions widely on the new challenges facing China's economy and show China's willingness to participate fully in the existing international financial and economic institutions. Predictably, the report argued that classic neoliberal measures were urgently needed in China: rapid privatisation of the banks, break-up and sell-off of the state sector and deregulation. It strongly opposed any further state-led stimulus and argued for a shift in emphasis from investment to consumption.[31]

The Chinese government officially greeted the report warmly, leading to great speculation that steps to dismantle the state-led economy would ensue. This did not happen, but efforts to decrease state-led investment, boost household consumption (primarily through above-inflation wage rises), liberalise the capital account and allow the development of a private banking sector protected by deposit guarantees created problems. Steps to deregulate the capital account facilitated substantial capital flight over the course of 2015, amounting to an estimated $750 billion in the year and major downward pressure on the RMB.[32] The boost in the share of household consumption in the economy and equivalent decline in savings – a policy broadly pursued from 2012 onwards – led to a parallel decline in investment and therefore some unnecessary slowing in China's rate of growth by 2015.

But, unlike Russia in the 1990s, the Chinese government was practical rather than dogmatic in pursuit of the World Bank's policies. Thus, for example, in August 2012, in response to the impact of renewed stagnation in the world economy, it announced a further $154 billion state-led investment programme – directly against the World Bank's advice.[33] Similarly, slower than anticipated growth in the first half of 2015 led to a raft of state investment announcements in June and again in 2016.

Nevertheless, the existence of a dynamic private – that is, capitalist – sector in China, the extensive influence of pro-neoliberal opinion in economics and business departments of Chinese universities, the exaggerated weight that continues to be given to Western ideas even within the higher echelons of the Chinese Communist Party (CPC), mean that there is a powerful internal lobby for such policies. The US puts huge direct and indirect effort into encouraging such views, providing them with ammunition – as with the World Bank report – and courting their most influential exponents with flattery and invitations to speak in the US.

These efforts have not effected a fundamental reorientation in China's economic policy. The 3rd Plenum of the CPC in November 2013 – which set the priorities for the Chinese government for the next decade and more – was greatly anticipated in the West as likely to propose an acceleration of 'market' reforms.[34] Instead it set out a strategy, which was, in its fundamentals, a continuation of that set out in 1978 by Deng Xiaoping, maintaining the 'dominant role of the public ownership system' in building a 'socialist market economy'. The Communiqué of the 3rd Plenum stated, inter alia,

> the basic economic system with public ownership at the core, jointly developing with many kinds of ownership systems, is the main pillar of Socialism with Chinese characteristics, and is the basis for the socialist market economy system. The publicly owned economy and the non-publicly owned economy are both important component parts of the socialist market economy … We must … persist in the dominant role of the public ownership system, give rein to the leading role of the state owned economy, incessantly strengthen the vitality, control, strength and influence of the state owned economy. We must … support and guide the non-publicly owned economy to develop, and encourage the economic vitality and creativity of the non-publicly owned economy.[35]

In other words, despite manifold pressures, attempts to persuade the Chinese government to change course on the fundamentals of its economic policy have so far failed and the US has continued to lose ground.

The Trans-Pacific Partnership, the US's 'economic pivot'

Obama's key economic counter to China was the TPP, a 12-country Free Trade Agreement that excluded China – primarily through its provision that state-owned companies constitute 'unfair competition'. The TPP aimed to include most of China's Pacific neighbours, locking the Asia-Pacific economies into preferential trading relations with the US and reducing their orientation to the growing China market. However, since the agreement would also open these Asia-Pacific economies to greater competition from tariff-free American goods and services, there were major problems in the negotiations, especially with Japan, which delayed agreement until autumn 2015.[36]

The TPP proposed much more than a simple free trade deal. Its central aim was to establish rules on 'anti-competitive practices' with supranational mechanisms to impose these rules on participating governments through penalties and exclusions. So if China felt it had to join the TPP, the price would have been the dismantling of its state-run economy. This led some China analysts to describe it as an 'economic NATO'.[37] But the TPP was dead in the water after the election of Trump, whose pledges to withdraw from the deal were implemented immediately.

China's riposte to the TPP had been to push ahead more rapidly with the Regional Comprehensive Economic Partnership (RCEP), a free trade agreement agreed in principle at the annual Association of Southeast Asian Nations (ASEAN) meeting in 2011, bringing together the ten member states of ASEAN, plus China, Japan, South Korea, India, Australia and New Zealand. Several TPP participants also joined the RCEP despite the US's tacit objections; other countries, like India, that had rejected the TPP, preferred the RCEP as it does not envisage setting new supranational economic rules for participants.

The military 'pivot' to China

The US's declining economic leverage means it is forced to rely more openly on military means to achieve many of its objectives. The US may be weakening, but it is still the greatest military power on the planet, its 2015 military spending constituted around 36 per cent of total world military spending, as great as the next eight largest military spenders combined.

Despite a budget squeeze, the US defence budget for 2016 was $585 billion. China's total military budget has tripled since the 1990s, so that it is now the world's second highest. However, even after several years of double-digit growth (for example, it rose 12.2 per cent in 2014–15 and by a further 10 per cent in 2015–16), at an estimated $215 billion to the US's $596 billion in 2015, China's defence spending was still only 35 per cent of the US level.

US military spending has averaged nearly 4 per cent of GDP since 2000, falling to 3.3 per cent in 2015 as a result of Obama's spending cuts, which Trump has pledged to reverse; while Chinese defence spending has averaged and remains at just below 2 per cent. In per capita terms China's military expenditure in 2015 was only the 55th highest in the world, at $156 per head compared to the US's $1,854. Between 1990 and 2013 the US's total military spending was $12.5 trillion (constant 2011 dollars), while China's was less than 13 per cent of that at $1.6 trillion in the same period. Or, just taking the more recent years, between 2000 and 2013 the US spent $8.1 trillion while China spent less than 17 per cent of that, $1.4 trillion.[38]

There is no comparison between the two in accumulated materiel and hardware. There are 20 aircraft carriers on active service worldwide, of which 10 are American and one is Chinese with a second under construction. China's carrier is a retrofitted, ex-Soviet ship originally built in the late 1980s, which it describes as a 'test platform' primarily for training. The second will be built in China, but it will be years before it is fully operational. The US has 9600 nuclear weapons to China's 240, twice the number of combat aircraft (3318 to 1500), 71 nuclear submarines to China's 10. While more evenly matched in tanks and smaller warships, the US has a huge arsenal of attack heli- copters (6400), which China does not, and at least 900 drones.[39]

China has made some technological advances on the US; for example, in 2011 China conducted the first test flight of the Chengdu J-20, its new-generation stealth jet fighter.[40] And China has an advantage in people power: the People's Liberation Army (PLA) is the largest in the world with an estimated 2.3 million troops compared to around 1.5 million marines and soldiers.[41] But the US army is vastly better equipped and has recent experience of active duty in a number of different environments.

However quickly China catches up with the US economically, the US will enjoy a global military advantage for decades. Therefore, deploying this advantage has been at the centre of the US effort to constrain China, and even more so under Trump. As a first step the US began ramping up its military presence around China's eastern and southern seaboards. Obama's core decision – to base 60 per cent of nuclear and high- tech naval vessels in the Pacific, including at least six aircraft carriers – was implemented. The US has greatly expanded its bases in South Korea; opened a new base in Darwin, Australia; and negotiated the use of bases in the Philippines. It has developed a raft of military exercises with regional partners that have China as the thinly veiled potential target.[42] And plans to surround China with stealth planes – B-2 bombers and F-22 and F-35 fighter-bombers – are on track.[43]

However, fully carrying through this redeployment towards the Pacific requires a ruthless shift from existing priorities, particularly ending the 'immense resources' absorbed by the Middle East and Afghanistan since 2002.[44] The attempt to make such a shift explained Obama's insistence on reducing US military commitments to Afghanistan and Iraq and refusal to play the leading role in the 2011 assault on Libya – the first time that the US did not directly lead a North Atlantic Treaty Alliance (NATO) oper- ation.[45] In Syria the US repeatedly ruled out any 'boots on the ground' intervention. In Mali and Côte d'Ivoire the US ceded the lead role to France, which has increasingly been taking the lead for the West and NATO in several African conflicts. Obama doggedly stayed out while South Sudan descended into bloody civil war. And the US was clear on staying out of any direct military role in support of Kiev in the Ukraine conflict.[46]

Despite this drawdown from other theatres to focus on Asia, events – such as the emergence of ISIS, Russian support for Assad and the crisis in Ukraine – constantly conspired to pull the US back to old problems. But while this meant US foreign policy was not able to entirely focus on Asia, military redeployment to the Pacific went ahead relentlessly.

For China to respond by dramatically speeding up the growth of its own military capacities would mean diverting resources from social and developmental priorities. Such a choice would not just have a hugely destabilising effect on its regional relations, but would further ratchet up tensions with the US. China has made it clear it will not go down this route. But the build-up of US forces and missile systems in the region, coupled with a rise in defence spending by many of its neighbours, has put pressure on China to enhance its own military capabilities.

A new Cold War?

There is no evidence that any influential US policy-makers, even the most extreme neocons, including Donald Trump and his advisors, seriously contemplate an actual war with China; such a conflict between nuclear powers would inflict an intolerable degree of destruction. The core of the US strategy has been to encircle China with a compelling series of de facto or de jure military alliances with China's neighbours, encouraging and aiding their rearmament and ratcheting up local disputes with China so as to constrain and pressure it.[47] The endgame is a pro-US military, economic and diplomatic noose around China that can be tightened to veto, punish, pressure or threaten China and narrow its options on a range of issues.[48]

Of course, there is more than one opinion on how to deal with China within the American politico-military establishment. There is an influential cohort that favours collaborative relations with China. Thus Joseph Nye, an assistant secretary of defence under Bill Clinton, says that 'an appropriate policy response to the rise of China must balance realism and integration' and that 'conflict is not inevitable'.[49] Or former secretary of state, Henry Kissinger, who called on Trump to soften his tone towards China, argues that 'a period of prolonged coexistence' with China is possible and preferable.[50]

But an even more powerful current, very weighty in the Republican establishment, among liberal interventionists in the Democratic Party and at the heart of the Pentagon, advocates a much more confrontational stance to China. This contingent starts from what is the shared credo of the entire US foreign policy elite: that America's world leadership underpins global order and must be defended at all costs. This American 'exceptionalism' holds that the interests of the US – from its very foundation as a nation – have been uniquely aligned with those of democracy and a 'free world'. As American founding father Thomas Paine put it: 'The cause of America is in great measure the cause of all mankind.'[51] Or as George W. Bush contended 200 years later: 'The story of America is the story of expanding liberty … Our nation's founding commitment is still our deepest commitment: In our world and here at home we will extend the frontiers of freedom.'[52]

Many serious studies of both the left and the advocates of 'liberal imperialism' have debunked this self-justifying and ultimately fictitious account of America's destiny and global role. From the left, works from William Appleman Williams' powerful 1959 *Tragedy of American Diplomacy* to Perry Anderson's 2013 essay 'Imperium and consilium' have exposed the self-serving character of US foreign policy, in the end defending the interests of US companies and capital flows rather than peace and democracy.[53] On the right works such as Niall Ferguson's 2005 *Colossus* have also argued that there is nothing 'wholly unique' about US foreign policy and that 'Americans need to recognise the imperial characteristics of their own power' – a power which he supports.[54] As these and other analysts argue, not only was the US expansionist from its birth, but once it had completed its internal colonial expansion to the Pacific and seized California and Texas from Mexico, it turned to expelling Spain and the other European powers from South America. From the late nineteenth century, its leaders began to nurse the desire to replace Britain as the dominant power in the world if without its vast formal empire.[55] Contrary to myths of the US as the 'reluctant superpower' prone to bouts of 'isolationism', it is the zealous pursuit of such dominance that has driven US policy.

But such critiques have not affected the memes of the US foreign policy establishment. As Perry Anderson contends: 'That US paramountcy is at once a national prize and a universal good is taken for granted by policy-makers and their counsellors, across the party-political board.'[56] Or as former French Foreign Minister, Hubert Védrine observed, 'most great American leaders and thinkers have never doubted for an instant that the United States was chosen by providence as the "indispensable nation" and that it must remain dominant for the sake of humankind'.[57] America is the one 'indispensable nation' because its interests – according to this mythology – are uniquely indivisible from those of all; no other nation occupies this peculiar material position, and all alternatives will reduce the world to warring gangs.[58] Entering the world family of nations is defined by acceptance of this US global leadership.

Of course, just because US policy elites across the board share this myth does not mean that they agree on how to maintain US leadership. And there is always the question of whether the American people accept the burdens of such world leadership willingly.[59]

Given its head, the policy advocated by the extreme neocons and Trump supporters towards China would be analogous to the tactics the US pursued against the USSR over the course of the twentieth-century Cold War. From the 1950s to the end of the 1980s – alongside periods of thaw, détente, and balancing – the USSR was variously surrounded by a tightening iron noose of US military alliances, forward bases, border interventions (Afghanistan in particular), cruise missiles and naval exercises. Economically it was shut out of international trade organisations, subjected to bans and boycotts and excluded from collaboration on scientific and technological developments. It was diplomatically isolated, excluded from the G7 group of major economies and awarded an international pariah status. It was designated as uniquely undemocratic. Any opponents of this 'Cold War' and accompanying nuclear arms race were stigmatised as disloyal apologists, closet 'reds' or spies and subjected to McCarthyite witch-hunts. The ideological isolation of the USSR and military strangulation walled it off behind an 'iron curtain', subjected to what became crushing military and strategic pressure.

This book suggests that this has some useful parallels for what the most bellicose wing of the US establishment would like to achieve in relation to China, although in a very different international context: a new Cold War, that contains China within a ring of hostile alliances, while isolating it from international support through a recycled set of anti-communist tropes. While this vision of an America redux triumphing over an isolated and subordinated China is particular to Trump and the neocons, the whole US political establishment aspires to maintain US leadership. Hence there is a tendency for the differences on how to deal with China to be reduced to rhetoric, and to dissipate before the actual foreign policy initiatives that a declining US power can actually take.

For example, there has been a broad US establishment consensus on the need to shift foreign and military focus to Asia, and to set about reinforcing and constructing a chain of regional friends and allies encircling China. Even a 'dove' like Nye agreed with this: 'China was welcomed into the World Trade Organization, but the US–Japan security treaty was revived to insure against China becoming a bully … American allies help shape the environment that encourages responsible behaviour.'[60]

Primarily this means toughening up the stance of close allies Japan, South Korea, Singapore and the Philippines, plus, at a slight remove, Australia and New Zealand. It means shoring up some relations that have weakened, such as with Thailand and the province of Taiwan. Additionally, the US has sought to court Vietnam by exploiting tensions in the South China Sea; been quick to move in on the opening-up of Myanmar; and attempted to defuse tensions that have built up with Malaysia and Indonesia. But crucially, for the US to establish a long-term favourable relationship of forces with China in Asia, it needs to divide Russia and India from China and lock them into alliance with the West.

China's uneasy international role

While for the US the rise of China has raised the issue of its own declining position and how to maintain its determining role in the political and economic world order, it has also posed problems for China. Until recent years, China's foreign policy was guided by Deng Xiaoping's dictum 'Hide our strength, bide our time'. This had meant seeking to play a non-controversial role in international forums, largely going along with the majority – that is, US – line in the UN, and deploying its low-key diplomacy to maintain a, sometimes uneasy, status quo on a series of long-standing border and maritime disputes with a number of its neighbours.

All this is both changed and changing. From joining with Russia at the UN to prevent an intervention in Syria to providing satellites for Chavez's Venezuela, launching the AIIB to the proposal for a pan-Asian new silk 'road and belt', China has begun pursuing a bolder international policy. At the same time, American encouragement after 2010 gave some of China's neighbours a heady confidence to pursue old disputes with China more vigorously, forcing China into some more edgy and determined responses – in the South China Sea, for example. This has been useful to the US in its reorientation to Asia. Under a hostile lens, any tensions, mistakes or missteps by China can be jumped on and exploited internationally to suggest it has expansionist ambitions.

While conscious that it is now a global player and more openly pursuing an independent foreign policy course, China still substantially lags behind the West in living standards and overall development. It would prefer to broker an agreement with the US that accepts the gradual emergence of a multipolar world, allowing China to continue to concentrate on social and economic development.

This approach was reflected in Xi Jinping's meeting with Obama in June 2013, where China proposed a 'new type of great power relationship', based on avoiding conflict and emphasising dialogue, respect for each other's 'core interests', and seeking cooperation and advancement of areas of mutual interest. Initially, Washington seemed warm to this; Obama echoed the idea of 'new major power relations' in several contexts, while his national security advisor, Susan Rice, repeated Xi's precise formula in a major speech: 'When it comes to China, we seek to operationalise a new model of major power relations.'[61] But foreign policy advisors and pundits reacted with alarm and strongly urged steering clear of any implied acceptance of a multipolar world and China's great power status within it, lest it give credence to a 'narrative of the United States' weakness and China's inevitable rise'.[62] The administration adjusted to these warnings and by the time of Obama's return trip to China in 2014 he studiously avoided any repetition of this.[63]

What does America want?

The immediate steps in the US's shift to Asia were straightforward and agreed across the US foreign policy and defence establishment. They included reinforcing American military presence in the Pacific to maintain its current strategic superiority – or 'balance' as this is usually euphemistically described; reassuring allies that the US remained a vital and proactive presence in the region; and reinvigorating and extending its regional alliances.

For China hawks such steps were to be just the opening sally in a campaign to force China into compliance with the demands of the US-led world. On the economic front these demands include opening up China's markets on terms favourable to the West, privatisation of key industries, revaluing the RMB, deregulating its capital account and not developing production in areas of more advanced technology that would directly compete with the West.[64] Overall the most desired outcome is for China's growth to stall, reducing China's economic leverage, making it easier for the US to keep China's neighbours in its own sphere of influence and depriving China of the resources to come to the aid of other 'recalcitrant' regimes like Venezuela or Iran. By the by, failing Chinese growth would also condemn the Chinese people to live forever at a standard of living roughly a quarter of that of the US, which would likely begin to make their government unpopular, creating instabilities, including possibly the potential for an end to Communist Party rule.

Politically, the US and the West have always more or less openly demanded 'regime change' in China: replacing the Communist Party with a reliably pro-Western govern-ment, euphemistically described as 'political reform' or the 'transition to democracy'. The flag-bearer for this particular US mission has been the National Endowment for Democracy (NED) – tagline: 'supporting freedom around the world' – which, tellingly, funds activity right across the Middle East except in semi-feudal Saudi Arabia. The NED led the enthusiastic support in the West for the 1989 movement in Tiananmen Square, promoted the use of Western symbols – like the Statue of Liberty – as metaphors for its demands. More recently it spurred on the wildly exaggerated excitement in the Western media at the 'democracy' campaign that appeared in Hong Kong in autumn 2014.

The US also makes a series of strategic and military demands: that China reduce its defence budget, accept a more proximate US military presence, retreat from its territorial claims in the East and South China seas, abandon any aspiration to 'blue water' naval capabilities and accept a naval sphere of influence confined to home waters to which, moreover, the US navy has free access. And, as proof of good faith, China should vote with the US in the UN Security Council.

But for the US hawks even a stalled Chinese economy, regime change and military containment are not enough. Their concern is not only to contain China now, but to weaken it permanently to prevent any threat that it might, in future, challenge the pre-eminence of the US. As a 2015 Council on Foreign Relations Special Report on China put it:

> Only a fundamental collapse of the Chinese state would free Washington from the obligation of systematically balancing Beijing, because even the alternative of a modest Chinese stumble would not eliminate the dangers presented to the United States in Asia and beyond.[65]

The devastation inflicted upon Russia following its defeat in the Cold War is a lesson in what that might look like. The disintegration of the USSR meant a state with a population of 288 million was reduced to a state – Russia – with roughly half that at 143 million. Russia then faced IMF economic 'shock therapy' that crashed its economy wiping out 60 per cent of GDP and reducing living standards by a similar degree. Russia's average GDP growth from 1993 to 1998 averaged a devastating –5.5 per cent, so that even after growth picked up from 1999 it meant average growth for the 19 years from 1993 to 2012 was only 2 per cent a year.[66] Life expectancy plummeted by 7.5 years for men and 3.5 for women between 1989 and 1994.[67] In 2013 Russia's population was still 4.6 million less than in 1992. Much of its manufacturing industry was destroyed and it was driven back on exports of raw materials. The rapid, corrupt privatisations saw the creation of a 'fifth column' of semi-criminal oligarch rentiers that 'own' the bulk of the economy, the profits of which end up in in Switzerland, Cyprus, the Cayman Islands and elsewhere and who have a powerful vested interest in defending the status quo, particularly against any temptation to renationalise these stolen assets. The dismemberment of the country also left large ethnically Russian populations as minorities in countries whose borders were agreed when part of a single federation. It saw NATO advance from Western Europe right up to its borders, accompanied by a proposed 'missile defence shield' that might give the West a nuclear first-strike capacity. All this ravaged Russia's global position and undermined the security of its borders, where, inter alia, it has faced civil war in Chechnya, war in Georgia over South Ossetia, and crisis in Ukraine.

Given the continuing decisive rejection of such a course by the Chinese government, this is not remotely on the cards unless China could be first economically crushed and subjected to overwhelming international pressure. But the contours of such a defeat can be seen in the US's de facto support for a range of separatist movements related to China. These include the US's ongoing arming of Taiwan and support for political parties that demand it is recognised as an independent state within the UN, given greater prominence by Trump's initial threat to break with the 'one China' policy on Taiwan; promotion of the Dalai Lama and those advocating separatism in Tibet; US opposition to China's efforts against al-Qaeda-affiliated terrorist groups in Xinjiang; and its succour to external organisations calling for secession of Chinese Mongolia that have not the slightest echo in China. The West would also insist on Hong Kong being allowed to act as a de facto independent city-state. Externally, elements of such a design for China include a new settlement on the Korean peninsula absorbing North Korea into South Korea and allowing the advance of the US army to China's land frontier. And a surrounding 'missile defence shield' giving the West a potential first-strike capacity, through the expansion of the Terminal High Altitude Area Defence (THAAD) missile defence system to Japan and South Korea.[68]

China's alternative

While such utter defeat is not in prospect, China is bound to reject such an outcome. Its alternative was set out clearly by Fu Ying, chair of the Foreign Affairs Committee of the China National Peoples' Congress (NPC):

> The two giants on the two sides of the Pacific Ocean are engaged in differing debates on the future international order. In the United States, the focus is on how to maintain American leadership. … In China, the discussion revolves around how to improve the international order and global governance.[69]

In other words, China proposes that international relations, including those between China and the US, should be conducted on the basis of equality and mutual benefit.[70] China's argument is simple: inevitably mistakes will be made and not all disagreement avoided, but if there is an approach of equality and understanding of each other's concerns, errors can be corrected through discussion and real conflicts of interest resolved through fair compromise.

The dominant sections of the American political, military and economic establishment reject any such concessions on its exclusive claim to lead the world, harder and harder though it may be to sustain. And those who favour good relations with China tend to see these as being achieved partly through coercion. Even Nye argues that it is the fact that America's network of alliances shapes the international environment that ensures China's 'responsible behaviour'.[71]

Eventually the US may be forced to accept a multipolar world of equality with China, and in the future India and others. But for the time being it is chasing the chimera of US 'leadership', and that means pressing China into line economically and militarily.

The structure of this book

This book examines the military, economic and diplomatic means that the US has deployed in its 'pivot' to Asia, and assesses its successes and failures in building an encircling ring of pro-Western alliances around China.

Firstly, in Part I, it considers China's economic achievements, debunks some myths about the alleged human cost of this advance and refutes the case that China faces an imminent collapse, arguing that this amounts to Western wishful thinking. The West's 'China problem' is not about to solve itself through China's implosion under its own internal contradictions. The book goes on to assess China's foreign policy, arguing that the claim that China has embarked on a dangerous, revisionist foreign policy in the Asia-Pacific region accords with neither its stated aims, nor its actions or interests. In this context it surveys the differing policies advocated towards China across the US foreign policy and military establishment, concluding that while they differ on what precise steps to take against China, all are united in the belief that China must be brought to heel irrespective of the facts of China's own foreign policy stance.

In examining the geopolitical consequences of this the book takes a sweep around China's long borders, assessing the US's success or otherwise in its attempts to construct a new Cold War-style set of alliances against China among its neighbours in the economic and political conditions of the twenty-first century. This begins with Russia. Whether Russia is more allied with the US or with China is probably the single most important factor in geopolitical developments in the coming years. So far the US has failed to drive a wedge between Russia and China on the model of the 1972–89 China–America relationship that was so critical to the success of the Cold War, while events in Ukraine have driven them closer together. Trump's proposed reset of US–Russian relations was partly an attempt to address this issue; but a comprehensive deal to draw Russia back towards the West is hard to achieve.

The book then considers US strategies to China's east where key US-ally Japan guards China's eastern seaboard and its gateway to the Pacific, flanked to the north and south by South Korea and the island of Taiwan. The US aims to compose these into a continuous military ring around China's east, bristling with missiles, home to large deployments of US marines and covered by missile defence. This ring would remain igneous with numerous conflicts: separatism in Taiwan; between South Korea and the North; over sovereignty rights; and with rising Japanese nationalism. But the analysis finds that these do not all lead to conflict with China, nor supersede the economic advantages that friendly relations with China can offer.

The discussion next moves to China's south, where the island nations skirting the South China Sea and the states of the Mekong peninsula are increasingly strongly organised together in ASEAN. In a region of conflicting loyalties, the US has had only one entirely reliable friend – the Philippines – and even that has begun to look shaky under its new president Rodrigo Duterte. Disputes over rocks and seabed rights stirred up tensions with China, which the US was quick to exploit, not only stepping up its military presence in the region, but inflicting a defeat on China over its claims in the Sea at the international court of arbitration in The Hague. The US even made some progress in courting Vietnam, which is torn between affinity with China and current and historic conflicts with its larger neighbour. But long-standing US allies such as Thailand and Singapore have been lukewarm about joining an anti-China club. Further west a struggle for the heart of Myanmar has begun as the US-backed democracy movement moves into government.

The book then considers one of the most important issues for US strategy – the tricky relations of India with both China and the US. In this context it also looks at China's Himalayan borders, and the problems of China's vulnerable remotest regions of Tibet and Xinjiang. Finally, it looks at the current state of Great Power play in Central Asia.

The book concludes that, despite its warnings of China's alleged expansionist ambitions in Asia, encouraging India and Russia to contest China for 'Asian leadership', sounding the alarm at China's military and naval advances, and urging a common front to contain China, the US has signally failed to convince the nations of Asia that they face an imminent threat. Its turn to Asia has led to elements of an arms race and has seen a significant sharpening of China's long-standing disputes with Japan and in the South China Sea, but the US has not proved able to set an Asian agenda where defensive concerns about China trump the attractions of collaboration with it for trade and investment. However, rather than retreat, and seek a basis for common development with China, the US remains unreconciled to China's rise. It is caught between its desire to respond more forcefully and its declining economic position, which restricts its capacity to do so. The result is that stability and peace in the region and worldwide are threatened as the US vainly seeks its implausible 'Pacific century' through militarising political relations in Asia, threatening a trade war and fomenting what looks extremely like a new Cold War, with China as the target.

Notes

1 See Chapter 7.
2 T. Phillips, '"Brutal, amoral, ruthless, cheating": how Trump's new trade tsar sees China', *The Guardian*, 22 December 2016.
3 K. Bradsher, 'In China-U.S. trade war, Trump would have weapons', *New York Times*, 10 November 2016.
4 FT reporters, 'China hawk or isolationist? Asia awaits the real Donald Trump', *Financial Times*, 20 November 2016.
5 D. Brunnstrom and M. Spetalnick, 'Trump team struggles for cohesion on tougher China policy', *Reuters*, 14 January 2017.
6 H. R., Clinton, 'America's Pacific century', *Foreign Policy*, 189, 11 October 2011.
7 G. Dyer and T. Mitchell, 'Hillary Clinton: the China hawk', *Financial Times*, 5 September 2016.
8 For more details, see J. Chen, *Mao's China and the Cold War*, University of North Carolina Press, Chapel Hill, 2001.
9 I. M. Destler, *American trade politics*, Institute for International Economics, Washington, DC, 1995, pp. 211–13.
10 See, inter alia, I. C. Cohen, *America's response to China: a history of Sino-American relations* (5th edn), Columbia University Press, New York, 2010; J. A. G. Roberts, *A history of China* (3rd edition), Palgrave Macmillan, Basingstoke, 2011.
11 J. Ross, 'China has overtaken the US to become the world's largest industrial producer', *Key Trends in Globalisation*, 2 September 2013. Available at: http://ablog.typepad.com/keytrendsinglobalisation/2013/09/china-has-overtaken-the-us.html (date accessed 17 February 2017).
12 IMF World Economic Outlook Database (WEO), 2016. GDP 2007–15, current US$. The IMF statistical databases are available at: http://www.imf.org/external/pubs/ft/weo/2016/01/weodata/index.aspx (date accessed 1 March 2017).
13 IMF WEO 2016. GDP 2014, $PPPs: China $17,961 billion; the US $17,348 billion.
14 China's National Bureau of Statistics expressed reservations about the PPP measure used by the World Bank, but measures in current dollars clearly underestimate the relative size of China.
15 IMF WEO 2016. GDP per capita, $PPPs.
16 Forbes Global 2000, 2016 list. China's 15 top companies include 11 banks/insurance companies, two oil, one telecoms and one property developer. The US's 39 top companies include Apple, Google, IBM, Intel, Microsoft and Cisco, to name a few.

17 J. Anderlini, 'Pretoria defends China's Africa policy', *Financial Times*, 24 August 2010.

18 J. F. Kennedy, Commencement Address at American University, Washington, DC, 10 June 1963.

19 G. Kolko, *The politics of war: the world and United States foreign policy, 1943–45*, Pantheon, New York, 1990, pp. 618–19.

20 For a full discussion of the post-war development of the US economy and its global role, see R. Desai, *Geopolitical economy: after hegemony, globalisation and empire*, Pluto, London, 2013.

21 J. Anderlini, 'UK move to join China-led bank a surprise even to Beijing', *Financial Times*, 26 March 2015.

22 US Department of Defence, 'Quadrennial Defence Review Report', Washington, DC, 6 February 2006, p. 29.

23 US Census Bureau 2016. US trade in goods with China, 2008. US Census Bureau international trade data. Available at: https://www.census.gov/foreign-trade/data/index.html (date accessed 1 March 2017).

24 J. Whitesides and C. Bohan, 'Obama and Clinton vow to get tough with China', *Reuters*, 14 April 2008.

25 *US export competitiveness in China: winning in the world's fastest-growing market*, American Chamber of Commerce in Shanghai, Shanghai, 2010.

26 P. Kellogg, 'Contours of a multipolar century', *Rethinking Marxism*, 27:4 (2015), 558–70.

27 J. Stiglitz, *Globalisation and its discontents*, Penguin, London, 2002, p. 143.

28 World Bank, *China 2030: building a modern, harmonious, and creative society*, 23 March 2013, pp. 16–17.

29 Agence France-Presse, 'China says no room for "western values" in university education', *Guardian*, 30 January 2015; S. Tiezzi, 'China's quest for global influence – through think tanks', *The Diplomat*, 22 January 2015. Available at: http://thediplomat.com/2015/01/chinas-quest-for-global-influence-through-think-tanks/ (date accessed 17 February 2017).

30 World Bank, *China 2030*.

31 J. Ross, 'Fundamental errors of the World Bank report on China', *Key Trends in Globalisation*, 18 September 2012. Available at: http://ablog.typepad.com/keytrendsinglobalisation/2012/09/fundamental-errors-of-the-world-bank-report-on-china.html (date accessed 17 February 2017).

32 A. Back, 'Why China's hefty trade surplus is dwarfed by outflows', *Wall Street Journal*, 13 January 2016.

33 World Finance, *The stunted superpower*, World Finance, Special Report, London, 10 January 2013.

34 The third meeting of the full Central Committee of the Chinese Communist Party (plenum) takes place about a year into its five-year term of office. The third plenum following a change of leadership sets overall economic and political direction for the new leadership. Deng Xiaoping's key reforms were introduced at the third plenum of the 11th Central Committee in December 1978, for example.

35 Decision of the Central Committee of the Communist Party of China on some major issues concerning comprehensively deepening the reform, adopted at the Third Plenary Session of the 18th Central Committee of the Communist Party of China on 12 November 2013.

36 The TPP is discussed in detail in Chapter 9.

37 S. Wu, 'Why the TPP is an "economic NATO"', *Huffington Post*, 19 October 2015. Available at: http://www.huffingtonpost.com/wu-sike/tpp-economic-nato_b_8328014.html (date accessed 17 February 2017).

38 All figures from the Stockholm International Peace Research Institute military expenditure database (SIPRI) 2016. SIPRI databases are available at: https://www.sipri.org/databases.

39 These are estimates from several sources, primarily the Centre for Strategic and International Studies and SIPRI.

40 J. Page and J. E. Barnes, 'China shows its growing might: stealth jet upstages Gates, Hu', *Wall Street Journal*, 12 January 2011.

41 International Institute for Strategic Studies, *The military balance 2012*, Routledge, Washington, DC, 2012.

42 J. Perlez, 'Panetta outlines new weaponry for Pacific', *New York Times*, 1 June 2012.

43 Z. Keck, 'US is encircling China with fighter jets and stealth bombers', *The Diplomat*, 30 July 2013. Available at: http://thediplomat.com/2013/07/us-is-encircling-china-with-fighter-jets-and-stealth-bom bers/ (date accessed 17 February 2017).

44 Clinton, 'Pacific century'.

45 For a discussion of the consequences of the 'pivot' on US policy in the eastern Mediterranean see R. N. Haass, 'The irony of American strategy: putting the Middle East in proper perspective', *Foreign Affairs*, 92:3 (May/June 2013), 57–67.

46 D. McManus, 'Chuck Hagel: the Asia pivot is still on', *LA Times*, 30 March 2014.

47 See, inter alia, J. Glaser, 'The ugly truth about avoiding war with China', *The National Interest*, 28 December 2015. Available at: http://nationalinterest.org/feature/the-ugly-truth-about-avoiding-war- china-14740 (date accessed 17 February 2017).

48 M. E. Manyin, 'Pivot to the Pacific? The Obama administration's "rebalancing" towards Asia', Congressional Research Service report R42448, 28 March 2012.

49 J. Nye, 'Only China can contain China', *Huffington Post*, 12 March 2015. Available at: http://www.huffi ngtonpost.com/joseph-nye/china-contain-china_b_6845588.html (date accessed 17 February 2017).

50 T. Perry, 'Kissinger warns Donald Trump to change his posture on China', *CBS News*, 19 December 2016. Available at: http://www.cbsnews.com/news/kissinger-warns-donald-trump-to-change-his- posture-on-china/ (date accessed 17 February 2017).

51 T. Paine, *Common Sense*, pamphlet published 10 January 1776.

52 President George W. Bush, Acceptance speech to the Republican Party convention, New York City, 2 September 2004.

53 A. W. Williams, *The tragedy of American diplomacy*, W.W. Norton & Sons, New York, 1959; P. Anderson, 'Imperium and consilium', *New Left Review*, 83 (September–October 2013), 5–167.

54 N. Ferguson, *Colossus: the rise and fall of the American Empire*, Penguin, London, 2009, p. 2.

55 See, for example, Desai, *Geopolitical economy*.

56 Anderson, 'Imperium', 117.

57 H. Védrine, 'Creating a new international community', *Times Change*, 19 (spring 2000).

58 W. J. Clinton, Inaugural address, 20 January 1997 (inter alia).

59 A 2006 survey found that only 10 per cent of the American public favoured the US retaining a pre- eminent global role, with 75 per cent preferring it shared this role with other nations and 12 per cent preferring total isolation. The Chicago Council on Global Affairs and WorldPublicOpinion.org, *World public opinion 2007*, Chicago Council on Global Affairs, Chicago, 2007, pp. 28–35.

60 Nye, 'Only China'.

61 The White House, Office of the Press Secretary, 'America's future in Asia', remarks as prepared for delivery by national security advisor Susan E. Rice, 21 November 2013.

62 A. S. Erickson and A. P. Liff, 'Not-so-empty talk: the danger of China's "new type of Great Power relations" slogan', *Foreign Affairs*, 9 October 2014. Available at: https://www.foreignaffairs.com/arti- cles/china/2014-10-09/not-so-empty-talk (date accessed 17 February 2017).

63 C. Li and L. Xu, 'Chinese enthusiasm and American cynicism over the "new type of Great Power relations"', *Brookings*, 4 December 2014. Available at: https://www.brookings.edu/opinions/chinese- enthusiasm-and-american-cynicism-over-the-new-type-of-great-power-relations/ (date accessed 17 February 2017).

64 R. Desai, 'Is there a new Cold War?', *Defend Democracy Press*, 4 March 2016. Available at: http:// www.defenddemocracy.press/1738/ (date accessed 17 February 2017).

65 R. D. Blackwill and A. J. Tellis, *Revising US grand strategy towards China*, Council on Foreign Relations, Special Report No. 72, March 2015.

66 United Nations Conference on Trade and Development Statistics database (UNCTADStat), 2016. GDP growth rates. UNCTAD statistical data is available at: http://unctadstat.unctad.org/wds/ReportFolders/reportFolders.aspx?sCS_ChosenLang=en (date accessed 1 March 2017).

67 Male life expectancy fell from 64.5 years in 1989 to 57 years in 1994. It did not recover to 65 until 2012. The equivalent figures for women are 74 years falling to 71 years, and recovering by 2008. Source: Rosstat.

68 'Missile Defence for Korea', *Wall Street Journal*, 15 October 2015.

69 Y. Fu, 'Under the same roof: China's concept of international order', *New Perspectives Quarterly*, 33:1, 2016. Fu Ying is Chair of the Foreign Affairs Committee of the National People's Congress.

70 J. P. Xi, 'Towards a community of common destiny and a new future for Asia', Speech at 2015 Boao Forum for Asia, 28 March 2015.

71 Nye, 'Only China'.

Part I

Is a US–China conflict inevitable?

2

China: a doomed and distorted growth model?

China's advance towards overtaking the US economy in absolute size and eventually in fundamental strength heralds the end of more than a century of American pre-eminence. This is not a small matter. No one living can remember a time when the US was not the largest economy. The last such transition in the modern world was when America itself overtook Britain in the 1870s.[1] Within 70 years the Pax Britannica – based on sterling and the gold standard – had yielded before US attempts to establish a Pax Americana and the dollar as the world currency. This involved fending off other contenders, particularly Germany and in a different way Japan, and two bloody and costly world wars. Given this history, contemplating such a shift leads to understandable anxieties about what the coming decades will bring.

The speed of China's development has been such that it has taken most observers by surprise. In GDP per capita terms its achievement is astonishing: following initial take-off in the 1980s China's GDP per head doubled in a single decade, whereas it took Britain six decades to achieve the same after the Industrial Revolution in the late eighteenth century and America five decades after the Civil War.[2] Western popular ideas of China lagged far behind this change, and still do. Until recently the popular imagining of China saw millions of Mao-suited cyclists when in reality Chinese urbanites were reading *Vogue* and dealing with downtown traffic gridlock. Modern China did not really arrive in Western popular consciousness until 2008, the year of the Beijing Olympics, a US presidential election and the financial crash.

For China, the Beijing Olympics were an opportunity to mark the end of 150 years of conquest, war, humiliation, post-1949 isolation and internal focus required to rebuild its shattered economy and to celebrate its renewed engagement. Film director Zhang Yimou's Opening Ceremony offered a panorama of 4000 years of Chinese culture, science and history, organised to convey that China was open to the world. The show unfolded from the initial projection of the first line of Confucius' *Analects*: 'How delightful it is to welcome friends from afar.'

But despite such efforts and a much-expanded interest in China – including an explosion in Chinese-language classes and increased tourism in both directions – accurate ideas about China remain limited by distance and a lack of cultural currency. The ubiquitous Hollywood and rock 'n' roll culture of the post-war twentieth century means that while most people have not actually been to the US, they do have a largely accurate image of what it is like. Contemporary China is only just beginning to appear in mainstream Western culture and it remains a closed book to the mass of the population in the West.

In this context a negative establishment discourse and a generally hostile mainstream media narrative are subject to little informed scrutiny, and can create and drip feed popular anxieties and prejudices about China that are useful in ensuring popular accept-ance of a Cold War-type agenda against China.

It is not just at the level of popular discourse that fictions and half-truths about China are perpetuated. Serious discussions about China's growth model are also distorted by the determination not to question the canons of neoliberal economics. To sustain the myths of the 'Washington consensus' it has to be claimed that China's economic growth is exaggerated, unsustainable, about to crash or has only come at immense human cost.

This chapter considers some of the myths and exaggerations that inform popular prejudices about China and tackles some misconceived theories that distort more influential opinions, including in assessing China's economic achievements and prospects.

Distorted, damaging growth?

Almost every year the announcement of China's GDP growth figures is met with a chorus of claims that they are not reliable and that China's growth has been over-estimated.[3] But few accounting errors have actually been uncovered, and the World Bank and IMF's assessment of China's growth rates have been virtually identical to those of China itself.

A more sophisticated case holds that China's growth is real but deeply distorted, with huge waste in excessive and unproductive infrastructure investment. A recurring favourite is the claim of weird 'ghost towns' where empty freeways circle unoccupied factory space, malls and housing estates. Some of this is straightforward misinformation. A classic example was a 2013 CBS 60 Minutes programme entitled 'China's Ghost Cities', focusing on Zhengzhou, a fast developing city in Henan province which was selectively filmed to show empty roads, buildings and malls.[4] Journalist Wade Shepard exposed this deceit when he went to the exact places shown a few weeks later and found them full of people; while the 'deserted mall' was just built and businesses were yet to move in.[5] There have been real cases of new urban developments that have stood empty for a while, but such problems have been temporary and they were occupied and functioning within a couple of years.[6]

There also have been examples of over the top and wasteful civic investments – over-large sports stadia and city halls, grand squares, heroic statuary, half-empty exhi-bition halls and ridiculous vanity projects; but such instances of local boosterism or semi-corruption are dwarfed by vital investments in modern metro systems, high-speed rail, metalled roads to every village, an efficient power grid, a network of polyclinics, world-class museums and ground-breaking architecture.

Given the persisting underdevelopment of China's infrastructure there is still vast scope for major investment without this being at all wasteful or unnecessary. Despite its similar geographic size, the total length of China's roads is only 62 per cent of the US's, and its railways only 38 per cent. Rail freight in tonnes per kilometre per capita in China is 23.5 per cent that of the US. Internet use in China is only 53 per cent of the US per capita total.[7] With more than four times the population, China's per capita electricity consumption is only 32 per cent of US levels. And China's 'excessive' per capita fixed investment is only $3,199 annually compared to the US's $10,017.[8]

Other arguments focus on questions of quality of life: ecological problems; that personal consumption has been sacrificed to investment-driven growth; or that only a privileged few have benefited.

An environmental disaster?

Undoubtedly there are major ecological problems. Most well known are those besetting the air quality in the larger cities, where foggy miasmas and invisible pollutants seriously impact on quality of life and adversely affect life expectancy in the most afflicted cities.

Without minimising the seriousness of this challenge – which China's governing organisations have made a central concern, setting high targets by Western standards for the reduction of carbon emissions – they are not exclusively Chinese problems.[9] A World Health Organization (WHO) 2014 report found that New Delhi was the most polluted city in the world, and that the next three worst cities for air quality were also in India.[10] Moreover, these are problems that Western countries were themselves familiar with in the not-so-distant past. London's 'pea-soupers' were a product of rapid, dirty development and were eventually addressed. And while undesirable, neither London's smogs nor China's pollution outweighed the improvement in the population's living standards or general well-being.

It is true that in the context of global warming, reducing China's use of coal in particular has become urgent. China is rising to this challenge, investing $90 billion in renewable energy in 2015, installing more solar power capacity in one quarter than exists in the whole of France, and achieving a record 23 gigawatt of wind power in 2014. China is already the 'superpower of low carbon industries'.[11] In 2016 its consumption of coal was set to fall for the third year in a row, after falling by 2.9 per cent in 2014 and 3.7 per cent in 2015. This decline is primarily due to reduction in coal-fired power plants, but also greater energy efficiency in industry; in 2015 China's power consumption grew by only 0.5 per cent while its economy grew by nearly 7 per cent. China has pledged to eliminate domestic use of coal in the countryside by 2020.[12]

China has also begun to play a decisive role internationally, crucially ensuring terms emerged from the Paris 2015 climate change talks that allowed the developing world to sign up to the agreement.[13] It had prepared the ground for this in 2014 by establishing the South–South Climate Cooperation Fund for climate change initiatives in the developing world to which it pledged $3.1 billion before the Paris talks. China's commitment is demonstrated by the scale of this pledge – similar in size to the US's $3 billion pledge to the UN's Green Climate Fund set up after the 2010 Copenhagen climate change talks to garner contributions from the developed world.

The human cost of growth?

On measures such as rising life expectancy, the elimination of poverty and growth in personal consumption, China has done better than any other country, not only now, but ever. Increases in life expectancy offer the clearest criteria for judging social well-being, as they are the product of the combined impact not just of a rise in per capita GDP but also of environmental, educational, sanitation, health and other considerations.

Correlation of per capita GDP and life expectancy shows that differences in per capita GDP account for 71 per cent of the differences in life expectancy and that on average a doubling of GDP per capita adds four and a half years to male life expectancy and five years to female.[14] However, while per capita GDP accounts for 71 per cent, the balance is down to other social and environmental factors, which explain why life expectancy in individual countries is above or below the international mean for their level of development (see Figure 2.1).

Table 2.1 compares per capita GDP and life expectancy for the major economies – the G7 plus the Brazil, Russia, India, China (BRIC) developing economies. This shows that China not only has a higher ranking in life expectancy than GDP per capita, but it is the best performing in real life expectancy of any of the BRIC economies even though its per capita GDP is not yet as high as Russia or Brazil. Russia's per capita GDP is more than double China's and Brazil's 29 per cent higher, but life expectancy is 69 years in Russia, 73 years and 5 months in Brazil and 73 years and 6 months in China. Overall in the world China ranks 75th in life expectancy, but 86th in GDP per capita, that is, its life expectancy is 11 places higher than would be expected from its level of economic development.[15]

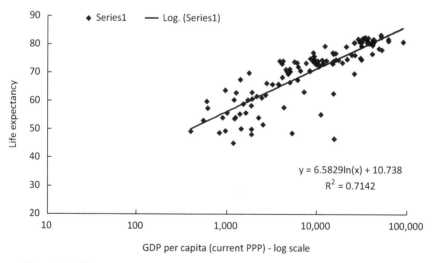

Figure 2.1 *GDP per capita and life expectancy in 2011 (GDP per capita in current PPPs, life expectancy in years)*

Source: *Calculated from World Bank World Developments Indiators, all 117 countries for which full annual data exists in 1960–2011*
© *John Ross*

Table 2.1   *Comparison of world rank in life expectancy and GDP per capita for G7 and BRIC economies in 2011*

Country	World life expectancy rank	Life expectancy rank compared to GDP per capita rank
Developing economies		
China	75	11
Brazil	78	−10
Russia	104	−60
India	119	−3
Advanced economies		
Japan	3	22
Italy	6	20
France	12	12
Canada	18	−1
UK	21	2
Germany	23	−4
US	34	−23

Source: *Calculated from World Bank World Development Indicators*
© *John Ross*

This contrasts with the US, which has the highest per capita GDP of any major developed economy but the lowest life expectancy: average life expectancy is 83 in Japan, 82 in Italy and France, 81 in the UK and Germany, 80 in Canada but less than 79 in the US.

These differences result from the impact of other factors, such as diet, health care, discrimination, sanitation, environmental problems, social support and so on. In other words, contrary to claims that China's growth has been at the cost of human welfare, in China people live three years longer than the global mean for its level of economic development, whereas in the US they live two years less. Of course, China's life expectancy is still significantly lower than that in the US let alone Italy or Japan. For China's people to have the same life expectancy as those in the more advanced economies primarily it needs to continue to raise its GDP per head, while also maintaining and improving the environmental, welfare and social factors that further boost life expectancy.

Elimination of poverty and growth in living standards

These improvements in life expectancy are underpinned by China's progress in the elimination of poverty and improving living standards. Few would deny the global significance of China's achievement in the reduction of poverty. The World Bank's data shows that between 1981 and 2010 the number of people in China living in its definition of 'extreme poverty' fell from 878 million to 150 million – in other words 728 million people were lifted out of extreme poverty in China in the 29 years to 2010. By contrast, in the same period the number of people living in such extreme poverty in the rest of the world outside China only fell by 150 million.[16] Figure 2.2 presents the difference China has made to the elimination of world poverty.

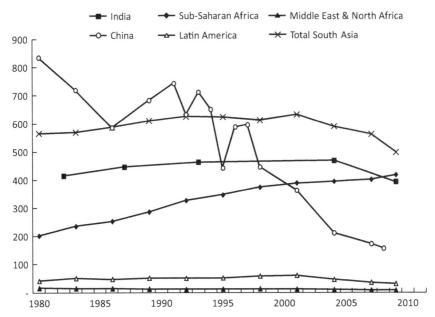

Figure 2.2 *Number living on expenditure of $1.25 a day or less (million people – income measured in PPPs)*
Source: *Calculated from World Bank World Development Indicators*
© *John Ross*

A further measure of China's achievements is its relative level of GDP per capita compared to the rest of the world over time. In 1978 China's population was at the bottom of the global heap; less than 1 per cent of the world's population lived in countries with a per capita GDP lower than China's while 74 per cent lived in countries where GDP per capita was higher. By 2012 China had risen to above the middle with 50 per cent living in countries with lower GDP per capita and only 30 per cent in countries with a higher GDP per capita.[17] This transition is shown in Figure 2.3.

However, the meaning of this achievement is constantly challenged, and not just by the right-wing media. Thus, for example, Wang Chaohua, writing in *New Left Review*, argued that China's successful economic reform and rapid growth had *adversely* affected both rural and urban workers. The rural population, she claimed, suffered the 'pauperisation of villages' turning 'hundreds of millions of peasants' into a deprived 'sub-proletariat'.[18] As for urban workers, despite the introduction of a minimum wage in 2008, 'nowhere has it kept pace with subsequent inflation'.[19] None of these claims are backed up by facts, figures or sources; but even a cursory examination of the statistical information reveals they are simply false.

Long before 2008 wage growth was far outstripping inflation. From 2003 to 2008 the annual growth rate of monthly wages in real terms, that is, adjusted for inflation, was 10.5 per cent in manufacturing, 9.8 per cent in construction and 10.2 per cent for all 'migrant' workers (urban workers with rural residence registration). In the agricultural sector the daily wage paid in the same period rose even faster – 15.1 per cent in grains, 21.4 per cent in larger pig farms and 11.7 per cent in cotton. The rise in real wages

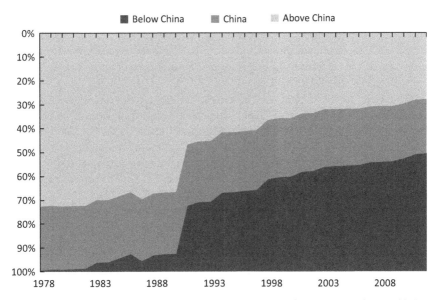

Figure 2.3 *Percentage of world population living in countries with GDP per capita above and below China, 1978–2012 (current US$ – countries for which data exists for all years)*
Source: *Calculated from World Bank World Development Indicators*
© John Ross

slowed from 2008 to 2009, but in 2010 the real wages of migrant workers increased by 19 per cent.[20] These figures are adjusted for inflation, but just for clarity, inflation in China over the same period (2003–10) averaged 3 per cent.[21]

An alternative critique focuses on the sharp rise in inequality over the last decade and a half, suggesting that China's success has only substantially benefited a minority at the top. Inequality has indeed been growing rapidly in China owing to a combination of factors, including the extremely steep rise in the incomes of the top 20 per cent of earners compared to the slower rise in incomes of the bottom 20 per cent, the disparity between rural and urban incomes particularly in the poorer west of the country and the weakness of the welfare safety net.[22] Nonetheless, given the continuous rise in living standards of all sections of the population, it would be radically false to argue from this that only a wealthy top layer has benefited from China's growth. Moreover, there are reasons to be optimistic about the future course of inequality in China.

For example, Milanovic argues: 'The causes of inequality in China are … primarily due to a transition of labour from low-productivity agriculture to a higher productivity industry, not dissimilar from the evolution in the United Kingdom between the mid-1800s and early 20th century or for that matter in the United States between the late 1800s and 1927.'[23] He points out that this transition in both the US and the UK led to an intense upswing in inequality, but this was followed by a downswing as more 'equalising' elements kicked in: reduced urban–rural gap as agriculture became more productive, spread of education across the population reducing the skills premium, and other factors such as the ageing of the population leading to increased demand for social welfare and thus to some greater redistributive taxation and welfare policies. While stressing the difficult and costly challenges this will pose for China in the future, he concludes that 'one can be optimistic: there are strong forces that may curb it in the future. We already see some first signs of it: from rising wages to the demand to extend the social safety net beyond urban state-sector workers.'

That these disparities need to be addressed has been clearly acknowledged, particularly since the 2006 CPC Central Committee Plenum which made building an 'harmonious society' the framework for government policy.[24] More recently, the 13th Five Year Plan proposed by the November 2015 Plenum set targets to reduce income inequality; to raise the proportion of 'middle income' earners in the population; and to lift a further 100 million people out of poverty by 2020, including all the 70.17 million people in rural areas living on an annual income of less than 2,300 RMB ($376).[25]

Given these trends in life expectancy and poverty reduction it is evidently ridiculous to argue that China's growth has been at the expense of its people.

The *hukou* system

The *hukou* system is often a particular focus for critique. This is the residence registration system tied to place of birth (and parents' place of birth) which means workers migrating to the cities for work are not entitled to many welfare benefits, pensions, medical treatment or education for their children in their city of actual residence. In 2013 China's urban population was around 54 per cent, but registered urban residents constituted only 36 per cent or two-thirds of all city dwellers, leaving approximately 260 million people living in Chinese cities without an urban *hukou*.[26]

This can lead to significant hardship and discrimination. In particular, the children of such migrants are often left behind either with one parent or with grandparents leading to long separations. These separations drive the millions of people who are on the move across China at the beginning of the annual two-week Spring Festival (Chinese New Year) holiday.

The *hukou* system interlocks with a factory system in the big cities in the east where the larger employers generally provided onsite accommodation and other facilities. Some – notoriously Foxconn, the Taiwanese components manufacturer – even regulated whether employees could leave the site during non-working hours.[27] Foxconn aside, living offsite without an urban *hukou* to access public housing can be more precarious than living onsite. However, while these are harsh conditions compared to the West, compared to other developing countries such as India, Brazil, Bangladesh and Vietnam, China's pay, working conditions, urban accommodation for the poor, sanitation and other services stand up very well – as they do to the alternative of life in the villages, scratching a living from a smallholding or in rural employment.

Part of the relative smoothness of China's urbanisation has been the restraint of the *hukou* system. Based on historic Chinese traditions of household registration, the current *hukou* was introduced in 1958 as a measure specifically to hold back migration from the land. From the 1980s its straightforwardly repressive aspect – forced removal of unauthorised internal migrants – was progressively relaxed. The rising need for urban workers led the authorities to cease most forcible removals and allow a build-up of unregistered residents in the cities, while in the 1990s the introduction of 'temporary urban residency permits' allowed such workers to regularise themselves for a small cost.

With the rapid growth of China's cities and the higher incomes available in its expanding manufacturing sector acting as a powerful magnet, the *hukou* system was retained to prevent an uncontrolled rush of migrants leaving the land for the cities – the type of human avalanche that has typically produced the slums and shantytowns that disfigure India, Brazil and Egypt.[28] Today these pressures are changing and as a result the *hukou* system is being progressively eliminated. Above-inflation pay rises, weighted towards the manufacturing hubs like Shenzhen and Guangzhou where rises have been even higher than the average, have improved the standard of living of all categories of workers in these centres.[29] This has also driven a shift in some of the most labour-intensive industries to the less developed west of the country where wages are lower, meaning workers migrating from the countryside further west can increasingly choose to remain closer to home, reducing the social impact of migration. These changes meant that from 2011 factories in the east began to report some problems with recruitment, especially after the Spring Festival break as workers failed to return having found other employment.[30]

The growing labour shortage in the east accelerated the discussion on reforming the *hukou* system. From 2013 the government began setting out a framework to abolish the *hukou* and start moving towards a 'place of work'-based registration system. However, there is a huge price tag attached to this for city administrations, as they will become responsible for the costs of health, education and pensions provision for this previously unregistered population. For the big cities in the east this could mean an increase in budgets and provision of up to 50 per cent. This cannot be put in place overnight without crashing city finances. *Hukou* reform is therefore planned in stages: rapidly in smaller towns and cities; moving on to medium-sized cities; with restrictions in place for the larger cities for some time to come. The initial goal is to increase the number with urban registration to around 75 per cent of all city dwellers by 2020.[31]

While the *hukou* system has led to undoubted hardships, many critiques do not accurately consider the alternatives, counterposing this flawed system to a utopian idea that would in practice lead to a whole different set of failures and injustices. In China's major cities there are certainly areas of very poor housing, but not the shanty-towns and temporary dwellings that we recognise as Third World slums. Such slums as these that did begin to develop in the course of the mass rural to urban migrations of the 1990s were all but eliminated through vast programmes of public housing. Some of this 'slum clearance' even went too far, with the destruction of large areas of the historic courtyarded *Hutongs* (Beijing's ancient alleys) or *Shikumen* housing in Shanghai due to their lack of sanitation. This was eventually slowed by popular and conservation movements.

There are many inevitable problems in China, but the question is the degree and speed with which they are being addressed, how the population's welfare is improving over time and how that compares to trends both in the past and elsewhere today. Setting the right measures for what China has achieved means looking at China's poverty reduction compared to other developing economies today or those at a similar stage of development or per capita income. Is its life expectancy higher or lower than the average for its level of development? Explaining China's development in these terms paints an image that is far from unattractive and alien. Rather than a people living in grotesque and repressive conditions, it reveals rapidly rising living standards, increased social mobility and a near universal sense of optimism and hope for the future. Thus, for example, in response to the question as to whether they anticipated that children would be better off in the future than themselves, the 2014 Pew Research Global Attitudes survey found 85 per cent of Chinese believed they would, whereas only 30 per cent of Americans did.[32]

The debate on 'consumption'

A widespread critique of China's growth model alleges that its economy is 'unbalanced' due to an excessively high share of investment and too low a share of consumption in GDP and that, to avoid a crash in demand, China's planners should shift to a new model of 'consumption-led growth'.[33] Such arguments often start from a comparison between investment and household consumption as a share of GDP in the US and China. The contrast is indeed stark. Whereas in 2013 investment constituted 19.8 per cent of GDP in the US, and household consumption 68.6 per cent, in China investment stood at 47.7 per cent and household consumption at 36 per cent, and the proportions have been similar for two decades.[34]

Calls on China to address this 'imbalance' have emanated from some of the most important newspapers and magazines in the West including the *Wall Street Journal*,[35] *The Economist*[36] and the *Financial Times*.[37] Leaving aside their economic merits, such arguments appear attractive, implying China should speed up the growth of household incomes and make everyone better off more or less instantly. But there is an arithmetical confusion behind this suggestion because it is not the *share* of household consumption in GDP that shows whether average living standards are rising and at what rate. A large share of a stagnant economy will leave living standards just as stagnant; for example, the percentage of consumption in GDP of Malawi is 96 per cent, far above China's, but it is the poorest country for which World Bank data exists.

Between 1990 and 2012, as Table 2.2 shows, China's per capita household consumption increased by an annual average 8.1 per cent, or by 8.5 per cent including state expenditure on items such as education and health – the fastest of any major economy. But the *share* of consumption in China's economy did not rise.[38] Table 2.2 shows growth rates of household and total consumption for the major economies – the G7 and BRIC.[39] A high-investment economy that is also a high-growth economy can deliver greater absolute increases in household consumption; and while household income is not the only determinant of quality of life, it is nonetheless the fundamental one.

While increasing living standards has been the aim of economic policy in China since 1949, this cannot be achieved without GDP growth, as this is what propels consumption levels upwards. As a significant 2013 paper on the Chinese economy pointed out:

> Low consumption means high savings levels, which makes high investment possible …
> Indeed, these are among the most important factors behind China's rapid growth. From

1990 to 2010, GDP grew at an average of almost 10.5% a year, while consumption grew at 8.6% (both adjusted for inflation) – no laughing matter when the world average was less than 3%.[40]

Even well-known neoliberal economist Jeffrey Sachs has argued that: 'When American economists advise China to boost consumption and cut savings, they are merely peddling the bad habits of American culture, which saves and invests far too little for America's future.'[41]

In other words, a major shift in resources from investment to consumption would amount to trading in continuous improvement in living standards for a one-off bonus. As Zhang Jun and Zhu Tian put it: 'It may sound paradoxical, but China's relatively low consumption rate is one reason the growth in the rate of its consumption has been so high.'[42]

Moreover, while this discussion on increasing the share of consumption in China's GDP may appear to be about improving living standards, it is not altruism that leads it to be such a persistent theme in Western commentaries on China. It is of a piece with other campaigns – for an appreciation of the RMB, privatising state companies, ruling out further stimulus programmes, stepped up intellectual property protection (IPP) – that all aim at shifting the playing field in China in favour of Western imports and investment and reducing the competitiveness of China's own production. A sharply expanded consumer market in China, within which China itself became progressively less competitive due to a corresponding decline in investment, is a seductive prospect for Western companies facing near stagnant home markets. But even considered as a measure for boosting Western imports into China, its effect would be short-lived as China's economy would slow, disposable incomes would rise more slowly and the domestic market would contract.

Rather than China's economy being about to fail because of a shortfall in consumer demand, maintaining a high level of savings and therefore investment has driven its

Table 2.2 *Consumption – annual percentage change (measured in inflation adjusted 2005 dollars)*

	Household Consumption		Total Consumption	
	1978–2012	*1990–2012*	*1978–2012*	*1990–2012*
China	7.7%	8.1%	7.9%	8.5%
India	5.3%	5.9%	5.4%	5.9%
Russia	n/a	4.1%	n/a	3.2%
Brazil	3.2%	3.7%	3.2%	3.3%
US	3.0%	2.9%	2.7%	2.6%
Canada	2.7%	2.8%	2.4%	2.5%
UK	2.8%	2.4%	2.4%	2.3%
France	1.8%	1.5%	1.9%	1.6%
Germany	1.6%	1.2%	1.5%	1.3%
Japan	2.1%	1.1%	2.3%	1.4%
Italy	1.7%	0.8%	1.6%	0.8%

Source: Calculated from World Bank World Development Indicators
© John Ross

rapid growth. A contraction – of around 1 per cent of GDP – in the overall savings level in China from 2014 is one of the reasons why its growth slowed from a steady 8–9 per cent to 7.7 per cent in 2013, 7.4 per cent in 2014 and 6.9 per cent in 2015.[43]

Is China's economy about to collapse?

Other distortions attributed to the Chinese economy include rampant debt, shadow banking, property bubbles, excessive investment and over-reliance on exports. Whichever argument is popular at particular points in time or with particular lobbies, the conclusion is the same: China's economy rests on unstable foundations and will imminently crash. A crash has been repeatedly and regularly predicted for two decades, often by exactly the same people, with each unfulfilled prediction leading to no greater adjustment in their failed analysis than a shift in what is meant by 'imminent'.

This 'economic fantasy literature' includes *The coming collapse of China* by Gordon Chang – frequently rolled out as chief China pundit by *Bloomberg* and others.[44] His 2001 book claimed that China had 'run out of time' and predicted collapse by 2011.[45] When that did not happen he extended it to 2012. In fact from 2002 to 2012 China experienced a decade of the fastest growth ever recorded in a major economy. Similarly *The Economist's* special supplement on China in 2002 was entitled 'A dragon out of puff'.[46] Fourteen years later it was still arguing: 'It is a question of when, not if, real trouble will hit China.'[47] More recently Will Hutton described the Chinese economy as 'a giant Ponzi scheme', 'an edifice waiting to implode'.[48]

Every kink in the Chinese economy is greeted with catastrophist headlines. When the Shanghai stock market fell sharply in mid-2015, *Bloomberg* claimed this 'could do even more damage than the US subprime crisis'.[49] The *Wall Street Journal* pronounced it was 'scarier than Greece' and that 'the global repercussions could be more severe'.[50] Factually such claims were pure nonsense: the 2008 US subprime crash bankrupted the entire US banking system and created the 'Great Recession'; in Greece all the banks were closed for weeks. In Shanghai, not very many people lost some money and it had zero impact on the real economy. But the 'end is nigh' headlines kept coming.

Response to the 2008 financial crisis

Of course, in 2008 a great crisis did occur, but the tsunami in the world financial system originated in and primarily affected the West, not China. While China suffered a steep decline in exports, it rapidly responded with a $586 billion stimulus package, mainly allocated to infrastructure investment plus some social programmes.[51] As a result China not only avoided slowdown, stagnation and recession through 2008 to 2010, but on the contrary enjoyed strong growth after the initial shock.

But rather than compare this favourably with the stagnation afflicting the West, every slight blip in the Chinese economy after 2008 – an incipient real estate bubble, some ill-judged investments, some expansion of inventories, a rise in inflation, some overheating – was presented as a sign of impending catastrophe. When these problems were overcome, the doom mongering focused on the relative slowdown of the Chinese economy compared to its previous growth rates. Somehow this was presented as redounding to the US's credit even though US growth had virtually flat-lined since 2008.[52]

China's annual average growth coming out of the crisis over the seven years from 2008 to 2014 was 8.9 per cent compared to 1.4 per cent in the US, 0.7 per cent in Japan and 1.1 per cent in Germany.[53] The 13th Five Year Plan, announced in autumn 2015, projected a minimum of 6.5 per cent per year from 2015 to 2020. Even this reduced rate of growth is nonetheless approaching three times that of the best projections for the US of 2.6 per cent per year. While it is true that the US emerged from the crisis rather better than most of the other Western economies, China's economy has enjoyed by far the best overall performance of any major economy since 2007.

Comparing the actual growth in each case gives a sense of proportion. Figure 2.4 demonstrates the relative post-crisis growth performance of China compared to the US, Europe and Japan to 2014. Over the seven years from 2007, China grew by 80.5 per cent, compared to 7.3 per cent for the US, 0.6 per cent in Japan and 5.2 per cent in Germany.[54] Saying that China's growth is 'slowing', but not noting that China's total growth has been more than ten times that of the US since 2007, distorts the truth.

Given this outcome, the obvious conclusion would be to learn from what China did. Instead China has been urged to abandon the policies responsible for this success, reduce its level of investment and privatise its state sector. It was state companies which carried out a major part of the stimulus programme and state ownership of the banks that allowed China to instruct its financial system to engage in countercyclical investment programmes while all that Western governments could do was to plead with non-compliant private banks and companies.

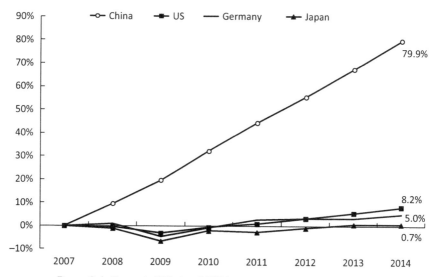

Figure 2.4 *Change in GDP since 2007 (percentage change in constant prices)*

Source: *Calculated for China from IMF World Economic Outlook October 2014 & National Bureau of Statistics, other countries calculated from OECD GDP data*
© John Ross

An ageing population will undermine growth?

With the publication of UN figures showing that China's fertility rate had fallen to 1.56 – less than is necessary to maintain the population – implying an ageing population and declining workforce, it was argued that these demographic factors are a time bomb under China's growth.[55] For example, *The Economist* proposed: 'Unlike the rest of the developed world, China will grow old before it gets rich.'[56]

This argument holds up no better than the others. Although a decline in the working-age population would shave a little off China's growth, this is not decisive. Research by Singapore-based economist Vu Minh Khuong shows that increases in China's working-age population made only a relatively small contribution to its economic growth, of which 94 per cent was due to factors other than increase in the labour supply.[57] Figure 2.5 shows the result of Vu's calculations for China's GDP growth from 1990 to 2010, concluding that 64.2 per cent of China's growth was due to investment increases, 29.7 per cent to increases in productivity and only 6.1 per cent to increases in labour supply.[58]

China's average growth rate was 9.8 per cent in the period, based on Vu's calculations labour contributed around 0.7 per cent and investment and productivity 9.1 per cent. In other words, without any increase in labour supply, average growth in the period would have been 9.1 per cent rather than 9.8 per cent. That would have been a slower rate of growth, but not a 'deadly point of unseen weakness'.[59] Moreover,

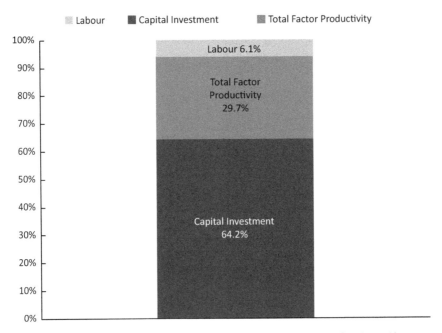

Figure 2.5 *Sources of China's GDP growth, 1990–2010 (percentage of total growth)*

Source: *Vu (2013) Table 4.1*
© John Ross

Vu's calculations are supported by simple arithmetic: the annual average increase in China's GDP was 9.8 per cent, but its working-age population (15–64) only grew at an annual average of 1.7 per cent, thus this could not possibly have been the main motor of China's rapid economic growth.[60]

The UN estimates China will reach its peak population in 2026 (not including potential increases in immigration).[61] If it sustains investment and productivity improvements, then the impact of demography will slow it somewhat but there is no reason for it to lead to collapse. However, a contracting workforce does add to the reasons why China has grown out of the possibilities of a successful economic strategy based simply on low wages. This is why the next phase of Chinese economic development is already focused on stepped-up investment in R&D and technology to maintain its price advantage through innovations in production techniques.

China's alleged lack of innovatory world-leading high-tech companies – 'China has no Apple or Microsoft' or 'China produces jobs but not Jobs' – is another reason proffered for why China's growth is not sustainable.[62] In fact, while it is hardly surprising that at China's level of development it does not challenge in novel, high-tech consumer products like the iPhone, in areas of innovation related to low-cost production techniques China is currently the unchallenged world leader.

Debunking the idea that China is weak on innovation and pointing to its strength in developing new production methods, Dan Breznitz and Michael Murphree's *Run of the Red Queen* makes the case that:

> As China has become the global centre for many different stages of production, it has also developed a formidable competitive capacity to innovate in different segments of the research, development, and production chain that are as critical for economic growth as many novel-product innovations.[63]

Chinese innovation is directed at reducing production costs and developing production flexibility that allows its companies to continue to compete on price despite rising labour costs. It will be sometime before China moves beyond competing on price, but China is building up a formidable capacity in 'cost innovation', using innovations in technology and management to maintain a global price advantage despite strongly rising wages.[64]

China is not a balloon about to burst

In sum, rather than collapse, long-term trends in both the American and Chinese economy would suggest that – barring a catastrophic change of policy, a new international crisis with unforeseen consequences or a major war – China will continue to grow faster than the US for a considerable time to come. It is the imminent threat that China will overtake it – not the imminent threat of a Chinese economic crisis – that has driven the US 'pivot to Asia' and reorganised its defence priorities.

Notes

1 A. Maddison, *The world economy: a millennial perspective*, Vol. 2: Historical statistics, OECD, Paris, 2006, Tables 1b and 2b.

2 Ibid., Tables 1c and 2c. (Later, during the Second World War, 1939–45, US per capita GDP doubled in five years, but this was not sustained.).

3 See, for example, E. Cary, 'The curious case of China's GDP figures', *The Diplomat*, 5 March 2013. Available at: http://thediplomat.com/2013/03/the-curious-case-of-chinas-gd-figures/ (date accessed 19 February 2017).

4 CBS, 'China's ghost cities', *60 Minutes*, 3 March 2013. Available at: http://www.cbsnews.com/videos/chinas-real-estate-bubble-4/ (date accessed 20 October 2016).

5 W. Shepard, 'A journey to Zhengdong, China's largest ghost city', *Vagabond Journey*, 13 March 2013. Available at: http://www.vagabondjourney.com/zhengzhou-zhengdong-china-largest-ghost-city/ (date accessed 20 October 2016).

6 W. Shepard, *Ghost cities of China*, Zed Press, London, 2015.

7 All figures calculated from CIA World Factbook 2014, except Internet use which is calculated from http://www.internetlivestats.com/internet-users-by-country/ (July 2014). CIA World Factbook data and statistics available at: https://www.cia.gov/library/publications/the-world-factbook/ (date accessed 1 March 2017).

8 Calculated from World Bank world development indicators, 2015, gross fixed capital formation in current US$. World Bank development indicators can be found at http://databank.world bank.org/data/reports.aspx?source=world-development-indicators (date accessed 1 March 2017).

9 Report on the work of the Government, delivered at the third session of the 12th National People's Congress on 5 March 2015 by Li Keqiang, Premier of the State Council, p. 33.

10 G. Harris, 'Cities in India among the most polluted, WHO says', *New York Times*, 8 May 2014.

11 A. Evans-Pritchard, 'Even if the global warming scare were a hoax, we would still need it', *Daily Telegraph*, 16 December 2015.

12 S. Yeo, 'Analysis: decline in China's coal consumption accelerates', *Carbon Brief*, 29 February 2016. Available at: https://www.carbonbrief.org/analysis-decline-in-chinas-coal-consumption-accelerates (date accessed 17 February 2017).

13 S. Tiezzi, 'China celebrates Paris climate change deal', *The Diplomat*, 15 December 2015. Available at: http://thediplomat.com/2015/12/china-celebrates-paris-climate-change-deal/ (date accessed 17 February 2017).

14 Calculated from World Bank indicators 2016. Life expectancy and per capita GDP (in $ppp) for 117 countries, 2011. Courtesy: John Ross.

15 Other countries outside this group also show variations. For example, from the same data as used for Table 2.1, Zambia ranked 99th in GDP per capita, but 111th in life expectancy; Spain, ranked 24th in GDP per capita, but 5th in life expectancy.

16 Calculated from World Bank indicators 2016. Those living on $1.90 a day (in 2011 $PPPs). Courtesy: John Ross.

17 Calculated from World Bank indicators 2016. Per capita GDP, current $. Courtesy: John Ross.

18 C. H. Wang, 'The Party and its success story', *New Left Review*, 91 (January–February 2015), 35–6.

19 Ibid., p. 33.

20 C. Wang, 'China's rising wages', *East Asia Forum*, 5 September 2011. Available at: http://www.eastasiaforum.org/2011/09/05/chinas-rising-wages/ (date accessed 17 February 2017).

21 Worldwide Inflation Data, Triami Media BV, Utrecht, 2016. Available at: http://inflation.eu/inflation-rates/china/historic-inflation/cpi-inflation-china.aspx (date accessed 16 February 2017).

22 S. Cevik and C. Correa-Caro, 'Growing (un)equal: fiscal policy and income inequality in China and BRIC+', IMF Working Paper, WP/15/68, IMF, March 2015.

23 B. Milanovic, 'Inequality in the United States and China', *Harvard Business Review*, 27 January 2014. Available at: https://hbr.org/2014/01/inequality-in-the-united-states-and-china (date accessed 17 February 2017).

24 M. Fan, 'China's party leadership declares new priority: "harmonious society"', *Washington Post*, 12 October 2006.

25 Xinhua, 'China unveils 13th Five Year Plan roadmap', *China Daily Asia*, 3 November 2015.

26 B. An, 'Hukou reforms 2020 target official', *China Daily*, 18 December 2013.

27 'Foxconn: working conditions in Chinese factories', *Facing Finance*, 2012. Available at: http://www.facing-finance.org/en/database/cases/working-conditions-in-foxconn-factories-in-china/ (date accessed 10 July 2015).

28 M. Davis, *Planet of slums*, Verso, London, 2006.

29 'China wages seen jumping in 2014 amid shift to services', *Bloomberg News*, 6 January 2014. Available at: https://www.bloomberg.com/news/articles/2014-01-06/china-wages-seen-jumping-in-2014-amid-shift-to-services- (date accessed 17 February 2017).

30 W. Li and R. Lu, 'Factories struggle to find, keep workers', *China Daily*, 21 February 2013.

31 'China's cities: the great transition', *The Economist*, 22 May 2014.

32 Pew Research Centre, Global Attitudes Survey, 2015.

33 See, for example, M. Pettis, *Avoiding the fall: China's economic restructuring*, Carnegie Endowment for International Peace, Washington, DC, 2013.

34 World Bank indicators, 2015.

35 C. Tejeda, 'ChinaRealTime', *Wall Street Journal*, 20 January 2012.

36 'Rebalancing China: China's consumer-led growth', *The Economist*, 20 October 2012.

37 'Editorial, China still awaits genuine reform', *Financial Times*, 7 November 2013.

38 J. Ross, 'China has the world's fastest growth in living standards', *China.org.cn*, 27 September 2013. Available at: http://www.china.org.cn/opinion/2013-10/24/content_30391004.htm (date accessed 17 February 2017).

39 Table 2.2 compares rates of growth in consumption from the beginning of China's reform in 1978 to 2011 – as the relevant data for Russia is only available from 1990, a comparison for 1990–2011 is also included.

40 J. Zhang and T. Zhu, 'Re-estimating China's under-estimated consumption', *Social Science Research Network*, 7 September 2013. Available at: https://ssrn.com/abstract=2330698 (date accessed 17 February 2017).

41 J. D. Sachs, 'The global economy's marshmallow test', *Project Syndicate*, 8 February 2016. Available at: https://www.project-syndicate.org/commentary/global-economic-recovery-higher-investment-by-jeffrey-d-sachs-2016-01?barrier=accessreg (date accessed 17 February 2017).

42 Zhang and Zhu, 'Re-estimating China's consumption'.

43 J. Ross, 'Why China can achieve its 6.5 per cent growth rate target', *China Daily*, 10 March 2016.

44 J. Ross, *Yī pán dà qí? Zhōngguó xīn mìngyùn jiěxī* (The great game of Go: new perspectives on China's future), Jiangsu Phoenix, Beijing, 2016, ch. 2.

45 G. C. Chang, *The coming collapse of China*, Random House, New York, 2001.

46 J. Miles, 'A dragon out of puff', *The Economist*, 13 June 2002.

47 'The coming debt bust', *The Economist*, 7 May 2016.

48 W. Hutton, 'Why are we looking on helplessly as markets crash all over the world?', *The Guardian*, 17 January 2016.

49 W. Pesek, 'If China isn't a global risk, what is?', *Bloomberg*, 16 July 2015. Available at: https://www.bloomberg.com/view/articles/2015-07-16/if-china-isn-t-a-global-risk-what-is- (date accessed 17 February 2017).

50 R. Sharma, 'China's stock plunge is scarier than Greece', *Wall Street Journal*, 7 July 2015.

51 'Supporting China's infrastructure stimulus under the INFRA programme', World Bank INFRA Update, June 2010.

52 M. Pettis, 'Revisiting my 2011 predictions', 24 September 2013. Available at: http://blog.mpettis.com/2013/09/revisiting-my-2011-predictions/ (date accessed 20 October 2016).

53 UNCTADStat 2016, GDP growth rates.
54 Calculated for China from IMF WEO & National Bureau of Statistics, other countries calculated from OECD GDP data 2016, courtesy John Ross.
55 United Nations, 'World population prospects: the 2012 revision, key findings and advance tables', United Nations Department of Economic and Social Affairs, Population Division, Working Paper No. ESA/P/WP.227, United Nations, 2013.
56 'Demography, China's Achilles heel', *The Economist*, 21 April 2012.
57 M. K. Vu, *The dynamics of economic growth: policy insights from comparative analyses in Asia*, Edward Elgar, Cheltenham, 2013.
58 Ibid.
59 'Demography, China's Achilles heel'.
60 Calculated from World Bank indicators 2016, courtesy John Ross.
61 UN World population prospects, 2012 revision, 2013.
62 Kellogg, 'Contours'.
63 D. Breznitz and M. Murphree, *Run of the red queen: government, innovation, globalization, and economic growth in China*, Yale University Press, New Haven, CT, 2011, p. 4.
64 Z. Ming and P. J. Williamson, *Dragons at your door: how Chinese cost innovation is disrupting global competition*, Harvard Business School Press, Boston, MA, 2007.

3

Can China rise peacefully?

The case that China must be contained rests on the premise that it is – or is about to be – engaged in a coercive expansion of its influence in 'Central Asia, the South China Sea, the internet and outer space'.[1] And that it is only a matter of time before China tries 'to push the United States out of the Asia-Pacific region, much the way the United States pushed the European great powers out of the Western Hemisphere in the 19th century'.[2] China's rise is cast as dangerous for the security of its neighbours and world peace, with the maintenance of the leading role of the US, especially in Asia, the only guarantee of regional and global stability.

China has indeed perceptibly shifted to a more assertive foreign policy since the mid-2000s and particularly since the change of leadership in 2013, pursuing its general international interests more emphatically, especially where its energy and trade security are at stake. However, as this chapter will argue, this is about greater confidence and growing influence, not a new aggressive stance.

Peaceful co-existence

The first period of foreign policy of the PRC under Mao, from 1949 to 1976, was extremely turbulent. After 1949 the PRC immediately became a target of US Cold War policies including internal destabilisation, threats of invasion and nuclear attack, international isolation and sanctions. This period included the hot war with the US in Korea, the 1962 border war with India and the anti-colonial and US wars in Vietnam. The Sino-Soviet split in the 1960s added border wars and tensions with the USSR to this stormy scenario. Throughout the US sought to 'triangulate' the tensions between Moscow and Beijing, first encouraging the USSR against China, and then, after the Nixon 'thaw' in 1972, binding China as a quasi-ally to many of its own international policy operations.

From 1949 until his death in 1976 Chinese foreign policy was the responsibility of Zhou Enlai, premier and second only to Mao in the post-1949 PRC. He steered the PRC through the international consequences of the Sino-Soviet split in the 1960s and then took the astonishing step of secretly meeting Kissinger and inviting Nixon to China in 1971–72, resetting relations between the PRC and the US.

Zhou had set out China's distinctive approach to foreign policy – within which the later thaw with the US sat quite logically – in 1954 when, at a meeting with president Nehru of India, he put forward 'Five Principles of Peaceful Co-existence', as a guide to the conduct of international relations between developing countries.[3] These five principles – mutual respect for territorial integrity and sovereignty; mutual non-aggression; non-interference in each other's internal affairs; equality and mutual benefit; and peaceful co-existence – still inform Chinese foreign policy.[4] They are frequently put forward as the explanation for China's position on issues today, for example in opposing sanctions on countries in response to the internal actions of their governments, or refusing to condemn the domestic behaviour of regimes.

These principles informed the PRC's approach to the multiple border disputes that confronted it – the bequest of the many foreign encroachments on China's territory in the 100 years to 1949. Adventurist attempts to reclaim lost territories were precluded and, instead, China pursued compromises based on the de facto existing borders, while being prepared to use force to resist any attempt to encroach on those borders, as in the 1962 confrontation with India.[5]

This approach also applied to the territories of Taiwan, Hong Kong and Macau which, at different times, had been occupied by Japan, Britain and Portugal. Taiwan had been handed back to China in 1945 but the retreat of the GMD to the island in 1949 meant it was once again separated from the administration of mainland China. This has never been accepted, although realpolitik also dictated that while the GMD was protected by the US there was little that could be done to change it.[6] Hong Kong and Macau were not handed back in 1945, as the UK and Portugal insisted they had treaty rights to occupy the islands. China accepted waiting for the leases agreed under the nineteenth-century 'unfair treaties' to expire.

Away from China itself, the PRC supported the post-war anti-colonial struggles – colonialism was an offence to Zhou's five principles, let alone the CPC's ideological opposition to imperialism.[7] But China's low level of development meant it could extend little material aid, and its support for such struggles, including for pro-Chinese or Maoist currents within them, remained largely political, except in Vietnam and Cambodia.[8]

'Hide strength, bide our time'

As Zhou succumbed to illness in 1973, he urged Mao to recall Deng Xiaoping from Cultural Revolution exile.[9] Deng was an admirer of Zhou's cautious and tactically astute foreign policy, but Mao had not entirely abandoned the leftist politics of the Cultural Revolution period and it was not possible for Zhou or Deng to pursue exactly the more conciliatory foreign policy that both favoured.[10] In 1974 Deng made the first speech by a Chinese leader to the UN – to which China had been admitted in 1971 as part of the growing thaw with the US – but the policy he outlined was Mao's. It called for unity of the 'third world' against the 'two superpowers' (the US and the USSR) who were the 'biggest international exploiters and oppressors of today', an approach that did not help the normalisation of China's relations with either.[11] Only after the death of Mao in September 1976 and the ousting of the 'Gang of Four' who had driven the ultra-left politics of the Cultural Revolution was Deng Xiaoping able to fully direct China's foreign policy.

When Deng became the PRC's de facto leader in 1978 his core priority was to address China's failing domestic economic policy through what became known as 'reform and opening up'. As this crucially involved increasing China's engagement with the world market and stepping up trade, he sought greater stability in foreign relations, both to facilitate this and to allow the CPC leadership to focus on domestic growth.[12] Deng's approach was summed up in his famous phrase: 'hide strength, bide our time' (tāo guāng yōng huì).[13] This meant, alongside minimising disputes with its neighbours, in other conflicts where China did not have a direct interest, it either took a neutral stance or, given the thaw with the US from 1972, more usually aligned itself with the US.

Apart from the brief invasion of Vietnam in 1979 (discussed in Chapter 11) – which Deng believed was necessary to prevent China's encirclement by hostile, pro-Soviet states after Vietnam's overthrow of the pro-Chinese Khmer Rouge in Cambodia – he avoided international confrontations.[14] He eased tensions with the USSR, Japan and China's other neighbours.[15] Most important however was the long-awaited 1979 normalisation of relations between the US and China under president Carter, when Deng reached agreement with the US despite its continued support for Taiwan.

Deng successfully negotiated compromise deals on the outstanding land frontier disputes in all but two cases (with India and Bhutan), where Indian intransigence made a compromise agreement impossible.[16] He maintained and deepened the approach of 'mutual inaction' on China's various maritime sovereignty disputes. This allowed the 1978 normalisation of relations with its old enemy Japan, with which there had been no peace treaty after 1945. Deng saw Japan as an important regional partner in China's economic development; therefore, he set about a typical 'Deng-style' compromise to deal with the outstanding obstacles to normal relations. On the key outstanding issue between them, the disputed sovereignty over the Diaoyu/Senkaku islands, Deng said:[17]

> It is true that the two sides maintain different views on this question … It does not matter if this question is shelved for some time … Our generation is not wise enough to find common language on this question. Our next generation will certainly be wiser. They will certainly find a solution acceptable to all.[18]

In 1991 China normalised relations with Vietnam, which had been troubled since their conflict in 1979 and by ongoing differences in Cambodia. In 1992 China agreed mutual recognition with South Korea, finally normalising relations following the Korean War. In the 1990s high-level visits put relations with India on to an even keel, with agreements on how to manage the disputed borders. The Sino-Soviet split had formally ended with Gorbachev's visit to China in 1989 and was sealed with the 2001 Treaty of Good-Neighbourliness and Friendly Cooperation between China and the Russian Federation. But Deng did not take China into any new military treaties or formal alliances, meaning its only such treaty today is with North Korea.

Deng's approach continued to determine Chinese foreign policy throughout the 1990s and into the new century. In the UN China abstained on the 1991 Gulf War. It voted for the ultimatum to Iraq on allowing weapons inspectors access and the surrender of alleged weapons of mass destruction (WMDs) in the lead-up to the 2003 Iraq

War. It was generally understood that China would have abstained had a resolution authorising force against Iraq gone to the Security Council. Despite being a significant importer of Iranian oil, it voted for sanctions on Iran in 2006, 2007 and 2010. It abstained on the Security Council motion authorising a no-fly zone over Libya.

From 1978 China had begun to engage more actively in other international institutions, particularly those bearing on the world economy and global trade. It took up the China seat at the World Bank in 1980; became an observer at GATT from 1986; and lobbied for membership of the World Trade Organization (WTO), which it achieved in 2001. It also supported a range of UN-sponsored international initiatives, on genocide, race discrimination, torture, women's rights and other issues. Regionally, in the 1990s, it stepped up its engagement with ASEAN, from 1997 helping to establish ASEAN plus three (APT), which brought China, Japan and South Korea into formal relations with the ASEAN group of countries.

In other words, from 1978 to the new century, the emphasis in China's foreign policy was to ease its relations and extend its cooperation with neighbours; it made no new military alliances, but did conclude friendship agreements and other exchanges with a range of countries, avoiding conflict with the US in particular. As one Chinese expert put it: 'This [policy] means for the last 20 years or so China has stood alone on the world stage, a completely neutral power without allies and assiduously avoiding making enemies, insularly focused on its internal development in the shadow of the US-led global system.'[19]

'Peaceful rise'

By the time of the 2002 change in leadership to Hu Jintao and Wen Jiabao, a new narrative was needed to explain China's foreign policy. Its runaway economic growth for more than two decades meant that China needed a way of expressing its continuing neutral and unassertive foreign policy direction, while acknowledging its growing strength and more visible international role, particularly in trade. The phrase 'peaceful rise' emerged from the 16th Congress of the CPC in 2002, first used by CPC theoretician and leadership advisor Zheng Bijian. He explained:

> Our path is different from both the paths of Germany in World War I and Germany and Japan in World War II, when they tried to overhaul the world political landscape by way of aggressive wars. Our path is also different from that of the former USSR during the reign of Brezhnev, which relied on a military bloc and arms race in order to compete with the United States for world supremacy.
>
> Our brand new path relies upon … reciprocity and mutual benefit with other countries for the purpose of win-win relations.[20]

This did not mean abandoning 'hide strength, bide our time' and all it implied for collaboration, neutrality and trade, but did mean acknowledging that China was now under greater international scrutiny and would have to tread more carefully and explain its views more clearly than before. China began to play a more active role in multilateral initiatives, while still avoiding conflict with or challenge to the US.

Emergence

The 2008 financial crisis marked a new shift. As the world economy lurched into a recession – with world GDP registering negative growth of –2.01 per cent in 2009 – affecting the advanced economies worst, China's continuing dynamic growth was in stark contrast. Observers no longer pondered whether China would overtake the US, but when.

The early vibrations of this seismic shift had already been troubling the old world order, reflected in the increasing attention China received from Pentagon planners and White House strategists, but after 2008 they became impossible to ignore. Even before the crisis American power was perceptibly declining, belying the triumphalism that only 15 years earlier had swept through US neocon elites when, following victory in the Cold War, US pre-eminence superficially seemed so secure and its power to shape the world order so unrestricted. The 1997 founding of the mememetically named think tank Project for a New American Century had given expression to this wave of American hubris, urging the US to overthrow Saddam Hussein in Iraq as an initial demonstration of its new untrammelled power.[21] With many of its founders – including Cheney, Gaffney, Rodman, Rumsfeld and Wolfowitz – becoming central to the George W. Bush administration, their strategy was put to the test in 2003 with the launch of 'shock and awe' against Iraq. But the global response to this unilateral action rapidly became a demonstration not of US dominance, but rather its declining influence. With almost no advanced countries, apart from Britain, joining Bush's 'coalition of the willing', 'the rest of the world rejected American leadership to an extent that had no precedent in the annals of US hegemony'.[22] Although the US was able to recoup its position with a unanimous October 2003 Security Council resolution endorsing its occupation of Iraq, the failure of the US war machine to deliver a resounding victory against the weak, ill-armed, divided and unseasoned resistance in Iraq further undermined claims that the world was entering a new American century.

The financial crash of 2008, originating in the US financial system and expanding outward to take in most of its closest allies and collaborators, shattered any residual belief in an unchallenged US-led unipolar global power system and undermined the authority of the West in general. If the failures of the 'war on terror' had demonstrated the frailties of even the US's continuing global military leadership, 2008 exposed its more fundamental economic decline. Above all, the financial crisis revealed how important China had become to the world economy as its growth helped avert an ongoing global recession.

The 2009 meeting of the G20, which had been a sop to the developing world and a sideshow to the G7/8, superseded the latter to become the more important meeting in the informal economic governance of the world. The summit meeting between Obama and Hu Jintao in 2009 was referred to as the 'G2' and Obama described China and the US as the relationship that would 'shape the course of the 21st century'.[23] This flattery of course went hand in hand with the preparations for the mighty shift in foreign policy towards containing China that was the US's real response to this emergence of Chinese influence. But in the immediate aftermath of the crisis that was subordinated to tying China into helping solve the West's problems. China was courted by the EU, was asked to bail out Greece (which it helped), developed a special relationship with Germany (which voted against EU sanctions on Chinese solar panels), was pursued for inward investment by France and the UK and was welcomed across the developing world.[24]

This coincided with what had been an observable shift in Chinese foreign policy to a more active role in regional and global developments that bear on its interests. This was particularly well put by David Finkelstein:

> Relative to previous periods, Chinese diplomatic activities in recent years seem to be increasingly proactive and flexible … in the sense that China is no longer willing to merely react to changes in the external environment; rather, when possible, it attempts to shape the external environment—especially the regional environment … Overall, Beijing now seeks a seat at the international and regional tables of note where the rules of the road are being developed, in order to shape outcomes favourable to its interests.[25]

Before the 2008 crisis China had already been more proactively engaging in a range of multilateral frameworks, like the APT, and had even begun to play a significant role in kick-starting such initiatives, as with the six-nation talks on Korean denuclearisation; the Shanghai Co-operation Organisation (SCO), bringing together Russia, China and four of the Central Asian republics; and the Bangladesh–China–India–Myanmar (BCIM) Forum for Regional Cooperation. In another sign of the changing times, from 2009 the four BRIC countries (Brazil, Russia, India and China), originally grouped by Goldman Sachs simply as the four most successful developing economies, formalised their links with the first of what became annual summits.

The Security Council veto

There was also a marked change in China's role in the UN Security Council, as it increasingly broke with its long-standing semi-neutral position, using its veto six times after 2011 to block UN-backed sanctions or military strikes against Syria. This was an unprecedented level of activity given that between assuming its seat in the Security Council in 1971 and 2011, it had used its veto only five times, and only once before 1997.[26] By contrast, the US had used its veto 83 times, the UK 32 times, France 18 times and the USSR/Russia 128 times.[27]

The roots of China's strong stand on Syria lay in the growing importance of its relations with Russia and in its objections to the way the US and its allies had used the 2011 vote on Libya to pursue 'regime change'. China saw the claims of Western liberal interventionism as destructive of stable international relations in general, while the lesson of Iraq was that such Western 'regime change' led to a dangerous spread of chaos and terror. China and Russia had understood the Libya resolution would simply allow enforcement of a 'no-fly zone' instead it was used to justify a bombing campaign aimed at the overthrow of Gaddafi. At the height of the NATO action the Russian and Chinese presidents, Dmitry Medvedev and Hu Jintao, issued a joint statement calling on other nations not to 'allow the wilful interpretation and expanded application' of the resolutions.[28]

This experience fed directly into the new firmer stance taken on Syria, a country where China has few direct interests and hence the type of issue on which it would have abstained in the past. China's unequivocal position undoubtedly undermined international support for any new 'coalition of the willing' to intervene outside the UN such as that Obama attempted to construct in August–September 2013. Although Russia led the international diplomatic offensive on Syria, China made a decisive difference by ensuring that the US could not present it as simply a matter of predictable and nugatory Russian support for an erstwhile ally.[29]

The setback for US policy on Syria in 2013 was pivotal, demonstrating how a globally influential and more proactive China might create significant future problems for the world's most powerful nation.

'Striving to make a difference'

The 2013 leadership transition to Xi Jinping and Li Keqiang had thus rapidly marked a further toughening of China's international stance. Its overall approach was described by Yan Xuetong, a Beijing foreign policy specialist close to the Chinese leadership, as 'striving to make a difference' (fèn fā yǒu wéi), implying that China would more frequently seek to influence the direction and outcome of events.[30] As Chinese Foreign Minister Wang Yi explained:

> as its comprehensive national strength expands steadily, expectations on China by the international community have also grown … As a permanent member of the UN Security Council and the world's second biggest economy, China can be expected to play a due role in maintaining world peace and stability and resolving regional conflicts.[31]

This did not imply a break with caution and non-interference. As one spokesman put it: 'as our influence grows we are even more reluctant to take sides or make strong statements because we understand that the more important we are the more likely our interference will complicate things and make them worse.'[32]

It could be claimed that any rising power inevitably describes its own advance as peaceful, whether true or not. However, China's emphasis on initiatives to facilitate trade, energy security and develop wider economic partnerships – through projects such as the AIIB, the New Development (BRICS – Brazil, Russia, India, China, South Africa) Bank and its 'Belt and Road' Asian development proposals – rather support China's claims. Moreover, while China has expanded military relations with its neighbours, this has not been its main emphasis, nor has it forged any new military alliances. Furthermore, China's foreign policy statements accord with any empirical analysis of China's material interests: maintaining a secure international environment in which to trade and a stable regional situation so that it can continue to direct its resources to domestic development.

China's proposal that China–US relations should be recast on more equal terms – the 'new major power relations' that Xi proposed to Obama in 2013, as discussed in Chapter 1 – did demonstrate a new assertiveness. However, the concrete steps that China envisages are also supported by many other developing countries, such as, for example, reorganising the governance of the IMF and the World Bank to give more weight to emerging economies. In 2015 Congress eventually agreed a limited reform to voting in the IMF, which increased the vote of China and some others, giving China a 6.14 per cent share, the third largest after Japan. But the US retains a veto in the IMF, where any important decision can be blocked by more than 15 per cent of the vote – the US is the only country with a voting share greater than 15 per cent. The US and the West have also refused to end the protocol that of the heads of the World Bank and IMF one is always American and the other European.

Despite the US's defensive response to Xi's proposal to reset their relations more generally, China proceeded with a number of steps that implement change in the international environment irrespective of the views of the US. The Asian Infrastructure Investment Bank was the most important of these.

The AIIB

The Chinese-proposed and largely Chinese-funded AIIB was launched in 2014 by 22 countries, with the agreed aim of raising $100 billion for infrastructure investment in Asia. This compares very well, given the respective sizes of the economies involved, to the capital base of the IMF's Asian Development Bank (ADB) of just over $160 billion and the World Bank's $336 billion.[33]

The US made no secret of the fact it saw the AIIB as a challenge to the US-led international financial architecture around the IMF and World Bank, and pressured its allies against signing up. Nonetheless Thailand, the Philippines and Singapore were among the initial founders. Worse, the UK, its oldest ally and international financial and military junior partner, announced – without prior consultation – that it was applying to join. The UK's eye was on maintaining the City of London as the pre-eminent financial entrepôt in Europe, particularly for the emerging international market in the RMB. The US establishment was horror-struck and warned that 'constant accommodation' to China was not the way to deal with a 'rising power'.[34] But, like tumbling dominoes, Germany, France, Australia, South Korea and even the Province of Taiwan followed suit. Only Japan and Canada among the G7 have stood apart. This disaster for US diplomacy was described as 'Washington's big China screw-up'.[35]

The AIIB is just the most striking of several steps that China has taken to establish alternative sources of emergency liquidity and investment to the developing world, including bilateral currency swaps, the Chiang Mai initiative, the BRICS New Development Bank, the investment funds for the 'Belt and Road' projects, the South-South Climate Cooperation Fund and many specific projects like the BCIM corridor.

The AIIB has been widely welcomed in Asia, both because the continent is estimated by the ADB to need $8 trillion in infrastructure investment until 2020, and because AIIB funds will not come with the neoliberal conditionalities of the IMF and World Bank. The AIIB's independent governance mitigates political problems that might arise from major direct Chinese investment in the national infrastructure. This has been a sensitive issue on some occasions, where the impression that another country, especially one that could be seen as a regional rival, might be accruing major control over infrastructure and communications crucial to national security has led to political opposition. For China, it delivers trade benefits from improved transport, communications and energy infrastructure, while also finding a productive home for some of its $3.21 trillion in foreign exchange reserves.[36] Altogether it is a classic example of what China calls its 'win-win' approach to foreign policy and regional relations.

Bilateral diplomacy

Over the course of 2013, the new Chinese leadership of Xi Jinping and Li Keqiang made a series of international trips that indicated the core concerns of China's foreign policy.

Russia – the destination for Xi Jinping's first state visit as president – was in top place. As discussed later, the Sino-Russian relationship is becoming the single most important international relationship for both countries. It gives greater strength to stand up to US pressure and meet the challenge of nationalist Japan, provides energy security for China and alternative markets for Russia and aids security in Central Asia. From Russia, Xi went to South Africa for the BRICS summit, underlining both China's priority to its relations with other rising economies and its growing trade and investment links with Africa. The focus was on successfully advancing the agreement to establish the $100 billion New Development (BRICS) Bank between the five participants.

Equally significantly, Li Keqiang's first foreign visit as premier was to India, where it was noted that this was the first time that a new Chinese leadership had visited India *before* Pakistan, with which China has had exceedingly close relations since 1950 when it became the third non-communist country to recognise the PRC. The keynote proposal of the visit was to seek progress on the existing loose agreement on the development of the BCIM overland trade route.[37]

The huge effort that China was prepared to invest in relations with the US was demonstrated when, in May 2013, Xi Jinping became the first Chinese president to visit America in his first year of office.[38] The meeting was widely flagged as a success in deepening the 'Xi–Obama personal relationship', but little else came out of it. As discussed in Chapter 1, the initial warm response to Xi Jinping's proposal for a fundamental reset in China–US relations did not long outlast the meeting.

Visits by both Xi Jinping and Li Keqiang to Central Asia in 2013 included a meeting of the SCO.[39] Alongside addressing ongoing security concerns that might spill over from instability in Afghanistan and elsewhere in this volatile region, the visits focused on proposals to develop direct overland transport and communications infrastructure to eventually link China's east coast to Central Asia and beyond to Moscow and Western Europe.[40]

Xi Jinping's visits to Indonesia and Malaysia and Li Keqiang's visits to Brunei, Thailand and Vietnam – all in October 2013 – underlined China's concern with its security and trade around the South China Sea. These visits potentially raised some tricky issues as – apart from the conflict with Japan over the Diaoyu/Senkaku islands – the manifold maritime territorial issues in the South China Sea are the most intractable of China's border disputes and potentially pit China against most of its southern neighbours. The overarching initiative in these crucial visits was the proposal for a 'maritime Silk Road' through South East Asia, improving and expanding port facilities and their overland links, to strengthen and secure the trade routes through the South China Sea across the Indian Ocean to the Gulf, Suez Canal and East Africa.[41] This potentially provides a framework for China's relations with most of the ASEAN countries, and with Sri Lanka and Pakistan where China is developing extensive port facilities.

This 2013 activity was rounded off by a visit by Li Keqiang to Germany and a highly successful visit to Beijing by Park Geun-hye, then president of South Korea.

This carefully judged whistle-stop diplomacy set out a clear Chinese agenda of improving its bilateral relationships with its near neighbours while putting its weight behind a range of multilateral initiatives primarily aimed at improving trade and aiding development.

Japan and the Philippines in the cold

There were two notable exceptions – Japan and the Philippines. These were not only the two closest allies of the US in the region but became the main purveyors of the allegation that China has become intimidating in its assertion of territorial claims.[42] The Japanese prime minister Shinzo Abe caused a mini-scandal at Davos in 2014 when he described the relations between Japan and China as similar to the relations between Britain and Germany before the First World War.[43] But even he was outdone by the then president of the Philippines, Benigno Aquino III, who claimed China in the South China Sea was behaving like Hitler over the Sudetenland.[44]

Nor did Japan and the Philippines stop at name-calling. In 2012 Japan broke its three-decade-long informal agreement to take no action on the disputed Diaoyu-Senkaku islands and instead first threatened to prosecute Chinese fishermen apprehended in the islands' waters, then 'nationalised' them.[45] In the same year, the Philippines similarly broke the peace with China over the disputed Scarborough Shoal (also known as the Huangyan island in Chinese and the Panatag shoal in Filipino) rejecting bilateral talks with China and instead, in a calculated act of conflict escalation, referred the issue to the UN for international adjudication. China believed both countries had been egged on by the US, which shifted from formal neutrality on the disputes to positions closer to those of Japan and the Philippines.

These disputes, the two countries' defence build-up, stepped-up military coordination with the US and their attacks on China, together with Japan's revisionism on its war crimes meant China's relations with both became decidedly wintry. There were no state visits to either country, very limited aid for the Philippines after Typhoon Haiyan in 2013 and no new trade or investment deals.[46] This chill, which continued through 2014, appeared to be the other side of the new, more active, foreign policy described by Yan Xuetong:

> In the future, China will decisively favour those who side with it with economic benefits and even security protections. On the contrary, those who are hostile to China will face much more sustained policies of … isolation.[47]

However, in 2015 China took steps to thaw relations with Japan. Annual trilateral talks between China, Japan and South Korea were resumed in March 2015 after a three-year gap, following the first high-level security talks between Japan and China for four years. And, following the replacement of Aquino with Duterte, there was a similar warming of relations with the Philippines.

Sino-British relations were also put into a 14-month 'deep freeze' following David Cameron's 2012 meeting with the Dalai Lama. Promised Chinese investment in the UK nuclear power industry and high-speed rail was delayed and relations only got back on track when Cameron made what was universally acknowledged as a grovelling retreat.[48]

All civilisations are equal

Chinese foreign policy doctrine for the last ten years, implemented with increasing clarity since the change in leadership in 2013, has not been regional or global aggrandisement, but, in Xi Jinping's words, has been to seek relations of 'mutual benefit' serving 'the long-term and fundamental interests of all people of the world'.[49] Or, as it is usually and popularly put, to seek 'win-win' international relations. This framework is in clear contrast to the 'zero-sum game' philosophy of the foreign policy of the so-called 'realists' of the West, which sees the inevitable course of international relations as rivalry, beggar-my-neighbour conflicts and competition, which can only be restrained through the superior threat of force by a 'benevolent' superpower.[50] China instead proposes that the aim should be to 'turn our global village into a big stage for common development, rather than an arena where gladiators fight each other'.[51]

Rather than seeking to replace American pre-eminence with Chinese leadership, China propounds an idea of common development within which, as a major power, China will have greater responsibilities not an exclusive say: 'Being a big country means shouldering greater responsibilities for regional and world peace and development, as opposed to seeking greater monopoly over regional and world affairs.'[52]

As Jamil Anderlini put it in the *Financial Times*:

> in many ways China's position in international affairs is rather noble. In a nutshell, China stands for non-interference, dialogue, negotiation, peaceful resolution of conflict, respect for sovereignty and territorial integrity and a voice for all nations no matter their size. Chinese diplomats argue, quite reasonably, that when foreign powers meddle in the internal conflicts of other countries they almost always make the situation worse.[53]

While such an approach to foreign policy is not aggressive, it might be claimed that it is utopian. However, in an increasingly interdependent world the common interests of nations – in trade, in transport and communications, in the international division of labour, in mitigating spillover from localised financial or liquidity crises, in environmental protection – mean that a rational foreign policy would precisely seek out the means to common development rather than to crush opponents.

In his keynote speech to the 2015 Boao Forum – China's equivalent for Asia of the annual Davos forum – Xi Jinping explained his approach:

> To build a community of common destiny, we need to seek win-win cooperation and common development … The old mindset of zero-sum game should give way to a new approach of win-win and all-win cooperation. The interests of others must be

accommodated while pursuing one's own interests, and common development must be promoted while seeking one's own development. The vision of win-win cooperation not only applies to the economic field, but also to the political, security, cultural and many other fields.[54]

The propensity of things

Despite the evidence of its actions and its words, China's commitment to a policy of 'peaceful rise' and 'win-win cooperation on the basis of mutual respect' is frequently dismissed as either a meaningless mantra or a cover for its 'real' intentions. And it is true that US liberals also deploy such language of 'mutual benefit', without proposing policies meaningfully distinct from realist and neocon ones. However the best measure of China's real intentions is to assess what is in China's national interests and how this measures against its professed policy.

The overwhelming priority for China is to continue to increase the capacities of its economy so that it can raise the general living standards of its population.[55] It is not only the morally correct goal of its government, but even the most cynical Western observers comment that the continued authority of the CPC substantially rests on its capacity to carry on improving social conditions for the mass of the population.[56] And on this front, the in-tray remains rather full. In 2014 Chinese GDP per head was still only about a quarter that of the US, half that of Russia or Malaysia, two-thirds of Bulgaria or Kazakhstan and three-quarters of that of Brazil or South Africa. Moreover, the gains of growth have been unevenly distributed between the cities and the countryside, the east and the west of the country, between 'migrant' workers and urban residents and they have not yet delivered a comprehensive health system or welfare safety net.

China has yet to achieve Deng Xiaoping's goal of building a 'moderately prosperous society'; a society with incomes at the level of those in the West is still further off. Xi Jinping reaffirmed that these are China's most important goals for its people and society over the next two or three decades; they were formally adopted by the 18th Congress of the CPC in 2012, and the first of these goals was embedded in the 13th Five Year Plan proposed in 2015:

> We have set the goals of completing the building of a moderately prosperous society in all respects by the centenary of the CPC in 2021 and building China into a modern socialist country that is prosperous, strong, democratic, culturally advanced, and harmonious by the centenary of the PRC in 2049 so as to realize the Chinese Dream of the rejuvenation of the Chinese nation.[57]

These goals are achievable if China maintains its projected rate of growth of at least 6.5 per cent a year. First and foremost this requires the pursuit of appropriate economic policies internally, but given China's position in world trade and the internationalised character of its economy it also places a premium on global stability, peace and open trading links. China has nothing to gain, now or in the foreseeable future, from provoking confrontations with its neighbours – still less with the US.

China may now engage more actively and attract more attention, and the first half of Deng's dictum – 'hide strength' – may no longer be a choice, but its approach remains to 'bide its time', awaiting the 'propensity of things' to achieve its goals.[58] This means continuing to avoid embroiling itself in contentious issues except where these press most closely on its own core concerns. This general framework has guided Chinese foreign policy since 1978 and still does for entirely logical reasons. Its over-arching aims are to seek stability, mitigate conflict and develop good relations with its neighbours and beyond, while standing firm on its core interests, including the security of its borders, littoral waters and shipping lanes, its territorial integrity (especially Taiwan, Tibet, Xinjiang and Hong Kong), and where its claims to sovereignty are shelved indefinitely, but not abjured. Within this framework it is ready to compromise, and eager to enter into positive-sum games, but will not accept being bullied by the US or anyone else.

As Xi Jinping explained:

> What China needs most are a harmonious and stable domestic environment and a peaceful and tranquil international environment. Turbulence or war runs against the fundamental interests of the Chinese people … China has suffered from turbulence and war for more than a century since modern times, and the Chinese people would never want to inflict the same tragedy on other countries or peoples. History has taught us that no country that tried to achieve its goal with force ever succeeded. … China will work to promote a new type of international relations of win-win cooperation and will always remain a staunch force for world peace and common development.[59]

This book seeks to demonstrate that China's foreign policy deeds accord with these stated principles and sentiments, and the sceptics who claim that these are just emollient words to disguise a relentless march towards regional hegemony cannot present a convincing case that this is so.

Notes

1 D. Cheng, 'America needs a comprehensive strategy for countering China's expanding perimeter of national interests', The Heritage Foundation, Issue Brief No. 4397, 28 April 2015.
2 J. J. Mearsheimer, 'The gathering storm: China's challenge to US power in Asia', *Chinese Journal of International Politics*, 3:4 (2010), 381–96.
3 Ministry of Foreign Affairs of the People's Republic of China, China's initiation of the five principles of peaceful co-existence. Available at: http://www.fmprc.gov.cn/mfa_eng/ziliao_665539/3602_6655 43/3604_665547/t18053.shtml (date accessed 19 February 2017).
4 This later formed part of the basis of the Non-Aligned Movement.
5 N. Maxwell, 'Sino-Indian border dispute reconsidered', *Economic and Political Weekly*, 34:15 (1999), 10–16.
6 Taiwan is discussed in Chapter 7.
7 Z. Mao, 'Apologists of neo-colonialism', Comment on the open letter of the central committee of the Communist Party of the Soviet Union (IV), 22 October 1963.
8 See Chapter 11.
9 On Deng's exile and eventual recall, see R. Deng, *Deng Xiaoping and the Cultural Revolution*, Foreign Language Press, Beijing, 2002.

10 A. V. Pantsov and S. I. Levine, *Deng Xiaoping: a revolutionary life*, Oxford University Press, Oxford, 2015, ch. 16.

11 Ibid., pp. 278–83.

12 For Chinese foreign policy in the Deng era, see E. Vogel, *Deng Xiaoping and the transformation of China*, The Belknap Press of Harvard University Press, Cambridge, MA, 2011, chs 9–11 and 17 in particular.

13 This was first used by Deng to describe Chinese foreign policy in the 1980s and is variously translated. The four characters literally mean something like 'lie low, hide talents'.

14 See Chapter 11.

15 Each of these are discussed in detail in the chapters relating to the specific countries or provinces concerned.

16 M. Taylor Fravel, 'Regime insecurity and international cooperation: explaining China's compromises in territorial disputes', *International Security*, 30:2 (2005), 46–83.

17 See Chapter 6.

18 C. K. Lo, *China's policy towards territorial disputes: the case of the South China Sea islands*, Routledge, Oxford, 1989, ch. 7.

19 X. T. Yan, 'China's new foreign policy: not conflict but convergence of interests', *New Perspectives Quarterly*, 31:2 (2014), 46–8.

20 B. J. Zheng, *China's peaceful rise, speeches of Zheng Bijian*, Brookings Institution Press, Washington, 2005, p. 5

21 'Statement of Principles', Project for the new American century, 3 June 1997. Available at: http://www.rrojasdatabank.info/pfpc/PNAC---statement%20of%20principles.pdf (date accessed 11 April 2017).

22 G. Arrighi, *Adam Smith in Beijing*, Verso, London, 2007, p. 185.

23 Remarks by the president at the US/China strategic and economic dialogue, Office of the Press Secretary, the White House, Washington, DC, 27 July 2009.

24 J. Mezo and B. Udvari, 'Effects of the debt crisis on EU-China relations', Munich Personal RePEc Archive, paper no. 40367, posted 6 August 2012. Available at: https://mpra.ub.uni-muenchen.de/40367/1/31-Effects_of_the_debt_crisis_on_the_EU-China_relations.pdf. A. Willis, 'Beijing promises to buy Greek bonds', *EUObserver*, 4 October 2010. Available at: https://euobserver.com/china/30949. S. Tiezzi, 'China and Germany's "special relationship"', *The Diplomat*, 8 July 2014. Available at: http://thediplomat.com/2014/07/china-and-germanys-special-relationship/ (date all accessed 15 February 2017).

25 D. M. Finkelstein, 'Commentary of China's external grand strategy', Centre for Naval Analyses-China Studies, Alexandria, DA, January 2011, p. 3.

26 1972 admittance of Bangladesh; 1997 authorising UN observers to verify the peace process in Guatemala; 1999 extending the authority for the UN force in Macedonia; 2007 sanctions on Myanmar; 2008 sanctions on Zimbabwe.

27 UN Security Council fast facts, CNN Library. Available at: http://edition.cnn.com/2013/09/03/world/united-nations-security-council-fast-facts/ (date accessed 9 January 2014).

28 K. Rapoza, 'Russia and China team up against NATO Libya campaign', *Forbes Magazine*, 17 June 2011. Available at: http://www.forbes.com/sites/kenrapoza/2011/06/17/russia-and-china-team-up-against-nato-libya-campaign/#71d924772561 (date accessed 19 February 2017).

29 'Iran, China finalise roadmap to double bilateral trade', *Tehran Times*, 23 February 2014.

30 Yan, 'China's new foreign policy'.

31 L. Zhang, 'Transcript of interview with Wang Yi', *Financial Times*, 29 January 2014.

32 J. Anderlini, 'Ukraine stand-off puts China on the spot', *Financial Times*, 14 March 2013.

33 S. R., 'Why China is creating a new "World Bank" for Asia', *The Economist*, 11 November 2014.

34 G. Dyer and G. Parker, 'US attacks UK's "constant accommodation" with China', *Financial Times*, 12 March 2015.

35 S. S. Roach, D. J. Zha, S. Kennedy and P. Chovanec, 'Washington's big China screw-up', *Foreign Policy*, 26 March 2015. Available at: http://foreignpolicy.com/2015/03/26/washingtons-big-china-screw -up-aiib-asia-infrastructure-investment-bank-china-containment-chinafile/ (date accessed 19 February 2017).

36 State administration of foreign exchange, PRC, January 2015 figures.

37 Joint Statement on the State Visit of Chinese Premier Li Keqiang to India, 20 May 2013, Ministry of External Affairs, Government of India.

38 Deng Xiaoping visited the US in January 1979, within a year of becoming de facto leader of China, but he never formally held the office of either president or premier. Jiang Zemin and Hu Jintao each visited several times but not in their first year in office.

39 See Chapter 15.

40 S. Denyer, 'China envisions new "silk roads" to west by land and by sea', *Japan Times*, 1 November 2013.

41 J. Wu and Y. Zhang, 'Xi in call for building of new "maritime silk road"', *China Daily*, 4 October 2013.

42 See Chapter 6 on Japan and Chapter 10 on the South China Sea.

43 L. Zhang, 'China rejects Abe's WWI comparison with Pacific tensions', *Financial Times*, 24 January 2014.

44 K. Bradsher, 'Philippine leader sounds alarm on China', *New York Times*, 4 February 2014.

45 See Chapter 5.

46 See Chapters 6 and 10 for a discussion of these events.

47 Yan, 'China's new foreign policy'.

48 J. Anderlini, 'Britain wins little reward from China in retreat on Tibet', *Financial Times*, 1 December 2013.

49 Xi, 'Towards a community of common destiny'.

50 K. Waltz, *Theory of international politics*, Waveland Press, Long Grove, IL, 1979 (reprinted 2010).

51 Xi, 'Towards a community of common destiny'.

52 Ibid.

53 Anderlini, 'Britain wins little reward'.

54 Xi, 'Towards a community of common destiny'.

55 See targets on poverty elimination and achieving 'low high income' economy in 13th Five Year Plan, November 2015.

56 See, inter alia, J. Anderlini, 'How long can the Communist Party survive in China?', *Financial Times*, 20 September 2013; H. F. Hung, A. R. Kroeber, H. W. French and S. S. Zhao, 'When will China's government collapse', *Foreign Policy*, 13 March 2015. Available at: http://foreignpolicy.com/2015/03/13/ china_communist_party_collapse_downfall/ (date accessed 19 February 2017).

57 J. P. Xi, *On the governance of China*, Foreign Language Press, Beijing, 2014. Speech at a discussion session with model workers, 28 April 2013. Ebook location 749.

58 F. Julien, *The propensity of things: towards a history of efficacy in China*, trans. by J. Lloyd, MIT Press, Cambridge, MA, 1995.

59 Xi, 'Towards a community of common destiny'.

4

America's exceptional empire

In contrast to China's proposed 'international relations of win-win cooperation', the parallel US discussion about China has been dominated by arguments that conflict is inevitable, and indeed necessary.

The Obama administration's 2010 announcement of a strategic turn in US foreign policy to the Pacific was prefigured by rising agitation in the most influential US foreign policy circles calling for a stronger response to China and followed by an equally intense discussion of the necessary steps for this to succeed. This chapter argues that from all sides this discussion has been framed by a shared perception: that the rise of China presents an existential challenge to the US's leading global position and this must be prevented. Most predict conflict. Some argue this is an inevitable consequence of any state achieving similar strength to that of the US – a new 'Thucydides trap'; others propound that coercion is a necessary response to China's rejection of neoliberal economic rules or its one-party system or its alleged regional expansionist aspirations. It is alleged that China's navy presents a threat to 'freedom of navigation' in the South China Sea and to unfettered access to the 'global commons', which must be repulsed. Trump focused on the economic challenge from China for US industry, and made sweeping claims of unfair Chinese competitive practices. Whatever the argument, whether starting from a neocon or liberal perspective, or whether chiefly concerned about the US's economic, military or geopolitical position, all arrive at the same conclusion: China must be contained and brought into line with the national and international interests of the US.

This chapter looks at this US foreign policy discourse on China and related Pentagon discussions, drawing out the most prevalent theoretical, strategic and military arguments that justify the policies pursued towards China.

American exceptionalism

American 'exceptionalism' originated with its founding fathers who conceived their country's mission as defining liberty and democracy for all times and for all peoples.[1] In Adams' words: 'Our pure, virtuous, public spirited, federative republic will last forever, govern the globe and introduce the perfection of man.'[2] This 'Manifest Destiny' was first applied to the rest of the American continent. Having expelled the British, the new expansionist republic attempted to annex Canada in 1812, seized half of Mexico in 1845 and purchased Alaska in 1867. The Spanish-American war of 1898 ended the Spanish empire on the continent, while Portuguese influence had all but collapsed after the independence of Brazil in 1825. But its high-minded rhetoric against the old empires was always aimed at creating a new American one. When, by the early twentieth century, it became clear that territorial acquisition was now largely out of the question, it settled for trying to create an informal empire instead.

From around 1820 to the end of the century, the US achieved an unprecedented rate of GDP growth averaging over 4 per cent, which was double that of even the fastest growing European economy. After a dip during the Civil War, from 1865 the US economy saw steady advance, overtaking the previous largest economy – the UK – by around 1870; and by 1910 its economy was greater in size than the next two largest economies – the UK and Germany – put together.[3] Such prodigious economic success served only to reinforce belief in the US's historic superiority and global mission.

Of course, this 'megalomania of Manifest Destiny' was never uncontested; this imperial interpretation of the nation's founding values was countered by a narrative that the US could 'preserve its unique virtues only by remaining a society apart from a fallen world'.[4] But such views never held real sway over the conduct or goals of US foreign policy, although its tactics in pursuit of its ultimately Brobdingnagian global project ranged from active to passive persuasion. And such arguments allowed the construction of a myth of the US as a 'reluctant superpower', an anti-colonial state, when it was in fact pervasively seeking to coercively influence greater and greater spheres of the world.[5]

Its project reached its apogee when the US emerged from the Second World War as the victor in a global struggle that saw Germany and Japan defeated and the UK indebted and subordinated. By contrast, the US itself had had a good war; as a result of vast state investment to deliver the materials and goods needed for war, its economy doubled in size between 1939 and 1944.[6] In 1945 its economy was larger than the sum of all 29 countries of Western Europe as well as Japan, Canada, New Zealand and Australia; and it was only marginally smaller than all these *and* the USSR.[7] Its share of industrial production was even greater. And the bombs that fell on Hiroshima and Nagasaki had announced it as the greatest military power yet seen on Earth.

This gave it an unprecedented advantage from which to embed its interests and leadership in the post-war political and economic settlement agreed at Potsdam, Bretton Woods and Dumbarton Oaks. At Bretton Woods the IMF and World Bank were set up, with inbuilt US vetoes, and the dollar was established as the reserve currency. Dumbarton Oaks set up the Security Council of the future UN, whose permanent members and veto-holders were to be the US and its key allies at the time – the UK, Chiang Kai-shek's China and the USSR – alongside a General Assembly in which two-thirds of the delegates would be from the US's client states in Latin America.[8]

With this international architecture in place, the framework for the US post-war approach to foreign policy was set; equating the stability of the capitalist world with preserving its own predominant role within it. This defined the tasks of US foreign policy in the entire post-war period: attempting to prevent further encroachment by directly anti-capitalist forces; subduing 'rogue' regimes that sought too great an independence from this US-defined world; and subordinating potential rivals from within the advanced countries themselves. It was the first of these that was most immediate. By 1946 it had launched the 'Cold War', turning from alliance with to containment of the USSR, it imposed sanctions on post-1949 China, fought a war on the Korean peninsula and by 1962 was at war in Vietnam.

However, the US was never as great as its directing ambitions, which always out-stripped its actual power to control the realities of the post-war world.[9] And by the 1970s its long relative decline had set in. Japan and Germany had not only outstripped its growth rate, which had fallen to around 3 per cent, but were growing faster than the US had done in the past. By the time the US admitted defeat in Vietnam in 1975 it was already seeing the emergence of independently minded nationalist regimes in the Middle East, socialist movements in Central and Latin America, and countless problems that posed lesser and greater challenges to its configuring of the world.

But despite these limits to the reality of its power, the dialogue of retreat in US foreign policy circles, engendered by defeat in Vietnam, was short-lived, and America's global assertiveness resumed with Reaganism in the 1980s. The Contra War in Nicaragua, invasions of Panama and Grenada, cruise missiles in Europe and covert war in Afghanistan were coupled with the championing of economic neoliberalism. Moreover, at the end of the decade the fall of the USSR became the launch pad for renewed US hubris under the banner of 'a new American century'.

It is this post-1989 American vision that has been dramatically disrupted by the rise of China, and which now presents the US with an economic challenger on a scale far exceeding that of either Germany or Japan, and, worse, it is communist. This has led to a mighty rehashing of familiar American establishment tropes regarding the historic responsibilities laid upon US foreign policy, within which China today is cast as a singular but similar problem to that posed previously by Germany, Japan and the USSR. China has to be cajoled, threatened, persuaded or forced to become what the US State Department calls a 'responsible stakeholder', a new 'status quo power', a loyal upholder of US leadership, the capitalist system and its existing world order.[10]

A conflict is inevitable?

In these discussions on China it is variants of the 'neorealist' view in international rela-tions that have had the most backing of powerful lobbies within the US foreign policy establishment. In realism's Hobbesian framework, no state can ever be sure of another state's intentions, rendering the international system anarchic, obscure and insecure. Rather than international relations between states being understood as the working through of material, economic forces and contradictory interests driving comprehensible and ultimately predictable developments, instead fear and suspicion rule. This drives states to take pre-emptive and coercive action against possible and potential threats, irrespective of whether there is an objective basis for these anxieties as this cannot be determined. The only constraint is superior force. It is like the Wild West, in which mutually contradictory concerns and fears clash constantly, controlled only by the threat of the superior force of a global 'sheriff' to police relations, hence the indispensable role of the US.[11] This intellectual platoon argues that if China reaches a point where its economic and military strength is to any degree comparable to that of the US, it must inevitably contest for regional and then global leadership.[12] From this perspective, the necessary pre-emptive task of the US is a precautionary attempt to contain or halt China's rise.

Such academic theorisations of inevitable conflict in international relations reinforce and often justify the prejudices of the US neocon-dominated foreign policy establishment.[13] They deploy the arguments of the academy to support an ideologically driven discourse that China presents a looming threat to the 'democratic' West from dark forces of autocracy, the 'free market' from 'state socialism', capitalism from communism, and the Pax Americana from global conflict and war. Drained of any accounting 'for the material bases of international conflict or cooperation, and focusing instead on the pursuit of essentialised "national interests" in an "anarchic" international system, realism performed yeoman service in malleably justifying the Cold War, military build-ups and the international actions of the United States.'[14]

In the academic field, probably the most prominent voice for the inevitability of conflict with China has been John Mearsheimer, originator of the theory of 'offensive realism'.[15] He argues that 'the mightiest states attempt to establish hegemony in their region of the world, while making sure that no rival great power dominates another region.'[16] In 2004 he wrote in the explicitly titled essay *Why China's rise will not be peaceful*:[17]

> The question at hand is simple and profound: can China rise peacefully? My answer is no. If China continues its impressive economic growth over the next few decades, the United States and China are likely to engage in an intense security competition with considerable potential for war.

Mearsheimer's case rests on the US's own rise to superpower status: its subordination of its neighbours and the expulsion of the European powers from the continent, establishing itself as regional hegemon; and then defeating global challenges from Germany, Japan and the USSR, while also reining in many lesser potential opponents usually by force. Based on this historical experience, he concludes that China must similarly drive for regional hegemony in Asia-Pacific by subordinating its neighbours and driving out the US. As ceding regional hegemony would mean that America could no longer claim a universal, global authority, it must try to prevent China from achieving such strength.

Mearsheimer's case does not rely on evidence that China actually has any such expansionist regional goals, as he 'privileges theory over political reality'.[18] In fact he admits: 'If you look at all the crises that have arisen in East Asia over the past 10 years, it is China's neighbours, not China, that have started almost all of them.'[19] But as he believes the adoption of such hegemonic goals is a priori inevitable as China grows stronger, then the US has no choice but to seek to contain China.

Others echo Mearsheimer's arguments. For example, influential writer and defence advisor Robert Kaplan argued in his seminal 2005 essay 'How we would fight China':[20]

> Whenever great powers have emerged or re-emerged on the scene (Germany and Japan in the early decades of the twentieth century, to cite two recent examples), they have tended to be particularly assertive – and therefore have thrown international affairs into violent turmoil. China will be no exception …

> Given the stakes, and given what history teaches us about the conflicts that emerge
> when great powers all pursue legitimate interests, the result is likely to be the defining
> military conflict of the twenty-first century: if not a big war with China, then a series of
> Cold War-style standoffs that stretch out over years and decades.

Kaplan, alert to the dangers in an outright military clash with China and drawing negative lessons from the war in Iraq, advocates a policy of military and diplomatic containment through developing the US's system of Pacific military alliances to include India and beyond, coupled with a reorganisation of the US navy particularly, to strengthen its capacities for patrolling the Chinese coasts. And, he argues: 'We will have to continually play various parts of the world off China, just as Richard Nixon played less than morally perfect states off the Soviet Union.'[21]

For these 'realists' the US and China are caught in a contemporary form of the 'Thucydides trap', derived from Thucydides' comment on the Peloponnesian War that: 'It was the rise of Athens and the fear that this inspired in Sparta that made war inevitable.'[22] References to Thucydides have become ubiquitous in US foreign policy discussion on China, both as a warning and as an explanation of inevitable conflict.[23] The analogy between China/Athens, the US/Sparta has one value; it at least suggests that a US war to prevent the rise of China would be ultimately tragic and founded purely on paranoia. But, in reality, to try to make the relations between Sparta and Athens an analogy for those between the US and China today means wrenching one aspect of the situation – Athens was a rising power – out of the overall material situation which led to that historical conflict. Ancient Greece was not at all similar to the world that faces the US and China today, particularly economically. In a world where economic growth was insignificant – possibly under 0.1 per cent a year – war to seize assets created by others, enslave populations or steal land was a rational route to enrichment.[24] This is not the case today. As Xi Jinping argues: 'There is no such thing as the so-called Thucydides trap … But should major countries time and again make the mistakes of strategic miscalculation, they might create such traps for themselves.'[25]

A clash of civilisations?

In the realists' framework the inevitability of conflict flows from features of the relations between all major states, whatever their ideologies or political systems – hence the 'tragedy' of great power politics.[26] But others argue that the need to contain China flows from its rejection of liberal democracy in favour of a single-party regime, its continued adherence to communism and embedded characteristics of historical Chinese political culture that cannot be accommodated. The US has a responsibility to defend the 'free world' against this threat of autocracy and 'statism'.

One such advocate was Samuel P. Huntington, famous for positing that international politics in the twenty-first century would be dominated by a 'clash of civilisations'.[27] His thesis of a world dominated by a confrontation between an encroaching 'backward' Islam and the allegedly more advanced West gained particular authority after 9/11, but his original analysis also suggested a similar clash between the West and 'Sinic' civilisation centred on China, and an emerging 'Sino-Islamic connection'. Subsequently his acolytes have been active principally in arguing against 'multiculturalism' and an alleged dangerous accommodation to Islam, but they have also taken up the cudgels against China.

Aaron L. Friedberg is a particularly influential exponent of this view applied to China, developed extensively in his book *A contest for supremacy: China, America and the struggle for mastery in Asia*.[28] He argues that containment is the only possible response to China given a series of factors making conflict inevitable. The most fundamental is China's internal regime: 'It is … not China's rise alone, but the nature of its political system that is at the root of Washington's mistrust and hostility.'[29] This is reinforced by what he suggests are problems in China's historic culture, such as an alleged 'penchant for deception' rooted as far back as the thinking of Sun Tzu, the c.500 BCE philosopher and author of *The Art of War*.[30] But it is China's government that is the greatest concern: 'if it continues to be ruled by a one-party authoritarian regime, its relations with the United States are going to become increasingly tense and competitive.'[31]

In evidence for this Friedberg suggests that: '[The US's] most important friends and military allies have tended to be democracies with whom it did the great bulk of its business, while its strategic rivals were authoritarian regimes.'[32] This is self-evidently contentious, as the US's close friends and allies have always included dictatorships and quasi-dictatorships: Saudi Arabia, Sisi's Egypt, Pinochet's Chile, Apartheid South Africa, Suharto's Indonesia, Somoza's Nicaragua, Thailand for most of the last century, South Korea until 1987, Franco's Spain, Turkey under the Generals, the list could go on. Nonetheless, on this basis his book argues that 'regime change' must fundamentally drive US policy towards China: 'Stripped of diplomatic niceties, the ultimate aim of the American strategy is to hasten a revolution, albeit a peaceful one, that will sweep away China's one-party authoritarian state and leave a liberal democracy in its place.'[33]

Clearly if the US were to openly adopt such a goal this would become the chief driver of conflict with China, which is why less febrile heads have prevailed in the White House. But even if recent US administrations have played down attacks on the political system in China, because 'there seemed little to be gained by reminding the Chinese leaders that the ultimate aim of US policy was to someday put them out of a job', this remains the unspoken goal across the political spectrum, from those who believe that trade liberalisation will eventually lead to political liberalisation to those who advocate an openly coercive course.[34]

While the 'defence of democracy' has never been the actual basis of US foreign policy, the idea of a conflictual contradiction between an American concept of 'democracy' and the system in place in China has popular purchase and helps to ensure domestic support for a US build-up in the Pacific.

The 1914 analogy

Another pervasive argument for the inevitability of conflict with China – originating in hawkish US defence circles, but particularly promulgated by *Financial Times* chief foreign affairs commentator Gideon Rachman – contends that:

> The analogy [of China] with Germany before the first world war is striking …
>
> Some historians argue that in 1914, the German government had concluded that it needed to fight a war as soon as possible … China now, like Germany 100 years ago, is a rising power that fears the established great power is intent on blocking its ascent.[35]

There is indeed one parallel between today and the period leading up to 1914: this was the last time that the dominance of the previous largest economy in the world – the UK – was replaced by that of a new largest power – the US. Today the US stands on the brink of being overtaken by China. But rather than China being a candidate today for Germany's 1914 alleged warmongering role, the homologies more closely fit the US itself.

The traditional thesis of culpability for the First World War – which is used in applying this analogy to China – suggests that the German ruling elites deliberately launched the war as they believed Germany's position was weakening, its 'moment was about to pass' and war was needed 'the sooner the better'.[36] In Europe Germany's growth had outstripped the UK's, but internationally it was falling behind the US economically, whose average GDP growth rate from 1870 to 1913 was 3.9 per cent compared to Germany's 2.8 per cent.[37] Dominating Russia could give Germany the edge, but it was in danger of falling behind Russia militarily as the German military budget was becoming very squeezed.

Comparing China's position today to this case against Germany in 1914, the analogy simply does not hold. Rather than China being outstripped by a more dynamic global economy – as Germany was – China's position is closer to that of the 1914 US when it was the most dynamic economy of the time. Nor is China in imminent danger of being outstripped by a rising military rival; insofar as the US (or Japan) plays that role vis-à-vis China, China is catching up – albeit slowly – but it is certainly not falling behind. China is not running out of money to develop its military defences; it is the US that faces a military budget squeeze.[38] Rather than its moment being about to pass, time is on China's side.

It could be more strongly argued that it is the US – facing relative economic decline, openly discussing the need to pre-empt China before it is 'too late' and with a considerable history in military intervention against regimes it objects to – which has a greater interest in risking solutions on the military field.

In any analogy with Germany in 1914 it is not possible to credibly cast China in the role of the belligerent. As the influential Singaporean scholar and former diplomat Kishore Mahbubani explained: 'Beijing has pulled off a near geopolitical miracle by emerging as the number two power without shaking the world order … If the West could emulate China's strategic restraint, it might finally end its decade of geopolitical failures.'[39]

Nonetheless, the most strident voices for containment of China insist that China has *already* embarked on a policy of regional aggrandisement: 'China claims that its rise is intended to be peaceful, but its actions tell a different story: that of a revisionist power seeking to dominate the western Pacific.'[40] Such a view requires seeing the strengthening of China's navy and seaboard defences as of a predominantly aggressive rather than defensive character and blaming China for all new tensions related to its long-standing island disputes in the East and South China Seas.

Accommodating China

An alternative view – that China and the US can forge a long-term collaborative future even as China catches up – does have supporters within the US establishment.

In the first instance there are the most internationally oriented sections of US business – such as Apple, Walmart, Hewlett Packard, Microsoft, Ford and General Motors – which look to China for future expansion and, with their political supporters on Capitol Hill, make the case for engagement with China. These constitute a powerful lobby, which had a strong hearing in the Obama White House particularly on trade and other economic relations. China hawks, of course, allege that such pro-China business lobbies are fundamentally venal and self-serving; for example, Jim Mann argues that a 'deluge of money has ... skew[ed] American discussions towards an upbeat pro-business viewpoint' on China.[41] But in truth such emollient voices are more than balanced by other sections of US business that are feeling the heat from China, and which are particularly influential upon Trump – components manufacturers, the steel and tyre industries and others – that call for protectionist measures. And the US defence industries are more than happy to see a push in Asia that leads to sharp increases in arms spending by US friends and allies.

Despite Trump's rhetoric against outsourcing and his allegations of unfair competition, in reality the respective strengths of the economies of the US and China complement each other in many ways. China is a major market for US high value added products, while China supplies medium-technology products at prices the US cannot match due to its far higher wage levels. These complementarities of their respective stages of economic development will continue for some time. On present rates of growth China will not catch up with the US in terms of productivity – and therefore its capacity to compete across the entire economy in high value added production – for 20 years or more.[42]

As Justin Lin Yi Fu, former chief economist and senior vice president at the World Bank, argues, it is by taking advantage of such constantly changing complementarities, not just with the US and more advanced countries but also with less advanced economies, that China's model of mutually beneficial growth and technological advance can last for several decades:

> As China undergoes industrial upgrading to more sophisticated product markets, it will leave the market space for other developing countries to enter the more labour-intensive industries. Chinese enterprises are expected to relocate their existing production to other lower-wage countries as they upgrade to higher value-added industries, like Japan and East Asian economies did a few decades ago.[43]

Moreover, for the US, there is no comparable source for price-competitive medium-technology products. In 2014, China-US trade stood at $640 billion, second only to the US's trade with Canada and the largest between any two countries outside the North American Free Trade Area – Canada, Mexico and the US. And US trade has been increasing more rapidly with China than with Canada. From 2007 to 2014 US trade with Canada grew by $94 billion, while that with China grew by $256 billion.[44] In other words, restrictions on trade between the two countries is fundamentally not in the interests of either; although, of course, weaker and less productive sections of US industry that are experiencing the impact of competition from China do not see it this way.

The economic complementarities are not limited to trade. In the words of Nobel economist Paul Krugman, the US developed an 'addiction' to Chinese purchases of US debt, as 'Dollar purchases [of US debt] by China and other foreign governments have temporarily insulated the US economy from the effects of huge budget deficits.'[45]

Such facts have led some to argue that the scale of bilateral trade, RMB holdings in US government debt and the interests of those companies heavily invested in China, such as Walmart and Apple, will be enough to mitigate future conflict.[46] Others go further, suggesting China is merely the US's 'head servant', 'diligently serving – and being held hostage by – the US': 'Despite occasional squabbles, the two elite groups on either side of the Pacific share an interest in perpetuating their respective domestic status quos, as well as the current imbalance in the global economy.'[47]

The premise that the 'complex interdependence' between states today, particularly as a result of such economic and other non-state relations, negates the role of the military in resolving disputes is at the heart of the contemporary liberal position on foreign policy.[48] In fact, such arguments have a longer history; for example, before the First World War it was compellingly and erroneously argued – most famously in Norman Angell's 1909 bestseller *The Great Illusion* – that conflict between Germany and Britain was impossible because the economic interconnections between them meant such a war would be disastrous.[49] But, as Aaron Friedberg correctly points out: 'History suggests that when the chips are down, politics trumps trade. … Strong economic ties could not slow the deterioration in Anglo-German relations that led eventually to war.'[50]

Or, as Perry Anderson argues, the US state acts 'not primarily as a projection of the concerns of US capital, but as a guardian of the general interest of all capitals, sacrificing – where necessary, and for as long as needed – national gain for international advantage, in the confidence of ultimate pay-off'.[51] According to such a perspective pre-emptively halting the rise of China is vital to protect the interests of global capital, and will have a longer term 'pay-off' for US domestic industry by preventing China reaching the point of competing at US levels of productivity and technology.

Nevertheless there are serious voices within the US foreign policy establishment who believe that major conflict with China can and should be avoided and argue powerfully for a strategy of engagement and compromise. One such voice is Joseph Nye, who co-authored the liberal riposte to realist international relations theory. He reasons that:

> The United States and China (as well as other countries) have much to gain from cooperation on a range of transnational issues … If power is the ability to affect others to obtain the outcomes one wants, it is important to remember that sometimes our power is greater when we act with others rather than merely over others.[52]

Henry Kissinger, the great architect of the Cold War Sino-American rapprochement also argues that 'containment won't work' and warns that a confrontational approach to China will backfire in Asia, as the 'vast majority of nations will seek to avoid choosing sides'.[53] Moreover, such a confrontation would solve nothing:

> In an actual conflict, both sides possess the capabilities and the ingenuity to inflict cata- strophic damage on each other. By the time any such hypothetical conflagration drew to a close, all participants would be left exhausted and debilitated. They would then be obliged to face anew the very task that confronts them today: the construction of an international order in which both countries are significant components.[54]

Even Kissinger's old sparring partner Brzezinski, Carter's national security advisor, has become a convert to the position that the US should accept reality and, 'as its era of global dominance ends', should 'take the lead in realigning the global power archi- tecture' to accommodate China and other rising powers.[55] This is a 180-degree turn from his brutally expressed 1997 position that: 'the three grand imperatives of imperial geostrategy are to prevent collusion and maintain security dependence among the vassals, to keep tributaries pliant and protected, and to keep the barbarians from coming together.'[56]

Of course, in Brzezinski's, as in Kissinger's, case, their dove-like conversions on China are driven by realpolitik, with the aim of preserving as much as possible of the US's leading role and the position of the dollar. But Kissinger's conclusion, that the US should propose to China that they build a new 'world order as a joint enterprise' has fallen on deaf ears.[57] And Brzezinski's volte-face on the issue has been studiously ignored.

Such voices are not alone, but none of these arguments make much headway against the aggressive thrust of the 'realist' neocon position on China, not least because their premise is the same. Thus Hillary Clinton, reviewing Kissinger's 2014 book *World order*, pointed to their shared 'belief in the indispensability of continued American leadership in service of a just and liberal order'.[58] Similarly Nye's more consciously liberal position nonetheless insists on the US's 'indispensable' world leadership role, and he argues for much the same 'persuasive' steps towards China, just stripped of the aggressive rhetoric. Overall, such voices for a more conciliatory policy towards China are hard to hear above the storm of articles and books sounding the looming inevitability of conflict and dire warnings of China's expansionist agenda.[59]

Pre-eminence at sea

Some of the strongest voices for a pre-emptive build-up against China have come from the defence, and especially the naval, lobby.[60] Since the end of the Cold War the freedom of the US navy to patrol the world's oceans, including right up to the coasts of every continent, has been unchallenged.[61] Soviet submarines no longer range the deep Atlantic and Pacific, leaving the US untroubled by who or what might be in the vicinity of its fleet deployments and exercises. Hence the US defence establishment has become rattled by the noticeable improvement in China's naval capacities, extrapolating a future limitation on the US navy's free access to the world's oceans, but in particular fearing that China is developing the ability to exclude the US from its littoral waters.

The world's media first remarked upon the impact of China's 15-year-long invest-ment in developing its navy in 2008 when the PLA navy undertook anti-piracy activities off the Horn of Africa and in the Gulf of Aden, its first active operation so far from home waters.[62] In 2011 PLA navy ships were on operational duty in the Mediterranean for the first time, evacuating Chinese citizens from Libya; in 2012 *Liaoning*, China's first aircraft carrier, was launched; 2013 saw China's first Indian Ocean submarine deployment; in 2014 it contributed to the hunt for missing Malaysian Airlines flight 370 in deep oceans; and 2015 saw participation in the international evacuation from Yemen, announce-ment of plans to build a second carrier and negotiations with Djibouti for a permanent Chinese naval facility.[63]

A debate on China's ultimate intentions seized US navy strategists, who worry that China aims to 'challenge US naval dominance on the high seas'.[64]

China's return to the sea

Until the alleviation of tensions with Russia in the 1980s, China's defences were pri-marily directed at securing its vast continental land borders. As discussed in the next chapter, this was driven by concerns that the USSR might try to carve out pieces of its territory from the north and east or that a hostile Soviet-Indian-Vietnamese alliance could significantly dismember it.[65] The military strategies that flowed from this relied in the first instance on the PLA land forces and the development of China's own nuclear deterrent.

From the 1990s, with its land borders more or less secure and it having become a major oil and gas importer, China's strategic priorities shifted towards defending its extensive and vulnerable seaborne trade and its eastern seaboard. On the one hand it built up land-based assets – missiles and launchers – to repel attack from its eastern seas. On the other it invested in developing its naval capabilities, primarily focused on coastal operations and its near seas.[66] But, alongside this, the PLA navy has also begun to develop the initial elements of a 'blue water' capacity, that is the ability to operate over long distances in the vast waters of deep oceans.

This contemporary turn to the sea reversed at last China's historically disastrous 1430s Ming dynasty decision to suppress the record of the remarkable sea voyages of Admiral Zheng He, destroy his fleet, institute a ban on overseas trade and place limits on the size and capacity of ships that could be built.[67] A scant 60 years later Vasco da Gama rounded the Cape of Good Hope and Columbus landed in the 'new world'. Just as seagoing technology was opening up the world to new levels of trade and development China abandoned the far oceans to the Europeans, with hugely negative consequences for China's development.

The key focus of China's naval investment has been on developing a navy capable of repelling a seaborne threat in or from its near seas. Its far seas naval capabilities are limited and will remain so for a long time to come. Alarmist claims, such as those by Peter Navarro in his potboiler *The coming China wars*, that China's navy threatens the US at home and at sea are pure fantasy aimed mainly at persuading a reluctant US public to support a new round of American warmongering directed at China. Among such *Boy's Own* yarns is the claim that:

> Running silent and deep, China's latest subs can now 'nuke' American cities – from Los
> Angeles and San Francisco to Chicago and Detroit. China's new subs are … specifically
> designed to attack and sink US aircraft carriers – from the Taiwan Strait and Strait of
> Malacca to the Strait of Hormuz. … China is developing a significant 'deepwater navy'
> capabilities replete with aircraft carriers to challenge the only other deepwater navy on
> the planet, that of the United States.[68]

With its existing naval technology, shipbuilding capacity and its proposed pace of development, China will not challenge the US in the far seas for many decades to come, even if it were pursuing that goal. Moreover its limited but growing deep-ocean capacity is clearly directed at defending its maritime trading and energy supply chain from threats of piracy or terrorism, as in the Gulf of Aden; or more generally being able to 'show the flag' at the ports of its key trading partners or where ex-pat Chinese communities come under threat, as in Libya. Moreover, China has shown no interest in extending its naval operations out towards the Eastern Pacific and America's seaboards.

Looking in detail at China's current and projected naval capacities, experts have convincingly made the case that:

> The bottom line is that China's present naval shipbuilding program aims to replace aging
> vessels and modernise the fleet, not to scale-up a modern fleet to the size and com-
> position necessary to support and sustain high-end blue water power projection. China
> is building a two-layered navy with a high-end Near Seas component and a limited,
> low-end capability beyond, not the monolithic force that some assume.[69]

China does not yet have one combat-ready aircraft carrier, nor does it have its own aircraft carrier launch technology or trained and seasoned naval pilots and mariners that could operate in combat conditions. A challenge from China to the US on the high seas is a figment of fevered imaginations.

'Access denial' and Air-Sea Battle

However, while it has not tried to catch up in global naval power projection, the development of China's capacity to counter the US in its littoral waters is much more advanced. Challenging the US navy in deep oceans would require a similar naval capability, but effective defence in China's home waters can be achieved even from a position of overall naval inferiority. As the US Air-Sea Battle Office put it:

> In certain scenarios, even low-technology capabilities, such as rudimentary sea mines,
> fast-attack small craft, or shorter range artillery and missile systems render transit into
> and through the commons vulnerable to interdiction by coercive, aggressive actors,
> slowing or stopping free movement.[70]

China's major maritime development has been directed at constructing land- and sea-based defences over the East China Sea and the Taiwan Straits that can 'clear rival navies out of designated waters – or deter them from entering in the first place', repel or keep a hostile naval force out of a particular area, for example to prevent a blockade, or to stop the secession of Taipei.[71] Shore-based ground-to-air, anti-ship and air defence missiles, improved fighter aircraft, radar and tracking increasingly extend a protective umbrella over the operations of the Chinese navy in coastal seas. China aims to project this umbrella to the 'first island chain' – the sweep of islands that enclose China's seas from the Japanese archipelago in the north, arcing south through Taiwan, the Philippine and Indonesian island chains and on through Singapore and Malaysia to Indochina (see Map 1).

The US naval and military strategists dub the potential impact of this defensive build-up as 'Area Access/Area Denial', or A2/AD for short, and claim it is creating putative 'no-go zones' in the seas off China's coasts. But of course in this looking-glass world there are no such 'no-go zones' around the US's Pacific or Atlantic coasts.

More seriously for the Pentagon, China's strong perimeter defences mean that, unlike in Iraq or Afghanistan, the US could not deploy forces into a projected Chinese theatre 'with little risk of hostile interference'.[72] Moreover, given the vulnerability of Okinawa and Guam to Chinese missile defences, the US would not necessarily have regional bases that were safe from attack, rendering its huge geographical extension a fundamental disadvantage despite China's inferior forces overall. While not preventing US 'power projection' into the East China Sea these developments would dramatically escalate the potential costs in mounting a plausible threat let alone carrying out an actual operation against China. Andrew F. Krepinevich, US defence analyst and military advisor, summarised the situation as follows:

> As the great Chinese military theoretician, Sun Tzu, observed, the acme of generalship is being able to win without fighting. It appears the PLA is incorporating this philosophy in its efforts to create an A2/AD network, whose ultimate goal appears to be to raise the US cost of power-projection operations in the Western Pacific to prohibitive levels.[73]

In response to these developments, the Pentagon tasked a combined US marine, air force and navy command to come up with a strategy – Air-Sea Battle – for a US seaborne attack on an 'extensively armed major state'.[74] Although the Pentagon avoided naming a specific target of this new strategy, others are more open that it can only apply to China.[75]

The starting point of Air-Sea Battle is a scenario in which the US cannot safely launch a proximate seaborne attack as its fleet and even its nearby bases would be vulnerable to the missile and other airborne defences of its opponent. The highly controversial proposal of Air-Sea Battle is to protect US naval assets approaching China's coasts through a massive pre-emptive strike on missile command and control centres – described as 'a blinding campaign against PLA battle networks' – followed up by 'long-range penetrating strike operations' to take out missile launchers, satellite systems and air defence.[76]

The whole plan is a destructive adventure, placing the US military strategy against China in a logic of escalation. As with Germany and the Schlieffen Plan in 1914 – which locked Germany into an immediate invasion of France – Air-Sea Battle locks the US into an exponential escalation to total war, also raising the real risk of any conflict leading to a nuclear exchange.[77] This explains the widespread controversy about the projected strategy, not just from China but from other neighbouring states.[78]

Vulnerable sea trade

Apart from homeland defences China is mainly concerned about protecting its ocean trade, and particularly its seaborne energy supply chain, from threats like piracy or blockade. China's oil primarily arrives by sea from the Gulf via the Malacca Strait thence to Hong Kong or on to eastern seaboard ports like Shanghai, Qingdao and Tianjin. Access to the Malacca Strait and free passage across the South China Sea are thus crucial strategic considerations (see Map 2).

The route from the Gulf through the Malacca Strait is the only direct one. The routes through the island chain in and out of the South China Sea are limited and alternatives require long detours to the south or negotiating straits that are less suitable for modern deepwater shipping. Thus domination of the Malacca Strait gives the possibility of closing the main sea route between China and the West. This features in US strategic discussion:

> One example of an indirect approach is to attack Chinese merchant shipping and resources transiting the Strait of Malacca. Since 80% of China's imported oil passes through these waters, the Strait is arguably a potential decisive point for US and Chinese forces in a western Pacific conflict.[79]

'Distant blockade operations' are envisaged as part of the third phase of Air-Sea Battle.[80] Defence strategists such as T. X. Hammes, research fellow at the Institute for National Security Studies, have argued that blockade – or what Hammes more euphemistically calls 'offshore control' – offers the most effective strategy for the US to take the offensive against China.[81] Although the US Department of Defense does not officially acknowledge that it is pursuing the capacity to blockade China, as one commentator wryly put it, Obama did not shift over half of American naval assets to the Asia Pacific 'to contain pirates'.[82] The stepped-up US military presence in Singapore and Singapore's own upgrading of its air-sea capability create further unease, reinforced by the sharply increased US naval presence in the South China Sea.[83] And Tillerson, Trump's Secretary of State, went so far as to threaten that the US navy might consider blockading China from access to its installations in the South China Sea.[84]

Not surprisingly therefore: 'Chinese leaders fret that the United States will deploy naval might to deny China access to the commons, retaliating against some Chinese transgression or even conceivably on the whim of an American president.'[85] As a result 'China has been forced to confront a central geopolitical dilemma: can it rely on a rival to protect the country's economic lifeline?' It has concluded that safeguarding these sealanes is not something it is prepared to subcontract to anyone else.[86]

Mitigating its dependence on these sea routes has also driven a flurry of Chinese deals with Russia and the Central Asian republics for new overland pipelines; Chinese investment in an overland link to the Gulf via Pakistan; and its commitment to improved land-based transport infrastructure across Asia. But none of these can

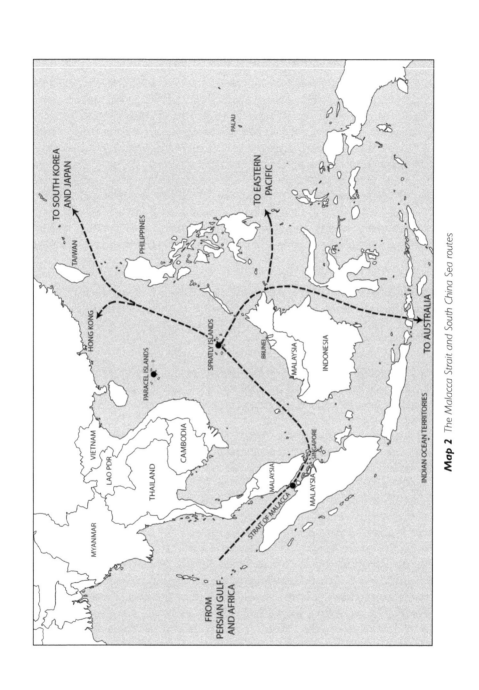

Map 2 *The Malacca Strait and South China Sea routes*

substitute for the sea. Safeguarding the route from the Gulf remains a high-level priority, driving China's investment in longer range naval capacity, in a series of ports along
this route (the maritime Silk Road) and its defensiveness about its airstrips and docking
points in the South China Sea that can position its navy close to its mercantile shipping
lanes.[87]

'Win-win' or 'zero-sum game'

China has been building up its navy, but the twin aims of this have been transparently to
defend its own coastal seas and patrol its extensive ocean trade routes, as demanded
by China's own historical experience and current vulnerabilities. In the 'century of
humiliation' it was via the oceans that Western imperialist 'gunboat diplomacy' forced
it to hand over territory and sign up to unfair treaties. As Robert Kaplan put it: 'China's
very urge for an expanded strategic space is a declaration that it never again intends
to let foreigners take advantage of it, as they did in the previous two centuries.'[88]
This historical lesson has been amplified by its reliance on its export trade and on oil
imported by sea.

China's overall foreign policy approach has been crystal clear. It requires stability, trade, secure and open seas, and the minimum necessary transfer of resources
from productive growth to a military build-up in order to pursue achieving a 'moderately
prosperous' standard of living for its people. It has no objective interest in provoking
conflicts or in territorial expansion. It is very far from a level of military development that
could challenge the US, either in equipment or in experience and is not trying to catch
up. As one commentator put it accurately: 'The US upgrades its military capabilities
through war, China through military drills. The difference here is like that between corporate executives and corporate governance scholars.'[89]

While China will not retreat from what it considers are strategic defensive
positions – for example in the South China Sea – it is willing to seek 'win-win' compromises with its neighbours. It rejects any US role as 'big brother' enforcer, but has
proposed that they should seek a new type of 'major power relations' that could
improve dialogue, ease conflict and find mutually beneficial ways forward. Despite this,
every new step by China is interpreted through a distorting lens of US paranoia about
its declining world role. Any success by China in negotiating good relations with its
neighbours is viewed as part of an advancing regional domination that challenges US
hegemony. Any improvement in its military capacities must be aimed at an eventual
challenge to the US.

But it is the US that deploys the language of aggression against China, not vice
versa. It is US government advisors that have written articles arguing: 'The fact is that
China is our enemy, now and in the future. A failure to recognise this fact has serious
national security implications for our great nation.'[90] It is US military officers that refer
to China as 'Voldemort' and the Pentagon that has drawn up plans for Air-Sea Battle,
which are a scarcely disguised military blueprint for total war against China.[91] It is senior
defence analysts, like Krepinevich, that argue for 'discouraging Chinese adventurism'
through 'the prospect of punishment, in the form of air strikes and naval blockades'
and call for a 'series of linked defences along the first island chain' to militarily contain

China.[92] It was Steve Bannon, the Trump White House's chief strategist, who stated unequivocally that 'We're going to war in the South China Sea in 5 to 10 years … There's no doubt about that.'[93]

Many factors do weigh against war between China and the US, not least the posses-sion of nuclear weapons. But given the huge adjustments in the international relationship of forces, the rhetoric issuing from the Pentagon, the escalated threats from Trump, the US's actual build-up in East Asia, and China's refusal to retreat in the face of threats there is a growing danger of conflict. Driven by Trump's rhetoric or the neuroses of the military establishment the US could be tempted to try to deliver pre-emptive blows that it conceives as limited, but with dynamics it cannot necessarily control. Or it could encourage China's neighbours into over aggressive steps, even proxy wars. These are all real and present dangers that have progressively deepened since Obama's original 'pivot to China'.

But China has risen peacefully for three and a half decades and has overwhelm-ing objective interests in avoiding conflict and maintaining stability with its Asian neighbours and the US. And even among the China hardliners in the US there are few who advocate an attempt to simply militarily cow China. Armed conflict is not the most likely outcome and the stronger China becomes the less likely it is. For eight years under Obama a battle of wills rather than arms played out between the US and China in Asia-Pacific, which primarily turned on the struggle for influence over all the countries that surround China. This book considers the main features of the multiple interactions and contestations between the US and China in the Asia-Pacific region that have contributed to how this struggle has developed so far.

It concludes that whether the US can succeed in launching something that looks like a new Cold War against China or whether China has already outstripped the possibility of containment is yet to be determined; but nothing suggests that the US is giving up on the attempt, still less with Donald Trump at the helm pledged to 'make America great again'.

Notes

1 R. Kagan, *Dangerous nation: America's foreign policy from its earliest days to the dawn of the twentieth century*, Vintage Books, New York, 2006, p. 39.

2 John Adams, Second President of the US, statement to Thomas Jefferson, 1813.

3 Maddison, *The world economy*.

4 Anderson, 'Imperium', 6–11.

5 Desai, *Geopolitical economy*, pp. 64–91.

6 Ibid., p. 87.

7 Maddison, *The world economy*, Vol. 2. 1945 GDP (measured in 1990 Geary Khamis dollars): US GDP $1.65tr; total GDP of other countries listed (ex. USSR) $1.37tr; inc. USSR $1.70tr.

8 De Gaulle's France became the fifth permanent member against the wishes of the US.

9 Kolko, *The politics of war*, p. 625.

10 Robert B. Zoellick, Deputy Secretary of State, Remarks to National Committee on US–China rela-tions, New York City, 21 September 2005, US Department of State archive.

11 See, inter alia, H. J. Morganthau, *Politics among nations: the struggle for power and peace*, McGraw-Hill, New York, 1948 and Waltz, *Theory of international politics*.

12 J. J. Mearsheimer, 'Why China's rise will not be peaceful', http://mearsheimer.uchicago.edu/pdfs/A0034b.pdf, 17 September 2004 (date accessed 20 October 2016).

13 See Anderson, 'Imperium'.

14 Desai, *Geopolitical economy*, p. 55.

15 J. J. Mearsheimer, *The tragedy of great power politics*, W.W. Norton & Co., New York, 2001.

16 Mearsheimer, 'China's rise'.

17 Ibid.

18 Arrighi, *Adam Smith*, p. 309.

19 C. Chen, '"Peaceful rise" will meet US containment', *Global Times*, 6 November 2013.

20 R. D. Kaplan, 'How we would fight China', *The Atlantic*, 295:5 (June 2005), 49–64.

21 Ibid.

22 J. R. Holmes, 'Beware the "Thucydides trap" trap', *The Diplomat*, 13 June 2013. Available at: http://thediplomat.com/2013/06/beware-the-thucydides-trap-trap/ (date accessed 5 June 2016).

23 See, inter alia, L. Whyte, 'The real Thucydides trap', *The Diplomat*, 6 May 2015. Available at: http://thediplomat.com/2015/05/the-real-thucydides-trap/; G. Allison, 'The Thucydides trap: are the U.S. and China headed for war?', *The Atlantic*, 24 September 2015. Available at: https://www.theatlantic.com/international/archive/2015/09/united-states-china-war-thucydides-trap/406756/ (both accessed 15 February 2017).

24 J. Ross, 'Why a US-China "Thucydides trap" can be avoided', *John Ross economics,* September 2016. Available at: http://www.johnrosseconomics.com/why-a-us-china-lsquothucydides-traprsquo-can-be-avoided.html (date accessed 17 February 2017).

25 Full text of President Xi speech on China-US ties, *China Daily*, 24 September 2015.

26 As in Mearsheimer, *The tragedy of great power politics*.

27 S. P. Huntington, *The clash of civilizations and the remaking of world order*, Simon & Schuster, New York, 1996.

28 Aaron L. Friedberg is professor of politics and international affairs at Princeton and was a signatory to the 1997 Project for a New American Century.

29 A. L. Friedberg, *A contest for supremacy: China, America and the struggle for mastery in Asia*, W.W. Norton & Co., New York, 2011, p. 135.

30 Ibid., p. 43.

31 Ibid., p. 38.

32 Ibid., p. 265.

33 Ibid., p. 184.

34 Ibid., p. 95.

35 G. Rachman, 'The shadow of 1914 falls over the Pacific', *Financial Times*, 4 February 2013.

36 D. Fromkin, *Europe's last summer: who started the Great War in 1914?*, Vintage Books, New York, 2005, p. 88. But this traditional account of the First World War is challenged; see, for example. C. Clark, *The sleepwalkers: how Europe went to war in 1914*, Penguin, London, 2012.

37 Maddison, *The world economy*, Vol. 2, p. 262.

38 Budget cuts saw US defence expenditure fall as a share of GDP from 5.6 per cent in 2010 to 4.3 per cent in 2014 Source: The US Bureau of Economic Analysis, National Income and Product Accounts, Table 1.5.5. GDP, expanded detail.

39 K. Mahubani, 'Look to China for wisdom on dealing with Russia', *Financial Times*, 21 March 2014.

40 A. F. Krepinevich, 'How to deter China', *Foreign Affairs*, 94:2 (March–April 2015), 78–86.

41 J. Mann, *The China fantasy: how our leaders explain away Chinese repression*, Viking Penguin, New York, 2007, pp. 62–3.

42 J. Y. F. Lin, *Demystifying the Chinese economy*, Cambridge University Press, Cambridge, 2012, chs 1 and 6.

43 J. Y. F. Lin, 'China and the global economy, luncheon address', *Federal Reserve Bank of San Francisco Asia economic policy conference*, 29–30 November 2011, pp. 213–29.

44 US Census Bureau, 2015. Values in nominal dollars.

45 P. Krugman, 'The Chinese connection', *New York Times*, 20 May 2005.

46 See, for example, A. Follett, 'The USA and China: destined to cooperate?', *The Diplomat*, 24 June 2014. Available at: http://thediplomat.com/2014/06/china-and-the-us-destined-to-cooperate/ (date accessed 19 February 2017).

47 H. F. Hung, 'America's head servant', *New Left Review*, 60 (November–December 2009), p. 25.

48 R. Keohane and J. Nye, *Power and interdependence: world politics in transition*, Little, Brown & Co., Boston, MA, 1989.

49 N. Angell, *The great illusion*, William Heinemann, London, 1909.

50 Friedberg, *Contest for supremacy*, p. 47.

51 Anderson, 'Imperium', p. 43.

52 D. Gavel, 'The second term: Joseph Nye on US-Chinese relations', *Harvard Kennedy School of Government*, 22 January 2013. Available at: https://www.hks.harvard.edu/news-events/news/articles/second-term-series-nye (date accessed 17 February 2017).

53 H. Kissinger, 'China: containment won't work', *Washington Post*, 13 June 2005.

54 H. Kissinger, 'The future of US-Chinese relations: conflict is a choice, not a necessity', *Foreign Affairs*, 91:2 (March–April 2012), 44–55.

55 Z. Brzezinksi, 'Towards a global realignment', *The American Interest*, 11:6 (2016), 7–11.

56 Z. Brzezinski, *The grand chessboard: American primacy and its geostrategic imperatives*, Basic Books, New York, 1997, p. 40.

57 H. Kissinger, 'Avoiding a US-China Cold War', *Washington Post*, 14 January 2011.

58 H. R. Clinton, 'Hillary Clinton reviews Henry Kissinger's "World order"', *Washington Post*, 4 September 2014; H. Kissinger, *World order*, Penguin Books, New York, 2014.

59 See, for example, J. Holslag, *China's coming war with Asia*, Polity Press, Cambridge, 2015.

60 H. Holst, 'Blue means blue: China's naval ambitions', *The Diplomat*, 7 January 2014. Available at: http://thediplomat.com/2014/01/blue-means-blue-chinas-naval-ambitions/ (date accessed 17 February 2017).

61 T. Yoshihara and J. R. Holmes, *Red star over the Pacific: China's rise and challenge to U.S. maritime strategy*, Naval Institute Press, Annapolis, MD, 2013, ch. 9.

62 A. S. Erickson and A. M. Strange, 'No substitute for experience: Chinese anti-piracy operations in the Gulf of Aden', *Naval War College CMSI, China Maritime Study 10*, November 2013. Available at: https://www.usnwc.edu/Research---Gaming/China-Maritime-Studies-Institute/Publications/documents/CMS10_Web_2.aspx (date accessed 17 February 2017).

63 C. Bodeen, 'China sends navy ship to protect Libya evacuees', *Washington Post*, 25 February 2011.

64 Holst, 'Blue means blue'.

65 See Chapter 5 this volume and J. Chen, *Mao's China and the Cold War*, University of North Carolina Press, Chapel Hill, NC, 2001.

66 For a detailed discussion of China's naval developments and military strategies, see A. J. Nathan and A. Scobell, *China's search for security*, Columbia University Press, New York, 2012; and Yoshihara and Holmes, *Red star over the Pacific*.

67 E. L. Dreyer, *Zheng He: China and the oceans in the early Ming dynasty, 1405–1433*, Longman, London, 2007.

68 P. Navarro, *The coming China wars: where they will be fought, how they can be won*, Financial Times Press, Upper Saddle River, NJ, 2008, p. 152.

69 A. Erickson and G. Collins, 'China's real blue water navy', *The Diplomat*, 30 August 2012. Available at: http://thediplomat.com/2012/08/chinas-not-so-scary-navy/ (date accessed 16 February 2017).

70 'Air-Sea Battle: Service Collaboration to Address Anti-Access and Access Denial Strategies', Air-Sea Battle Office, US Department of Defense, Virginia, May 2013, p. 2.

71 Yoshihara and Holmes, *Red star over the Pacific*, p. 73.

72 C. J. McCarthy, 'Anti-Access/Area Denial: the evolution of modern warfare', *Lucent, US Naval War College Student Journal*, 2010. Available at: https://www.usnwc.edu/Lucent/OpenPdf.aspx?id=95 (date accessed 20 October 2016).

73 A. F. Krepinevich, *Why Air-Sea Battle?*, Centre for Strategic and Budgetary Assessments, Washington, DC, 19 February 2010.

74 2010 Quadrennial Defence Review.

75 J. Van Tol, M. Gunzinger, A. F. Krepinevich and J. Thomas, *AirSea Battle: A point-of-departure operational concept*, Centre for Strategic and Budgetary Assessments, Washington, DC, 18 May 2010.

76 Ibid.

77 A. MacKinnon, *Falling eagle, rising dragon*, Campaign for Nuclear Disarmament, London, 2013.

78 In January 2015 Air-Sea Battle was renamed Joint Concept for Access and Manoeuvre in the Global Commons.

79 McCarthy, 'Anti-Access/Area Denial'.

80 Van Tol et al., *AirSea Battle*.

81 T. X. Hammes, 'Offshore control is the answer', *Proceedings*, 138:12 (2012), 1318.

82 P. Porter, 'Thucydides trap 2.0: superpower suicide?', *The National Interest*, 2 May 2014. Available at: http://nationalinterest.org/feature/thucydides-trap-20-superpower-suicide-10352 (date accessed 16 February 2017).

83 P. Ghosh, 'Singapore: little tiger with a big military roar', *International Business Times*, 15 May 2012.

84 D. Brunnstrom and M. Spetalnick, 'Tillerson says China should be barred from South China Sea islands', *Reuters*, 12 January 2017. Available at: http://www.reuters.com/article/us-congress-tillerson-china-idUSKBN14V2KZ (date accessed 16 February 2017).

85 Yoshihara and Holmes, *Red star over the Pacific*, p. 10.

86 G. Dyer, 'The US v China: is this the new Cold War?', *Financial Times*, 20 February 2014.

87 For the disputes in the South China Sea, see Chapter 10.

88 R. D. Kaplan, *Asia's cauldron: the South China Sea and the end of a stable Pacific*, Random House, New York, 2014, p. 21.

89 X. T. Yan, 'Why a bipolar world is more likely than a unipolar or multipolar one', *New Perspectives Quarterly*, 32:3 (2015), 52–6.

90 T. D. Naegele, 'China is America's enemy: make no mistake about that', 13 January 2011. Available at: https://naegeleblog.wordpress.com/2011/01/13/china-is-americas-enemy-make-no-mistake-about-that/ (date accessed 20 October 2016).

91 Dyer, 'The US v China'.

92 Krepinevich, *Why Air-Sea Battle?*.

93 B. Haas, 'Steve Bannon: "We're going to war in the South China Sea … no doubt"', *The Guardian*, 2 February 2017.

Part II
Containment without Russia?

5

Russia: facing west or east

Russia and China share a long, permeable land border, stretching 4195 km along China's north-eastern and western frontiers (see Map 1). The state of Sino-Russian relations has determined whether such an extended border between two such mighty states is a source of strategic anxiety or security.

In the context of the high tensions and mutual suspicions between China and the USSR after the Sino-Soviet split, these facts of Sino-Soviet geography helped the US 'triangulate' their relations to its own advantage, first courting Russia to isolate and threaten China and then drawing China into its Cold War strategies against the USSR. If, rather than exploiting Sino-Soviet divisions, the US had faced them united, the outcome of the Cold War might have been quite different. Today a newly arisen China and a resource-rich and militarily powerful Russia acting in concert could offer each other critical mutual economic and military support, and exercise a formidable geopolitical influence.

Hence it is well understood across the US foreign policy spectrum that success in containing China requires preventing Russia and China coming together, and instead redeploying the old Cold War triangular strategies for today's circumstances. As a *Heritage Foundation* publication put it, it is 'in America's interest to shape relations between the largest country and the most populated country on the planet to prevent their alignment against the US.'[1] According to an article published by *Foreign Policy*: 'One of Washington's long-term geopolitical priorities should be driving a wedge between Moscow and Beijing.'[2] Or as the managing editor of *The Diplomat* pointed out, a US 'alliance with Russia would undoubtedly make it easier for the US to contain China's expansion in the Western Pacific and beyond', as it would force Beijing 'to concentrate its military resources on its borders with countries like Russia, India and North Korea, as well as its western autonomous regions' rather than the Pacific.[3]

Given the enormous tensions that blew up between the US and Russia from 2014 – primarily over Ukraine – binding Russia into Western projects against China seemed an unrealistic goal, particularly as Russia responded to the Ukraine crisis by intensifying its already deepening orientation towards China. For example, in its midst, in May 2014, Putin signed a ground-breaking $400 billion, 30-year deal to supply China with gas via thousands of miles of new pipelines across Siberia.[4] Sino-Russian naval exercises in the East China Sea in the same month sent a similar message.

However, this relationship has taken time to mature and, before the conflict over Ukraine, it was not at all a foregone conclusion that Russia would look primarily to China rather than the West. The long post-war history of tensions between Russia and China gave US foreign policy experts grounds to be hopeful of implicating Russia in its goal of containing China. Though Sino-Soviet tensions eased from the 1980s, the foreign policy focus of both Gorbachev and Yeltsin suggested that post-Soviet Russia was moving into the ambit of the West, not closer to China. Initially Putin, elected in 2000, was also positively oriented to the US and Europe, with China playing a secondary and uncertain role. But, with NATO's 2002 decision to install the US's interceptor missile shield in former Warsaw Pact countries, Putin's relations with the West began to falter, until they completely broke down over Ukraine in 2014.

This chapter reviews US–China–Russia relations in the post-war period, and considers how their recent development affects prospects for the US in Asia. It outlines how those driving US foreign policy towards China saw the confrontation with Russia in Ukraine as a dangerous and diversionary adventure, bewailing the resulting Sino-Russian convergence, deploring the distraction of US attention from East Asia and warning that this would undermine confidence among the US's Asian allies of its commitment to the region.[5] In sum: 'If the US is to maintain primacy in the 21st century, it must … recognise that China is its primary geostrategic rival and subordinate other foreign policy goals to the paramount objective of containing its rise.'[6] The US's failure to do this, instead pitting itself against both Putin in the West and China in the East, drove Russia and China together, quite possibly sacrificing the more vital need to contain China for a lesser goal of uncertain outcome in Ukraine. From this point of view, Trump's proposal to 'reset' US–Russia relations made sense; far from being a personal idiosyncrasy, his suggestion of a possible 'grand bargain' with Russia to settle Syria and Ukraine played to a strategic agenda of driving a wedge between Russia and China. Trump's price for a deal with Putin would undoubtedly include at the very least acquiescence by Russia to US policy to contain China.[7]

Post-1949 Sino-Soviet unity vs US containment

The 'Sino-Soviet split' – which not only drove the USSR and China into conflict but rent the worldwide communist movement between supporters of Mao and those of the USSR – can be taken to have begun in 1959, but in fact tensions had existed for decades before this date.

Although the immense authority of the Russian Revolution made the Russian communists' advice highly influential in the infant CPC, founded in 1921, disagreements with the USSR's representatives grew over the next ten years. Disputes emerged over the communists' tactics towards the GMD nationalist forces after the death of Sun Yat-sen, when the rightist Chiang Kai-shek emerged as its new leader and bloodily suppressed the Shanghai workers' uprising in 1927. Following this defeat, the CPC's armed forces (reorganised as the Red Army) retreated to rural areas in the south where Mao developed the strategy of the 'countryside surrounding the cities'; this led to his first major dispute with the CPC leadership and the representatives of the Comintern in China. The decisive fight, however, came over military tactics after the Red Army was defeated in 1934, for which Mao blamed the Soviet representatives because of their insistence on a suicidal offensive against the GMD.[8] At a special CPC conference called in January 1935 at Zunyi, during the course of the Long March as the Red Army was forced to flee the GMD, Mao and his supporters routed the existing leadership of the CPC and Otto Braun, the Comintern representative, on the military question. The Soviet representatives were pushed out of any future leadership role and Mao assumed the helm of the party.[9] Although fraternal relations were maintained, and Mao always expressed the highest respect for Stalin, Soviet views were never again paramount in the CPC.

Mao and Stalin's views reconverged over the forging of a united front between the GMD and the Chinese communists to resist the Japanese invasion in 1937, but Stalin clearly expected that the GMD would emerge as the dominant force in liberated China. When instead the communists began to win the civil war, Stalin accepted the outcome. The USSR became the first state to recognise the PRC within days of its declaration on 1 October 1949. In February 1950 the USSR and the PRC signed a Treaty of Friendship, Alliance and Mutual Assistance, committing them to mutual defence and non-aggression for 30 years, abrogating Stalin's 1945 treaty with Chiang Kai-shek's defeated Republic of China (ROC), which by then was essentially confined to the island of Taiwan.[10] The new treaty included a $300 million loan to China, transferred ownership of the crucial Changchun Railway to China and pledged technical help and expertise in defence and other industries – although not including access to the Soviet nuclear programme, which had seen the USSR successfully test its first nuclear bomb in August 1949.

This alliance between the PRC and the USSR convinced Washington that it confronted a new strategic threat in Asia. With the Truman administration facing fierce domestic criticism for having 'lost China' – though there was little that it could have done to affect the outcome – the US refused to recognise the PRC, imposed a trade embargo (that continued until 1971) and strengthened its support for Chang Kai-shek in Taiwan.[11] In 1950 it moved its Seventh Fleet into the Taiwan Strait, allegedly to prevent any extension of the Korean War southwards, but effectively blocking any military action by the PRC to retake the island. The US rapidly penned military alliances with Japan, Australia, New Zealand, the Philippines (1951) and South Korea (1953).[12] In September 1954 it added Thailand and Pakistan to its treaty allies through the misnamed Southeast Asia Treaty Organization (SEATO) – of which only two members were South East Asian countries.[13] The US expanded its pre-war Pacific bases from Hawaii via Wake, Midway and Guam to the Philippines; and added new air and naval bases in South Korea and Japan, facing China's eastern coast. A mutual defence treaty with the ROC in Taiwan in 1954 completed the encirclement. China and the USSR opposed this containment, which threatened both countries.

But Sino-Soviet tension mounted after Stalin's death in 1953, coming to a head in 1954 when the PRC attempted to drive GMD troops off some small Chinese coastal islands – including Jinmen (2 miles off the Chinese coast) and Mazu (10 miles). The US immediately came to Chiang Kai-shek's aid. The US Joint Chiefs of Staff even recommended the use of nuclear weapons against China; Secretary of State John Foster Dulles warned that the American people should prepare for a nuclear attack on China; and President Eisenhower famously dismissed concerns about the potential consequences: 'A-bombs can be used … as you would use a bullet.'[14]

There was no equivalent support for the PRC from the USSR. Stalin's successor, Khrushchev, had reoriented Soviet foreign policy towards 'peaceful coexistence' with the US. This meant mitigating points of potential conflict with the West, encouraging its allies to compromise on disputes and discouraging communist parties worldwide from engaging in frontal struggles for power. Since it was clear Khrushchev did not intend to risk a war with the US, China had to make a tactical retreat.[15]

The Sino-Soviet split

This crisis reinforced Mao's view that China needed its own nuclear weapons. However, only it was only when the US stationed missiles capable of carrying nuclear warheads on Taiwan in 1957 that the USSR agreed to help China develop a nuclear capability and China began uranium enrichment.[16] But on 20 June 1959 Khrushchev abruptly withdrew from China's nuclear programme, and in July 1960 all Soviet technical support and personnel were pulled out of China without prior consultation.

Behind this move lay Khrushchev's determined orientation towards a rapprochement with Eisenhower's US, including his 1958 proposal for an international ban on nuclear testing, to be initially agreed between the USSR, the US and Britain.[17] Withdrawing China's access to Soviet nuclear technology strengthened Khrushchev's hand before meeting Eisenhower at Camp David later in 1959. These events precipitated the Sino-Soviet split, which was to poison their relations for the next 25 years and allowed the US to manipulate each country against the other, weakening both.

There is still major debate on the reasons for the Sino-Soviet split. Earlier discussions, before the partial opening of Soviet archives in 1992, tended to reflect Cold War divisions, with Western non-Marxist commentaries presenting it as a struggle of rival empires; Soviet writers ascribing it to great Han chauvinism and Chinese nationalism; and Maoists to Soviet revisionism and Russian expansionism. More recent contributions are more balanced but still do not agree. For example, L. M. Luthi concludes it was because Mao was moving in a leftist direction, just at the point that Khrushchev was seeking more 'pragmatic' international and domestic approaches.[18] J. Chen argues that Mao deliberately drove the split as he thought the USSR was holding China back economically, therefore 'radicalising domestic policy' with the Great Leap Forward.[19] S. Radchenko suggests more multidimensional causes, including massive blundering by Khrushchev, particularly his failure to understand the nationalist sensibilities of a country long dominated by foreign powers.[20] J. Friedman argues the split was born of a fundamental strategic contradiction between an 'anti-capitalist' orientation of the USSR and an 'anti-imperialist' orientation of the PRC.[21]

However, whatever other causes are ascribed for the split, the withdrawal of support for China's nuclear programme – which Mao considered critical – was decisive in precipitating it.[22] Khrushchev's subordination of China's future defence to agreements between the USSR and the West was unforgiveable in Mao's eyes, particularly given the ongoing international isolation of the PRC, still excluded from the UN and recognised by only a small minority of countries. The fury of the ideological debate reflected this sense of fraternal betrayal.[23]

The USSR had launched the first space satellite – Sputnik – in 1957 and successfully tested the world's first intercontinental ballistic missile, the R-7, capable of delivering a nuclear warhead over 5500 miles to an accuracy of 3 miles, putting it temporarily ahead of the US in the nuclear arms race.[24] China did not have nuclear weapons and had been directly threatened with nuclear attack, a threat that was repeated in the Second Taiwan Strait Crisis of 1958–59, when once again the PRC unsuccessfully tried to drive the GMD from the islands adjacent to the Chinese coast.

China did eventually test its own A-bomb in 1964, but the split in 1959 began nearly three decades of bruising relations between the USSR and China. From 1965 both countries progressively increased border military deployments, rising to several hundred thousand on each side by the end of the decade.[25] In 1969 bloody conflicts broke out over disputed borders along the Ussuri River in north-east China and along the western border with Xinjiang, where Russia was also intervening to encourage pro-Soviet political currents among China's Kazakh and Uyghur populations. Soviet troops were stationed in the quasi-independent Mongolian People's Republic, militarising China's entire northern border. As the two countries teetered towards all-out war, the USSR privately informed the US that it might make a pre-emptive nuclear strike against China's infant nuclear capacity.[26]

Nixon in China

Through the 1960s China sought to create a 'third force' in world politics, a pro-Chinese coalition opposed to both US imperialism and Soviet 'social imperialism', as Mao dubbed it, based on the wave of liberation struggles that was sweeping through the colonial world.[27] China won many friends in the developing world through these efforts, but in the end China could not substitute for the support offered by the USSR crucially to Vietnam – at war with the US – and India, which signed a comprehensive treaty with the USSR in 1971 in the context of its war with Pakistan over Bangladesh.[28] Feeling vulnerable on all sides, China was drawn into a rapprochement with the US.

In 1971–72, when Kissinger and Nixon visited China, American prestige was at a significant post-war low, with the country already facing probable defeat in Vietnam; international opprobrium for its use of napalm, Agent Orange and carpet-bombing; and a growing anti-war movement at home. In 1971 the weakening of the US economy was signalled by its first-ever trade deficit and the dollar devaluation that followed abandoning the gold standard. China's apparent embrace of America's Cold War aims reinvigorated US leverage across the globe.

The crucial gain for China was replacing the ROC in the UN, including on the Security Council in 1971, thus legitimising the PRC internationally for the first time, ending its 20-year isolation and putting it on a par with the USSR in having a UN veto.

However, the policies that China pursued internationally following this rapprochement with the US served to profoundly undermine the esteem in which it had been held by progressive opinion and potential allies worldwide.[29] It lost the support of the developing world and the international allegiance of the left as it scaled back its support for Third World guerrilla movements, vetoed Bangladesh's entry to the UN, maintained relations with Chile after the overthrow of Allende, refused to condemn Israel in the UN after the Six Day War and – most decisively of all – continued to arm the National Union for the Total Independence of Angola (UNITA) when it was backed by the apartheid regime in South Africa and was fighting the Soviet- and Cuban-backed Movement for the Liberation of Angola (MLPA).[30]

Through the 1980s China remained broadly aligned with the US, although China still did not use its veto in the UN. This facilitated trade and other support as China implemented its economic reform, using the rapprochement with the US to improve its relations with Japan in particular, South Korea and even Taiwan.

The West's reorientation to post-Cold War Russia

The importance of China in American international strategies came to an abrupt end in 1989 with the fall of the Berlin Wall and the events in Tiananmen Square. The first obviated the imperatives of the previous two decades of maintaining an alliance with China against the USSR, while the US saw the defeat of the Tiananmen Square movement as a blow to their hopes for a similar fall of communism in China.

The early post-communist period in Russia could not have gone better for the US, with Boris Yeltsin defining Russia's national interest as integration into Western security and economic institutions, banning the Communist Party in 1991 and embarking on the economic 'shock therapy' recommended by the 1990 World Bank and IMF report on Russia.[31] Yeltsin did not object when NATO established the 'Partnership for Peace' as a pathway for the integration of former Soviet allies in Eastern Europe in 1994, nor when it formally invited Poland, Hungary and the Czech Republic to join in 1997. Russia's acquiescence to the priorities of the West was tested by the conflict in Yugoslavia, which was a Russian ally, but it took no concerted counteraction apart from raising formal objections and aborting a visit to Washington in 1999 in response to NATO bombing of Serbia.

But shock therapy devastated the Russian economy leading to a fall in annual GDP of 45 per cent between 1989 and 1999 and inflicting financial ruin on a huge section of the population whose jobs, savings and pensions were eliminated. It also created a widely despised layer of semi-criminal profiteers from the sale of undervalued state assets (the 'oligarchs').[32] This national disaster utterly undermined the lure of the West in the minds of a large majority of the population. By the mid-1990s Yeltsin's support was plummeting and the refounded Communist Party was gaining support, as were right, left and centre Russian nationalist currents. From the late 1990s openly pro-Western parties consistently failed to gain much more than single-digit shares of the vote.

The 2000 election win by Putin, a self-described conservative Russian nationalist, was not what the West sought. Putin's priority, alongside restoring domestic economic stability, was to prevent any further encroachment upon Russia's borders.[33] While not necessarily shifting away from a primary orientation to the West, Putin would clearly no longer simply capitulate to its every behest, as Yeltsin had.[34]

Almost immediately Bush's hawkish policies began to encroach on Russia's strategic interests. Putin tolerated the 2001 invasion of Afghanistan due to shared concern over safe havens for al-Qaeda-type forces in Central Asia; but this brought the US military closer to Russia's southern borders, which Putin was not prepared to accept indefinitely.[35] Missile defence and NATO proposals to incorporate the Baltic States, raised tensions more sharply.[36] As frictions grew, Putin began to pay increasing attention to Central Asia and to China.

Putin and tensions with the West

The 2002 NATO decision to develop a European 'missile defence shield', involving, inter alia, the deployment of long-range interceptor missiles and radar tracking systems in the Czech Republic and Poland, badly affected relations with Putin, as this constituted a clear military threat to Russia.[37] By 2007 relations reached a nadir as negotiations with Poland and the Czech Republic on missile defence proceeded apace.

Disagreements over the Middle East and Central Asia were also increasing. Russia did not support the invasion of Iraq; objected to US interference in Georgia, and the suggestion it might join NATO; and did not share Bush's hostility to Iran, seeing it instead as a regional ally and counterweight to American influence.

For a brief period of time, after the election of Obama, it seemed that a more conciliatory line might prevail. Coupled with Putin's 2008 replacement by Medvedev as president of the Russian Federation, elected on a platform of a reinforced Russian orientation to the West, there was a renewed spirit of engagement. Obama's September 2009 announcement that the Czech and Polish missile interceptor deployments would not go ahead looked like an attempt to compromise – even though they would be on warships instead.[38] The incoming NATO general secretary, Rasmussen, even projected a fundamental 'strategic partnership' between Russia and NATO on global security issues.[39] Russia returned to collaboration with the West on a number of fronts, particularly in persuading China to accept the 2010 Security Council resolution expanding the sanctions on Iran, in return for which Obama lifted the US sanctions on the Russian arms export agency (which had been imposed as it supplied arms to Iran). Russia also supported the 2011 UN no-fly zone over Libya.

But the thaw was short-lived, with disagreements rapidly re-emerging over many issues including the stationing of missile defence interceptors in the Black Sea, the pursuit of 'regime change' in Libya, Russia's offer of asylum to Edward Snowden and the US proposal to intervene in Syria against Assad. Nonetheless, until the crisis in Ukraine erupted in 2014, it appeared that Putin would continue to use Russia's close links with Germany in particular to retain a priority orientation towards Europe and the US, while at the same time stepping up initiatives to engage with China to its east as a counterweight, not as an alternative.[40]

Healing the split with China

Sino-Russian relations had begun improving in the mid-1980s, with both Deng Xiaoping and Mikhail Gorbachev keen to put the hostilities of the Sino-Soviet split behind them. A speech by Gorbachev in 1986 offering talks with China at 'any time and at any level' led to a rapid thaw and in 1989 Gorbachev visited Beijing for the first Sino-Soviet summit meeting since 1959, where he carefully declined to comment on the Tiananmen Square events that happened to coincide with his visit. The USSR announced unilateral reductions in the Soviet garrisons on the Chinese borders and the 1991 Sino-Soviet Border Agreement, subsequently confirmed by the Russian Federation, finally resolved the outstanding issues. In 1994 President Jiang Zemin visited Moscow, the first visit by a Chinese head of state since 1957.[41] These developments led to the 2001 comprehensive cooperation and friendship treaty between the two countries.[42] Since 2001 Russia and China have held annual high-level meetings leading to further agreements covering military cooperation, cross-border trade and financial transactions among others.

China has made clear the importance it attaches to relations with Russia. Both Hu Jintao in 2003 and Xi Jinping in 2013 made Moscow the destination for their first state visits as presidents of the PRC. Putin was given equal ranking with George W. Bush as top international guests at the 2008 Beijing Olympics.[43] China placed its ties with Russia in fighting Japan in the Second World War at the centre of its 70th anniversary commemorations in 2015. And while the US boycotted the Russian 70th anniversary events in retribution for Ukraine, Xi Jinping attended as guest of honour.

Increasing trade has reinforced these diplomatic ties. Between 2000 and 2014 trade between Russia and China increased 12-fold from $8 billion to $95.4 billion. Russian exports to China increased 7-fold from $5.8 billion in 2000 to $41.6 billion in 2014, while imports from China rose 24-fold in the same period from $2.2 billion to $53.8 billion annually.[44] China has become Russia's number-one trading partner. Although Russia is only China's ninth largest trading partner, dwarfed by the EU, the US and Japan, its trade with Russia is much more significant than this ranking might imply.[45] Russia is increasingly essential to China's future energy security, providing a source of oil and gas that does not rely on vulnerable sea lanes.

In January 2011 the East Siberia–Pacific Ocean pipeline, Russia's first eastward-facing oil pipeline, was opened and by 2013 was operating at full capacity with expansion planned. In January 2012 the Chinese state grid began importing Russian electricity. In March 2013 Rosneft, Russia's state-owned oil company, announced it had reached 'agreement in principle' to more than triple its annual oil exports to China to 45–50 million tonnes – which would make China the largest consumer of Russian oil. The deal included joint development of deposits in east Siberia and offshore near the Barents Sea.[46] In November 2013 Rosneft signed a deal with Kazakhstan's state oil company to use the Kazakhstan–China oil pipeline, opened in 2006 and since expanded, to export Russian oil to China. In May 2014 Russia signed a 30-year deal to supply gas to China – worth over $400 billion it was the largest in Gazprom's history.[47]

This increasing cooperation on energy supply works for both countries, bringing China greater energy security while reducing Russian reliance on European energy markets, which became more urgent with the sanctions resulting from the Ukraine crisis.

The US loses Russia

Despite these fast-evolving diplomatic and economic relationships between Russia and China, most US foreign policy analysts suggested that mutual suspicions and security concerns would preclude a Sino-Russian strategic partnership, and that Russia would remain chiefly concerned to 'balance' China's growing influence in Asia.[48] The view that 'the relationship between Moscow and Beijing seems characterised more by common antipathies than shared sympathies' was mass marketed in the media.[49] Headlines claimed: 'Russia fears China, not Japan' (*Wall Street Journal*); 'Russia and Vietnam team up to balance China' (*The National Interest*); 'Why Putin fears China' (*Bloomberg*); 'Russia fears embrace of giant eastern neighbour' (*Guardian*).[50]

But the events in Ukraine in 2014 reset the overall direction of Russian foreign policy. As the director of the Carnegie Moscow Centre Dimitri Trenin put it succinctly:

> The Ukraine crisis that began in 2014 has shifted the geopolitical axis of Eurasia. Russia, which during the previous quarter century had tried to integrate into the West and become a full-fledged part of Europe, has moved back to its traditional position as a Eurasian power sitting between the East and the West. Moreover, faced with political and economic pressure from the United States and its allies, Russia has tilted toward China.[51]

The US's determination to integrate Ukraine into NATO inevitably led to a far greater breach with Russia than any previous tensions.[52] In the context of German reunification the West had made undertakings not to seek NATO expansion to Russia's borders.[53] In 1990, Secretary of State James Baker had assured Gorbachev that NATO would not expand 'one inch' to the east and West German Foreign Minister Hans-Dietrich Genscher said it would not expand 'closer to the borders of the Soviet Union'.[54] Russian objections to the earlier incorporations of 12 East European countries into NATO had been muted because this had left a neutral 'buffer zone' of Finland, Belarus and Ukraine between Russia and NATO along almost all its European border. But Russia had always made it clear that NATO expansion to include Ukraine (or indeed Georgia) was an issue of an entirely different order.

NATO in Ukraine would present a game-changing security challenge for Russia, particularly if this had included Crimea, home to Russia's main Black Sea naval bases.[55] Even a super-realist like Mearsheimer could understand how US policy was driving an uncompromising Russian response that would disrupt its relations with the West:

> Putin's actions should be easy to comprehend … Ukraine serves as a buffer state of enormous strategic importance to Russia. …Washington may not like Moscow's position, but it should understand the logic behind it … After all, the United States does not tolerate distant great powers deploying military forces anywhere in the Western Hemisphere, much less on its borders. … Officials from the United States and its European allies contend that they tried hard to assuage Russian fears … [but] it is the Russians, not the West, who ultimately get to decide what counts as a threat to them.[56]

Moreover, Ukraine's eastern regions are highly economically and culturally integrated with Russia.[57] As events have shown, while the ethnically Russian Ukrainian population had accepted neutrality, they did not acquiesce to a reorientation of the country from Russia to Europe and the US; the resulting resistance to the new government in Kiev placed Russia and the West on opposite sides in a de facto civil war.[58]

Whatever had been the truth of previous Western speculation that Sino-Russian relations were hampered by mutual suspicions, after 2014 Russia faced a stark choice between international isolation and agreement with China. US commentators may have urged that 'much as Nixon and Kissinger sought the "dragon" to balance against the stronger "bear", the United States must consider the reverse'; but rather than the deft tactics of the 1970s, when the US played into Sino-Soviet fears and rivalries to its own advantage, it had forced Russia to turn to China.[59]

Russia, Japan and the Kuril islands

Engaging Russia in a US-led network of Asian alliances to contain China met a further major obstacle in the intractable antagonism between Russia and Japan, the US's chief ally in the North Pacific.

In 1945, with Hitler defeated in Europe, the USSR, as agreed with the Allies, turned east to take on Japan. This offensive successfully drove the Japanese out of Manchuria and the north of Korea, and the USSR took control of Sakhalin Island off the Russian coast and the Kuril archipelago running south from Russian Kamchatka to just north of Japan.

The Kurils had changed hands between Russia and Japan at various points in the nineteenth century; but after Japan had used them as the springboard for invasions of Kamchatka and Siberia in 1904–05 and 1918, Russia came to see them as crucial to securing its north-east littoral, hence, the Yalta agreement of February 1945, which committed the USSR to enter the war against Japan undertook that:

> The former rights of Russia violated by the treacherous attack of Japan in 1904 shall be restored, viz.: (a) The southern part of Sakhalin as well as the islands adjacent to it shall be returned to the Soviet Union; ... The Kuril Islands shall be handed over to the Soviet Union.[60]

However, with the advent of the Cold War and the victory of the communists in China, the terms of the 1951 San Francisco peace treaty with Japan were actually determined by the US and the UK, without consultation with the USSR and ignored many of its demands. China was entirely excluded. The treaty did insist that Japan surrender its claims to Sakhalin and the Kurils, but did not specify Soviet sovereignty over them, as had been promised at Yalta. This was one of a number of reasons why the USSR refused to sign it.[61] No peace treaty has been signed since between Japan and the USSR/Russia, and Japan continues to dispute Russia's control of the islands, particularly the four nearest to Japan. Attempting to tease out the contending claims to the islands from the disputed historical evidence on both sides is thankless and adjudication on some alleged objective historical basis would not resolve the matter anyway, as Russia has no intention of ceding its control of the islands unless the international security situation should change entirely. However, as with China's claims to the Diaoyu/Senkaku islands or the archipelagos in the South China Sea, what can be said is that had China not been excluded from the San Francisco negotiations and had the US and the UK applied the same rigour to Soviet and Chinese claims as they did to their own, the treaty emerging in 1951 would have been clear, giving an international legal framework for the islands' sovereignty today.[62]

The Kurils, girdling the Sea of Okhotsk, turn it into a Russian controlled 'lake' from which its nuclear submarines and other naval forces can operate securely, with safe underwater access to the open Pacific via the deep channels between the southern islands (see Map 3). They are perhaps even more indispensable to Russia's security interests today than they were in 1945. Even Yeltsin, who was very keen – at the urging of the US – to make terms with Japan, in the end did not dare cede any of them despite offers of major economic assistance if he did so.[63] Medvedev, when president of Russia, described the Kurils as an 'inalienable' part of Russia's territory.[64]

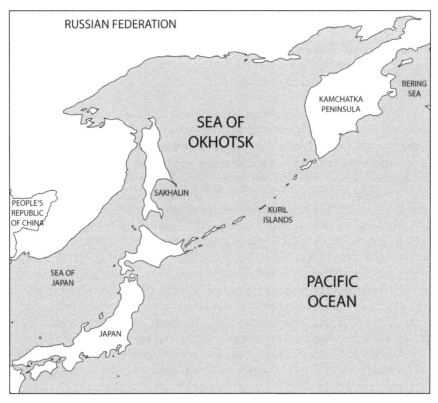

Map 3 *Russia, Sea of Okhotsk, Japan and Kuril islands*

Japan's minimum demand is to retake at least the four southernmost islands, breaking Russian control over the Sea of Okhotsk and moving Russia further away from its mainland islands. But for Japan's nationalists, sovereignty over *all* the islands is a matter of national honour.

Western hopes have occasionally been raised that a compromise could be found; after a 2013 exchange of visits between Abe and Putin it was reported that: 'Both sides expressed an understanding that the solution … can only be based on the principle that there are no victors or losers.'[65] But what this would mean in practice is far from clear. Russia handing over the two smaller islands to Japan is the 'compromise' advocated by the West. But without a huge incentive, offering reliable security guarantees, Putin would not consider such a move, especially given Japan's sharp nationalistic turn and the US's Pacific build-up. And even if it was offered, no Japanese government, let alone Abe's hardline nationalists, would agree that gaining just two of the islands settled the issue.

So, despite joint military exercises and trade deals, the disagreements and security concerns dividing Russia and Japan have continually outweighed the positives; and the potential benefits to Russia from better relations with Japan have not come close to those offered from relations with China.

Mongolia

Mongolia for a while looked like a promising target for the US to advance its strategic position between China and Russia. The Republic of Mongolia's vast territory of empty steppe and deserts is remarkably rich in minerals. In 2015 it finalised a deal with Rio Tinto to develop the Oyu Tolgoi copper mine complex, set to be the largest in the world.[66]

But above all it has a vital geographic importance for its two neighbours. If the US could get agreement for a military base in Mongolia it would be a strategic blow to China, forcing it to divert military attention towards its northern land borders.

Mongolia was completely isolated from the West during the Cold War. Although never actually part of the USSR its policies were indistinguishable and Soviet troops were permanently deployed there from 1967. Mongolia first began to build relations with the US in the 1980s, alongside Gorbachev's turn to the West. With the impact of shock therapy during the 1990s, Russia paid little attention to Mongolia; its previous subsidy, amounting to around 37 per cent of Mongolian GDP, came to an abrupt end and Mongolia stepped up its search for what it called 'third neighbours'.[67] By the mid-1990s, the US had built up a comprehensive engagement, which included everything from the International Institute of the Republican Party, the Soros Foundation and the Peace Corps to a plethora of American advisors and extensive military collaboration.[68] From 2006 the US held annual military exercises – Khaan Quest – in Mongolia; and in 2012 it awarded Mongolia special partnership status with NATO.

Like the West, China also had virtually zero relations with Mongolia from the 1960s owing to the Sino-Soviet split. Alongside the Soviet military presence in Mongolia, China was concerned that the USSR was using it as a base to stir up separatism in China's inner Mongolian territories; but in fact pan-Mongolian nationalism had very little purchase in China. From the late 1980s China took rapid steps to rebuild relations with Mongolia, partly in pursuit of its 'good neighbour' regional policy, but also as a counterweight to the growing US presence.[69] It settled outstanding border disputes in a 1988 agreement and in 1994 signed a friendship and cooperation treaty.

Russia too has re-engaged with Mongolia, welcomed back both as an old friend and as a balance to China's growing influence.[70] Both Putin and Xi Jinping visited Mongolia in 2014, and trilateral meetings were held in 2014 and 2015.

Despite its overtures to the US, Mongolia knows relations with its two mega-neighbours will determine its future. In 2015, 84 per cent of Mongolia's exports were to China, and 62 per cent of total trade, followed by Russia on 14 per cent, with Japan and South Korea trailing on 3.2 per cent and 3.1 per cent respectively.[71] China is already Mongolia's second largest investor (after the Netherlands) with a stake of 26.7 per cent of total foreign direct investment (FDI) in Mongolia, way ahead of the US with 2.2 per cent.[72]

When Defense Secretary Chuck Hagel visited the country in April 2014, the Mongolian newspaper *News Today* alleged that the US had made a renewed request for a base in the country. This was denied but the story served as an opportunity for the Mongolian government to draw attention to its 1990 constitution ruling out foreign bases, and thus to reassure China.[73]

In the final analysis, while Mongolia may collaborate with the US and seek out 'third neighbours', it is not going to do anything in northern Asia that would seriously upset either China or Russia. It has too much to gain from China and too much to lose from introducing insecurity to the region. So far the assiduous courting of Mongolia by the US has delivered little in the way of aiding its goals to apply pressure to China.

A 'Cold War' without Russia

If the events in Syria and Ukraine from 2013 onwards reveal anything, it is that Russia remains an international power to be reckoned with. Despite the depths to which post-communist Russia sank in the 1990s and the impact of international sanctions from 2014, in 2016 its economy remained the sixth largest in the world, while its GDP per capita was $26,109, when China's was still only $15,424 for example.[74] Although heavily reliant on the export of raw materials – especially oil and gas – its advanced technological and scientific capacity has not disappeared, reflected in its nuclear, military, rocket and satellite capabilities.

Russia's conventional military power is greater than any other state apart from the US and possibly China. Russia's military budget at $90 billion in 2014 was well behind that of the US, and China's too, but was nearly double that of Japan or India.[75] Russia has over 1 million soldiers on active service. Its nuclear arsenal of an estimated 8000 weapons is greater than the US's estimated 7300, although the US has more fully deployed – 1920 to Russia's 1600. Both are way ahead of China, which has an estimated 250 nuclear weapons, none of which are fully deployed.[76] Russia's accumulated materiel includes 33 nuclear submarines, nearly 2000 combat aircraft and a huge arsenal of tanks and attack helicopters as well as land-to-sea and intercontinental ballistic missiles. Its intervention in Syria has demonstrated the combat utility of its state-of-the-art weaponry and systems, which is why it is the world's second largest arms exporter after the US.[77] While the US military budget may dwarf either those of China and Russia individually, the two together constitute a formidable opponent.

Nonetheless, the Russian Federation today is not a power on anything like the scale of the Cold War USSR when Russian presidents had a hotline to the White House and the world appeared to turn largely on the relations between Moscow and Washington. Quite aside from the impact of the economic disaster of the 1990s, at 143.4 million, the population of the successor Russian state is today roughly half that of the USSR's 287 million in 1989. Millions of ethnic Russians are now outside its current borders. Putin, reflecting the deep feelings of the Russian population, described this as a 'geopolitical disaster'.[78]

But Russia's decline is open to exaggeration, and some of the ways that the US behaved towards Russia in recent years precisely appeared to reflect such a misappraisal.[79] In 2013 Zachary Keck, at the time associate editor of *The Diplomat*, wrote an article headlined, 'Putin's Russia: the pretend great power'. Claiming Russian weakness meant it was being sidelined in the discussion about possible international intervention in Syria, the usually perspicacious Keck wrote:

> The fact that the US doesn't feel at all compelled to consider Russia's position before intervening, and that Russia can do little to stop or impede Washington from proceeding, underscores Moscow's weakness. Such a development would have been

unthinkable during the Arab-Israeli conflicts during the Cold War, for instance, when Russia could still claim the great power mantle.[80]

This was written on the eve of a Russian diplomatic coup that proved precisely the opposite, when Putin dramatically reset the scene on Syria with a deal on dismantling Assad's chemical weapons stocks, effectively deferring American military action against Assad indefinitely by removing its stated casus belli. Russia rapidly moved on to broker an international deal with Iran, in the face of resistance from a reluctant US. Moreover such views as Keck's ignored the capabilities Russia had already demonstrated in 2008, when NATO and the West had been unable to prevent Russian military support for the breakaway of Abkhazia and South Ossetia from Georgia. This was shortly to be shown again in 2014 with Russia's decisive intervention in Ukraine to secure the Crimea and prevent the pro-Russian opponents of the Kiev regime being simply crushed.

In believing that a weakened Russia could be pushed around, the US both misjudged its residual strength and propelled it closer to China. Unlike in its Cold War triangula-tions with China and the USSR, today the US cannot simply manipulate the fears of the weak, in the case of either China or Russia.

A US strategy to contain China without the participation of Russia cannot achieve the degree of isolation of China that was imposed on the USSR after 1971. Therefore the question US China strategists ask is whether NATO's attempt to advance towards Russia's borders in Ukraine will end up exacting too high a price for US strategy in the Pacific? Trump clearly believed this was so, and indicated he was prepared to ride roughshod over German objections to make a deal on Ukraine with Russia, for which the minimum price from Putin would be to abandon Iran and break with China. Even under Obama, the White House's most strategic advisors considered policy on China so vital and Russia so central to it, that they advocated avoiding conflict with Russia:

> Washington should try to avoid having disputes in other regions of the world affect its ties with Russia in the Pacific ... at some point the US will have to make a choice about whether the issues in other regions are important enough to scuttle ties with Russia in the Pacific. In the Asian Century, the answer to this question should almost always be 'no'.[81]

Hence the most intelligent proponents of the US's policy in Asia shook their heads in disbelief and growing despair at the US's alienation of Russia under Obama. Kishore Mahbubani is just such an informed and subtle advocate. He spelled out the entire problem of US policy towards Russia in a succinct paragraph:

> Unwise western expansion of NATO has not enhanced western security. It has only alienated Russia. Yet when the West finally wakes up to deal with a rising China, Russia would provide just the sort of geopolitical heft needed to balance Beijing's power. Today, in direct violation of its own long-term geopolitical interests, the west is driving Russia towards China ... This compulsion to act against its own interests perfectly illus-trates declining western geopolitical wisdom.[82]

Whereas in the first Cold War the US showed considerable skill in weaving together unlikely alliances, particularly successfully 'triangulating' relations between the USSR and

China, so far in this putative new Cold War it has singularly failed to do so. Instead it clumsily drove Russia and China closer together, even, in the view of some commentators, sacrificing the struggle to maintain global leadership for a prize of uncertain outcome on Russia's western border. Despite all its declarations of a turn to Asia, the US's eyes remained fixed in the west, fighting battles that may prove fatal to its greater objectives. At the time of writing, it remained to be seen whether Trump's overtures to Russia were the start of a fundamental reset in these triangular relations.

Since 2010, and the US declaration of its 'pivot' to Asia, it has been the realpolitik of Putin rather than the 'triangular' diplomacy of the US that has emerged as the more dexterous in their global interrelations. Rather than fearing the embrace of China, Putin has seen the advantage to Russian security and its future geopolitical influence of a strong Sino-Russian partnership, and has undertaken his own 'pivot to Asia' to balance the offensive Russia faced in the west. Even if a new modus vivendi between the West and Russia can eventually be salvaged from the confrontation in Ukraine, the dynamic between China and Russia is now so well established and has already served both well that it is hard to see the US having much purchase between them. That means that the US attempt to contain China has suffered a major blow before it has really got off the ground.

Notes

1 D. Cheng and A. Cohen, *How Washington should manage US-Russia-China relations*, The Heritage Foundation, Washington, DC, 2013.

2 G. Dyer, 'In the battle for Crimea, China wins', *Foreign Policy*, 12 March 2014. Available at: http://foreignpolicy.com/2014/03/12/in-the-battle-for-crimea-china-wins/ (date accessed 15 February 2017).

3 Z. Keck, 'Russia as a US-China battleground state', *The Diplomat*, 20 November 2013. Available at: http://thediplomat.com/2013/11/russia-as-a-u-s-china-battleground-state-3/ (date accessed 15 February 2017).

4 A. Anishchuk, 'As Putin looks east, China and Russia sign $400-billion gas deal', *Reuters*, 22 May 2014. Available at: http://www.reuters.com/article/us-china-russia-gas-idUSBREA4K07K20140521 (date accessed 15 February 2017).

5 P. Sullivan, 'Ukraine threatens to undermine Obama's delayed Asia "pivot"', *The Hill*, 20 April 2014. Available at: http://www.thehill.com/policy/international/203907-ukraine-threatens-to-undermine-obamas-delayed-asia-pivot (date accessed 20 October 2016).

6 J. D. J. Brown, 'Ukraine and the Russia–China axis', *The Diplomat*, 2 April 2015. Available at: http://thediplomat.com/2015/04/ukraine-and-the-russia-china-axis/ (date accessed 15 February 2017).

7 J. Pomfrett, '45 years ago, Kissinger envisioned a "pivot" to Russia. Will Trump make it happen?', *Washington Post*, 14 December 2016.

8 For a full account, see A. V. Pantsov, *Mao: the real story*, Simon and Schuster, New York, 2012.

9 For a first-hand account, see E. Snow, *Red star over China: the rise of the Red Army*, Victor Gollancz, London, 1937.

10 For documentary sources, see A. Lawrance, *China's foreign relations since 1949*, Routledge, Abingdon, 1975 (reissued 2005).

11 See 'The China White Paper' August 1949 prepared by secretary of state Dean Acheson for president Truman. Published by Stanford University Press, Stanford, 1967.

12 Chen, *Mao's China*.

13 B. P. Farrell, 'Southeast Asia Treaty Organization (SEATO)', in *The encyclopaedia of war*, John Wiley and Sons, Hoboken, NJ, 2011.

14 Dwight D. Eisenhower, presidential news conference, 16 March 1955.

15 S. H. Hu, 'Assessing Russia's role in cross-Taiwan Strait relations', *Issues and Studies*, 43:4 (December 2007), 39–76.

16 J. Lewis and L. T. Xue, *China builds the Bomb*, Stanford University Press, Stanford, 1991.

17 J. van Oudenaren, *Détente in Europe: the Soviet Union and the West since 1953*, Duke University Press, Durham and London, 1991, pp. 170–1.

18 L. M. Luthi, *The Sino-Soviet split: Cold War in the communist world*, Princeton University Press, Princeton, 2008.

19 Chen, *Mao's China*.

20 S. Radchenko, *Two suns in the heavens: the Sino-Soviet struggle for supremacy, 1962–1967*, Woodrow Wilson Centre Press, Washington, DC, 2009.

21 J. Friedman, *Shadow Cold War: the Sino-Soviet competition for the Third World*, University of North Carolina Press, Chapel Hill, 2015.

22 N. Horsburgh, *China and global nuclear order: from estrangement to active engagement*, Oxford University Press, Oxford, 2015, ch. 1.

23 For material of the international communist movement related to this period, see 'The great debate, documents of Sino-Soviet Split'. Available at: https://www.marxists.org/history/international/comintern/sino-soviet-split/ (date accessed 2 February 2017).

24 See the history and archive pages of the S. P. Korolev Rocket and Space Corporation. Available at: http://www.energia.ru/english/ (date accessed 2 February 2017).

25 R. van Dijk, W. G. Gray, S. Savranskaya, J. Suri and Q. Zhai (eds), *Encyclopaedia of the Cold War*, Vol 1, Taylor and Francis, New York, 2008, p. 147.

26 US State Department Memorandum of Conversation (between Boris Davydov of the Soviet Embassy in the US and William Stearman, Nixon's special advisor on Vietnam), 18 August 1969.

27 Friedman, *Shadow Cold War*.

28 Ibid., pp. 119–39.

29 Anderson, 'Imperium', pp. 69–70.

30 Friedman, *Shadow Cold War*, pp. 209–12.

31 *A study on the Soviet economy*, IMF, World Bank, OECD and European Bank for Reconstruction and Development, Paris, 1991 (published).

32 S. Menshikov, 'Russian capitalism today', *Monthly Review*, 51:3 (1999), 82–6.

33 R. Sakwa, *Putin: Russia's choice* (2nd edn), Routledge, Abingdon, 2008, ch. 10.

34 R. E. Kanet (ed.), *Russian foreign policy in the 21st century*, Palgrave Macmillan, Basingstoke, 2010, p. 30.

35 See Chapter 15.

36 Kanet, *Russian foreign policy*, ch. 10.

37 'Putin: US missile defence aimed at neutralising Russia nukes, N. Korea & Iran just a cover', *Russia Today*, 10 November 2015. Available at: https://www.rt.com/news/321434-us-missile-shield-putin/ (date accessed 15 February 2017).

38 B. Lo, 'Medvedev and the new European security architecture', *Centre for European Reform Policy Brief*, July 2009.

39 'NATO chief reaches out to Russia', *BBC News*, 18 September 2009. Available at: http://news.bbc.co.uk/1/hi/world/europe/8262515.stm (date accessed 15 February 2017).

40 Kanet, *Russian foreign policy*, chs 9 and 13.

41 C. M. Chao and B. Dickson, *Remaking the Chinese state: strategies, society, and security*, Routledge, London, 2003, p. 235.

42 Treaty of Good Neighbourliness and Friendly Cooperation between the People's Republic of China and the Russian Federation, 16 July 2001.

43 A. Devyatov, 'Symbolism of new Chinese president's visit to Moscow', *Pravda*, 11 June 2003; 'Xi's Russia visit enhances mutual trust', *Xinhua*, 31 March 2013.

44 United Nations Commodity Trade Statistics database, July 2015 published figures.

45 In 2014 China's total trade in goods with: the EU was €467 billion (European Union, Directorate-General for Trade, November 2016); US $592 billion (US Census Bureau, January 2017); Japan $344 billion (Japan External Trade Organisation, February 2015).

46 'Rosneft to triple oil supplies to China', *Reuters*, 22 March 2013. Available at: http://www.reuters.com/article/us-rosneft-china-oil-idUSBRE92L13020130322 (date accessed 15 February 2017).

47 'Russia signs 30-year gas deal with China', *BBC News*, 21 May 2014. Available at: http://www.bbc.co.uk/news/business-27503017 (date accessed 15 February 2017).

48 M. De Haas, *Russia's foreign security policy in the 21st century: Putin, Medvedev and beyond*, Contemporary Security Studies, Routledge, Abingdon, 2010, p. 172.

49 Cheng and Cohen, 'How Washington should manage US–Russia–China relations'.

50 M. Auslin, 'Russia fears China, not Japan', *Wall Street Journal*, 4 March 2011; D. Tweed, 'Why Putin fears China', *Bloomberg*, 16 February 2015. Available at: https://www.bloomberg.com/news/articles/2015-02-15/putin-fearing-russian-subservience-to-china-casts-wider-asia-net; S. Blank, 'Russia and Vietnam team up to balance China', *The National Interest*, 7 April 2014. Available at: http://nationalinterest.org/commentary/russia-vietnam-team-balance-china-10195; L. Harding, 'Russia fears embrace of giant eastern neighbour', *The Guardian*, 2 August 2009 (online articles accessed 15 February 2017).

51 D. Trenin, *From Greater Europe to Greater Asia: the Sino-Russian Entente*, Carnegie Moscow Centre, Moscow, 2015.

52 A leaked phone call by US assistant secretary of state Victoria Nuland to the US Ambassador in Ukraine revealed the US opposed attempts by the EU to defuse the crisis and broker a compromise.

53 For a full discussion on NATO expansion, see M. D. Nazemroaya, *The globalisation of NATO*, Clarity Press, Atlanta, 2012.

54 J. M. Goldgeier, *Not whether but when: the US decision to enlarge NATO*, Brookings Institution Press, Washington, DC, 2010, p. 15.

55 E. Götz, 'It's geopolitics, stupid: explaining Russia's Ukraine policy', *Global Affairs*, 1:1, 2015.

56 J. J. Mearsheimer 'Why the Ukraine crisis is the West's fault: the liberal delusions that provoked Putin', *Foreign Affairs*, 93:5 (September–October 2014), 77–89.

57 B. Kagarlistky (trs. R. Clarke), 'Ukraine: a country that might have been', *Links International Journal of Socialist Renewal*, 12 June 2014. Available at: http://links.org.au/node/3911 (date accessed 4 February 2017).

58 Ibid.; see also the website 'The new Cold War: Ukraine and beyond', available at: www.newcoldwar.org (date accessed 1 March 2017).

59 G. R. Lawson, 'Beyond the reset: reverse "Nixon goes to China"', *The Atlantic Sentinel*, 12 May 2012. Available at: http://atlanticsentinel.com/2012/05/beyond-the-reset-reverse-nixon-goes-to-china/ (date accessed 14 February 2017).

60 The Yalta Conference 1945, The Avalon Project, Documents in law, history and diplomacy, Yale Law School.

61 Statement of the First Deputy Minister of Foreign Affairs of the USSR, A. A. Gromyko, at the Conference in San Francisco (1951), Joint compendium of documents on history of territorial issue between Japan and Russia, iv. San Francisco Peace Treaty, Ministry of Foreign Affairs of Japan.

62 S. Lee, 'The 1951 San Francisco Peace treaty with Japan and the territorial disputes in East Asia', *Pacific Rim Law and Policy Journal*, 11:1 (2002), 65–146.

63 'Relations thaw over Kuril Islands', *BBC News*, 12 November 1998. Available at: http://news.bbc.co.uk/1/hi/world/asia-pacific/212865.stm (date accessed 15 February 2017).

64 'Russia escalates row with Japan over Kuril islands', *The Guardian*, 9 February 2011. Available at: https://www.theguardian.com/world/2011/feb/09/russia-kuril-islands-dispute-japan (date accessed 15 February 2017).

65 'Putin, Abe agree "no winners or losers" in island row', *Japan Today*, 6 September 2013. Available at: https://www.japantoday.com/category/politics/view/putin-abe-agree-no-winners-or-losers-in-island-row-kremlin (date accessed 15 February 2017).

66 M. Neems, 'Rio Tinto, Mongolia sign Oyu Tolgoy deal', *The Australian Business Review*, 19 May 2015.

67 In 1991, US secretary of state, James Baker, described the US as Mongolia's 'third neighbour'.

68 M. Goleman, 'Mongolia and the US: from acquaintance to strategic cooperation', *New Eastern Outlook*, 31 May 2015. Available at: http://journal-neo.org/2015/05/31/rus-mongoliya-i-ssha-ot-znakomst-va-k-strategicheskomu-sotrudnichestvu/ (date accessed 16 February 2017).

69 A. Campi, 'Sino-Mongolian relations from Beijing's point of view', *Jamestown Foundation*, China Brief, 5:10 (2005). Available at: https://jamestown.org/program/sino-mongolian-relations-from-beijings-viewpoint/ (date accessed 3 February 2017).

70 D. Sneath, 'Russia's borders: Mongolia looks to its old Big Brother to counterbalance China', *The Conversation*, 26 January 2015. Available at: http://theconversation.com/russias-borders-mongolia-looks-to-its-old-big-brother-to-counterbalance-china-36721 (date accessed 15 July 2015).

71 CIA World Factbook 2017, Mongolia economy.

72 Invest Mongolia Agency, Statistics, FDI by country, 1990–2013. Available at: http://investmongolia.gov.mn/en/?page_id=757 (date accessed 3 February 2017).

73 M. Goleman, 'Mongolia and the US are strengthening their ties within the defence industry', *New Eastern Outlook*, 12 August 2014. Available at: http://journal-neo.org/2014/08/12/rus-mongoliya-i-ssha-krepyat-sotrudnichestvo-v-oboronnoj-otrasli/ (date accessed 15 July 2015).

74 IMF WEO 2015. GDP per capita, PPP$.

75 SIPRI 2015.

76 SIPRI 2014, world nuclear forces. For comparison, the UK has 225 weapons, 160 deployed; France has 300, 290 deployed. Other known nuclear states (India, Pakistan, Israel, North Korea) have smaller numbers of weapons and none deployed.

77 R. K. Simha, '5 weapons that are driving up Russian arms exports', *Russia Beyond the Headlines*, 24 December 2015. Available at: http://rbth.com/blogs/continental_drift/2015/12/24/5-weapons-that-are-driving-up-russians-arms-exports_554147 (date accessed 15 February 2017).

78 President of Russia, annual address to the Federal Assembly, Kremlin Archives (English), 25 April 2005.

79 T. Atlas and M. Talev, 'Obama snubs Putin in sign of tensions in US-Russia ties', *Bloomberg*, 8 August 2013. Available at: https://www.bloomberg.com/news/articles/2013-08-07/obama-snubs-putin-in-sign-of-tensions-in-u-s-russia-ties (date accessed 15 February 2017).

80 Z. Keck, 'Putin's Russia: the pretend great power', *The Diplomat*, 30 August 2013. Available at: http://thediplomat.com/2013/08/putins-russia-the-pretend-great-power/ (date accessed 15 February 2017).

81 Keck, 'Russia: battleground state'.

82 K. Mahbubani, 'Look to China for wisdom on dealing with Russia', *Financial Times*, 21 March 2014.

Part III

Containment from the east

6

The rise of Japanese nationalism

Japan has played a critical role in the post-war US power system. While Japan's 'pacifist' constitution – imposed after 1945 – did not permit it to play a military role on a par with NATO members, its contribution to the US security system was just as crucial. Throughout the post-war period America's overseas military deployment to bases in Japan was second only to that to Germany and from 2010 Japan became home to its largest overseas military presence, with 49,396 personnel.[1] Japan has always been at the heart of US Asian strategy and the rise of China has only increased its importance: 'No other US relationship approaches that with Japan in maintaining the current balance in Asia and dealing with the rise of Chinese power. Indeed, without close and enduring US-Japan security cooperation, it is difficult to see how the United States could maintain its present power and influence in Asia.'[2]

By contrast, Japan's relationship to China – and its other near neighbours – is deeply coloured by the experience of Japanese imperialism; its colonisations and the atrocities carried out by its occupying forces between 1894 and 1945 left a legacy of high sensitivity to any sign of Japanese nationalist recidivism. This has been kept inflamed by the vocal presence of a revanchist component within Japanese politics, that denies its egregious treatment of its former colonies; views Korea and China as insubordinate subaltern states which should be put back in their place; resents the influence and military presence of the US; and rails at the constraints imposed on its military capacities. Such views have been a constant, though minority, presence in post-war Japanese politics, but had never seized the mainstream in Japanese politics until recently.

Indeed, through the last decades of the twentieth century Japan enjoyed rather harmonious relations with its neighbours in North East Asia. Its economic success from the 1970s onwards had a positive impact on development firstly in South Korea and Taiwan and then in China. The 'flying geese' development model described by Japanese economists at the time accurately suggested that neighbouring countries could deploy comparative advantage due to their lower level of development – primarily cheaper labour – to advance on the coattails of Japanese success. This synergy led to growing trade and other links with South Korea, Taiwan and China, while domestically Japan saw a strengthening of political currents more strongly oriented to Asia rather than just the US.

The rise of Japanese nationalism in the new century and especially since the financial crisis in 2008 is both an indicator and a product of changes in these regional economic

synergies. From the end of the 1990s, a combination of factors began to create economic dissonances that were soon reflected in political divisions. The onset of the
well-documented long secular stagnation of the Japanese economy in the 1990s both
coincided with and contributed to some South Korean and Taiwan companies beginning
to catch up, compete with and even overtake those of Japan, while the rapid advance of
China meant it began to replace Japan as their top regional trading partner.

Within Japan, revisionist and nationalist currents started to become more clamorous
and more influential as successive governments failed to find a solution to the problems besetting its economy. The 2012 election of Shinzo Abe to the leadership of the
Liberal Democratic Party (LDP) – the party that has governed post-war Japan almost
continuously – put a variant of these politics in the driving seat, with a particularly negative impact for Japan's relations with its neighbours, especially China and South Korea.[3]

This chapter appraises Japan's crucial role in US policy towards China against the
background of the evolution of post-war relations between Japan, the US and China. It
argues that the rise of Japanese nationalism has encouraged Japan to challenge China,
but its overly belligerent tone has made problems for the US in pulling together a North
East Asian 'anti-China' bloc, comprising the US, Japan and South Korea.

The subordination of Japan

From 1945 to 1952 Japan was practically a vassal state; its infrastructure had been cat-
astrophically destroyed by US bombardment, including by the atomic bombs dropped
on Hiroshima and Nagasaki. Japan had to accept a US occupation force under General
MacArthur and the establishment of US air and naval bases, the largest at Okinawa at the
southern tip of the Japanese archipelago. It was dependent on the US for post-war aid and
reconstruction. Japan only began to emerge from its post-war crisis when the US used it as
the headquarters for operations in the Korean War, which fortuitously also had the effect
of kick-starting the Japanese economy owing to its place in the supply chain for the war.[4]

The formal US occupation ended with the 1951 peace treaties, but the US nonetheless held on to various islands that hosted its bases – until 1972 in the case of
Okinawa. These bases number 23 today, giving the US a military presence on both
sides of the Pacific, which it could thereby conceive as a 'moat' protecting its west
coast; an American ocean from California to the east Asian archipelagos.[5] The 1951
peace treaties required Japan to renounce the right to wage war and to maintain only a
purely 'defensive' army. Japan's resulting military dependence on the US was reinforced
by its 1967 adherence, under US pressure, to the NPT. While these obligations did not
prevent Japan from developing a very substantial military arsenal, until the second
decade of the twenty-first century – when China's exponential growth began to force a
rethink – the US discouraged Japan going beyond certain defensive limits. And so far it
still prefers Japan to rely on the US nuclear deterrent.

This military dependence on the US has not gone unopposed. As the Japanese
economy recovered in the 1950s, a popular movement objecting to the US bases
began to develop, strengthened in the 1960s by opposition to their use for operations
in Vietnam. The base at Okinawa in particular has remained controversial, flaring up
periodically into major confrontation, as in 1995 when a 12-year-old Japanese girl was

raped by three US marines. But opposition to the bases has always foundered on the combination of US intransigence and successive Japanese governments' unwillingness to force the issue with their military protector.[6]

While a left pacifist movement has opposed the US bases, on the right nationalistic currents have opposed the military limits imposed by the US, arguing for rearmament and the development of a Japanese nuclear weapons capability. But the mainstream of Japanese politics – based on globally successful Japanese big business – has ensured that to date neither of these trends has been allowed to disrupt relations with the US.[7] But, in the context of China's ascent and the perceived relative weakening of America, with concerns about the US's long-term ability to maintain a high-level military capability in the North Pacific, Japan has begun to think more seriously about how to reduce its reliance on the US.

The economic rise and decline of Japan

Between 1960 and 1990 – the period of the Japanese miracle – the Japanese economy grew at an historically unprecedented average of 8.6 per cent per annum compared to an average 3.5 per cent in the US over the same period. The Japanese economy doubled in size every 8.5 years.[8] Driven by high levels of investment – 30 per cent of GDP per annum in the 1960s and reaching a peak of 35 per cent in the 1970s (compared to a US average of 18–20 per cent) – Japan's GDP grew from $44 billion in 1960 to $1.1 trillion in 1980 and to £3.1 trillion in 1990, overtaking both Germany and the USSR to become the world's second largest economy by 1980.[9]

Over this period Japan also powered up the value chain, transforming its 1960s advantage in low-value mass production – when Made in Japan had the ubiquity of Made in China today – to innovation in high-tech production that by the 1980s came to challenge the entire US-originated Fordist model. Toyota, the poster child of post-Fordism, invested heavily in robotisation, allowing more flexible, short-run customised outputs.[10] US car companies – the epitome of the global success of US manufacturing – eventually found themselves challenged by Japan not just in Asia but also in their home markets.

From the mid-1960s the export success of Japan began to provoke vociferous demands from American big business that Japan should open up its market, revalue the yen and take other measures to reduce competitive pressure from cheap Japanese imports on producers in the US.[11] Initially Japan resisted these demands, dragging out trade talks and agreeing to limited steps, but rejecting any fundamental adjustments.

However when, in 1971, Japan's overall trade surplus hit $4.3 billion while the US recorded its first-ever trade deficit since the nineteenth century, including a deficit of $3.3 billion with Japan, the US forced the issue.[12] 'Ultimately … the most decisive weapon in the incipient competitive struggle was a drastic devaluation of the dollar in relation to the Japanese yen and German mark.'[13] In the so-called 'Nixon shock' the US unilaterally withdrew from the gold standard leading to a devaluation of the dollar. The dollar's fall applied huge pressure for a revaluation of the yen, and after initial efforts to resist – by buying $5.2 billion dollars in the two weeks following the 15 August announcement – Japan had to allow the yen to rise over 13 per cent against the dollar by the end of 1971. Following a further two years of attempts to find new fixed exchange rates, in 1973 a further major dollar devaluation heralded the ultimate end of the Bretton Woods fixed-rate exchange system in favour of floating rates, and saw another 15 per cent added to the yen's upward climb against the dollar. The yen rose 28.2 per cent against the dollar from 1971 to 1973, the beginning of a revaluation of a yen that pushed it up by 50 per cent against the dollar in the 12 years from 1971 to 1983.[14]

But still the US trade deficit with Japan ballooned, from $10 billion in 1980 to $46 billion in 1985, and the pressure in the US for a further devaluation became irresistible, despite the opposition of hard-line monetarists around president Ronald Reagan. In the 1985 Plaza Accords, Japan and the other G5 countries agreed to engineer a further round of dollar devaluation.[15] From 1985 Japan allowed a remarkably steep revaluation of the yen, which rose by more than 275 per cent against the dollar in the 11 years to its first peak in 1994, before falling back slightly and then resuming its trend back up until the introduction of Abenomics in 2013 (see Figure 6.1). The scale of the yen revaluation – or rather the fall in the dollar – had a devastating impact on the Japanese economy. This was also accompanied by a sharp decrease in the rate of investment, which fell from its peak of 36 per cent of GDP in 1973 to 28 per cent in 1995, and from 25 per cent in 2000 down to 21–22 per cent since 2004.[16]

On top of this, in the 1990s Japan's export-led economy began to suffer from rising competition from South Korean companies (for example, the rise of Samsung and the decline of Sony) and the other Asian tigers, and in the most recent period from the beginnings of problems from Chinese companies moving up the value chain.

As its exports struggled, the Japanese economy fell into prolonged secular stagnation, slowing to a meagre 1.03 per cent per annum average growth through the 1990s and becoming mired in the deflationary pressures that beset it through and beyond the global financial crisis of 2008, when the overall contraction in world trade put additional pressure on its exports.[17]

Figure 6.1 *Increase in the exchange rate of the yen vs US$ (percentage change January 1971 to December 2012)*

Source: *Calculated from IMF International Financial Statistics*
© John Ross

All this pain for Japan only temporarily reduced the trade surplus with the US. Therefore, alongside these revaluations, Japan had also mitigated the impact of the US's declining competitiveness on the US balance of payments by buying up US government debt, becoming the world's leading holder of US debt by the late 1980s – a position it held until it was overtaken by China in 2008 and resumed again in 2016 as China reduced its exposure to US debt. China's holdings fell from $1.27 trillion in November 2015 to £1.1 trillion in November 2016.[18]

China and Japan: economic synergies

An alternative direction for Japan economically and politically would be to turn towards greater integration in Asia, in particular taking advantage of the opportunities to deepen trade and investment links with China. Support for such a strategy gained weight in Japan from the 1980s with the Asian 'economic miracles' in South Korea, Taiwan, Hong Kong and, later, China.

In 1978, when Deng Xiaoping agreed a Treaty of Peace and Friendship with Japan, he also sought Japanese engagement in China's economic reform. As a result, throughout the 1980s, with the US's tacit blessing Japan played a key role in China's economic development.

China's reform and opening up were well timed as, following the rapid yen appreciation in the 1980s, Japanese companies were looking for price advantages through offshoring and China rapidly became the destination of choice. The Japan External Trade Organization (JETRO) opened offices in China helping Japanese companies to identify business opportunities.[19] Japanese factories in China became the standard by which China measured its own progress towards more efficient production. Both Japanese FDI in China and the two countries' bilateral trade relationship soared, as China became the hub initially for the assembly of Japan's high-value commodities and then for the direct production of components and increasingly for value added inputs. The synergies of their respective specialisations – Japan's in high-tech, high value added machinery and commodities and China's low cost, efficient assembly and production capacities – gelled perfectly. China's 'latecomer advantage' also allowed it to pick up lower-value production from South Korea, Taiwan and Hong Kong as they developed.[20] This symbiosis, fed by geographical proximity, put the China–Japan axis at the heart of a network of supply chains and trade and investment flows across East and South East Asia.[21]

By 2015 Japan and China's bilateral trade had reached $270 billion, the third largest trading relationship in the world.[22] Japan's main exports to China are cars, smartphone components and machinery, while it imports assembled smartphones, electrical components, photoelectric cells and iron and steel from China. China has been Japan's largest trading partner since 2006, accounting for 21.2 per cent of total trade in 2015, but the US remains Japan's largest export market (with 18.6 per cent of Japan's exports compared to the China's 17.5 per cent in 2015). China is by far the largest importer into Japan, with a 24.8 per cent share in 2015 compared to the US's 8.8 per cent.[23] Japan therefore runs a substantial trade deficit with China, but given the amount of Japanese production offshored in China the reasons for this trade deficit are not at all straightforward. Japan is also the largest investor in China. In 2012 its stock of FDI in China stood at US$93 billion compared to US FDI of US$51 billion (the next largest).[24]

But even these figures understate just how intertwined the Japanese and Chinese economies actually are, as their 'different levels of industrial and technological capability … generate business and investment on a scale not matched in any of China's other economic relationships, even that with the United States'. [25]

Although the US was happy for Japan to act as its proxy, seeing its close involvement in China's reform as pushing the country towards capitalism, it consistently opposed this role leading to any closer political integration of Japan with East Asia. Since 1945 the US has maintained 'implacable opposition to any moves towards Japanese involvement in an East Asian community' or any proposed reorientation of Japan's policies in Asia that might tend to make Japan more politically independent.[26] For example, when the Cold War ended Japan put forward a proposal for 'cross recognition' whereby China and Russia would normalise relations with South Korea, while Japan and South Korea normalised relations with North Korea, with the aim of laying the basis for a new 'East Asian commonwealth'. The US intervened to 'caution' against this and reasserted its veto over any independent Japanese diplomatic initiatives in the region.[27]

Similarly, the US objected when Japan's response to the Asian financial crisis of 1997 was to propose an independent Asian Development Fund as a source of loans and short-term liquidity outside of the IMF, whose prescriptions Japan believed had deepened the crisis. It dropped the suggestion.[28] It also gave in to US pressure to stay out of the AIIB.

This ultimate subordination to the demands of the US was most starkly illustrated by the failure of the 2009–12 Democratic Party of Japan (DPJ) government's short-lived attempt to plot just such an 'Asian' course. The electoral success of Hatoyama's DPJ in 2009 – virtually the sole break in the dominance of the pro-US LDP in post-war Japanese politics – was achieved on a platform of pursuing a foreign policy more independent of the US, symbolised by its pledges to close the base at Okinawa, to improve relations with China, and seek to develop a regional trade bloc with South Korea and China, an 'Asia-Pacific community' modelled on the EU.[29] The DPJ's 'new growth strategy', which was based on this turn towards Asia, made sense at many levels given the complementarities of China and Japan's economies and the stagnation in Japan's exports to the US.[30] But the attempt foundered in the face of intransigent US hostility. Locked out by the US, snubbed by Obama and forced to concede on Okinawa, Hatoyama was gone before 2010 was out, an outcome largely put down to the US.[31] The DPJ government limped on for a further two years, but resumed Japan's previous course, adopting the harsher toned policy towards China demanded by the US's rising priority to corral its Asian allies into a bloc against China. With the return to power of the LDP in 2012 all suggestion of a political and economic 'turn to Asia' was abandoned, and instead Abe took Japan into the TPP negotiations.[32]

The result has been that, despite the synergies between Japan's economy and those of China and its other neighbours, rather than emerging in the twenty-first century to play a leading role within a group of successful East Asian economies, instead Japan is politically distanced from its neighbours and a rather isolated if powerful presence in the region.

Under the US military umbrella

On every significant issue of dispute with the US, whether strategic, military or, most devastatingly, economic, for the entire post-war period Japan has ultimately complied with the core of whatever the US demanded. This was because, facing a potential combination of China, the USSR/Russia and North Korea, Japan always considered that its strategic defence was untenable without the nuclear and military umbrella of the US. As the US weakens economically and militarily, the contradictions for Japan in this dependent stance are multiplying. But, at least so far, no group capable of forming a government in Japan has suggested breaking from its time-honoured role as chief Asian proxy for the US.

For the US, Japan's dependence was not just about locking it into alliance against the USSR and China; in the post-Cold War world its aim was to prevent any of 'the advanced industrial nations … from challenging our leadership or seeking to overturn the estab-lished political and economic order', according to the notorious 1992 draft US Defence Policy Guidance by Undersecretary of Defense Paul Wolfowitz.[33] As the New York Times explained, this made the case for 'a world dominated by one superpower' with 'sufficient military might to deter any nation or group of nations from challenging American primacy'.[34]

This sheds light on the US's post-Cold War approach to the defence policy of Japan. Even as pressures in the Balkans, Afghanistan and the Middle East meant that the US wanted Japan to take more regional responsibility, this remained within limits, particularly nuclear limits.[35] While supporting a Japanese military build-up to improve its effectiveness in supporting US policy, this was not to be to a degree where Japan would feel released from military dependence; hence, while by 2015 Japan's military budget, of just over $40 billion per annum, was estimated to be the eighth largest in the world, it remained reliant on the US nuclear and military umbrella.[36] Compared to Russia alone, in 2015 Japan had 18 submarines (none nuclear) to Russia's 67; 777 combat aircraft to Russia's 3547; and no nuclear weapons to Russia's 12,000.[37]

Shifting focus to China

From 1945 to 1992 Japan's primary security concern was the USSR. Not only had they never agreed a peace treaty after the Second World War, but Japan was a non-nuclear state while the USSR bristled with nuclear warheads. Consequently, during the Cold War Japan's key bases and military deployments were in the north, facing Russia's east coast and guarding its gateway to the Pacific.

After 1992 the US tried to encourage a closer relationship between Japan and Russia, but, as we saw in the last chapter, such an alliance remained elusive. Nevertheless, the potential threat from Russia subsided, allowing Japan to shift its focus to China as it emerged as a credible military and economic power in the early 2000s.

As China's position perceptibly strengthened, Japan's 2004 defence review upgraded its concern with China, but only as a matter on which to 'remain attentive'. However, in line with the US's 'pivot', the December 2010 review found that China's rising mili-tary capabilities had 'become a matter of concern for the region and the international community'.[38] This underpinned a series of steps directed at China.[39] The framework of Japanese military strategy – with US agreement – was shifted from its long-standing passive/reactive 'basic defence' to a more assertive and proactive policy described as 'dynamic defence'. This included planning to increase its submarines from 16 to 22 and to collaborate with the US on missile defence. Japan's overall defence focus was shifted from the north (Russia) to the south-west (its sea border with China), and included beefing up the Japanese army and navy presence on remote islands facing the Chinese coast.

The 2010 defence review coincided with a sharp rise in nationalistic politics in Japan, which saw Shinzo Abe take the helm of the LDP, leading it back into government in 2012.

The bases of Japanese ultra-nationalism

Ultra-nationalism has deep roots in Japanese society and has been a background component of its politics throughout the post-war period. It has classical features: racism – with the small ethnically Korean and Chinese populations within Japan the particular targets; revivalist, imperialist projections and fantasies; and revisionism regarding the record of Japanese colonialism in the region. Gavan McCormack has described how the post-war settlement imposed by the US deliberately reinforced a state ideology of Japanese singularity, distanced from the rest of Asia and therefore tied to the US.[40] But this also kept alive nostalgia for pre-war imperial Japan and a reluctance to admit responsibility for its conquest of most of China and East Asia in the first half of the twentieth century. In some ways the rise of China, while making any imagined colonial reconquest absurd, has fed this reactionary recidivism – in the same way that a Britain in decline produces political currents that mourn its loss of empire and its 'leading global role'.

This ideology is not without contradictions in terms of its relations with the US, as it includes a strong strand of resentment at the continued sway of the 1945 victor, but this so far remains a preoccupation of the far right. A classic example is the former (1999– 2012) governor of Tokyo, Shintaro Ishihara, who became notorious for his anti-foreigner, homophobic and misogynist views.[41] He first came to prominence for his 1991 book *The Japan that can say no*, opposing what he described as the Caucasian supremacism of the US and arguing for a reorientation of Japan towards Asia, but with dominion in view, not the progressive content of the DPJ's 'Asian' policy. Rather than conquest, he claims Japan's imperial expansion was in fact a resistance to Western colonialism and denies its crimes – such as the 1937 massacre of 300,000 Chinese in Nanjing.[42]

Ishihara, however, is something of an isolated maverick. The nationalist politics that won the leadership of the LDP, first with the election of Koizumi in 2001 and then Shinzo Abe from 2006 to 2007 and again from 2012, is similarly revisionist on Japan's imperial past, but is strongly in favour of a close military alliance with the US. Nonetheless while Abe's security agenda may suit Washington, his parallel agendas on history and culture have created some alarm.[43] Abe was elected on pledges to revise the 'pacifist' 1946 constitution, make 'patriotism' part of the compulsory curriculum in schools and adopt a 'no-compromise' policy on the various island disputes with China, Korea and Russia. Upon his election as leader he said: 'Our land and seas are threatened, and the economy has deteriorated after years of deflation. We must break free from this difficult situation and make a strong Japan, and that is my mission.'[44]

While Abe has presented himself as a 'mainstream' nationalist, it has been alleged that several of his ministers have links with the Zaitokukai, neo-Nazi-type groups.[45] These extremist groups have been linked to a rise in violent attacks on Koreans, liberal academics and others seen as 'traitors'.

This twenty-first-century growth in popular support for extreme nationalism in Japan lies in a combination of factors. While the Japanese right articulates a vision for a resurgent Japan derived from its particular imperialist history, the immediate causes of its rise are similar to those that have propelled the emergence of right-wing populist responses in Europe and the Tea Party and Trumpism in the US: the absence of a coherent progressive response to falling real wages, declining living standards, and the erosion of in-work benefits and 'jobs for life'.[46] But it also gains strength from specific economic and social characteristics of Japan.

A particular feature of Japan's social structure is the continued existence of a highly protected, numerically weighty – globally uncompetitive and highly subsidised – sector of small business in agriculture and in retail and manufacturing subcontracting.

> The country is known for its hugely successful technically sophisticated international firms, but in reality small and inefficient producers, farmers and retailers dominate much of the economy. Japan has some of the largest and most modern cities in the world, yet throughout Japan one sees farmers and their families … hand planting individual stalks of rice on their small one or two hectare farms.[47]

Thus Japan's rather high – for an advanced economy – proportion of the workforce in agriculture (4 per cent compared to 1.4 per cent in the US, 1 per cent in the UK, 1.5 per cent in Germany and 2.8 per cent in France, higher even than Italy at 3.6 per cent) is also very unproductive, contributing only 1.2 per cent of GDP.[48] Small business is also a feature of manufacturing and retail. Thus 72 per cent of Japanese manufacturing workers are in establishments with less than 250 people, compared to 59 per cent in Germany.[49]

The electoral strategy of the LDP – which kept it in power almost continuously for 60 years – was to form a political bloc between big Japanese business (mainly its steel, automotive, shipbuilding and high-tech industries) and this large petit bourgeois layer through protectionist trade policies, restricting foreign investment and other measures such as planning restrictions on large stores and chains.[50]

This is what led to the peculiarly 'closed' character of the Japanese economy and society. For example, for a country with such a profile in high-value exports, trade represents a very small proportion of GDP.[51] Japan's inward and outward flows of FDI have been much lower than other developed economies and even some developing countries.[52] This was not an accident, but the result of deliberate government policy; measures such as the 1950 Foreign Investment Law and 1949 Foreign Exchange Law meant even the largest foreign companies faced huge obstacles to investing in Japan.[53] Tourism to Japan is also very low.[54]

A policy of discouraging all immigration has led to a highly monocultural society, relative to other advanced economies.[55] In 2005 Japan's total migrant stock was an estimated 1.6 per cent compared to 12.9 per cent in the US, 9.1 per cent in the UK, 10.7 per cent in France, 12.3 per cent in Germany, 18.9 per cent in Canada,

20.3 per cent in Australia and even Italy's 4.3 per cent. Japan's 0.7 per cent minority Korean population is subject to extensive racism.[56]

Japan's inward-looking, internationally restrictive policies create a fertile ground for nationalistic, xenophobic, racist ideas, especially among Japan's protected small businesses and farmers. Not only does the atomised life of the 'family business' have an inbuilt tendency to create deeply conservative social and cultural ideas, but such small businesses are acutely vulnerable to foreign competition. These increasingly challenged petit bourgeois layers have given growing voice to rightist, revanchist responses to Japan's relative decline vis-à-vis both China and South Korea, and provided an electoral base for the nationalist politics of those such as Koizumi and Abe who have come to dominate the LDP and the orientation of its governments.

Japanese revanchism

The US encouraged the succession of Abe to the leadership of the LDP in 2012; after the DJP experiment with an anti-US/pro-China policy, Abe was seen as a safe pair of hands to deal with China.[57] The US hoped to limit any regional concerns provoked by Japan's stepped-up military capabilities by tripping China into a stance where it could be painted as the region's aggressor. But instead, Japanese steps to unilaterally 'resolve' the Diaoyu/Senkaku dispute were understood throughout the region as Japanese belligerence, and this pugnacity created increasing alarm in the eyes of its crucial neighbour, South Korea.[58]

Abe's revisionism further disrupted relations. South Koreans particularly objected to his allegation that 'many so-called ... comfort women ... are liars', alleging that Korean women had not been forced into prostitution under Japanese occupation, and rather they were prostitutes already as brothels or *gisaeng* 'permeated life' in Korea.[59] Both China and South Korea strongly object to visits to the Yasukuni Shrine since 14 'Class A' convicted war criminals were added to those honoured there in 1978. Emperor Hirohito refused to visit the shrine after this, a stance his son Akihito has upheld. Koizumi, in 2001, had been the first post-war Japanese prime minister to visit the shrine, provoking strong regional protest. Obama urged Abe not to visit the shrine and when he did, in December 2013, it provoked an unusual public rebuke from the US.[60]

While a less conciliatory Japanese policy towards China generally served the US's Pacific 'pivot', other aspects of Japanese nationalism posed significant problems. Truculent expressions of Japanese nationalism, visits to the Yasukuni Shrine, and the rewriting of Japan's historical record of invasion, occupation and atrocities created tensions between Japan and America's other key regional ally, South Korea, and drove a further wedge between Japan and any possible rapprochement with Russia. Revived Japanese nationalism is viewed with suspicion by former Japanese colony, the island of Taiwan, and has raised concerns among farther flung US allies such as Singapore and the Philippines. Rather than divide opinion regionally as to who is behaving aggressively, it has tended to unite opinion against Japan, including within China itself where pro-Western currents, especially in Hong Kong, which often take a political distance from Beijing, have backed China in the dispute over the Diaoyu/Senkaku islands.

Thus, reinforced Japanese nationalism has already proved an uncertain weapon for the US in a regional struggle against China. 'Ironically, therefore, while no post-war leader has done more than Abe to please the United States … His Japan is both solipsistic, intent on vindicating its troubled past at the cost of alienating its neighbours, and servile but also resentful towards the United States.'[61]

The Diaoyu/Senkaku dispute

The problems that could be posed by Japanese nationalism became especially clear in the escalation of tensions over the disputed Diaoyu/Senkaku islands. The five uninhabited islands were annexed by Japan in 1895, alongside Taiwan, at the start of its imperialist expansion into Asia.[62] For both China and Japan respectively they carry a heavy symbolism: as a last vestige of China's 'century of humiliation' and as a lingering outpost of Japan's lost empire. However, the fact that they are strategically located roughly halfway between Okinawa and Taiwan, and that control of them could be used to seal off China's access to the outer Pacific, means they are more than just a matter of historical grievance (see Map 4).

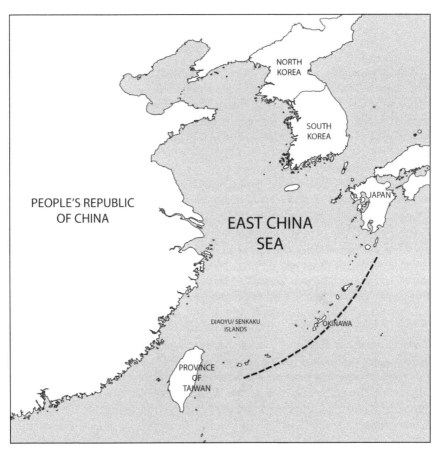

Map 4 *The Japanese archipelago and Diaoyu/Senkaku islands*

China had expected the islands to be handed back at the end of the Second World War, alongside Taiwan. The Cairo Declaration, agreed between China, Britain and the US, stated that: 'all the territories Japan has stolen from the Chinese, such as Manchuria, Formosa (Taiwan) and the Pescadores, shall be restored to the Republic of China. Japan will also be expelled from all other territories she has taken by violence and greed.'[63] But, instead, in the context of the civil war in China and the opening of Cold War hostilities, they were kept under US control. In 1972, as part of an agreement handing back sovereignty of Okinawa and the Ryukyu archipelago, the US transferred the Senkaku/Diaoyu islands to Japan's 'administration'.[64] While, whatever its pre-war promises, the US had no intention of handing the islands over to the PRC, the fact it passed them to Japanese 'administration' rather than as part of the sovereign state of Japan was an acknowledgement of the dispute, which Japan de facto accepted, refraining from developing or occupying them or stationing troops or navy ships. China meanwhile agreed to shelve the matter 'for the time being', as long as Japan did nothing to change the status quo.[65] Fishing in the disputed waters operated under 'flag state' rather than 'coastal state' law and apart from one or two minor flare-ups – provoked by Japanese nationalists or disputes with Taiwan over fishing – things were left as they stood.[66]

A coordinated escalation

The situation suddenly changed in 2010 when, in what looked like a coordinated escalation, Japanese coastguards arrested a Chinese trawler boat skipper after a collision near the islands – the first time a Chinese national had been arrested for an incursion in the area.[67] Claiming 'coastal state', that is Japanese, law applied to fishing activities in the islands' waters was an unprecedented assertion of Japanese sovereignty. China reacted strongly, imposing a ban on the export to Japan of 'rare earth' minerals vital for many high-tech manufacturing processes.

The arrest took place during the contested DPJ leadership election following the resignation of Hatoyama, which was partly over the relocation of the US base in Okinawa. Contender Naoto Kan had taken a pro-US line citing the need to counter China; the escalation of the trawler dispute favoured his candidacy and he duly became prime minister. As soon as the DPJ leadership contest was out of the way, the Japanese government backed down and released the Chinese skipper. A couple of weeks later, the US and Japan announced their largest ever joint military exercise scheduled for later that year in southern Japanese waters, adjacent to the Diaoyu/Senkaku islands.[68]

This initial clash over the islands worked out rather well for the US. The US had ratcheted up its East China Sea diplomatic and military manoeuvres, asserted its right to a presence in the area, engaged in a little sabre-rattling, reinforced an anti-China/pro-US political agenda within Japan, aided Kan's election and it had ended without problems.

Although peacefully resolved, the September 2010 incident was a clear indication of how the Diaoyu/Senkaku dispute with China would interact with a new wave of Japanese nationalism. But this rapidly proved not always so tractable for the US's calculated moves.

Undermining the 'pivot'

The issue exploded again in April 2012. Ishihara, the right-wing governor of Tokyo, thought the DPJ government had 'kowtowed' to China in retreating in 2010 and so he proposed that the Tokyo city government would 'buy' the land deeds to the islands from their private owners and begin oil and gas explorations. The proposal was entirely serious and a public subscription fund amassed ¥1.46 billion ($18.6 million) by September 2012 when the Japanese government stepped in. To block Ishihara, the faltering DPJ government of Yoshihiko Noda announced that the national government would itself purchase the titles for ¥2.05 billion ($25.95 million). But as Noda did not forewarn China of Japan's intentions, when two days previously he had met President Hu Jintao in Vladivostok, this had the look of a studied provocation.

In response, Chinese surveillance vessels began making daily sailings into the islands' waters and Chinese warships were regularly seen nearby. China pulled all its senior officials from attendance at the 2012 meetings of the IMF and World Bank in Tokyo, rendering the gatherings somewhat futile given China's role in the post-crisis stabilisation efforts. Protests against Japan spread across China to over 100 cities, mushrooming into the biggest popular demonstrations in China for many years. Japanese companies, car dealerships and factories were attacked and Japanese retail chains were forced to close for a few days. The Chinese government stepped in to halt the violence, but peaceful protests were not interfered with.

As the demonstrations petered out, a consumer boycott escalated. Japanese car companies were particularly hard hit, at a time when nearly one in four vehicles on the road in China were Japanese, with monthly sales of Japanese cars registering annual monthly falls in September and October of up to 60 per cent. Toyota cut output from its Chinese factories by 50 per cent for November and totally suspended exports of its luxury car, Lexus, to China.[69]

Tourism to Japan also plummeted. The number of Chinese visitors to Japan was second only to South Koreans; they were the biggest spenders and vital to the challenged Japanese tourist market. The Mount Fuji tourist area suffered a 70 per cent cancellation rate by Chinese visitors in September.[70]

Taipei also reacted strongly. A flotilla of nearly 100 Taiwanese fishing boats sailed to the islands to protest, which was favourably reported in China.[71] At the same time, the Taiwanese administration turned a blind eye to mainland nationalist protesters travelling to the Diaoyu via Taiwan, where they raised the Chinese flag.

Following his election at the end of 2012, Abe deepened this more combative Japanese stance on the islands. In a long interview with the *Washington Post* he insisted that they were 'under Japan's valid control' and China's challenge justified a stepped-up US military presence and increases in Japan's defence budget.[72] Japan's military budget was expanded by 3 per cent in 2013, the biggest increase for 22 years. In September 2015, amid rowdy scenes, Abe forced a vote in the Diet 'reinterpreting' Article 9 of the 1947 constitution to allow for 'collective self-defence'.

Not surprisingly this reinvigorated and rearmed Japanese nationalism increased regional insecurities, with both China and South Korea in particular expressing disquiet. South Korea's own dispute with Japan over the Dokdo islands (known as Takeshima in Japanese and Liancourt Rocks in English) had also blown up into a diplomatic spat in the summer of 2012. Alarmingly for the US, after being elected in April 2013, President Park of South Korea refused all invitations to visit Japan, while making a visit to China in the autumn of that year.

The nationalist offensive in Japan, encouraged by the US, was running dangerously too far, pushing both South Korea and Taiwan closer to China and presenting Japan as a potential aggressor.

Japanese nationalism and 'Abenomics'

It was not only Abe's foreign policies but also so-called 'Abenomics' that caused increased tensions with Japan's neighbours. Elected on a promise to end the long secular stagnation of the Japanese economy, Abe proposed to implement a combination of 'quantitative easing' to drive down the yen, reduced taxation on businesses to stimulate investment, high government spending and the promise of structural reform to reduce protection of uncompetitive small business.[73]

The first step was a sharp devaluation of the yen, which fell 20 per cent in 2013 and had fallen 50 per cent by mid-2015, after nearly four decades of appreciation.[74] This raised fears it would trigger destructive currency wars.[75] The devaluation was viewed particularly negatively in South Korea, which directly competes with Japan in a number of key sectors (cars, shipbuilding and electronics, for example).[76] Moreover, South Korea had few mechanisms to deal with this; a counter devaluation of the won might aid its manufacturers' export prices but would create problems in terms of the costs of their imports of raw materials. China's lower value production was less vulnerable, but its State Administration of Foreign Exchange commented that 'yen depreciation … could … have dangerous spill-over-effects'.[77]

The discord Abenomics created between Japan and its neighbours was exacerbated by parallels drawn between Abe's economics and those of the 1931 Japanese government, particularly in the context of the revisionist idiom of his nationalist narrative. Both governments devalued the yen, greatly expanded public spending, especially on the military, and cut interest rates. Japan's massive competitive 1931 devaluation of the yen – when the value of ¥100 fell by 69 per cent, from 2.4oz gold to 0.75oz in the space of a year – was accompanied by the invasions of Manchuria in 1931 and China in 1937.[78] Ultimately, the impact of these policies was not just disastrous regionally, but led to the Pacific War in 1941.[79]

Overall Abe's economic policy, as with his foreign policy, has reinforced Japan's orientation towards the US. Rather than the greater integration in North East Asia that had been the initial project of the 2009 DPJ government, Abe focused on the US market through increased price competitiveness and greater alignment of Japan's economy with the US. These imperatives meant Abe signed up to Obama's TPP despite the domestic problems that would have been created by its requirement to lift protection of Japan's unproductive agricultural sector.[80] Japan's support was vital, as while the projected deal included 12 countries, the US and Japan together comprised 78.5 per cent of the GDP of the proposed TPP, meaning their involvement was the crux of the whole deal.[81]

Cooling down

For the US, the rise of a more militant Japanese nationalism helpfully toughened up Japan's stance towards China, and allowed Abe to push through military reinforcement. But it also risked igniting conflict between Japan and its former colonies, especially Korea, and had united opinion within China, including Taiwan, against Japan. This was not what the US had been looking for at all, as Mike Green, a former policy advisor to George W. Bush, pointed out:

> There's no development that could do more to undercut the Obama administration's 'pivot' to the region. When Japan and South Korea are in a cycle of confrontation, it weakens US influence vis-à-vis China and North Korea, and makes coordination much harder.[82]

As a result, from 2013, there was a perceptible shift in US policy towards Japan with the aim of getting relations between Japan and South Korea in particular back on track. On the issue of Japan's war record, the US intervened several times to push Abe to use 'prudence and restraint in dealing with difficult historical issues'.[83] In January 2014 the *Wall Street Journal* reported that: 'US officials said they were looking for assurances from Mr. Abe that he would refrain from further comments and actions that ruffled Japan's neighbours … [and] said they were urging Japan to reach out to South Korea to end their bickering, which is complicating efforts for the key US allies to work together on broader regional challenges.'[84] Nonetheless, despite much urging, Abe did not apologise for Japan's past in his historic 29 April 2015 speech to the US Congress – nor for his own comments on 'comfort women'.[85]

But by the end of 2015, Abe seemed to have finally got the message; while continuing to pursue a change in Japan's constitution to ditch restraints on its military power, he also embarked upon a round of diplomacy aimed at reassuring allies and neighbours. The three-year-long freeze between Tokyo and Seoul eventually ended in November 2015 when Park met with Abe bilaterally. Relations between the US allies were restabilised and secured by Abe's December 2015 agreement to a deal on the 'comfort women' that acknowledged Japan's 'painful awareness' of its responsibility and included a payment of $8.3 million into a fund for surviving victims.[86]

The US also advocated that Abe reduce tensions on the Senkaku/Diaoyu Islands. In April 2014 Obama intervened directly, saying it would be 'a grave mistake' to allow the dispute to deteriorate, while sweetening this pill by declaring for the first time that: 'the Senkaku islands … fall within the scope of Article 5 of the US-Japan Treaty of Mutual Co-operation and Security and we oppose any unilateral attempts to undermine Japan's administration of these islands.'[87] This combination of push and pull had the desired effect as by the end of the year Abe's formulations had changed to say there were 'differing views' on the status of the islands, clearing the way for a first Xi–Abe summit in November 2014.[88]

In a similar vein, the US also attempted to progress its long sought after goal of a Russia–Japan link up. However, despite an initial meeting between Abe and Putin in 2014, goodwill broke down almost immediately with Japan's decision to follow Europe and the US in imposing sanctions on Russia over Ukraine, which Russia derided as demonstrating Tokyo's 'inability to pursue an independent foreign policy'.[89] In October 2015 a projected visit by Putin to Japan was cancelled indefinitely with both sides citing irreconcilable differences over the Kuril Islands. A Putin visit to Tokyo finally did take place in December 2016, after – and probably as a result of – the election of Trump. But despite warm words a much-heralded breakthrough on the Kurils failed to materialise.

This tactical reorientation to present a more conciliatory face to the world – while continuing to pursue Japanese rearmament – was crowned by Abe's decision to become the first Japanese leader to visit the site of the 1941 attack on Pearl Harbor. This symbolic step sought to reassure its neighbours and others that a militarily stronger and more bullish Japanese policy toward China does not augur a return to its expansive war-mongering of the past.[90]

Is it China or Japan that that their neighbours should fear?

Obama's strategy from 2014 was both to encourage Japanese remilitarisation and to persuade Abe into a more tactically astute presentation of Japan's goals that did not encourage associations with Japan's imperialist past. Steps like Obama's visit to the once-destroyed city of Hiroshima in August 2016 were partly aimed at persuading Abe's hawkish domestic base to mute their objections to such a superficially conciliatory approach, and allow Abe to reposition Japan's international image as a 'peacemaker' and unifying force in the region. Obama wanted Japan's military build-up and closer military coordination with the US against China – for example, participating in regular 'freedom of navigation' sailings in the South China Sea – to be seen as a necessary response to Chinese presumption, not the aggressive acts of a revisionist power. Having regional – and indeed world – opinion view Japan as in the grip of dangerous nationalism and potential revanchism did not suit Obama's purposes, especially if this obstructed coordination between the US, Japan and South Korea in dealing with China:

> If Abe's nationalism leads Japan to needlessly provoke China over the Senkaku/Diaoyu, it undermines Washington's confidence in Japan's reliability as an ally. If Abe's stance on … historical issues continues to undermine cooperation between Tokyo and Seoul, it greatly complicates US planning for dealing with military contingencies in the region and weakens US diplomatic efforts to present a strong, united allied front.[91]

Trump, as on other issues relating to China, was less circumspect, openly calling for more rapid Japanese rearmament. His well-publicised snipe that Japan could 'sit home and watch Sony television' if the US was attacked pointed to a possible change in their treaty relations to ensure Japan is more directly committed to military support for the US.[92] While Obama was also committed to the goal of Japan playing a more active military role alongside the US in Asia, his administration was constrained by understanding that, unless carefully presented, such a strategy could undermine support for the US's policy among other Asian allies for whom a remilitarised Japan strongly backed by America could appear no less overwhelming and threatening than a resurgent China.

For US policy in the northern Pacific to succeed, its regional friends and allies have to be bound together into a common diplomatic, military and political project aimed at China. At the centre of this, must be Japan – no other regional power approaches being sufficiently muscular to act as the lynchpin of such a strategy. So far the jury is still out on whether the US can both boost the capacities of Japan as its key regional military partner and at the same time convince Japan's neighbours that it can prevent Tokyo emerging as a parallel regional threat to the one that it conjures in Beijing.

Notes

1 US Department of Defense statistics, 31 December 2014.

2 Blackwill and Tellis, 'Revising US grand strategy', p. 28.

3 T. U. Berger, *Abe's perilous patriotism: why Japan's new nationalism still creates problems for the region and the US-Japanese alliance*, Centre for Strategic and International Studies, Washington, DC, 2014.

4 See Papers of the Office of the Historian, US Department of State, Occupation and reconstruction of Japan, 1945–52.

5 General D. MacArthur, Letter to the veterans of foreign wars, 17 August 1950.

6 G. McCormack, 'The end of the Postwar? The Abe government, Okinawa, and Yonaguni Island', *The Asia-Pacific Journal*, 12:49 (2014), 1–21.

7 G. McCormack, *Client state: Japan in the American embrace*, Verso, London, 2007, ch. 4.

8 J. Ross, 'Why Asia will continue to grow more rapidly than the US or Europe', 17 September 2008. Available at: http://socialisteconomicbulletin.blogspot.co.uk/2008/10/why-asia-will-continue-to-grow-more.html (date accessed 3 May 2015).

9 World Bank indicators 2016, Japan GDP (current US$).

10 T. Ohno, *The Toyota production system: beyond large-scale production*, Productivity Press, New York, 1988.

11 R. Taggart Murphy, *The real price of Japanese money*, Weidenfeld & Nicolson, London, 1996, pp. 86–7.

12 R. Brenner, *The economics of global turbulence: the advanced capitalist economies from long boom to long downturn, 1945–2005*, Verso, London, 2006, p. 125.

13 Arrighi, *Adam Smith*, p. 103.

14 T. Kanimori and Z. Xhao, *The Renminbi exchange rate revaluation: theory, practice and lessons from Japan*, Asian Development Bank Institute, Tokyo, 2006.

15 D. Flath, *The Japanese economy* (3rd edn), Oxford University Press, Oxford, 2014, p. 140; Desai, *Geopolitical economy*, pp. 173–81.

16 World Bank indicators 2016. GFCF (% of GDP).

17 For a full discussion of the long secular stagnation of the Japanese economy see, inter alia, R. Brenner, *Economics of global turbulence*, in particular, ch. 9.

18 US Treasury Department, major foreign holders of treasury securities. Available at: http://ticdata.treasury.gov/Publish/mfhhis01.txt (date accessed 5 February 2017).

19 Vogel, *Deng Xiaoping*, ch. 16.

20 J. Y. F. Lin, 'From flying geese to leading dragons: new opportunities and strategies for structural transformation in developing countries', *Global Policy*, 3:4 (2012), 397–409.

21 S. Armstrong, 'Sino-Japanese economic embrace is warm enough to thaw the politics', *East Asia Forum*, 27 September 2015. Available at: http://www.eastasiaforum.org/2015/09/27/sino-japanese-economic-embrace-is-warm-enough-to-thaw-the-politics/ (date accessed 5 February 2017).

22 Japan External Trade Organization (JETRO), 2016. International trade in goods (yearly). JETRO data is available at: https://www.jetro.go.jp/en/reports/statistics (date accessed 1 March 2017).

23 Ibid.

24 UNCTADStat 2014, Bilateral FDI statistics.

25 Armstrong, 'Sino-Japanese embrace'.

26 McCormack, *Client state*, p. 2.

27 Ibid., pp. 94–5.

28 Stiglitz, *Globalisation*, p. 112.

29 L. E. Easley, K. Tetsuo and M. Aki, 'Policy analysis: electing a new Japanese security policy? Examining foreign policy visions with the Democratic Party of Japan', *Asia Policy*, 9 (2010), 45–66.

30 H. Patrick, 'Japan's foreign economic relations', *East Asia Forum*, 31 October 2010. Available at: http://www.eastasiaforum.org/2010/10/31/japans-foreign-economic-relations/ (date accessed 5 February 2017).

31 J. Rogin, 'Did Obama bring down Hatoyama?', *Foreign Policy*, 2 June 2010. Available at: http://foreignpolicy.com/2010/06/02/did-obama-bring-down-hatoyama/ (date accessed 5 February 2017).

32 Japan joined in May 2013.

33 P. E. Tyler, 'Pentagon's document outlines ways to thwart challenges to primacy of America', *New York Times*, 8 March 1992.

34 'In the first draft of the 1992 Defence Policy Guidance ... it was unclear where the new rival to US supremacy would most likely emerge. Europe and Japan as well as China were among the candidates' (J. Gershman, 'Remaking policy in Asia?' *Foreign Policy in Focus*, November 2002.)

35 McCormack, *Client state*, pp. 55–89.

36 SIPRI 2016.

37 International Institute for Strategic Studies, *The military balance 2015*, Taylor and Francis, Abingdon, 2015.

38 National Defence Programme Guidelines for FY 2011 and Beyond, Japanese Ministry of Defence, 17 December 2010. Available at: http://www.tr.emb-japan.go.jp/T_06/files/National_Defense_Program_FY2011.PDF (date accessed 3 May 2015).

39 D. Fouse, *Japan's 2010 National Defence Programme guidelines: coping with the 'grey zones'*, Asia-Pacific Centre for Security Studies, Honolulu, 2011.

40 McCormack, *Client state*, ch. 6.

41 Interview in 2001 with women's magazine *Shukan Josei*.

42 D. Shenff, interviewer, 'Playboy interview: Shintaro Ishihara – candid conversation', *Playboy*, 37:10 (1990), 63.

43 McCormack, 'End of Postwar?'.

44 M. Foster, 'Ex-PM Abe wins vote to lead Japan's opposition party', *Deseret News*, 26 September 2012. Available at: http://www.deseretnews.com/article/765607027/Ex-PM-Abe-wins-vote-to-lead-Japan-opposition-party.html?pg=all (date accessed 5 February 2017).

45 J. McCurry, 'Japan's ruling party under fire over links to far right extremists', *Guardian*, 13 October 2014.

46 McCormack, *Client state*, pp. 39–45.

47 S. Steinmo, *The evolution of modern states: Sweden, Japan and the United States*, Cambridge University Press, Cambridge, 2010.

48 World Bank indicators 2016, Employment in agriculture, percentage of total workforce, 2010 figures; Statistical Handbook of Japan 2014, 2010 figures.

49 A. Demirgüç-Kunt, M. Ayyagari and V. Maksimovic, 'Small and medium enterprises across the globe', *World Bank*, March 2005. Available at: http://siteresources.worldbank.org/DEC/Resources/84797-1114437274304/SME_globe.pdf (date accessed 7 February 2017). Figures are 1990–99 averages. 52.5 per cent of the US workforce was in enterprises with fewer than 200 employees.

50 F. M. Rosenbluth and M. F. Thies, *Japan transformed: political change and economic restructuring*, Princeton University Press, Princeton, 2010, pp. 53–70.

51 World Bank indicators 2016. Trade (% of GDP) Japan compared with Germany, UK, France, Spain, Italy and so on. The US is not comparable due to the size of its internal market.

52 Outward FDI as percentage of GDP, 2005: Japan 12.4 per cent; US 20.2 per cent Germany 37.3 per cent; France 54.7 per cent; UK 61.5 per cent; China 3 per cent. Inward FDI 2005: Japan 10.1 per cent; US 15.1 per cent; Germany 19 per cent; France 40.1 per cent; UK 48.6 per cent; China 10.1 per cent. Calculated by John Ross from 2005 UNCTAD figures

53 G. Jones, *Multinationals and global capitalism*, Oxford University Press, Oxford, 2005, p. 206.

54 World Bank indicators 2010. International tourism, receipts (percentage of total exports), 2008 figures. Japan, 1.5 per cent; US 9 per cent; Germany 2.9 per cent; France 8.7 per cent; UK 6 per cent.

55 For discussion on multiculturalism in Japan, see C. Burgess, 'Multicultural Japan? discourse and the "myth" of homogeneity', *The Asia-Pacific Journal*, 5:3 (2007), 1–25.

56 South Korea estimates that there are 901,000 ethnic Koreans resident in Japan including students. The population of Japan is 127.3 million.

57 Rogin, 'Obama bring down Hatoyama?'.

58 McCormack, 'End of Postwar?'.

59 Ten-year-old transcript carries Japan prime minister's denial of 'comfort women', *The Hankyoreh*, 20 March 2007. Available at: http://english.hani.co.kr/arti/english_edition/e_international/197543.html (date accessed 2 May 2015).

60 G. Nishiyama, 'Abe visit to controversial Japanese shrine draws rare US criticism', *Wall Street Journal*, 26 December 2013.

61 McCormack, 'End of Postwar?'.

62 J. Lee, 'Senkaku/Diaoyu: islands of conflict', *History Today*, 61:5 (2011), 22–6.

63 Declaration of the World War II allies in Cairo, 27 November 1943.

64 Treaty of San Francisco and Japan–US Security Treaty 1951 and agreements to cede back sovereignty of the Amami Islands 1953, the Bonin Islands 1968 and the Ryukyu Islands (including Okinawa) 1972.

65 'Set aside dispute and pursue joint development', Ministry of Foreign Affairs of PRC. Available at: http://www.fmprc.gov.cn/mfa_eng/ziliao_665539/3602_665543/3604_665547/t18023.shtml (date accessed 5 February 2017).

66 1997 Bilateral Fisheries Agreement agreed 'flag state' rather than 'coastal state' law would apply to fishery related activities in the disputed seas.

67 The issue was not who was at fault (probably the Chinese boat) but how Japan appeared to be going to deal with it, i.e. prosecuting the captain under Japanese law.

68 J. McCurry, 'US and Japan begin joint military exercises', *The Guardian*, 3 December 2010.

69 J. Soble, 'Toyota to cut output in China by half', *Financial Times*, 5 October 2012.

70 N. Nakamoto, 'Chinese tourists give Japan a wide berth', *Financial Times*, 5 October 2012.

71 '75 Taiwan fishing boats sail to Diaoyu Islands', *China.org.cn*, 24 September 2012. Available at: http://www.china.org.cn/china/2012-09/24/content_26619633.htm (date accessed 6 May 2015).

72 'Transcript of interview with Japanese prime minister Shinzo Abe', *Washington Post*, 20 February 2013.

73 J. MacBride, J. and B. Xu, 'Abenomics and the Japanese economy', *Council on Foreign Relations Backgrounder*, 15 February 2016. Available at: http://www.cfr.org/japan/abenomics-japanese-economy/p30383 (date accessed 5 February 2017).

74 Bloomberg Business, Spot exchange rates, USD-JPY. Available at: https://www.bloomberg.com/quote/USDJPY:CUR (date accessed 7 February 2017).

75 D. Choyleva, 'Japan actions risk igniting currency war', *Financial Times*, 12 November 2014.

76 H. W. Jung, 'South Korea is caught between cheap Chinese goods and a plunging yen', *Business Insider UK*, 28 November 2014.

77 SAFE annual report 2012 cited in J. Mistral, 'Currency wars: this time is it for real?', *Brookings*, 10 April 2013. Available at: https://www.brookings.edu/opinions/currency-wars-this-time-is-it-for-real/ (date accessed 5 February 2017).

78 N. Lewis, 'Currency devaluations of the 1930s', *New World Economics*, 30 September 2012. Available at: http://www.newworldeconomics.com/archives/2012/093012.html (date accessed 20 October 2016).

79 P. Symonds, 'Japan's currency war, militarisation and monetary policy', *Global Research*, 26 January 2013. Available at: http://www.globalresearch.ca/japans-currency-war-militarization-and-monetary-policy/5320566 (date accessed 5 February 2017).

80 The TPP is discussed in Chapter 9.

81 IMF WEO 2015. 2014 GDP current $s. TPP signatories: Brunei, Chile, New Zealand, Singapore, USA, Australia, Peru, Vietnam, Malaysia, Mexico, Canada, Japan.

82 M. Dickie and S. Mundy, 'Seoul-Tokyo: a relationship on the rocks', *Financial Times*, 15 October 2012.

83 Daniel R. Russel, Testimony, Senate Committee on Foreign Relations Subcommittee on Asia and the Pacific, Washington, DC, 4 March 2014.

84 Y. Hayashi, 'US seeks Abe assurance he won't visit war shrine', *Wall Street Journal*, 23 January 2014.

85 R. Harding and G. Dyer, 'Abe stops short of apology in speech to Congress', *Financial Times*, 29 April 2015.

86 R. Harding and J. Song, 'Tokyo and Seoul agree "comfort women" settlement', *Financial Times*, 28 December 2015.

87 G. Dyer, 'Barack Obama says disputed islands covered by Japan pact', *Financial Times*, 24 April 2014.

88 Y. Reiji, 'Tokyo admits "differing views" on Senkakus, opening door to Abe-Xi meeting', *Japan Times*, 7 November 2014.

89 A. Martin, 'Japan announces fresh Russia sanctions', *Wall Street Journal*, 24 September 2014.

90 J. Sakurai, 'Shinzo Abe's act of peace at Pearl Harbor masks a hawkish intent', *Financial Times*, 21 December 2016.

91 Berger, *Abe's perilous patriotism*.

92 P. Lavender, 'Donald Trump: If the US is attacked, Japan "can sit home and watch Sony television"', *Huffington Post*, 6 August 2016. Available at: http://www.huffingtonpost.com/entry/donald-trump-japan-sony_us_57a638d8e4b03ba680128d39 (date accessed 5 February 2017).

7

The USS Taiwan?

If Japan is a bristling redoubt facing China's eastern seaboard, Taiwan and South Korea are bastions to each side. The US relies on all three to support its presence in the region and in the cases of Taiwan and South Korea, their support for the US is reinforced by the fact that the US has been the guarantor of their very existence. With major US bases in Japan and South Korea, and with Taiwan armed to the hilt to sustain its separation from mainland China, it would appear that the US already confronts China with a forti-fied arc around its east.

Throughout the Cold War Japan, South Korea and Taiwan acted in a sense as the extension of NATO in the Far East; alongside Australia, New Zealand, Singapore and the Philippines they were linked to NATO by 'military partnerships, affiliated gov-ernment agreements, a military network, and bilateral military agreements with the Anglo-American alliance'.[1] And they were closely engaged with each other, with strong personal ties between their post-war leaders and shared insecurities vis-à-vis the PRC, North Korea and the USSR.[2] Initially, despite the US rapprochement with the PRC in the 1970s, and the transfer of the Chinese UN seat from Taipei to Beijing in 1971, these close relations were unchanged.

From the mid-1980s these interrelationships began to shift. In the context of the US formal recognition of the PRC in 1979, coupled with the beginning of China's economic reform, mutually beneficial trade and economic relations with China began to take priority over anti-communist suspicions for all three US allies in the region. First Japan and then, in the 1990s, South Korea and Taiwan, became deeply economically engaged with China. Taiwan's engagement was especially encouraged by China, whose incen-tives to Taiwanese companies were aimed at fostering economic cooperation towards future political reintegration.[3] The exports of both South Korea and Taiwan to China have become crucial to their trade balances, while their companies are often reliant on Chinese-made components or assembly. With the fall of the USSR also reconfiguring regional security concerns, these multiple factors had the effect of driving both Taiwan and South Korea, in different ways, towards closer diplomatic and political relations with China.

At the same time South Korea and Taiwan began to experience some pressure in their relations with Japan. By the 1990s their rapid development along a similar path meant South Korea's high-tech and car companies and Taiwanese components were beginning to compete directly with Japan. In the new century these challenges were reinforced by growing militarism and rising nationalism in Japan.

This chapter and the next will examine how these pressures play out in influencing the policy of Taiwan and South Korea towards contemporary US goals towards China. In the context of a discussion of their post-war relations with the US, China and Japan, the chapters consider how each weighs its particular regional interests in responding to a rising China, a rearmed Japan and a declining US. This examination finds that while both South Korea and Taiwan continue to prioritise relations with the US and welcome a stepped-up US military presence, economic and strategic considerations have led them both to exercise considerable caution about signing up to US-led initiatives aimed at China.

An 'unsinkable aircraft carrier'

For the key protagonists – the US, China and Japan – it is Taiwan's strategic position that overwhelmingly determines their attitude to the island. Geographically and militarily the island is a key link in the US's 'defensive perimeter' running from Korea to the Philippines, and has been crucial to its Pacific security strategy since 1945. For China, it is dangerously close to a part of its coast that is hard to defend and completes a hostile armed ring around its east coast. Japan seized it from the Qing dynasty in 1895 partly to create a buffer between Japan and Chinese territory to its south; Taiwan is almost within sight of the southern extension of the Japanese archipelago;.[4] Not surprisingly, it was Taiwan that brought China and the US closest to war after 1949; and it remains a central strategic factor in the military planning and build-up on all sides.

Taiwan occupies a crucial role in US strategies towards China. If the goal of Obama's 'pivot' was to maintain the US's position as the leading power in the region, then ensuring its determining role in the future of Taiwan is critical. If the US abandoned Taiwan it would give China control over the Taiwan Strait, free access to the Pacific Ocean and send a signal to its other allies that US power in the region was an unreliable and fading guarantee.[5]

Taiwan's military reliance on the US was formative. Without the US's intervention – and China's diversion into the Korean War – the PRC army would undoubtedly have pursued the fight with the GMD in 1950, driving Chiang Kai-shek off the island. China's position on Taiwan has been consistent since 1949: the GMD illegally seized a part of internationally recognised Chinese territory, and eventually China will get it back.[6] The fear that China might militarily retake the province has sustained US leverage over Taiwan and kept it firmly within the US system of formal and informal alliances in the North Pacific.[7]

In 1949, confined to Taiwan, the defeated GMD elaborated the conceit that its ROC, government headquartered in Taipei, was the true government of all China, illegally expelled by a 'Communist rebellion'. Its claim to rule the whole of China (and Mongolia) was convenient for the West in the initial stages of the Cold War, especially as it meant that the pro-Western ROC held the China seat in the UN and Security Council rather than the PRC. The US even toyed with backing an attempt by the GMD to 'retake' China. However, the odds were never in Chiang Kai-shek's favour and after the 1950s it was not seriously considered.

The US approach to Taiwan was set out by US General MacArthur in 1950 justifying moving the US 7th Fleet to prevent Taiwan being retaken by Mao's victorious forces. He argued that in 'unfriendly' hands the island would 'constitute an enemy salient' in the US's Pacific 'defensive perimeter'. A Chinese-controlled Taiwan, he went on, 'could be compared to an unsinkable aircraft carrier and submarine tender [supply ship] ideally located to accomplish offensive strategy and at the same time checkmate defensive or counteroffensive operations by friendly forces based on Okinawa and the Philippines'.[8]

US defence policy expert Michael Mazza reiterated its same strategic significance for today:

> Even though no US troops are stationed on Taiwan, the island's continued de facto independence is crucial for America's forward defence perimeter, which since World War II has sought to keep would-be aggressors from approaching the United States via the Pacific Ocean. If Taiwan fell into unfriendly hands, moreover, America would find it increasingly difficult to defend its Asian treaty allies, notably Japan and the Philippines.[9]

Taiwan is thus the 'cork that keeps Chinese maritime and air forces bottled up within what China calls the "first island chain" – a string of islands running from Japan in the north, through Japan's Ryukyu chain to the Philippine island of Luzon, and then skirting the southern and western perimeters of the South China Sea'[10] (see Map 5). Taiwan would also make an ideal base for military action aimed at the Chinese mainland:

> A little more than a hundred miles from the Chinese coast, ... Across from a coastal part of China that is difficult to defend and increasingly prosperous, Taiwan is always in a position to threaten the mainland, especially if it were to offer military, intelligence or propaganda facilities to a great power.[11]

'One China'

Given Taiwan's critical position at the confluence of the East China Sea and the Pacific, the US, despite formally agreeing Taiwan is part of China, has in reality been determined it should remain separate, within its sphere of influence and not available for use by Chinese naval and air forces.[12]

While the US would like access to Taiwan's deepwater ports, the island's international status as a 'province of China' rules this out, as it cannot enter into treaty or military relations with third powers. While some hawks have always advocated the US should sponsor a change in Taiwan's international status, no US administration has seriously contemplated this. Instead US policy has flexibly tacked around Taiwan's status, ensuring that any concessions it made to China were paralleled by new initiatives to shore up Taiwan. Trump initially raised the possibility of abandoning the 'one China' policy in relation to Taiwan, but retracted this by the time of his first phone call with Xi.[13] This would have been a dangerous course, raising military tensions in the region to red hot and posing a serious risk of actual conflict – which also means it would not be a popular policy with the US's other regional allies. Whatever willingness China has shown to tolerate the present status quo or its flexibility on a possible settlement with

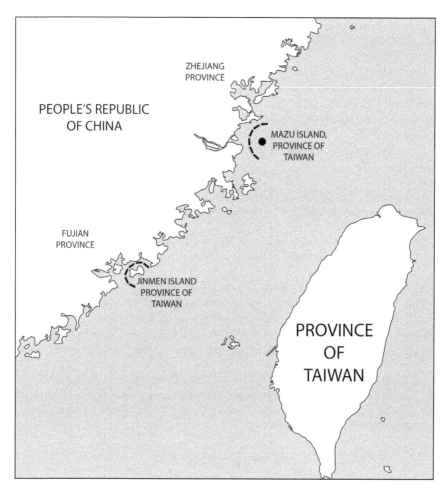

Map 5 *The Province of Taiwan and China's east coast*

Taiwan within the framework of 'one China', China has always been crystal clear that any step towards Taiwan 'independence' would be resisted with force. China will not budge on this: firstly because the island was seized illegally from China; and secondly because it believes that an 'independent' Taiwan would just be a bridgehead for a US military build-up aimed at bottling it up within the East China Sea.

The US role in maintaining Taiwan's separation has been decisive.[14] In 1950 Mao's proposal to drive the GMD from Taiwan was blocked by the US moving the 7th Fleet off the coast of Taiwan. Later in the decade China's attempt to drive the GMD off its island outposts close to the Fujian coast resulted in the first (1954–55) and second cross-Strait crises (1957–58), when the US threatened to use nuclear weapons against China in 'defence' of Taiwan.[15]

With the US's 1970s rapprochement with China, Taiwan feared – and China hoped – that the US would back reintegration of the island with the mainland.

The first blow to the ROC came in 1971, when it lost the China seat in the UN in 1971. Despite regular attempts by states friendly to Beijing to move resolutions in the UN General Assembly shifting the China seat to the PRC, they had always fallen short of the two-thirds majority needed. However, the entry of a number of newly independent developing nations into the UN in the 1960s, encouraged by the Nixon 'thaw' towards the PRC, suddenly produced an unexpected two-thirds majority for the PRC in the UN at the end of 1971. The vote, recognising the PRC as the government of 'all China', and redesignating Taiwan as 'Taiwan, province of China', was a surprise to both the US and the Chinese. The US had intended to insist upon keeping some status for the ROC in the UN as the price for agreeing the transfer; but the unanticipated outcome pre-empted the US's intentions and left the ROC with no status and outside the UN.[16]

Despite this the US had no intention of backing Taiwan's reintegration with the rest of China. From the initial meetings with Kissinger in 1971 Zhou and Mao understood – and Nixon confirmed verbally – that the US would 'sacrifice' Taiwan for the benefits of cooperation with China.[17] But this is far from what occurred. After tough negotiations, the Shanghai communiqué, issued during Nixon's historic 1972 visit to China, set out an 'agreed' US–Chinese position on Taiwan. However, the document contained two parallel declarations: the Chinese reaffirmed that Taiwan was China's 'internal affair' in which other countries had no right to interfere, while the US offered rather less:

> The United States acknowledges that all Chinese on either side of the Taiwan Strait maintain there is but one China and Taiwan is a part of China. The United States Government does not challenge that position. It reaffirms its interest in a peaceful settlement of the Taiwan question by the Chinese themselves … it affirms the ultimate objective of the withdrawal of all US forces and installations from Taiwan.[18]

These careful formulations, 'constructive ambiguity' in Kissinger's memorable words, set out an American 'one China' policy that the Chinese negotiators believed meant accepting Chinese sovereignty over Taiwan and ending US military support to the ROC, as verbally promised by Nixon.[19] But this was not Nixon's intent; indeed, by formalising US 'interest' in the eventual outcome in Taiwan the document had more strongly tied the US to defence of the ROC government, and gave this US 'interest' added legitimacy as the PRC had also put its name to it.

Formal US recognition of the PRC was delayed until 1979 as Nixon became mired in Watergate and his successor, Gerald Ford, was too weak for such a major step. It was under Carter that the US eventually formally recognised the PRC as the 'sole legal gov-ernment of China', ending the US defence treaty with Taiwan, withdrawing its military personnel and pledging to end military assistance. But in April 1979 Congress passed the Taiwan Relations Act that reasserted the US 'interest' in the 'future of Taiwan'; pledged to continue selling it sufficient arms to maintain its defences, guaranteed US support if it were attacked, including by China; and established a quasi-governmental framework that allowed it to continue what were effectively state-to-state relations with Taiwan except in protocol terms.[20] In 1982 the PRC and Reagan agreed a communiqué limiting arms sales to Taiwan, but once again the US used legalistic arguments to mitigate its impact and arms sales continued – although at a reduced level.

In other words, despite diplomatic recognition of the PRC, and the US's affirmation of 'one China', it remained the case that: 'Although separation is not the US policy's expressed intent … it has been the policy's effect.'[21]

Nonetheless, the UN and the US's changed relationship to Taiwan severely undermined the island's position. On the one hand US arms sales to Taiwan fell and became increasingly controversial. On the other, a wave of countries had already transferred their diplomatic relations from the ROC to the PRC after the 1971 UN decision: before 1971, 66 countries had recognised the PRC, but by 1979 this had grown to 117. More countries rapidly followed suit in the early 1980s; by 2014 Taiwan was recognised by only 22, mainly very small, states.[22]

The 1990s cross-Straits crisis and 'independence'

The US's continued commitment to Taiwan was tested in the third cross-Strait crisis of 1995–96, which also marked a decisive shift in the key drivers of China–Taiwan relations. The first and second Strait crises in the 1950s had seen Beijing and Taipei sparring over control of offshore islands. The conflict in the 1990s arose quite differently, in response to the emergence of political currents in Taiwan that for the first time did not aspire to 'take back' the mainland, but instead proposed to split away from mainland China altogether.

By the 1990s the province's economic success over the previous two decades – achieving growth rates of over 8 per cent for several years in the late 1980s – and the ageing of the generation that had fled to Taiwan in 1949, had weakened ties to mainland China. Chiang Kai-shek had died in 1975, and his son, Chiang Ching-kuo succeeded him. In the 1980s he began loosening the grip of the original émigré GMD forces over political life on the island, which was becoming increasingly unacceptable as the events of 1949 faded into the past.[23] Under Chiang Kai-shek the ROC government was composed of a National Assembly elected in China in 1949 and a legislative Yuan elected in 1947, neither of which had been re-elected since. Change was vital to maintain legitimacy. In 1984 Chiang Ching-kuo appointed Taiwan-born Lee Teng-hui as his deputy; martial law was lifted in 1987 and opposition parties were allowed; and the first elections to the Assembly and Yuan were held in 1991 and 1992 respectively.

The consequences of this were profound and led to a sharp deterioration in relations with Beijing. In 1991 the new opposition Democratic Progressive Party (DPP) came out for Taiwan independence. This was given a boost when Lee Teng-hui, who was now GMD president and looked set to win the first democratic presidential election in 1996, also began to favour some form of independence. It appeared Taiwan was about to make a sharp political shift away from its founding position of 'one China'.

In response to this growing separatist talk, the PRC decided that it had to prepare a military response; this was written into China's 1993 defence strategy.[24] From July 1995 it held a series of missile tests, PLA mobilisations and naval and amphibious assault exercises along the Chinese coast opposite Taiwan. But when, in March 1996 just before the elections, China held missile tests off the coast of Taiwan itself, the US moved two US aircraft carrier battle groups to the Taiwan Strait – the largest show of naval force in the region since the Vietnam War. While analysts suggest that the show of force on both sides was always symbolic, the clash demonstrated what might be unleashed by any attempt to unilaterally change the status quo of Taiwan.[25] And both the US and China rapidly moved to shore up this status quo.

Clinton took the opportunity of his 1998 visit to China – the first by an American president since the events of Tiananmen Square – to reaffirm the US position on Taiwan's status.[26] Known as the 'three no's', he said:

> We don't support independence for Taiwan, or 'two Chinas' or 'one Taiwan, one China', [and] we don't believe that Taiwan should have a membership in any organi- sation for which statehood is a requirement. So I think we have a consistent policy.[27]

But within Taiwan the pro-independence DPP continued to advance, based on fears of what the impact of reunification with China might be on its political system and buoyant economy, together with long-standing hostility to the mainland per se among sections of the indigenous population. In 2000 the DPP's Chen Shui-bian was elected president, ending more than 50 years of GMD control of the executive. In 2001 George W. Bush entered the White House on a hard-nosed foreign policy platform, led by Paul Wolfowitz, which was more pro-Taiwan than at any time since 1979. Bush's statements led many observers to conclude that he 'had abandoned the long-standing US policy of "strategic ambiguity" in favour of "strategic clarity"' and question whether he was 'pre- paring to change … position on Taiwan independence'.[28] In April 2001 Bush approved a major weapons sale to Taiwan – including submarines, which no previous administration had authorised – and senior Taiwan officials, including the president, were invited to visit the US.[29]

With such strong US backing Chen Shui-bian hardened the pro-independence line of his administration; in response, in 2005 China adopted an 'Anti-Secession Law' that authorised 'non-peaceful means … to protect China's sovereignty and territorial integ- rity'.[30] But with the US deeply embroiled in Afghanistan and Iraq, Bush did not want a crisis with China and began to urge moderation on both sides.[31]

The end of Bush's presidency coincided with the end of the pro-independence DPP's first period at the helm in Taiwan and the return of the 'one China' GMD to the presidency when Ma Ying-jeou won the 2008 election.[32] But the 2000–08 period of DPP leadership and the Bush-Wolfowitz pro-Taiwan policy had led – from China's point of view – to a dangerous strengthening of pro-independence currents in Taiwan. The election of Ma therefore also saw a shift in the tactics of the PRC from hardball rhetoric aimed at the island's leaders towards courting the 'hearts and minds' of Taiwan's population.[33]

Winning hearts and minds

In line with this, China's more recent strategy towards Taipei has been to exploit the growing synergies between their economies to encourage closer relations.

The exponential expansion of Taiwan's economy in the 1970s and 1980s, coupled with 'reform and opening up' in China from 1978, quickly made the restrictions on trade, travel and investment with mainland China an obstacle to their mutual economic potential. Under these pressures, in 1987 Taiwan eased travel restrictions to the mainland, and in 1994 China agreed a law that gave special protections to Taiwanese investments similar to those from Hong Kong.[34]

Trade and commercial links between Taiwan and mainland China grew rapidly. In 1995, 24 per cent of Taiwan's total exports went to the US compared to less than 1 per cent to the PRC, but by 2005 China was its largest trading partner.[35] Total trade with China grew to 22 per cent ($130 billion) by 2014, while the US share fell to 10.5 per cent ($62 billion). Moreover, China runs a trade deficit with Taiwan, which in 2014 was $75 billion, larger than Taiwan's total trade surplus of $39.4 billion in that year.[36] In other words Taiwan's trade surplus with China alone more than offsets a negative trade balance with the rest of the world.

China also became the chief destination for Taiwan's outward FDI; China's preferential terms, ease of communication and proximity made it attractive as competitive pressures forced Taiwan's companies to seek cheaper assembly and production abroad. By 2013 Taiwan's annual flow of FDI into China was $8.7 billion, around 63 per cent of its total FDI outflow, ahead of its investments in the US, South Korea, Germany, the UK and France.[37]

Taiwan's economy has become extremely dependent upon its links with the mainland and this is not susceptible to any mid-term change. As has been aptly said, the two economies flowed together like water running downhill.[38] Whatever the DPP thought about political relations with mainland China, in government they had taken no steps to undermine these economic synergies.

Ma's election to the Taiwan presidency in 2008 – and re-election in 2012 – combined with these deepening economic links drove a thaw in cross-Strait relations. Elected on a mandate of reducing tension with mainland China, Ma pledged there would be 'no independence, no unification, and no use of force'; while the PRC stressed economic, cultural and diplomatic cooperation rather than reintegration.[39] One immediate effect was a 'diplomatic truce' whereby Ma dropped Taiwan's campaign for entry into the UN and instead looked to China for support its participation in other international organisations, while China lifted its objections to Taiwan participating with special status as a 'customs area' in various international forums such as the WTO and WHO.[40]

In 2010 an Economic Co-operation Framework Agreement (ECFA) between the mainland and Taiwan further opened up the China market to Taiwan, on terms very favourable to Taiwan. Tariffs were reduced on 539 Taiwanese exports to China, and on 267 Chinese exports to Taiwan. It was estimated that in the first year almost $14 billion of Taiwanese goods exported to China would face lower or no tariffs, compared to just under $3 billion of Chinese exports to Taiwan.[41]

Within months of Ma's election the first regular, direct flight from mainland China for nearly 60 years landed at Taipei and flights from several Chinese cities to five different Taiwan airports were introduced.[42] In June 2015 China lifted entry-permit requirements for Taiwan residents visiting the mainland. High-level meetings increased culminating in an historic meeting between Xi Jinping and Ma Ying-jeou in November 2015, the first time that the leaders of the PRC and Taiwan had met since 1949.

The regional impact of this cross-Strait harmony became evident when both Japan and the Philippines provoked confrontations with China over disputed islets in 2012.[43]

Rather than Taipei rallying to the defence of the US's allies against China, stronger bilateral relations reinforced their shared view on these territorial disputes. Almost all forces on Taiwan reject Japan's claim to the Diaoyu, as they were administered out of Taipei under the Qing dynasty and are part of Taiwan's traditional fishing grounds. In the South China Sea, the ROC occupies Taiping, the largest of the disputed Spratly Islands.[44] The ROC's claim to Taiping is based on the same 1945 map that the PRC relies on; indeed, it was originally drawn up by the ROC government of Chiang Kai-shek to show territory surrendered to China as the Japanese retreated from South East Asia.[45]

Given this history it would always have been difficult to recruit Taiwan against China specifically on any of these island disputes. Indeed, the ROC's common position with the PRC on the disputed sovereignty of these islets is one reason why the US had been careful to be seen as neutral on the issues and had not encouraged Japan or the Philippines to pursue their claims. But Taipei's coolness towards the demands of Obama's turn to China went further; it kept its distance from the entire US propaganda campaign against China. So, for example, when in 2013 China announced it was implementing an Air Defence Identification Zone (ADIZ) over the East China Sea that overlapped with part of Taiwan's existing ADIZ, Taiwan's response was extremely mild despite the US urging the ROC to refuse to recognise it.[46]

The balance of arms

As Taiwan's relations with mainland China warmed under Ma, US China hawks began to raise the alarm. Thus Paul Wolfowitz warned that 'China hopes to embrace Taiwan more tightly through economic ties while also preparing military options if it decides to take action to accomplish its ultimate goal of unification'. Fearing Taiwan was heading dangerously towards eventual reunification with China, he urged that the US should 'take more ambitious steps', including challenging Taiwan's non-sovereign status by entering into direct trade agreements, or ignoring China's objections and making major increases in arms sales.[47] The *National Interest* suggested that Taiwan should be 'the first new TPP signatory after the agreement is implemented'.[48]

US arms sales to Taiwan had generally declined since the Taiwan Relations Act despite occasional breaches, such as those under George W, Bush. Obama did agree to substantial arms sales in 2010 and 2011 and a further lesser sale in 2015, but the deals did not include new fighter jets or help in replacing Taiwan's ageing submarine fleet, which it urgently wanted.[49] Future US arms sales remain a key indicator of the degree to which Trump and future US administrations are really prepared to confront China over Taiwan.[50]

Given Taiwan's insecurities its military spending has always been high. Despite their vast disparity in size, China's annual military spending only overtook Taiwan's in 1995.[51] However the difference in their year-on-year spending is now unbridgeable; China's military spending in 2015 was an estimated $215 billion compared to Taiwan's $10.3 billion.[52] Moreover, with the easing of relations with China and pressures on domestic budgets, Taiwan – under both the DPP and the GMD – allowed its defence spending to fall from 2.7 per cent of GDP in 2000 to 1.9 per cent in 2015. US strategists, and Trump's team in particular, have argued strongly this should be reversed.[53]

From the 1990s China's priority was to build up military capacity across the Strait to deter any hostile naval incursion and insure against any temptation for Taiwan to seek formal separation from China. This has involved a large arsenal of short- and medium-range missiles along the Fujian and Jiangsu coasts, missile defence systems, stealth jets and specialist coastal naval vessels. As a result China has, or is very close to having, an effective deterrence capability in relation to the East China Sea and Taiwan. As discussed in Chapter 4, this has become an almost obsessive concern of US military strategists who claim that China is pursuing 'Access Denial', threatening free access to the 'global commons'.[54] What they actually mean is that the US may no longer have the naval capacity to dominate China's coasts and littoral waters.

This poses the question as to what US military support could actually deliver if it did encourage Taiwan to formally break away from China. An authoritative 2009 report for the RAND Corporation found that the logistical problems posed by the geographic distance of the US from Taiwan, 'combined with the limited array of forward basing options for US forces – and China's growing ability to mount sustained and effective attacks on those forward bases – calls into question Washington's ability to credibly serve as guarantor of Taiwan's security in the long run'.[55]

This carries a serious message for all the US's weaker regional allies, not just Taiwan. If the US can no longer effectively defend them in a putative conflict with China, is it not wiser in the long term to seek stable relations with China rather than support a US policy to contain China that will inevitably lead to deteriorating relations in the region? As the Pentagon said in the 2010 Quadrennial Defence Review: 'Without dominant US capabilities to project power, the integrity of US alliances and security partnerships could be called into question.'[56]

The US strategy to counter this is the previously discussed Air-Sea Battle plan (see Chapter 4), which implies that in any conflict with China over the Taiwan Strait, the only response that the US has is a rapid escalation to all-out war with China. That is not a scenario that offers a great sense of security to Taiwan.

Taiwan and Japan

This weakening of the military relationship of forces with China has meant the US is drawing Japan more centrally into the military equation over Taiwan. Hence the 2005 round of US–Japan negotiations on their Mutual Defence Treaty, identified '[e]ncouraging a peaceful resolution of issues concerning the Taiwan Strait' as a mutual security concern.[57] While sounding neutral enough, it was the first time since 1960 that Taiwan had featured as a common security concern. This was subsequently reflected in Japan's build-up of monitoring and other facilities on Yonaguni Island, 70 miles off the coast of Taiwan.[58]

However, relations between Japan and Taiwan are not so simple. Although the island's 50-year occupation by Japan – from 1895 to 1945 – left no great stain of atrocities and corresponding grievance, its legacy does lead to suspicion of Japan's intentions. Conflicts have rumbled on over the Diaoyu/Senkaku Islands, particularly in the form of recurring disputes over fishing rights. During the 2012 dispute between China and Japan there was a surge of popular feeling in Taiwan against Japan; Chinese nationalists from both the mainland and Taiwan took part in protest actions. However, the US intervened to persuade Japan to make concessions to Taiwan, leading to a 2013 comprehensive Taiwan–Japan agreement on fishing rights around the islands.

The defeat of the GMD in 2016's presidential elections brought to an end the period of prolonged détente with China under Ma and the DPP's Tsai Ing-wen assumed the presidency on a policy of hardening up Taiwan's stance towards the mainland, coupled with ambiguous statements on possible future independence for Taiwan. To underline this reorientation, she made a point of visiting Japan in the run-up to the elections on a 'friendship tour' to strengthen 'our partnerships with the US, Japan, and other like-minded democracies from around the world'.[59] Joseph Wu, the DPP's secretary-general, described Japan as 'Taiwan's most important as well as the best friend in the region'.[60]

Bringing Japan into the cross-Straits equation reinforces the US military and strategic position over Taiwan, and was precisely the type of extension in the function of its regional alliances to increase the military pressure on China that the US foresaw in launching the 'pivot' in 2010.

Taiwan swings electorally against China

The strengthening of cross-Straits relations under Ma was not uniformly popular in Taiwan. Polls over two decades have shown a steady trend downwards in those identifying as 'Chinese' rather than 'Taiwanese' on the island, and a similar decline in the number favouring eventual reunification.[61] Such sentiments partly lay behind a 23-day student occupation of the island's legislature in March 2014 against a new service trade agreement with the mainland. Dubbed the Sunflower movement, and modelled on the 'colour' revolutions elsewhere, the students' representatives were welcomed by the US Congress. The Sunflower movement contributed to the landslide for the DPP in the November legislature elections that year and the victory for Tsai in the January 2016 presidential elections, giving the DPP control over both the executive and the legislature for the first time – and giving the ROC its first female president.[62]

However, despite the popular purchase of anti-China rhetoric, the real challenge facing Tsai's presidency lies in the six years of sluggish growth since the 2008 crisis that underlay the disenchantment with Ma's government. The period 2008–13 saw growth rates barely above 2.5 per cent, only picking up to 3.5 per cent in 2014, mirrored in a declining share of world trade.[63]

Tsai put joining the TPP centre stage in her economic alternative, appealing for US support for Taiwan's integration into the US trade pact. But even if the TPP had survived Trump's presidency, it is questionable whether Taiwan would have been able to join. But, in any event, given the sluggish state of the US market, the US does not hold the solution to Taiwan's trade woes. For that it will remain obliged to look to China.

Before the election Tsai also pledged that Taiwan would increase its defence spending to 3 per cent of GDP, which was strongly welcomed by the US and Japan, although this should be viewed with some scepticism as defence spending actually fell through most of the DPP's previous period in office.[64]

It is yet to be seen what this new period of DPP government in Taiwan will bring. Initially it has strengthened the US's position in East Asia by bringing in a pro-US government instead of one more oriented to China. But while the core of the DPP's support comes from that section of Taiwan's population that wants a complete break with China – 31.2 per cent favoured independence in a 2015 poll – this is not a majority. And polls show there is no particular taste in the population for provoking an international crisis over Taiwan's status – 56.2 per cent prefer to keep the status quo, and with that small section of the population, around 10 per cent, that still support reunification, it means two-thirds do not want a confrontation on the issue.[65] Therefore the DPP's support in 2016 was clearly boosted by the fact that Ma's GMD government was predictably blamed for Taiwan's prolonged post-2008 economic difficulties. To stay in power the DPP needs to retain support from those that voted for it because they want an improvement in their living standards, despite disagreeing on independence. Tsai will find – sooner rather than later – that solving this means less anti-China rhetoric and more China trade.

The 'cork in the bottle'

Taiwan's 'cork in the bottle' strategic position between the South and East China Seas means it occupies a crucial role both in China's future security and in the US's Pacific strategies.[66] 'Historically, Taiwan's pivotal location off the China coast and between Northeast and Southeast Asia has served a variety of strategic purposes for regional powers, both offensive and defensive. In the contemporary era, Taiwan remains geographically at the intersection of most of East Asia's danger points.'[67]

For China, Taiwan is both a potential gateway to the Pacific and the perfect base for a hostile power with malicious intent. China definitively wants to get Taiwan back and therefore has been prepared to be extremely flexible about the form that an eventual reunification might take. Deng Xiaoping set out a 'one country, two systems' solution for both Hong Kong and Taiwan in 1984.[68] Jiang Zemin reiterated this in 1995, including indicating that China was prepared to accept much greater autonomy for Taiwan than was agreed for Hong Kong from 1997.[69] But reintegration is not on the cards for now, and China has accepted a de facto separate Taiwan as long as it cannot be a base for potentially hostile operations by the US in the East China Sea. This has been guaranteed by Taiwan's international legal status, which prevents it from entering into treaty arrangements with other countries or allowing the stationing of foreign troops.

Similarly, the US would like direct access to Taiwan's deepwater ports, which would provide an ideal base for naval containment of China through dominating its routes out to the Pacific. But as this would mean a confrontation with China, it had not been openly advocated since 1979, until Trump's key advisor and former US ambassador to the UN, John Bolton, suggested the US should both increase 'military sales to Taiwan' and 'station military personnel and assets there'. But pursuit of such a confrontational policy does not make strategic sense for the US and it could well backfire in leaving the US more isolated in East Asia. Hence successive US administrations have pursued the second best option of the continued quasi-independence of Taiwan, ensuring that the Chinese navy cannot be based there either and taking comfort from the fact that support within Taiwan for reintegration into China is low and has been falling.

But what is certain is that the attractive power of the US economically is receding and its real ability to defend Taiwan is waning as China's capacities have grown. Taiwan's ties with continental China have become crucial not just to its advanced high-tech industries but to its entire economy. They share a language, writing system, history and culture, as well as extensive historic family links enriched by contemporary migrations of the young and ambitious to mainland China. Without a takeover threat from China, the US defensive shield has been declining in importance – and already is possibly not a credible defence at all.

These multiple factors make it likely that while the return to DPP government from 2016 has changed the rhetoric, it will not fundamentally reverse the deepening of cross-Strait ties. And the DPP itself acknowledged this when, as the elections approached, in April 2015, it clarified it would 'maintain the status quo' on Taiwan's status with the mainland and seek party-to-party dialogue with the CPC.[70]

As elsewhere in the region, in Taiwan the success of the US's policy in Asia relies on the perceived need for US military support outweighing the benefit of economic links with China. The reality is that hard economic facts have driven the island ever closer to the mainland, whatever the subjective intentions of its politicians or inclinations of its population. A hard-line orientation to a pro-American, anti-China policy of the type initially floated by Trump would damage its economy and threaten internal instability. As a result, even with a formally pro-independence DPP government in Taipei, Taiwan looks set to continue down a middle course, taking arms and military support from the US where it can, while continuing to avoid conflict with China.

Notes

1   Nazemroaya, *Globalisation of NATO*, ch. 11.

2   C. X. G. Wei, *China-Taiwan relations in a global context: Taiwan's foreign policy and relations*, Routledge, Abingdon, 2012, p. 115.

3   R. C. Bush, *Uncharted Strait: the future of China-Taiwan relations*, Brookings Institution Press, Washington, DC, 2013, pp. 10–11.

4   Yoshihara and Holmes, *Red star over the Pacific*, p. 67.

5   N. Bernkopf Tucker and B. Glaser, 'Should the US abandon Taiwan?', *The Washington Quarterly*, 34:4 (2011), 23–37.

6   Nathan and Scobell, *China search for security*, p. 215.

7   Bush, *Uncharted Strait*, ch. 2.

8   Draft Memorandum, General MacArthur's Message on Formosa, 17 August 1950, secretary of state file, Acheson Papers.

9   M. Mazza, 'Taiwan's crucial role in the US pivot to Asia', *American Enterprise Institute*, 9 July 2013. Available at: http://www.aei.org/publication/taiwans-crucial-role-in-the-us-pivot-to-asia/ (date accessed 12 February 2017).

10 Ibid.

11 Nathan and Scobell, *China search for security*, p. 213.

12 Ibid., pp. 212–39.

13 C. Bohan and D. Brunnstrom, 'Trump says US not necessarily bound by "one China" policy', *Reuters*, 12 December 2016. Available at: http://www.reuters.com/article/us-usa-trump-china-idUSK-BN1400TY (date accessed 12 February 2017).

14 Nathan and Scobell, *China search for security*, p. 215.

15 See Chapter 5.

16 L. Wei, *China in the United Nations*, World Century Publishing Corp, Hackensack, NJ, 2014, pp. 50–3.

17 Nathan and Scobell, *China search for security*, p. 101.

18 Joint Communiqué of the United States of America and the People's Republic of China, 28 February 1972.

19 Nathan and Scobell, *China search for security*, pp. 101–2.

20 R. C. Bush, 'Thoughts on the Taiwan Relations Act', *Brookings*, April 2009. Available at: https://www.brookings.edu/opinions/thoughts-on-the-taiwan-relations-act/ (date accessed 12 February 2017).

21 Nathan and Scobell, *China search for security*, p. 215.

22 Bush, *Uncharted Strait*, p. 20.

23 Ibid., ch. 2.

24 Ibid., pp. 14–16.

25 R. Pinsker, 'Drawing a line in the Taiwan Strait: "strategic ambiguity and its discontents"', *Australian Journal of International Affairs*, 57:2 (2003), p. 353–68.

26 US presidential visits to China: Nixon 1972; Ford 1975; Reagan 1984; Bush 1989; Clinton 1998.

27 R. Sutter, 'The "Three No's"; Congressional-administration differences and US policy issues', *Congressional Research Service 98-837F*, 30 June 1998.

28 K. B. Dumbaugh, 'Taiwan: recent developments and US policy choices', *Congressional Research Service Issue Brief*, IB98034, 24 January 2006.

29 M. McDevitt, 'Taiwan: the tail that wags the dog', *Asia Policy*, 1 (January 2006), 69–93.

30 Anti-Secession Law, 14 March 2005, Third session, 10th National People's Congress and CPPCC. Full text at http://news.xinhuanet.com/english/2005-03/14/content_2694180.htm (date accessed 14 May 2015).

31 Dumbaugh, 'Taiwan', p. 11.

32 The GMD had retaken a narrow majority in the parliament at the end of 2004.

33 Y. K. Wang, 'China's growing strength, Taiwan's diminishing options', *Brookings*, 2010. Available at: https://www.brookings.edu/research/chinas-growing-strength-taiwans-diminishing-options/ (date accessed 12 February 2017).

34 Law of the PRC on Protection of Investments by Compatriots from Taiwan, 5 March 1994.

35 D. K. Nanto and E. Chanlett-Avery, 'The rise of China and its effect on Taiwan, Japan and South Korea: US policy choices', *Congressional Research Service Report RL32882*, 13 January 2006.

36 Taipei, Bureau of Foreign Trade – Trade Statistics 2000–2015, value of exports and imports by country, US$.

37 Republic of China Yearbook 2014, Executive Yuan.

38 Nathan and Scobell, *China search for security*, p. 219.

39 R. C. Bush, 'Taiwan and East Asian security', *Orbis*, 55:2 (2011), 274.

40 B. A. Lindemann, *Cross-Straits relations and international organisations*, Springer VS, Wiesbaden, 2012.

41 'Historic Taiwan-China trade deal takes effect', *BBC News*, 12 September 2010. Available at: http://www.bbc.co.uk/news/world-asia-pacific-11275274 (date accessed 12 February 2017).

42 'Direct China–Taiwan flights begin', *BBC News*, 4 July 2008. Available at: http://news.bbc.co.uk/1/hi/7488965.stm (date accessed 12 February 2017).

43 See Chapters 5 and 10.

44 L. Kuok, *Tides of change: Taiwan's evolving position in the South China Sea*, Brookings Institution: Centre for East Asia Policy Studies, Washington, DC, 2015.

45 See Chapters 9 and 10.

46 J. M. Cole, 'China's ADIZ: Taiwan's dilemma', *The Diplomat*, 28 November 2013. Available at: http://thediplomat.com/2013/11/chinas-adiz-taiwans-dilemma/ (date accessed 12 February 2017).

47 P. Wolfowitz, 'US Taiwan policy threatens a face-off with China', *Wall Street Journal*, 9 October 2014.

48 A. Bernard and P. J. Leaf, 'The US, TPP and Taiwan', *The National Interest*, 24 April 2014. Available at: http://nationalinterest.org/feature/the-us-tpp-taiwan-10300 (date accessed 12 February 2017).

49 M. Forsythe, 'China protests sale of US arms to Taiwan', *New York Times*, 17 December 2015.

50 Bernkopf Tucker and Glaser, 'Should the US abandon Taiwan?'.

51 SIPRI 2016. 1995 figures: Taiwan $11,470 million, PRC $12,575 million (current $).

52 SIPRI 2016.

53 B. Glaser and A. Mark, 'Taiwan's defence spending: the security consequences of choosing butter over guns', *Asia Maritime Transparency Initiative*, 18 March 2015. Available at: https://amti.csis.org/taiwans-defense-spending-the-security-consequences-of-choosing-butter-over-guns/ (date accessed 17 February 2017).

54 Yoshihara and Holmes, *Red star over the Pacific*, pp. 6–7.

55 D. A. Shlapak, D. T. Orletsky, T. I. Reid, M. S. Tanner and B. Wilson, *A question of balance: political context and military aspects of the China-Taiwan dispute*, RAND National Security Research Division, Santa Monica, CA, 2009.

56 US Quadrennial Defence Review, p. 31.

57 Joint Statement US–Japan Security Consultative Committee, 19 February 2005, Ministry of Foreign Affairs of Japan.

58 P. Kallender-Umezu, 'Japan quietly builds limited counter A2/AD capabilities', *Defence News*, 17 September 2013. Available at: https://www.cigionline.org/articles/japan-quietly-builds-limited-counter-a2ad-capabilities (date accessed 6 June 2015).

59 Tsai Ing-wen speech to Democratic Progressive Party 29th anniversary diplomatic reception, Taipei, 22 September 2015.

60 S. Tiezzi, 'What Taiwan–Japan relations might look like in 2016', *The Diplomat*, 9 October 2015. Available at: http://thediplomat.com/2015/10/what-taiwan-japan-relations-might-look-like-in-2016/ (date accessed 12 February 2017).

61 R. C. Bush, *Taiwan's January 2016 elections and their implications for relations with China and the United States*, Brookings Institution Press, Washington, DC, 2015, p. 4.

62 Bush, 'Taiwan's elections'.

63 W. Wilson, 'Market solutions should be central to US's Taiwan policy', *The Heritage Foundation*, 14 August 2014.

64 Glaser and Mark, 'Taiwan's defence spending'.

65 L. S. Loa, 'Support for Taiwanese independence, identity: think tank poll', *Taipei Times*, 5 February 2015.

66 Taiwan/Formosa is 'the cork in the bottle of the South China Sea', attributed to Admiral Ernest J. King, Commander in Chief US fleet during the Second World War.

67 J. A. Bosco, 'Taiwan and strategic security', *The Diplomat*, 15 May 2015. Available at: http://thediplomat.com/2015/05/taiwan-and-strategic-security/ (date accessed 12 February 2017).

68 Deng Xiaoping, 'One country, two systems', 22–23 June 1984. Available at: http://en.people.cn/dengxp/vol3/text/c1210.html (date accessed 20 October 2016).

69 'On the premise there is only one China, we are prepared to talk to the Taiwan authorities about any matter': Continue to promote the reunification of the motherland, Speech by president Jiang Zemin, Beijing, 30 January 1995.

70 L. S. Loa, 'DPP vows to keep "status quo" going in cross-strait ties', *Taipei Times*, 10 April 2015.

8

Korea: divided nation, divided allegiances

The Korean peninsula has been described as 'a dagger, pointing either at China or Japan, depending on who is talking'.[1] It was here that Japan took the first significant step in its attempt to create an Asian colonial empire, annexing Korea in 1910 – having first ensured there would be no Russian resistance through defeating it in the 1905 Japan–Russia war. Korea became the launch pad for conquest of Manchuria and invasion of China.

Today the peninsula (see Map 6) is divided at the 38th parallel into the southern Republic of Korea (ROK) and the northern Democratic People's Republic of Korea (DPRK), a division originating in 1945.[2] Just as the 1945 turn from war to Cold War in the West was marked by the division of Germany into two states along a line where the Soviet and US armies met, so in the East it was marked by a similar line drawn through the Korean peninsula.[3] Both North and South Korea advocate reunification, but as the two states today embody different social and economic systems, as well as different political structures and international alliances, currently no untraumatic transition to a single state can be envisaged.[4]

For China, notwithstanding occasional tensions with the North, particularly under Kim Jong-un, and growing economic ties with the South, the existence of the DPRK prevents US troops from sitting on the Yalu River staring down at China's north-eastern industrial heartland and only 1000 km from Beijing. China's security would be severely challenged by a US-dominated united Korea born from a fall of the North into the arms of the South, so has little choice but to prop it up. Russia sees the issues similarly. Korea's other neighbour, Japan, in contrast, would *only* wish to see the reunification of the peninsula as long as it was under the influence of the US and not of China; a united Korean peninsula in alliance with China would be unnerving for Japan.

For South Korea the tense border with the North compounds other security concerns arising from proximity to China and Russia and lingering fears arising from its former occupation by Japan, rendering it entirely militarily reliant on the US. There would have been no South Korea in the first place had it not been for the US's 1945 occupation of the South and 1950 intervention launching the Korean War.[5] Similarly North Korea, facing a US-backed state in the South, is militarily reliant on China and to a certain extent Russia. Without Chinese intervention in 1950 the US forces backing Syngman Rhee's South Korea would have eliminated the North.

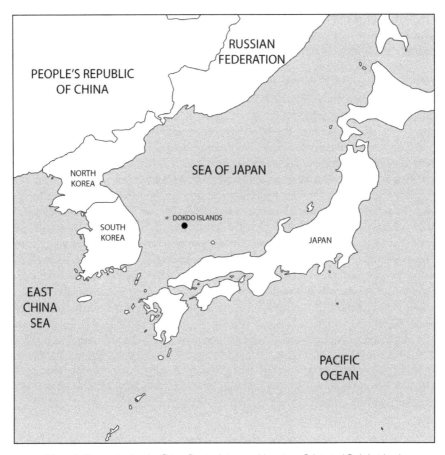

Map 6 *Korean peninsula, China, Russia, Japan and location of disputed Dokdo islands*

As with the intractable status of Taiwan, in this part of East Asia the Cold War, in a sense, never ended: post-1945 geographical divisions persist; the same claims to governmental legitimacy and territorial sovereignty are disputed; and opposing social and political systems still face each other gun in hand.

But little else is at it was in 1945. South Korea's economic success now sees it biting at Japan's heels as the premier East Asian producer of cars and other high-tech, high-value commodities.[6] North Korea, on the other hand, after a period of post-war economic success ran into its own version of the problems that beset other 'command' economies. With no equivalent of a Chinese 'reform and opening up' and bereft of Soviet support from the late 1980s, it tipped into deep crisis, from which it has not fully recovered.[7] Ironically, for both North and South, China today is not just their mightiest near neighbour, but their primary economic partner. For North Korea, its extreme international isolation creates a semi-dependency on Chinese trade and support. While China has risen from virtually zero trade in 1990 to become South Korea's top export market since 2003.

Thus two states occupy the strategically vital Korean peninsula: one weaker and reliant on China – though not very tractable to China's wishes; the other successful, but militarily dependent upon the US, while also deeply enmeshed economically with China.

South Korea merited prime billing in Obama's plans for the 'pivot' thanks to its military alliance with the US and strategic position in North East Asia.[8] But while US military collaboration with South Korea has proceeded apace, in other respects its integration into the US's strategic priorities for Asia has been less than satisfactory. It stayed out of the TPP, while signing up to the AIIB.[9] Its relations with Japan have often been hostile and distant, while those with China have become closer and warmer. And while South Korea has been perturbed by developments in North Korea, it has increasingly looked to China to influence the situation as much as to the US for its military protection.

This chapter considers how the post-war division of the peninsula threw the North and South respectively into the camps of the USSR/China and the US as guarantors of their existence, and analyses their changed relations to the world today. It assesses the impact of South Korea's economic success, its emerging competitive challenge to Japan and its increasing synergies with China. It questions to what degree North Korea is an actual threat to security in the region, or whether its demonisation is a convenient justification for a reinforced US presence in the South. And it weighs South Korea's concerns about a strengthened China against those provoked by Japan's more nationalistic stance under Abe.

The chapter concludes that these considerations have led South Korea to be cautious about rushing to sign up to US policies that are too explicitly cast against China. While it has continued to step up its military collaboration with the US, it has not become a cheerleader for pushing back against China in the style of some of the US's other regional treaty allies.

The division of Korea

Given the location of the Korean peninsula between Japan, Russia and China, and the historical power plays between them, it is perhaps surprising that Korea survived as a continuous unified independent state from the seventh century. For much of this time it had a type of tributary relationship with neighbouring China, but was not conquered and had its own social system, governing dynasties, language and culture.[10] Its history of invasions and occupations is a modern phenomenon.

A division at the 38th parallel has no basis in Korean history. In 1945 the Soviet army entered Korea to drive out Japan – as it had agreed to do at the Yalta conference earlier that year – but halted its advance through the peninsula at the 38th parallel at the behest of the US. If the Soviet armies had continued they would have faced no opposition from the US army, which was too tied up elsewhere to land substantial forces, and would have been welcomed by Koreans as liberators. But Stalin wanted to show good faith; prioritising the USSR's negotiating position in Eastern Europe, he stood aside as the US army arrived and set up its own military administration in the South.[11]

At the 1945 Potsdam conference the allies agreed to keep the peninsula under joint Soviet and American 'trusteeship' for five years to 1950, during which time a unified governmental solution for the whole peninsula would be found. But, in 1948, facing a generalised uprising against its military administration, which was widely seen as a renewed colonial occupation, the US reneged on this agreement. Amid riots and chaos it pushed ahead with elections in the South, resulting in the US-backed rightist Syngman Rhee forming a government and declaring the Republic of Korea (ROK).[12]

In the North a provisional government – the Provisional People's Committee for North Korea – led by anti-Japanese resistance leader Kim Il-sung had carried out a highly popular, sweeping land reform, seizing Japanese- and collaborator-held land and then supporting peasant mobilisations to break up all large landholdings.[13] In response to Syngman Rhee's 1948 declaration of the ROK, Kim Il-sung declared the Democratic People's Republic of Korea (DPRK). Each claimed authority over the entire peninsula.

During the course of 1949 the US and the USSR withdrew from Korea. But with Rhee's government facing popular mobilisations against the stitched-up elections and undertaking provocative military actions against the North, in June 1950 Kim Il-sung led a military offensive against Rhee aiming to reunify the country. With Rhee rapidly losing this civil war, the US turned to the UN, claiming that Kim had violated the sovereignty of a separate nation.[14] In January 1950 the USSR had begun a boycott of the Security Council, citing the 'lawlessness' of the UN decision not to transfer the China seat to the PRC. But the other members of the Security Council continued to meet without the USSR, hence there was no opposition to Resolution 83 in June authorising international military support for Rhee's Republic of Korea. Within a month the US had intervened under the UN banner and the Korean civil war became the Korean War.

The Americans drove the DPRK back and only the intervention of the one-year-old PRC in late 1950 prevented its defeat. In 1953 the country was again divided along the 38th parallel. This division of the country may make no historical or cultural sense, and may have arisen without planning or conscious intent, but nonetheless it has proved completely intractable. Once reaffirmed by the outcome of the Korean War, the geo-political realities of the Cold War meant the peninsula had become an object of big power contestation in which governments of North and South were reduced to bit parts. The divergent courses of economic development and extreme ideological and systemic differences between North and South, which have been reinforced since then, compounded the obstacles to reunification.

This line through the Korean peninsula has now become a key battlefront in a proxy war between the US and China, symbolised most sharply by their opposing relations with the DPRK. On the one hand China's sole mutual defence treaty is with the DPRK. On the other, the US has never established formal diplomatic relations with it, instead imposing what has become the longest lasting sanctions regime against any country. North Korea was excluded from the UN until both were admitted as full members in 1991 – the South had observer status from 1948.

South Korea: the US and military dependency

South Korea's strategic location inevitably places it at the heart of current US policy towards China. The US bases in South Korea are its only ones actually on the continent of Asia east of Islamabad; geographically they are the most proximate to China of all its bases, and its annual naval exercises with South Korea take place the closest to China's shores.[15] Only Japan is as militarily and strategically significant as South Korea.

At $36.4 billion per annum, and 2.6 per cent of GDP, South Korea's arms spending is the 10th highest in the world.[16] It has compulsory male military conscription, adding around 159,000 conscripts to its permanent force and giving it 687,000 troops on active service at any one time; only China, the US, India, Pakistan, the DPRK and Russia have more. It is well equipped with submarines, destroyers and attack aircraft, mainly supplied by the US, which is not constrained in its arms sales to South Korea in the way it is to Taiwan.

The 28 US army and air bases in the country are critical for the US's strategic position in North East Asia. Comprising 29,300 US troops in 2014, this was its third largest permanent overseas deployment after Germany and Japan; and will become its second largest, as its drawdown from Germany continues. Fort Humphreys, a new US base, will become the largest single US garrison in Asia. Despite reducing US defence expenditure by over 1 per cent of GDP between 2009 and 2015, Obama pledged to increase the US presence in South Korea.[17,18] A Senate Report found that the costs to the US of its military presence in Korea in 2012 amounted to nearly $3.1 billion, not including the 2012 South Korean contribution of $765 million.[19]

Given these costs, and Trump's general approach that all US allies would have to pay more towards defence, it was not surprising that he described South Korea as a 'free rider' that was not paying its way.[20] But attempts to make South Korea pay a greater share towards the costs of the US presence on the peninsular would run into popular opposition, including to the degree of control exercised by the US over the ROK's foreign and defence policies. Hence why Trump's Defence Secretary, 'Mad Dog' Mattis, who made Seoul the venue for the first overseas visit of a senior Trump official after the inauguration, took a much more emollient tone on the US's ongoing commitment to South Korea's defence.[21]

From 1950 until 1994 the US had complete day-to-day operational control – OpCon – over the ROK army. Until the 1980s this was largely uncontroversial, as fear of the North (potentially backed by the USSR or China) outweighed any incipient anti-American feeling.[22] But after the end of the Cold War, the receding sense of threat began to shift opinion in the ROK against the US having this degree of say, and the US surrendered peacetime control in 1994. But OpCon would still revert to the US in the case of war ('wartime control') and the transfer of this command to South Korea has been serially postponed. Latterly it was due to expire by the end of 2015, but in October 2015 the two countries postponed it *sine die* pending South Korea developing the 'core military capabilities' for such a transfer.[23]

The US's winning card in seeing off opposition to its military role in South Korea has been to play up the threat emanating from the DPRK. Demonising the North as an irrational rogue state, maintaining a 65-year-long sanctions regime against it and exaggerating the threat from its primitive nuclear weapons programme have all underpinned the US presence in South Korea, ensuring both the ROK's compliance and Congressional support for the huge budgets required.

Periodically the actions of the DPRK have indeed seemed to confirm allegations that it challenges regional security. But US inflexibility on the DPRK has been driven less by the actions of Pyongyang than by concern to maintain an internationally acceptable cover for the US military position in the South, for which the primary target is China, not North Korea.[24]

North Korea – the mouse that roars

The relationship of forces between the DPRK and South Korea has fundamentally shifted since 1953. While South Korea became one of the world's most successful economies and regional cultural draw – with South Korean brands, food, pop music and TV popular across North East Asia – North Korea is caricatured as an almost failed, oaf of a state with unpredictable and dangerous leaders. But this was not always the case.

When Korea was partitioned, the North was home to most of Korea's pre-war heavy industry and mineral resources, around 92 per cent of power generation, 90 per cent of metal and 83 per cent of chemical products.[25] It had also been spared the Japanese sabotage that reduced 1948 production in the South to 20 per cent of 1940 levels.[26] Using centralised control and Soviet aid to get the economy going again, for the two decades after the war it grew somewhat faster than the South overall. From 1950 to 1970 the DPRK's economy grew from $7 billion to $27 billion, while with slightly more than double the population South Korea grew from $16 billion to $63 billion.[27] GDP per head was roughly similar, but social provision and workers' conditions in the North were generally much better.

However, through the 1970s and 1980s the DPRK fell further and further behind as its economy stalled and South Korea's high investment and export-led growth turned it into an Asian 'tiger'. By 1990 the DPRK's GDP was $57 billion compared to the ROK's stunning $373 billion. This slippage reflected the underlying problems of the North's version of ultra-centralised economic state 'planning' – underpinned by its ideology of *Juche* or self-reliance that sought to turn US sanctions-enforced autarky into a virtue – which was incapable of propelling growth in the long run.[28] In the 1990s the collapse of support from the USSR, a series of natural disasters and tightened US sanctions exacerbated these problems leading to a devastating crash. Annual GDP growth between 1990 and 1997 averaged −4.6 per cent, and GDP fell by more than half to $25 billion, leading to widespread famine.[29]

Already by the mid-1970s the North had no serious perspective of the military reunification of the peninsula and its attempts to recruit China or the USSR to that cause also ended.[30] This did not mean the end of incidents along the tense demilitarised zone and around the disputed ocean borders – some quite bloody. In the 1980s an increasingly isolated and threatened North took a turn towards terrorist acts, including hijackings of civilian aircraft, the attempted assassination of ROK president Chun Doo-hwan in 1983 and the downing of Korean Air flight 858 in 1987. It also decided to shore up its position by speeding up its nuclear programme through investing in uranium enrichment. A nuclear capacity had been a goal since the 1960s, partly provoked by strong evidence that at that time the US had nuclear warheads stationed in South Korea, but progress had been slow.[31]

With the end of the Cold War, the US anticipated that North Korea could not survive long and a serious clash between the US and DPRK developed as the US stepped up the pressure through an international campaign against its nuclear programme. But, in June 1994, former president Carter persuaded the DPRK to back down. During what had been presented as a 'private' visit, but which was in fact at the behest of the new Clinton administration, Carter found a rapport with the ageing Kim Il-sung. They agreed points for a formal treaty, which Carter then announced, bouncing the Clinton administration into signing an 'Agreed Framework' with the DPRK in December of that year.[32] The US agreed to lift some sanctions, help the North build light water reactors and supply it with domestic fuel oil in return for ending its nuclear arms programme.[33] But the US never implemented it: Congress openly opposed it, and the Clinton administration believed the famine-struck state would collapse before the US had to make good on its side of the deal. The North, however, did suspend its weapons programme.

This did not stop Bush proclaiming the DPRK to be part of a global 'axis of evil' in his seminal post 9/11 2002 State of the Union address announcing the 'war on terror'. A year later, in a blinding display of military and technological might, Operation Iraqi Freedom overthrew Saddam Hussein. The next targets of the US war machine appeared to be Iran and the DPRK.

A troubled Pyongyang reacted with a precipitate withdrawal from the NPT and relaunched its nuclear weapons programme; which in turn has provided the justification for the US refusing to enter into talks and persuading the ROK to expand the US presence on the peninsula. This is accompanied by exaggerated and absurd claims implying the DPRK already has, or is close to attaining, the capacity to nuke the US itself.

Former US president Carter, who followed the issues closely from 1994, has convincingly argued that, if the US were willing, an agreement with the DPRK 'could be worked out … in half a day', because it would give up its nuclear weapons in return for US diplomatic recognition, a peace deal and aid for its power needs (as outlined in the 1994 Agreed Framework).[34]

South Korea and the US diverge on the DPRK

But while relations between the US and the North deteriorated, the end of the Cold War had the opposite impact on South Korea itself, which adopted a new spirit of engagement with the DPRK. For South Korea, peninsular stability had always been more important that the international strategic priorities that drive US policy, and from the 1990s this divergence became more open.[35]

The huge weakening of the DPRK as its economy first fell behind then slipped into devastating crisis in the 1990s, coupled with its military and strategic weakening due to the end of the USSR, reduced security fears in the South.[36] At the same time, within South Korea, economic success and rising living standards had led to increasing calls for democracy against the series of US-backed army regimes that had followed Syngman Rhee since 1961. This pressure built up through the 1980s and resulted in the first truly democratic election to the ROK presidency in 1988, although, due to a split in the opposition, Roh Tae-woo, the army's candidate, won.

With civilian rule the underlying cleavages in South Korean domestic politics began to emerge: 'Democracy released the constraints on the expression of conciliatory policies towards the North and politics in the South became strongly polarised between the conservatives who … insisted on the alliance with the US and those who sought reconciliation with the North.'[37] South Korea began to assert greater independence from the US on the North.[38] Under Roh the DPRK was admitted to the UN and North and South made an agreement on reconciliation and cooperation.[39]

Both the next two presidents of South Korea, Kim Young-sam (1993–97) and Kim Dae-jung (1997–2003), despite coming from the opposed right and progressive wings in South Korean politics, pursued further opening to the North. Kim Dae-jung initiated the economic and political 'Sunshine policy' towards the North, lifting restrictions on South Korean investments in the North, ending the prohibition on visits and attempting to broker an international deal to end sanctions in return for an end to its WMD programme. In 2000 he held an historic summit with Kim Jong-il in Pyongyang. His successor, Roh Moo-hyun, was elected in 2002 on a pledge to continue this approach, despite Bush having already declared the 'war on terror' targeting the DPRK.[40]

One result of this orientation to conciliation with the North was that the 1990s saw a sharp decline in border tensions and provocative actions by North Korea, creating a greater sense of stability and security on the peninsula. Therefore, when the declaration of the 'war on terror' resulted in the DPRK pulling back from international frameworks on its nuclear programme, this was viewed with alarm in South Korea, which tried to persuade Washington back into negotiations.[41]

South Korea's relations with China were already becoming closer as the synergies of their respective economic development were propelling China towards becoming its main export market, as it did in 2003. Now their common interests in calming relations with the DPRK began to draw them together in working to restore stability on the Korean peninsula.

Together they initiated the framework for 'six-party talks' involving the US, China, Russia, Japan and both Koreas, with the aim of getting the US to the table with the DPRK.[42] The US agreed to participate in the talks, which held several rounds between 2003 and 2007. But China had to drive the process and Bush constantly intervened to scupper any agreement.[43] In 2006 the DPRK was provoked into withdrawing from the talks when the US refused to release North Korean foreign assets, and when the talks resumed they were blocked again by the US claiming the DPRK had failed to fully disclose nuclear facilities. With Roh's government in Seoul increasingly working with China to keep the six-party talks going against US attempts to sabotage them, this was the worst period in ROK–US relations since 1953 and gave added impetus to the warming of ROK–China relations.[44] 'South Korea's interests seemed increasingly aligned with China's, with their common approach favouring engagement, reforms and eventual reunification.'[45]

This trend was interrupted for a period by the election of the right-wing Grand National Party's presidential candidate Lee Myung-bak in 2008 pledged to take a hard line on the North and reprioritise relations with the US.[46] Relations with China cooled, and the DPRK resumed its nuclear programme, including missile and nuclear tests in 2009 and 2013. In 2010, during US–South Korea naval exercises in disputed waters, the DPRK shelled a South Korean-held island. Also in 2010 the South Korean ship *Cheonan* sank during exercises, allegedly due to a North Korean torpedo – although this is strongly disputed.[47]

Park Geun-hye ousted Lee from the leadership of the Grand National Party (renamed Saenuri Party) and won the presidential election in 2013. Her leadership marked a resumption of the previous policy of collaboration with China on regional issues, including the North. But the deterioration in relations with the North from 2008 to 2013 under Lee, coupled with the US's 'pivot' and its associated regional military build-up, followed by a lack of decisive initiatives by Park, clearly persuaded the DPRK's new young leader Kim Jong-un to pursue an uncompromising policy on its nuclear programme and, despite China's urgings and offers of aid, continued with nuclear tests.

Despite this the pattern of closer cooperation between the ROK and China has continued, while ROK–US relations have frequently been tense over regional tactics.

The 'little tiger'

South Korea's economic take-off has been a significant factor in modifying its post-war relations in the region and with the US. As a trading partner, the US has been super-seded by China – both China's imports and exports with South Korea are double those of the US. And South Korea's most successful companies now compete with those of Japan.

The South Korean economic miracle took it from a per capita GDP similar to that of the Philippines, Malaysia, Congo and Tunisia in 1970 to a 2014 GDP per capita of $35,379, higher than Italy or New Zealand; and its economy of $1410 billion is the 13th largest in the world, greater than Spain or Sweden.[48] The foundations of this were laid in the 1960s when government policies to boost domestic savings and support industry saw some success by the end of the decade.[49] After faltering growth in the early 1970s, in 1972 the government launched a programme to boost investment, including a 200 billion won grant to the banks to support a radical reduction in interest rates and roll over existing loans. South Korea's investment levels hit an unprecedented 32 per cent of GDP in 1979, and average GDP growth was over 10 per cent.[50] Its trade expanded sharply, and its exports were aided by the increase in the exchange rate of the Japanese yen after the Nixon shock.[51] By the end of the 1990s globally successful Korean companies were beginning to challenge Japan in high-value exports such as cars and electronics.

At the same time, the impact of China's reform and opening up was also creating new economic synergies between South Korea and China. From virtually zero trade in 1990, China became its top export market in 2003, and is now its leading trading partner. In 2015 the value of South Korea's exports to China ($142.7 billion) was nearly double that of its exports to the US ($73 billion).[52] By 2012, nearly one-quarter, $51 billion, of South Korea's total stock of FDI was in China, compared to $83 billion in Europe and $35 billion in the US.[53] Chinese inward investment into South Korea also surged, jumping from $133 million to $631 million between 2013 and 2014.[54]

These developments on the economic field have a political refraction in South Korea's international and regional policy, making it wary of US initiatives aimed at China. This was seen, for example, in the ROK's rejection of the TPP; and in its refusal to join the US condemnation of China's actions in the South China Sea. It also means that Trump's threats of punitive tariffs against alleged South Korean 'unfair trading practices' and 'currency manipulation', were unwelcome but not likely to have much persuasive power over the ROK's policies on China. The ongoing shifts in South Korea's global export markets and economic relations mean there are strong internal pressures to resist US economic and political demands.

South Korea, the US and Japan

Economic factors have also played a role in why Seoul has remained distant from Tokyo, despite the desire of the US to see its two key treaty allies working in close step in the region. Growing competition with Japanese companies and Japan's long-term trade deficit with Korea ($18.1 billion in 2015) have reinforced political factors that keep the two countries apart.

Despite the closeness between their regimes during and after the Korean War, South Korea and Japan did not normalise their relations until 1965, and since civilian rule unresolved issues over the legacies of Japanese occupation have frequently been to the fore. South Koreans, alongside other victims of Japanese aggression, believe that Japan has never really accepted culpability for its past actions, not properly apologised, nor offered adequate compensation to individuals who suffered. The post Korean War military regime in South Korea was seen as tainted by apologism for Japan, as many collaborators were first protected by the US in 1945 and then integrated into Syngman Rhee's anti-communist dictatorship. The 1980s democratic movement that eventually led to civilian rule was both anti-military and anti-Japanese.[55]

The recurring bad feeling over Japan's war crimes is exacerbated by the disputed sovereignty of the Dokdo islands (known as Takeshima in Japanese and Liancourt Rocks in English) (see Map 6). Seized by Japan in 1905, they were reclaimed by Korea upon liberation in 1945; but despite South Korea having a permanent presence, including of private residents, Japan maintains its claim.[56] The ROK military commander on the Dokdo graphically illustrated the response this provokes: 'Whenever I hear Japanese saying Dokdo is Japanese territory, I feel so outraged that my blood boils. To put it in an extreme way, I want to kill them.'[57]

Despite synergies in their economic development in the 1980s and 1990s, steps to improve their bilateral relations remained very tentative. The highpoint was in 2002 when Seoul and Tokyo jointly hosted the World Cup and negotiations for a joint Free Trade Area began.[58] But in fact relations were already turning once again for the worse, with the growth of recidivist nationalism in Japan, Koizumi's visits to the Yasukuni Shrine and other evidence of revisionist interpretations of Japanese history. Attitudes to Japan in South Korea have been consistently negative. In 2015 a survey found that 78 per cent of South Koreans viewed Japan negatively, and 58 per cent saw it as a military threat, whereas only 38 per cent saw China in this way.[59]

Following Park Geun-hye's election in 2013 relations with Japan took a negative turn, with Park refusing to hold any bilateral meetings with Abe (because of his position on the 'comfort women') despite Obama's urgings, and despite making a highly success-ful state visit to China in July 2013. She even preceded an agreed three-way US, South Korea, Japan meeting in 2014 by attending an event to thank the Chinese for erecting a memorial to a Korean patriot who had assassinated a Japanese occupation official in Harbin.[60] The snub could hardly have been more pointed.

Park did eventually meet Abe in December 2015 when they negotiated what was seen as a breakthrough agreement on the issue of the 'comfort women'.[61] But South Koreans remained suspicious and distant from Abe's Japan and opposition to Park's deals – on the 'comfort women' and on sharing military information with Japan – became a theme of the crisis that beset her presidency in 2016. Moreover, despite the 2015 agreement, by December 2016 the issue was back on the agenda when, under pressure from hardline Japanese nationalists, Abe withdrew Japan's ambassador from South Korea in protest at a 'comfort women' memorial they thought was 'too close' to the Japanese embassy in Busan.

South Korea: balancing China and the US

The main trend in South Korean international relations since the 1990s has been towards collaboration with China, driven by economic ties, but also by common interests in maintaining peace and stability on the Korean peninsula. Over the same period there have been jarring notes in the ROK's relations with the US: on tactics towards the DPRK, on its attitude to Japan, and also on how far the ROK is prepared to go in antagonising China.

These shifting perspectives have not meant that South Korea's military relations with the US have been negotiable, but pressures on South Korea's governments against the role of the US in the country are deepening. Thus, while Park Geun-hye rebuked China for objecting to the US proposal to deploy the Terminal High Altitude Area Defence (THAAD) missile system in South Korea, the two main opposition candidates in 2017's elections called for it to be cancelled.[62] But despite popular opposition to the US and the weight of trade with China, the new US base will open, US wartime OpCon remains in place, and annual joint naval exercises go ahead – and are getting bigger despite regular protests from China and anger from Pyongyang. But South Korea is no longer simply a pawn of the US:

> South Korea is neither fully dependent nor fully independent. It is neither a pawn of empire nor a fully equal ally. The ROK's postwar history is a unique example of rapid economic development, modernisation, and eventual democratisation. As a consequence of this remarkable historical evolution, it has become a much more independent actor in the US-ROK alliance and in the larger international system. Nevertheless … with its security ultimately dependent upon the US … while South Korea has unquestionably enhanced its profile, it remains semi-sovereign.[63]

In other words, while the military alliance with Washington remains crucial, it is no longer the only factor in South Korea's considerations. It does not want a confrontation with China – its main economic partner – nor regional stability threatened by a revanchist Japan or an isolated DPRK. It wants a lasting solution on the Korean peninsula – by eventually absorbing the North – but it does not want constant crises or a nervy neighbour provoking border incidents. The result is:

> South Korea has to dually manage its security, which is grounded in the ROK-US alliance, and its economic wellbeing, which is dependent on the ROK-China strategic

cooperative partnership. The South Korean public tends to favour the diplomatic strategy of managing both bilateral relationships harmoniously.[64]

In this South Korea is an example of a pattern that emerges throughout this discussion of the US turn to the Asia-Pacific region. Although the US's traditional friends and allies want to retain the US military umbrella, they must weigh up the US's precise demands against both their trade and investment interests and their regional security concerns in both of which good relations with China are key. In proposing its 'new Pacific century' the US explained that updating its existing partnerships in the region to fit them to its new purpose in countering China would be the 'fulcrum for our strategic turn to the Asia-Pacific'. But these partners do not face a simple choice of the old Cold War type, but confront far more complex trade-offs between military security and economic interests. These choices will become even sharper if Trump truly implements a policy of 'America first' in trade and defence relations in the region.

These complexities have meant that the US attempt to reinforce its alliances around China's east coast have only met limited success. Apart from in Japan, there has been no zeal for confrontation with China and hopes that China might make missteps that unnerve its neighbours have foundered as it has played a considered hand in relations in the East China Sea. Nonetheless the US is relentlessly advancing its military position and jumping on any opportunity to drive a wedge between its allies and China, whether it is on Pyongyang's nuclear tests or existential fears in Taiwan.

Notes

1   T. Beal, *Crisis in Korea: America, China and the risk of war*, Pluto Press, London, 2014, ch. 1.
2   The ROK, South Korea and the South are used interchangeably, as are the DPRK, North Korea and the North.
3   B. Cumings, *The Korean War: a history*, The Modern Library, New York, 2010.
4   S. M. Jager, *Brothers at war: the unending conflict in Korea*, W.W. Norton & Co., New York, 2013, pp. 464–70.
5   G. Brazinsky, *Nation building in South Korea: Koreans, Americans and the making of a democracy*, University of North Carolina Press, Chapel Hill, 2007, p. 13.
6   U. Heo and T. Roehrig, *South Korea since 1980*, Cambridge University Press, New York, 2010, p. 78.
7   Jager, *Brothers at war*, pp. 450–5.
8   Clinton, 'Pacific century'.
9   A. Panda, 'South Korea joins the AIIB', *The Diplomat*, 28 March 2015. Available at: http://thediplomat.com/2015/03/south-korea-joins-the-aiib/at (date accessed 20 February 2017).
10 Cumings, *Korean War*, e-book location 240.
11 C. K. Armstrong, *The North Korean revolution, 1945–1950*, Cornell University Press, Ithaca, NY, and London, 2003, e-book location 1129.
12 Brazinsky, *Nation building*, pp. 14–20.
13 Armstrong, *North Korean revolution*.
14 For outbreak of the war, see Cumings, *Korean War*; I. F. Stone, *Hidden history of the Korean War*, Monthly Review Press, New York, 1969; Jager, *Brothers at war*.
15 The US has a small military presence in Thailand of c.100 personnel.
16 SIPRI 2016. 2015 figures.
17 US Bureau of Economic Analysis 2015, national income and product accounts, Table 1.5.5.

Available at: https://www.bea.gov/iTable/iTable.cfm?reqid=9&step=3&isuri=1&903=35#reqid=9 &step=3&isuri=1&903=35 (date accessed December 2015).

18 T. Capaccio and N. Gaouette, 'US adding 800 troops for South Korea citing rebalance', *Bloomberg*, 7 January 2014. Available at: https://www.bloomberg.com/news/articles/2014-01-07/u-s-adding-800-troops-for-south-korea-citing-rebalance (date accessed 20 February 2017).

19 'Inquiry into the US costs and allied contributions to support the US military presence overseas', Report of the Committee on Armed Services, US Senate, 15 April 2013.

20 B. Padden, 'Japan, South Korea brace for Trump protectionist policies', *Voice of America*, 23 January 2017. Available at: http://www.voanews.com/a/japan-south-korea-brace-trump-protectionist-poli cies/3687704.html (date accessed 20 February 2017).

21 M. R. Gordon and S-H. Choe, 'Jim Mattis seeks to soothe tensions in Japan and South Korea', *New York Times*, 5 February 2017.

22 R. B. Lee and W. Patterson, *Korean-American relations 1866–1997*, State University of New York Press, Albany, 1999, pp. 83–95.

23 S. Denney, 'South Korean politics drive OpCon transfer', *The Diplomat*, 28 October 2015. Available at: http://thediplomat.com/2014/10/south-korean-politics-drive-opcon-transfer/ (date accessed 20 February 2017).

24 Beal, *Crisis in Korea*, pp. 70–4.

25 Armstrong, *North Korean revolution*, ch. 5.

26 C. R. Frank Jr., K. S. Kim and L. E. Westphal, *Foreign trade regimes and economic development: South Korea*, National Bureau of Economic Research, Cambridge, MA. 1975, ch. 2.

27 Maddison, 2006, *World economy*, Vol. 2. GDP in 1990 Geary-Khamis dollars.

28 C. K. Armstrong, *The tyranny of the weak: North Korea and the world, 1950–92*, Cornell University Press, Ithaca, NY, and London, 2013, p. 253.

29 UNCTADStat 2016.

30 Armstrong, *Tyranny of the weak*, p. 230.

31 J. B. Lee, 'US deployment of nuclear weapons in 1950s South Korea & North Korea's nuclear devel-opment: toward denuclearisation of the Korean peninsula', *Asia Pacific Journal*, 7:8:3 (February 2009).

32 Beal, *Crisis in Korea*, p. 65.

33 Agreed Framework between US and DPRK, 21 October 1994, Geneva.

34 Beal, *Crisis in Korea*, p. 71.

35 G. W. Shin, *One alliance, two lenses: US-Korea relations in a new era*, Stanford University Press, Stanford, 2010, pp. 15–18.

36 Armstrong, *Tyranny of the weak*, ch. 7.

37 L. Buszynski, *Negotiating with North Korea: the six-party talks and the nuclear issue*, Routledge, Abingdon and New York, 2013, pp. 8–40.

38 Shin, *One alliance*, ch. 1.

39 W. K. Young, *Transforming Korean politics: democracy, reform and culture*, Routledge, London and New York, 2015, ch. 7.

40 Ibid., pp. 40–2.

41 Buszynski, *Negotiating with North Korea*, pp. 58–9.

42 Ibid.

43 E. Goh, *The struggle for order: hegemony, hierarchy, and transition in post-Cold War East Asia*, Oxford University Press, Oxford, 2013, pp. 80–96.

44 N. K. Choong, 'The Roh Moo Hyun government's policy toward North Korea', *East-West Centre working papers* No. 11, August 2005, East-West Centre, Honolulu.

45 Goh, *Struggle for order*, p. 95.

46 A. Khamidov, 'The Lee Myung-bak revolution: explaining continuity and change in South Korea's foreign policy', *SAIS US-Korea Yearbook 2008*, Johns Hopkins University, Baltimore, MD, 2008.

47 On the *Cheonan* incident, see Beal, *Crisis in Korea*.

48 IMF WEO 2016. GDP current prices & GDP per capita $PPPs.

49 Frank, Kim and Westphal, *Foreign trade regimes*, pp. 16–21.

50 UNCTADStat 2016.

51 Frank, Kim and Westphal, *Foreign trade regimes*.

52 CIA World Factbook, 2017. South Korea, economy.

53 UNCTADStat, Bilateral FDI statistics. ROK, Total stock of FDI abroad by geographical destination, 2012.

54 H. S. Toh, 'China's South Korea investment soars ahead of free trade pact', *South China Morning Post*, 15 March 2015.

55 K. J. Cooney and A. Scarborough, 'Japan and South Korea: can these two nations work together?', *Asian Affairs*, 35:3 (2008), 173–92.

56 Japan-Korea Protectorate Treaty, 17 November 1905. It was formally annexed in 1910.

57 M. Dickie and S. Mundy, 'Seoul–Tokyo: a relationship on the rocks', *Financial Times*, 15 October 2012.

58 Heo and Roehrig, *South Korea since 1980*, pp. 192–3.

59 Y. Kudo, 'Perilous perception gaps surge between Tokyo and Seoul 50 years after normalising diplomatic relations', *The Genron NPO*, press release, 30 May 2015. Available at: http://www.genron-npo.net/en/issues/archives/5191.html (date accessed 19 February 2017).

60 T. Escritt and L. Sieg, 'Obama brokers Japan, South Korea talks as Pyongyang fires missiles', *Reuters*, 26 March 2014. Available at: http://www.reuters.com/article/us-north-korea-missiles-idUSBREA2O1XM20140326 (date accessed 20 February 2017).

61 See Chapter 6.

62 S. Tiezzi, 'China warns THAAD deployment could destroy South Korea ties "in an instant"', *The Diplomat*, 25 February 2016. Available at: http://thediplomat.com/2016/02/china-warns-thaad-deployment-could-destroy-south-korea-ties-in-an-instant/ (date accessed 20 February 2017).

63 C. Work, 'South Korea: dependence in the age of OpCon', *The Diplomat*, 9 July 2014. Available at: http://thediplomat.com/2014/07/south-korea-dependence-in-the-age-of-opcon/ (date accessed 20 February 2017).

64 S. H. Han, *South Korea seeks to balance relations with China and the United States*, CFR Report, Council on Foreign Relations Press, New York City, November 2012.

Part IV

Containment from the southern seas

9

Asia's Mediterranean

From Taiwan southwards the US's strategic position relies on the support of countries along an arc around the South China Sea extending through the Philippines, Brunei, Indonesia, Malaysia to Singapore. Throughout the Cold War these long-standing friends supported the US, particularly in Vietnam, relied on it to defeat communist and other insurgencies domestically, and looked to the West for aid, trade and investment to support their weak and undeveloped economies.

But since 1989 these close relations with the US had been gradually atrophying. The US naval presence in the region had been in sharp decline from the 1990s. Political changes in the Philippines forced it to leave Subic Bay, its only remaining naval base in the South China Sea, in 1992, meaning that – unlike in the northern Pacific, where it has bases in Japan and South Korea and its own outpost in Guam – the US no longer had a permanent base in the South China Sea. Reassured by the fact that the USSR/Russia had also left its naval base in Vietnam's Cam Ranh Bay, by the new millennium the US presence in the Sea had declined to little more than regular flag-waving and routine exercises. Thus a key goal of Obama's 'pivot' was to reverse this semi-retreat from the South China Sea, particularly by securing a new local base for its naval and military forces.

Alongside this military retreat, the economic pull of the West had also weakened. The political relations between all the South East Asian states had grown closer, organised primarily though ASEAN, while trade among them and increasingly with China had become the main driver of their external economic relations. This was 'the "golden era" of China–ASEAN relations from 1991 to the end of 2010, during which bilateral cooperation flourished and trade ballooned nearly 37 times, from no more than $8 billion to $300 billion. During this period, China's GDP rose rapidly, and most South East Asian economies expanded more than five-fold.'[1]

Despite the US's declining economic weight in the region, Obama did not abandon this terrain, with his proposed TPP aimed at reorienting these economies towards the US market. But in trade the US is on weak ground vis-à-vis China; therefore, in seeking to reinstate itself as the key political and military pole in the external relations of all these countries, the US's chief tactic has been to shift priorities in regional relations from trade and development to security concerns and military balances.

In this it has sought to exploit the long-standing sovereignty disputes between China and neighbouring countries over islands in the South China Sea. These disputes had been successfully managed through a regime of compromise and interim settlements, via bilateral agreements or brokered by ASEAN, which had kept the peace. From 2010 the US intervened, particularly through the agency of the Philippines, to reject such locally negotiated compromises, instead insisting the disputes become subject to international arbitration, alleging that China's claims challenged 'freedom of navigation' through the South China Sea. This substituted a new state of tension and militarised confrontation for the relatively peaceable balance of the past. The US aim was to drive China back from its established positions in the South China Sea but also to boost regional support for its augmented military and diplomatic presence in the area through creating a sense of security threat.

This chapter and the next will look at US strategy in the South China Sea and China's responses: the unfolding and prospects for settlement of the island disputes; and the varying domestic and strategic concerns in these primarily island countries driving their responses to both the US and China.

These two chapters are linked to the one that follows on Vietnam, which has played a critical role in the shifting relation of forces in the South China Sea disputes. Alongside the Philippines, Vietnam has been the most determined in its contestation of China's claims and was where the US invested most hopes for a dramatic shift in regional alignments, aspiring to engage it in a US–Vietnam–Philippines axis to hem in China and encourage the more ambivalent states in the region to lean towards a US-led status quo for the Sea.

Assessing the US's progress, these chapters conclude that, despite its lack of a local ally with anything like the weight of Japan or South Korea and the immense geographic extension of American power involved in maintaining its presence in the region, in some respects the US 'rebalance' strategies have made more progress here to China's south than to its east.

A contested sea

The South China Sea is on the way to becoming the most contested body of water in the world, so much so that 'the map of the South China Sea is a classic document of geopolitics' (see Map 2).[2]

Half the world's maritime trade by merchant fleet tonnage passes through the Sea. In 2012, $1.2 trillion in US trade crossed the Sea, as did about 80 per cent of China's imported oil, 66 per cent of South Korea's and 60 per cent of Japan's imported energy supplies.[3] It is by far the most direct route for oil from the Gulf to East Asia and the western seaboard of the US. Lacking the US's geographical good fortune in facing both the Atlantic and the Pacific, East Asia's only maritime route to the ports of Europe is via the South China Sea and Indian Ocean to the Suez Canal. For China it is also the route for its increasingly important trade with Africa.[4] The South China Sea is 'as central to Asia as the Mediterranean is to Europe'.[5]

The only major shipping route from the South China Sea to the Indian Ocean is through the Malacca Strait, overlooked at its narrow south-eastern debouch by US-ally

Singapore. According to the US Energy Information Administration, in 2011, 12.9 million barrels of crude oil a day were passing through the Malacca Strait, 11 million of which were headed to China, Japan and South Korea. There are no alternative sea routes without extensive detours to the south.

From 1945 control of the routes through the South China Sea allowed the US to project naval power across the Pacific to the Indian Ocean and up to the Gulf. From its home bases it built a continuous military supply chain stretching from Honolulu to Guam – its westernmost territorial outpost in the Pacific and major military base – and on via Subic Bay in the Philippines, port and airbase facilities at Singapore controlling the Straits of Malacca, to its east–west-facing base deep in the Indian Ocean at British-held Diego Garcia, used for bomber operations in both the Iraq and Afghanistan wars. Were any other power able to control access through the South China Sea it would threaten this global reach. Part of the US's goal in its return to the South China Sea is to ensure that it is the US, not the PLA, navy that is the chief guarantor and therefore arbiter of the routes through the South China Sea.

The US navy's return to the Sea was extremely rapid. In 2012 the US negotiated an agreement with Australia for a US Marine base in Darwin, within striking distance of the South China Sea, which in 2016 it announced might also host US warships. In 2016 it gained agreement in principle to re-establish bases in the Philippines.[6] In the meantime, there had been an impressive increase in US naval visits; whereas in 2003 there were just six visits by US warships to ports in Malaysia, in 2012 there were over 50.[7] US navy visits to the Philippines jumped from 54 in 2011 to 88 in 2012, and 72 in just the first six months of 2013.[8] And more than 100 US planes began stopping over each month at Clark, the former US airbase in the Philippines.[9]

This growing US military presence was accompanied by a generalised rise in military spending in the region, which the US encouraged. Across South East Asia military spending increased by 13.5 per cent in 2011 to $24.5 billion, projected to rise to $40 billion by 2016.[10]

China has been forced to respond. As the South China Sea is the crucial and vulnerable route of most of its sea trade, as well as geographically its backyard – akin to the Gulf of Mexico for the US – it could not ignore this stepped-up US navy presence. Hainan Island, in the north of the Sea, was already the site of China's main underwater submarine base, and now increasingly hosts its whole southern fleet, which is being expanded with the most up-to-date ships and equipment.[11] China's 2015 defence policy proposed expanding the PLA navy's remit from coastal defence to protecting its 'maritime rights', noting that some 'external countries' are 'meddling in South China Sea affairs' including 'close-in air and sea surveillance and reconnaissance against China'.[12]

The US's South East Asian island alliances

The US's military and strategic relations with the island states around the southern perimeter of the South China Sea were put in place in the aftermath of the Second World War in the Pacific. As the US drove Japan back from its 1941–42 dramatic advance through South East Asia, it interacted with a variety of indigenous anti-Japanese resistance and independence movements with deep-rooted local support, some of which espoused wider anti-colonial or social demands. How the US negotiated these interactions was crucial to the form taken by the post-war settlements in each of these countries.[13]

Although Britain and the Netherlands (and France in Indochina) wanted to retain their substantial pre-war colonial interests in the region, the US favoured transitional forms of government brokered by the West that would secure pro-Western governments against more radical nationalist and communist oppositions.[14] This championing of 'independence' against the old colonial powers, while retaining the role of the comprador national elites, won it friends in the region. But the new regimes that the US helped bring to power had to crush independent anti-colonial movements, militant trade unionism and radical, often communist-led, guerrilla campaigns. The resulting authoritarian governments faced major social and political movements that challenged their ability to hold on to power without the backing of the US.[15] This was reinforced in the context of the Vietnam War, when a new wave of mass popular movements was radicalised by domestic economic and social failures and encouraged by the success of the resistance in Vietnam.

Chief among these quasi-independent protectorates was the US former colony, the Philippines, which won independence in 1946 – after over a million Filipinos had lost their lives in the resistance war against the Japanese. The Treaty of Manila, granting independence, secured a number of US bases on the islands, while the 1946 Bell Trade Act formalised trade relations favourable to American business. In 1951 the US-Philippines Mutual Defence Treaty brought the country into the US's Cold War alliances. It rapidly became America's most sycophantic ally in the region, sending troops to fight with the US in Korea, suppressing the communist-inspired Hukbalahap armed opposition movement that had developed from local anti-Japanese resistance forces and leading the foundation of the pro-American, anti-communist SEATO grouping of states, which the US proposed as the Asia-Pacific version of the Cold War NATO alliance in the West.[16]

The fate of radical forces in other states in the region was similar. The British colonial authorities put down a leftist revolt in Brunei in 1962 and independence was eventually granted in 1984 to an undemocratic Sultanate. Brunei remained a member of the Commonwealth, with a British base where the army trains in jungle warfare, and has a long-standing friendship treaty with the US originally signed in 1850. Indonesia saw the emergence of the largest communist party outside the USSR or China, a product of its long and fierce struggle for independence against the Dutch.[17] Eventually it was brutally suppressed, with US backing, in Suharto's 1965 de facto coup. At least 500,000 communists and their supporters were massacred and another million imprisoned. Indonesia, the fourth largest country in the world by population, became a Cold War bulwark of anti-communism in the region.[18]

In 1963 the British united its former colony of Malaya with sundry other territories to create Malaysia in 1963, after driving back a communist-led anti-colonial insurrection that rumbled on until 1989. Based on Malaya's 1957 monarchical constitution, Malaysia codified discrimination in favour of the 50 per cent Malay population, excluding the 40 per cent Chinese and 10 per cent Indian from full equality in the state. The ejection of Singapore in 1965 – on racist grounds – reduced the weight of the

Chinese population by a further 5 per cent.[19] The United Malays' National Organisation (UMNO) has held power at the centre of a variety of coalitions since Malaya's independence in 1957.

Meanwhile, in Singapore, the British colluded with Lee Kuan Yew's People's Action Party to defeat the left nationalists and communists and install an authoritarian de facto one-party regime. Lee Kuan Yew was prime minister for 30 years from 1959 to 1990 – and retained enormous influence until his death in 2015.

In the 1990s the end of the Cold War broke this holding pattern of authoritarian regimes reliant on the West against popular social discontent, often with large communist influence. Under the impact of the fall of the USSR, South East Asian communist currents – already fractured by the Sino-Soviet split – suffered disintegrating declines and became less a cause for concern. 'In the Third World, scarcely a government was left that any longer cared to call itself socialist.'[20]

Alongside this, political and economic stability in China from 1978 – notwithstanding the 1989 events – reduced concerns about insecurity emanating from the PRC. Deng Xiaoping's 'good neighbour' foreign policy, ending most Chinese support to armed oppositions in the region and resetting China's relations with the governments of its near neighbours, eliminated all but residual fears that the PRC might be seeking to overthrow them.[21] In the course of the 1990s the increasing weight of China as a trading partner also became a factor. From the mid-1980s Malaysia and Indonesia experienced strong growth rates – as had Singapore already – and, with employment and GDP per capita both rising, social stability improved. These changes reduced these countries' military dependence on the West.

In the 1990s the spread of various forms of Islamist politics became an increasingly important factor in the domestic politics of most of these countries. The majority Muslim populations of Indonesia and Malaysia and large minority in the Philippines, meant sensitivity to pro-Muslim sentiment increasingly affected not just domestic policy choices but attitudes to US policies in the Middle East and Afghanistan.[22]

And, as outlined above, the 1990s and early 2000s saw the US's overt presence and influence in the region in retreat, while that of China steadily rose.

ASEAN and US decline

The 5–6 per cent rate of 'South East Asian growth' enjoyed by these island economies (except Brunei) over the two decades to 2008 was underpinned by high investment rates and increased trade.[23] This led to growing regional economic integration, rising trade with Asian partners and China in particular, and a greater decoupling of their economic concerns from those of the US and its global institutions. The heavy-handed intervention of the IMF after the 1997–98 Asian financial crisis (discussed in more detail in Chapter 12) – when its neoliberal prescriptions of deregulation, spending cuts, reductions in social and job protection programmes and interest rate rises were seen to have deepened the crisis – strengthened the orientation of these countries to closer regional economic cooperation rather than relying on the West's global institutions.[24]

This greater economic independence was reflected in parallel political developments, particularly the trajectory of ASEAN. ASEAN was formed in 1967 by Indonesia,

Malaysia, the Philippines, Singapore and Thailand (and joined by Brunei in 1984) as a Cold War bloc united against domestic leftist insurgencies and the advance of communism.[25] However, after the end of the Cold War it sought a new role in developing greater regional integration. It was strengthened when Myanmar, Vietnam, Laos and Cambodia joined in the 1990s. Attempts to boost its economic impact by a 1993 proposal to establish an East Asian Economic Caucus involving China, South Korea and Japan were initially blocked by strong US objections.[26] But this gained renewed momentum with the onset of the Asian financial crisis, and in December 1997 an ASEAN summit meeting with China, South Korea and Japan agreed to set up the APT. By the new century ASEAN had moved beyond its origins towards becoming a framework for asserting an independent multilateral South East Asian economic and political perspective.[27]

Unhappy with the IMF response to the 1997 crisis, Japan proposed establishing new Asian financial infrastructure outside the IMF, dropping the idea when the US reacted furiously, perceiving it as 'posing a challenge to US hegemony in Asia'.[28] But in 2000 APT agreed to set up its own mechanisms to provide liquidity in the event of a future financial crisis, eventually launched formally as the Chiang Mai Initiative in 2010.[29] By 2012 this could call on funds of $120 billion in the event of a threatened default and was gradually delinking from the oversight of the IMF in approving loans.[30] An expansion of bilateral currency swaps using the major reserves of China, Japan and South Korea, again agreed outside the IMF, added to growing regional economic independence. The AIIB has further accelerated these divergences.

On trade, ASEAN lowered tariffs among member states and signed an ASEAN–China free trade agreement that came into effect in 2010, impelling an even faster pace of growth in its China trade. ASEAN has also proposed an extended free trade agreement – the Regional Comprehensive Economic Partnership (RCEP) – encompassing 16 countries: the ten members of ASEAN plus China, Australia, India, Japan, South Korea and New Zealand. There were obvious parallels between the RCEP and the TPP, as discussed below; however, unlike the TPP, the RCEP does not propose a regulatory framework that supersedes the national law of the participating countries. But despite this, the RCEP has been beset by the inevitable problems of finding agreement between 16 countries to remove tariffs, with India delaying agreement in early 2017 as it sought to postpone implementation dates for some products.

This growing regional autonomy is not just underpinned by the fact that these countries have grown stronger, but the US no longer has the attractive power that it did, and even less so since the 2008 crisis. As noted previously, expansion in US trade since 2008 has remained rather sluggish; while still a very large market it is not the most dynamic. Countries looking to their future trade relations do not see the US as necessarily offering the greatest opportunities for growth over the next decade, while trade within the region and with China looks to keep increasing. Nor is the US any longer the major source of inward investment for many of these countries. For example, US total flow of outward FDI only reached its 2007 pre-crisis peak of $394 billion in one year (2011) out of the eight following years, and fell back to $300 billion in 2015.[31] Dollar diplomacy to shore up alliances and keep out rivals is simply no longer possible today in the way it was in the past.

The Trans-Pacific Partnership

Obama's intended counterblast to this was the TPP, a preferential trade deal encompassing 12 Pacific Rim states.[32] Alongside tariff reductions the agreement also proposed stringent terms on issues from intellectual property rights to food standards.[33] The TPP was far from a traditional trade deal; it proposed extensive 'investor' rights, which could be enforced over the actions of national governments.[34] These regulations would have granted private companies the right to sue participating governments in special courts – the Investor-State Dispute Settlement (ISDS) system – the decisions of which would be binding. In US economist Jeffrey Sachs' opinion, these were '[t]he most egregious parts of the agreement', which constituted 'a dangerous and unnecessary … blow to the judicial systems of all the signatory countries'.[35] Thus the TPP was as much about setting the rules for governments on what would be deemed anti-competitive practice as it was about preferential tariff agreements.

As Obama explained: 'We have to make sure America writes the rules of the global economy. And we should do it today, while our economy is in the position of global strength. Because if we don't write the rules for trade around the world – guess what – China will.'[36] The TPP was to be the mechanism whereby the US set the rules for 'acceptable' economic policies and competitive practices. In this sense, as the *Washington Post* explained, the TPP was 'a much more central part of foreign policy and even domestic law-making' than traditional trade deals.[37] Or as *The Diplomat* put it commendably clearly, the 'TPP is as much about political and economic dominance in Asia as it is about reducing trade barriers.'[38] The *National Interest* went further, describing it as 'part of the broader American geostrategic goal of containing China'.[39] Which is why Ashton Carter, US defense secretary at the time, said it was as important as 'another aircraft carrier' in the Pacific.[40]

The fact that the TPP was conceived as a face-off with China partly explains why South Korea, Indonesia and Thailand opted out, although they also rejected the regulatory framework it proposed.[41]

While 12 countries were the initial participants in the TPP, the US and Japan were its indispensable heart, bringing together the first and third largest economies, between them comprising 30 per cent of the world economy.[42] Without the US there could have been no TPP at all, but without Japan its aspirations to set the rules for competition in Asia would have had no traction beyond its members, making it just another trade deal, of which there are over 500 globally.[43] But even with Japan, without the inclusion of China and the other larger regional economies such as India, South Korea and Indonesia, the TPP could not have been the framework for the Asia-Pacific economy as a whole. In reality the proposal was always dominated by the three G7 countries within it – the US, Japan and Canada – which together comprised 90 per cent of the GDP of the group, with a fringe of developing economies latched on. Moreover, these were neither the world's nor the region's most dynamic economies. The percentage of world GDP accounted for by the 12 TPP countries had fallen from 54 per cent in 1984 to 36.2 per cent in 2014, and their share of world merchandise trade had also been falling – from 33 per cent in 1984 to 25 per cent in 2014.[44] This contrasts with the RCEP for example, where the share of world GDP accounted for by these countries rose from 20 per cent in 1984 to 30 per cent in 2014, and their share of merchandise trade grew from 19 per cent to 31.3 per cent in the same period.[45]

The deal was deeply unpopular domestically in the US, due to the possible impact on US jobs of the tariff concessions that the US was making in order to persuade other countries, like Japan, to sign up.[46] It met huge resistance in Congress, which was intensively lobbied by labour unions and those industries most vulnerable to competition from East Asia. Abe also faced problems getting the deal through as it meant confronting the traditional base of the LDP, his own party – the disproportionately electorally strong, protected Japanese agricultural sector. Abe went ahead because: 'The TPP goes beyond just economic benefit. It's also about our security. Long-term its strategic value is "awesome".'[47] The deal was also opposed by labour movement organisations and sections of business in New Zealand and Australia in particular.

The popular opposition in the US meant all the main 2016 presidential candidates – Clinton, Sanders and Trump – came out against it. Commentators warned of the consequences of abandoning the TPP: 'America's Asian allies will feel badly let down. They have risked antagonising Beijing by signing up to the US-led initiative. Now Washington may jilt them at the altar.'[48] Nonetheless, one of Trump's first acts as president was to abandon the deal. Trump argued that in negotiating the TPP – as on other multi-partner trade deals – the US had made tariff concessions that it would not need to concede in bilateral deals where the US bargaining position would be stronger. But abandoning the TPP will significantly impact on the US's status in the region, particularly given the efforts some of the US's allies went through to get it agreed.

Indonesia – not playing the US game

Indonesia the largest of the countries bordering the South China Sea demonstrates the US's increasing difficulties in influencing the region. With a population of 250 million, and healthy economic growth since 2000, it is now the world's 16th largest economy.[49] No longer simply the weak, semi-dependency of the last century, Indonesia is becoming an influential regional force in its own right, pursuing an independent position on regional issues. It has tacked a deliberate path between the US and China, especially in the fraught South China Sea.

This is a sharp change from the relations between the US and Indonesia in the last century, when after the de facto coup in 1965–67, which brought US-backed strongman Suharto to power, it was one of the US's most important regional allies.[50] However, from the end of the Cold War, relations began to cool. The IMF's 'recovery' programme after the 1997 financial crisis was deeply unpopular as it meant spiralling unemployment, the end of food subsidies and falling wages, while a 13.5 per cent crash in Indonesia's economy made it the worst victim of the crisis. In 1999 this led to huge social upheaval and, deserted by the army and his US backers, Suharto finally fell.

Bad feeling towards the US deepened when in 1999 Clinton imposed sanctions on Indonesia because of its actions in East Timor. These were not lifted until 2005, as Bush punished it for its lukewarm support for the 'war on terror'. In the world's most populous Muslim country Bush's policy was deeply unpopular and support for it could have boosted homegrown jihadist groups which had already carried out bombings in Bali and Jakarta between 2002 and 2005.[51]

At the same time as its relations with the US faltered, Indonesia's relations with China improved, with a comprehensive 'strategic partnership' signed in 2005 setting out areas of collaboration.

Recovering from the devastating impact of the 1997 crisis Indonesia became the South China Sea's success story. With solid growth from 2000, it weathered the 2008 crisis better than neighbouring Malaysia or the Philippines and survived the impact of the 2014 fall in world commodity prices on its trade deficit, with only a small decline in growth from just over 6 per cent to around 5 per cent.[52] In this context economic synergies reinforced its closer relations with China, which edged ahead of Japan to become Indonesia's biggest trading partner in 2013 with 14.2 per cent of its total trade.[53]

Indonesia's success has been driven by high investment, hitting 35 per cent of GDP in 2012.[54] But its investment has been chiefly in manufacturing, and its infrastructure development has not kept pace, with an estimated $450 billion in infrastructure investment needed to maintain productivity and future growth.[55] This cannot be found simply from domestic savings, so Indonesia is looking to boost inward FDI, which was only about 7.6 per cent of gross fixed capital formation (GFCF) in 2015.[56] Historically Indonesia's key sources of FDI were the US, Japan, Singapore and South Korea, mainly in manufacturing and raw material extraction, but from 2008–09 China began to emerge as a significant regional investor, particularly in infrastructure. Of Indonesia's $29.27 billion in realised inward investment in 2015, $2.16 billion was Chinese, up from $141 million in 2012, and $22 billion in Chinese investment plans were approved, the highest from any country.[57]

Indonesia and China have also increasingly collaborated on defence and security. Indonesia's defence budget, targeted at counterterrorism and counterinsurgency capabilities and improving its coastal navy, grew by 53 per cent to $7.9 billion from 2011 to 2012, with a target spend of 1.5 per cent of GDP per year.[58] While still buying most of its arms from the US, its military upgrade has included joint training and exercises with Beijing and in 2012 Indonesia and China agreed to jointly develop anti-ship missiles. The US responded to this by adding loans for 24 F-16 fighter jets to a previously agreed package. But the collaboration with China offers opportunities for Indonesia to develop its own defence industries, as China has been willing to share and transfer technology and 'does not impose conditions'.[59]

Xi Jinping reinforced these relations during his state visit to Indonesia in 2013, when he became the first foreign leader to address the Indonesian parliament.[60] Xi's signature announcement was the proposal to provide Chinese investment for a 'Maritime Silk Road', improving port and other maritime infrastructure for trade from the South China Sea to the Gulf and Mediterranean. This gelled with Indonesia's own goal to build the country as a 'global maritime axis'.[61]

Fortuitously Xi's visit also underlined the changing geopolitical balances in the region, as it coincided with Obama's cancellation of a long-planned visit to the region because of his 2013 'fiscal cliff' confrontation with Congress. It was not lost on Indonesia, or the other countries of the region, that relying on good relations with the US rather than

China in the South China Sea might be a risky strategy. China did not have to 'pivot' to Asia; it is already there. By contrast, for all its promises and threats, the US could be distracted by other problems, domestic or international, and therefore absent at crucial moments.

Indonesia and Australia

Indonesia's rocky relations with its southern neighbour and major US-ally, Australia, have also created fissures where the US would rather see a seamless bloc confronting China. Their relations reached a low with the 2013 Snowden exposés showing Australia had attempted to monitor the phones of Indonesian president Yudhoyono and his wife.[62] But Indonesian suspicions that Australia treats it as a combination of upstart subordinate and potential security threat were of longer duration than that.

In the early 1960s Australia was involved, alongside the British, in an undeclared war with Indonesia to stop it integrating former British Borneo (the provinces of Sarawak and North Borneo) into Indonesia. Instead the territory was included in the British-brokered consortium state of Malaysia, which Britain and Australia considered 'safer' hands.[63]

East Timor has also blighted their relations. In 1975 Australia supported Indonesia's annexation of East Timor, but then in 1999, after international outcry against Indonesian repression, joined the US in promoting its separation from an unwilling Indonesia.

Australia's tough refugee policies under Tony Abbott led to further conflict. Australia had to apologise for multiple 'accidental' incursions into Indonesian sovereign waters in pursuit of Abbott's policy of intercepting boat-borne asylum-seekers at sea and towing them to Indonesia's maritime borders.[64] This unilateral dumping of a regional refugee problem on one poorer state incensed Indonesia.

There are positives: Indonesia is a key market for Australian cattle; Australia's influence in ASEAN and the wider region is largely brokered by Indonesian support; and Australia is Indonesia's largest source of international aid. But the relationship of forces between the neighbours is changing. Indonesia grew at twice the rate of Australia from 2005 to 2015 and this was predicted to continue. In 2005 Australia's economy was three times the size of Indonesia; in 2015 it was not even twice the size. Strategically, their roles have reversed. Rather than Indonesia looking southward to Australia as its bridge to the West, Australia now knocks on Indonesia's door to gain entry to Asia. 'Australia's dominance and transactional approach to the relationship will have to give way to a more balanced and strategic one.'[65]

All this means Indonesia has not proved fertile ground for the US's new China strategies. If anything, Indonesia has rather represented something of a Chinese bridgehead in the US drive to reinforce its relations with the South East Asian island states.

Malaysia bends to the headwinds

While China has made a particular effort towards Indonesia, for all these island states China has become a significant and growing trading partner and source of inward investment, and China has deployed this to foster closer relations with them all.

Apart from the Singapore city-state, Malaysia has been the most economically successful. Policies to boost industry and attract foreign investment, introduced by long-standing premier Mahathir bin Mohamed and his reforming finance minister, Anwar Ibrahim, saw Malaysia sustain high growth throughout the 1990s. Mahathir also rejected the IMF prescriptions following the 1997–98 Asian financial crisis, instead imposing capital controls, reducing interest rates, rescheduling loans, supporting the currency and aiding troubled industries. Despite dire warnings from the IMF to the contrary, foreign investment was maintained and growth rapidly resumed. This success meant by 2014 it had a GDP per head of $25,154 a year, double that of China ($13,224) and an even greater leap up from Indonesia and the Philippines at $10,651 and $6,974 respectively.[66]

China, with which Malaysia claims a 'special relationship' as the first ASEAN country to recognise the PRC in 1974, has become its main trading partner, with 15 per cent of total trade in 2013, ahead of Singapore (13.5 per cent) and Japan (9.7 per cent).[67] But Malaysia is highly dependent on inflows of FDI – 14 per cent of GFCF in 2014 – and the US, Japan, Singapore, South Korea and Taiwan remain its largest annual investors, holding large accumulated stocks; between 2005 and 2012 the US's cumulative FDI in Malaysia reached $5.6 billion and Japan's $10.5 billion.[68] China and Hong Kong only invested $1.3 billion in Malaysia in this period. By contrast, Malaysia's FDI in China was $6.3 billion, 20 per cent of its total FDI – an 'imbalance' that Malaysian government officials have pointedly raised.[69] In 2015 mainland China's total outward FDI reached $127.5 billion, on a par with that of Japan, and only behind the US.[70] With China now one of the world's three leading foreign investors, South East Asia is beginning to look more seriously to China not just as a trading partner, but as an investor.

As in Indonesia, China signalled its concern to build warm relations on all these issues through a 2013 visit by Xi Jinping. During the visit China announced a target of $160 billion in bilateral trade by 2017 and made a commitment to encourage investment into the underdeveloped north of the country, arrange currency swaps and promote greater military-to-military cooperation.[71] In 2015 a China General Nuclear $2.3 billion deal to acquire power assets from the debt-laden and scandal-hit Malaysian state investment fund 1MDB was announced during a visit by Li Keqiang. The higher than expected price was a major contribution to solving the 1MDB problem for the Malaysian government.

Although Malaysia has a dispute with China in the South China Sea, over the rights to the James Shoal off Borneo, it has chosen so far to deal with the issue privately and bilaterally. And it has intervened in ASEAN to prevent it adopting positions too critical of China in the South China Sea.[72]

But at the same time, Malaysia has a much stronger orientation to the West than Indonesia. American and British companies have major accumulated weight in its economy, and its historic English-speaking links make it an attractive destination for English-language call centres, such as British Telecom whose global service centre is based there. These priorities meant Malaysia put itself at the heart of the TPP. Its defence links with the West are also stronger, holding regular low-level military exercises with the US, which they plan to step up, and participating in the '5 power defence agreement' between Malaysia, Singapore, the UK, Australia and New Zealand.[73]

Although, like almost all majority Muslim countries, Malaysia opposed the 2003 Iraq War, it did support the 'war on terror' providing airspace and logistical support to the war in Afghanistan. Its provision of intelligence on al-Qaeda suspects in the country earned silence from Bush when it cracked down on internal Islamist oppositions.

Thus, Malaysia has faced in both directions, seeking to strengthen relations with the US, but working against the escalation of tensions with China on the US's chosen terrain for confrontation – the conflicting claims in the South China Sea.

Singapore – guarding the Malacca Strait

By global standards Singapore and Brunei are both very small for sovereign countries and at the same time, for rather contrasting reasons, are enclaves of privilege, enjoying Western levels of GDP per head, in an underdeveloped region.[74]

Singapore's exceptionally high savings and investment powered the city-state economy to annual growth rates of 10 per cent and higher before the Asian financial crisis, resuming growth at a 7.2 per cent average from 2002 until the 2008 global financial crisis since when it has slowed, growing only 2.9 per cent in 2014.[75] Trade between China and Singapore increased steadily from the mid-1990s and in 2013 China became its largest trading partner.[76]

But the core of Sino-Singapore economic relations is Singapore's outward FDI flows into China, which have mounted year on year. In 2013 Singapore FDI in China topped $77 billion, more than in Europe at $67 billion or the US at $7.5 billion.[77] However, when it comes to inward FDI, Singapore's main partners remain the US, the Netherlands, Japan and the UK.[78] Singapore may have substantial interests in China, but its main orientation is firmly to the West and Japan.

Singapore gains its strategic importance from its location overlooking the Malacca Strait – the only major shipping route between the South China Sea and the Indian Ocean, the unavoidable pinch point in all east-west ocean routes from the Gulf to the east coast of China, Japan or across the Pacific to the Americas. This is what led Tome Pires, the sixteenth-century Portuguese writer and trader to warn that: 'Whoever is the Lord of Malacca has his hand on the throat of Venice.' It remains as vital to east-west trade today, and the potential for it to be closed to Chinese shipping is a profound source of insecurity for China.[79]

Singapore hosts a small but strategically significant US military post and offers airbase and port maintenance facilities to the US military as required. From Spring 2012 it agreed to host a new class of US 'littoral combat ship', the first US military vessels to be permanently stationed in Singapore.[80] Singapore spends 3.7 per cent of GDP on arms, with its defence spending per head higher than all except the UAE, the US and Israel.[81]

Singapore has encouraged a more active US presence in the region and supported its hard line on the South China Sea. But Singapore wants the US in the mix to ensure regional stability, not to ramp up confrontation with China. It sees a US counterweight as insurance against China becoming too assertive; but an actual falling out with China would be bad for trade and business.

Brunei – wealth without growth

Brunei's economy is based entirely on oil and gas – it is the world's fourth largest supplier of natural gas. This fossil fuel wealth in such a tiny country has delivered GDP per capita that was fourth highest in the world, $73,233 in 2014.[82] But other sectors of its economy are undeveloped; its domestic investment rate has been low and its growth anaemic, barely topping an average of 1 per cent for the last 10 years.[83] While the Sultanate's exports to China are minimal – 0.8 per cent or $66 million in 2013 – its imports from China – 22 per cent or $2 billion of total imports – make it Brunei's third largest trading partner overall.[84] But Brunei still looks primarily to Japan for investment in its oil and gas fields, not least because that avoids having to negotiate around awkward issues of contested sovereignty and rights.

In recent years Brunei's old Cold War hostility to China has given way to increasing collaboration. And, like its neighbours Indonesia and Malaysia, Brunei has kept disagreement over claims in the South China Sea out of the fraught arena of international disputation involving the US, preferring to deal with any disputes with China quietly and bilaterally.

Facing two ways

Malaysia, Singapore, Brunei and Indonesia all count themselves as first and foremost allies and partners of the West. But if Trump pursued his threat to ramp up the conflict with China in the South China Sea, and if an attempted new Cold War against China became an international reality, it is not clear what position any of these states would take. Despite the growing role of Chinese commerce in the region, at present the global influence of the US together with its Western and Japanese allies can still exert considerable leverage. On the other hand, the mounting weight of China in their trade, investment and development strategies means that, unless faced with an unavoidable choice, they would rather face both ways. So, for example, while Malaysia and Singapore were at the centre of the TPP negotiations, they also pushed ahead on the RCEP that has China at the centre. They all strongly encouraged the renewed American attention to the area and have enhanced their own military spending. But at the same time they have encouraged Chinese engagement with ASEAN.

However, as will be discussed in the next chapter, despite these countries' cautious balancing between the US and China, in particular making efforts to prevent the disputes in the South China Sea becoming a full-blown regional confrontation with China, Obama's 'pivot to Asia' did find a focus and an alleged justification in these disputes. In this the US was especially helped by its ex-colony, the Philippines, which enthusiastically took up the charge that China is 'bullying' and aggressive in pursuit of its claims in the Sea. While this was not much welcomed by its other neighbours, it remains the case that as the US steps up the pressure to push back at China all these countries will face increasingly difficult choices.

Notes

1 Y. Fu and S. C. Wu, 'South China Sea: how we got to this stage', *The National Interest*, 9 May 2016. Available at: http://nationalinterest.org/feature/south-china-sea-how-we-got-stage-16118 (date accessed 17 February 2017).

2 Kaplan, *Asia's cauldron*, p. 170.

3 Ibid., p. 9.

4 China is Africa's largest trading partner. In 2013 Chinese (including Hong Kong) trade with Africa was $156 billion. Other East Asian trade with Africa via the Malacca Strait included Japan's c.$25.3 billion and South Korea's $22 billion. US-Africa trade was $72.1 billion. Source: UNCTADStat and IMF WEO 2016.

5 Kaplan, *Asia's cauldron*, p. 71.

6 S. Robson, 'US buildup in Philippines raises stakes in region', *Stars and Stripes*, 3 February 2016. Available at: https://www.stripes.com/news/us-buildup-in-philippines-raises-stakes-in-region-1.3919 12#.WK7r02SLTUo (date accessed 17 February 2017).

7 Kaplan, *Asia's cauldron*, p. 88.

8 M. Mogato, 'Manila plans air, naval bases at Subic with access for US, officials say', *Reuters*, 27 June 2013. Available at: http://www.reuters.com/article/us-philippines-usa-idUSBRE95P1EP20130626 (date accessed 17 February 2017).

9 J. O'Callaghan and M. Mogato, 'The US military pivot to Asia: when bases are not bases', *Reuters*, 14 November 2012. Available at: http://www.reuters.com/article/us-usa-asia-military-idUS BRE8AD05Y20121114 (date accessed 17 February 2017).

10 'Shopping spree', *The Economist*, 24 March 2012.

11 D. McDonough, 'Hainan Island and China's South Sea Fleet', *The Strategist*, 19 March 2015. Available at: https://www.aspistrategist.org.au/hainan-island-and-chinas-south-sea-fleet/ (date accessed 17 February 2017)

12 China's military strategy, State Council information office of the PRC, May 2015, Beijing.

13 Anderson, 'Imperium', p. 58.

14 Kolko, *Politics of war*, pp. 275–6.

15 G. Kolko, *Century of war: politics, conflicts and society since 1945*, The New Press, New York, 1994, pp. 437–41.

16 Ibid., pp. 351–64.

17 For Indonesian independence, see R. J. McMahon, *Colonialism and Cold War: the United States and the struggle for Indonesian independence, 1945–49*, Cornell University Press, Ithaca, NY, 1971.

18 Anderson, 'Imperium', pp. 59–60.

19 M. Jones, *Conflict and confrontation in South East Asia 1961–65: Britain, the United States and the creation of Malaysia*, Cambridge University Press, Cambridge, 2002.

20 Anderson, 'Imperium', p. 84.

21 S. L. Ye, *China's regional policy in East Asia and its characteristics*, China Policy Institute, Discussion paper 66, University of Nottingham, 2010.

22 C. Rubenstein, 'The role of Islam in contemporary South East Asian politics', *Jerusalem Letter no. 436*, Jerusalem Centre for Public Affairs, 15 August 2000.

23 UNCTADStat 2016. GDP annual growth rates. The Philippines' average growth rate was slower at just over 4 per cent in the period.

24 Stiglitz, *Globalisation*.

25 C. Chari (ed.), *War, peace and hegemony in a globalised world*, Routledge, Abingdon, 2008, pp. 175–88.

26 M. Richardson, 'Japan straddles fence on issue of East Asia caucus', *New York Times*, 26 July 1994.

27 Chari, *War, peace and hegemony*, ch. 15.

28 P. Lipcsy, 'Japan's Asian Monetary Fund proposal', *Stanford Journal of East Asian Affairs*, 3:1 (2003), 93–104.

29 Ibid.

30 C. Sussangkarn, 'Prevention and resolution of foreign exchange liquidity crises in East Asia', *Asian Development Bank Institute*, working paper 363, June 2012.

31 UNCTADStat 2016, annual inward and outward FDI flows.

32 The TPP founding countries: US, Australia, Brunei, Canada, Chile, Japan, Malaysia, Mexico, New Zealand, Peru, Singapore and Vietnam.

33 I. F. Fergusson, M. A. McMinimy and B. R. Williams, 'The Trans-Pacific Partnership (TPP): negotiations and issues for Congress', Congressional Research Service, Report R42694, 20 March 2015.

34 J. D. Sachs, 'TPP is too flawed for a simple 'yes' vote', *Boston Globe*, 8 November 2015.

35 Ibid.

36 Remarks by the president on trade, The White House, Office of the press secretary, 8 May 2015.

37 L. DePillis, 'Everything you need to know about the Trans Pacific Partnership', *Washington Post*, 11 December 2013.

38 M. Maidan, 'The TPP and China: the elephant that wasn't in the room', *The Diplomat*, 15 October 2015. Available at: http://thediplomat.com/2015/10/the-tpp-and-china-the-elephant-that-wasnt-in-the-room/ (date accessed 17 February 2017).

39 G.C. Chang, 'TPP vs RCEP: America and China battle for control of Pacific trade', *The National Interest*, 6 October 2015. Available at: http://nationalinterest.org/feature/tpp-vs-rcep-america-china-battle-control-pacific-trade-14021 (date accessed 17 February 2017).

40 H. Cooper, 'US defence secretary supports trade deal with Asia', *New York Times*, 6 April 2015.

41 D. Kirk, 'China, Russia, US: looming face-off in Asia over TPP with Korea at the vortex', *Forbes Asia*, 29 September 2015. Available at: http://www.forbes.com/sites/donaldkirk/2015/09/29/china-russia-u-s-face-off-in-asia-over-tpp-with-korea-at-the-vortex/#4eecefe92e88 (date accessed 17 February 2017).

42 IMF WEO 2015. GDP of TPP member countries in 2014, nominal $s.

43 M. K. Griffith, R. Steinberg and J. Zysman, 'Great power politics in a global economy: origins and consequences of the TPP and TTIP', Paper for conference: Unpacking the Transatlantic Trade and Investment Partnership (TTIP) Negotiations, *Université Libre de Bruxelles*, 17 October 2015.

44 J. Ross, 'The TPP – a slow growth Pacific club, 4 December 2015, available at: http://www.china.org.cn/opinion/2015–11/14/content_37056796.htm (date accessed 20 October 2016).

45 World Bank indicators, 2016. The calculation for 1984 does not include Cambodia, Myanmar and Vietnam as the data is not available, but their share would have amounted to less than 0.2 per cent.

46 G. Sargent, 'The Trans-Pacific Partnership is in trouble thanks to grassroots pressure', *Washington Post*, 13 February 2014.

47 E. Cheng, 'Japan's Abe to Congress: TPP's value is "awesome"', *CNBC*, 29 April 2015. Available at: http://www.cnbc.com/2015/04/29/japans-abe-to-congress-tpps-value-is-awesome.html (date accessed 21 May 2015).

48 G. Rachman, 'America's Pacific pivot is sinking', *Financial Times*, 19 September 2016.

49 IMF WEO, 2015. GDP in $s nominal rates, 2014 $888.5 billion.

50 W. S. Simon and E. Goh (eds), *China, the United States, and South-East Asia: contending perspectives on politics, security, and economics*, Routledge, Abingdon, 2008, p. 128.

51 Ibid.

52 UNCTADStat 2016, GDP annual growth rates.

53 CIA World Factbook 2015. Indonesia export and import partners 2013.

54 World Bank indicators, 2016, GFCF as percentage of GDP.

55 M. Henstridge, S. De and M. Jakobsen, 'Growth in Indonesia: is it sustainable? Drivers of recent eco-
    nomic growth', Oxford Policy Management, Client Report, March 2013.

56 Calculated from UNCTADStat 2016, GFCF and FDI inflows in current $: GFCF $289 billion; FDI
    inflow $22 billion.

57 National Coordinating Agency for Investment (BKPM), Indonesia, www.bkpm.go.id (date accessed
    20 October 2016).

58 T. Moss, 'Indonesia military powers up', *The Diplomat*, 18 January 2012. Available at: http://thedip
    lomat.com/2012/01/indonesia-military-powers-up/ (date accessed 17 February 2017).

59 Z. Hussain, 'Indonesia hikes defence budget, forges close ties with Beijing and Washington', *Straits
    Times*, 24 August 2012.

60 'China's Xi Jinping addresses Indonesia parliament', *BBC News*, 3 October 2013. Available at http://
    www.bbc.co.uk/news/world-asia-24361172 (date accessed 17 February 2017).

61 V. Shekhar and J. C. Liow, 'Indonesia as a maritime power: Jokowi's vision, strategies, and obsta-
    cles ahead', *Brookings*, November 2014. Available at: https://www.brookings.edu/articles/indone-
    sia-as-a-maritime-power-jokowis-vision-strategies-and-obstacles-ahead/ (date accessed 17 February
    2017).

62 E. MacAskill and L. Taylor, 'Australia's spy agencies targeted Indonesian president's mobile phone',
    The Guardian, 18 November 2013.

63 D. Easter, *Britain and the confrontation with Indonesia, 1960–66*, I.B.Tauris, New York, 2004.

64 L. Taylor and agencies, 'Indonesia demands suspension of Australia's asylum operations', *The
    Guardian*, 17 January 2014.

65 A. L. Halimi, 'The regional implications of Indonesia's rise', *The Diplomat*, 10 April 2014. Available
    at: http://thediplomat.com/2014/04/the-regional-implications-of-indonesias-rise/ (date accessed
    17 February 2017).

66 IMF WEO, 2015. GDP per capita, $ppp.

67 CIA World Factbook, 2015. Malaysia export and import partners 2013.

68 ASEAN statistical yearbook 2013, ch.VI, Foreign Direct Investment.

69 'More Chinese investment to Malaysia expected', *China Daily (Europe)*, 3 October 2013.

70 UNCTADStat 2016. Annual FDI outflows.

71 'President Xi Jinping holds talks with prime minister Najib Razak of Malaysia, deciding to establish
    China-Malaysia comprehensive strategic partnership', Ministry of Foreign Affairs of PRC, News
    report, 4 October 2013. Available at: http://www.fmprc.gov.cn/mfa_eng/topics_665678/xjpfwynmlx-
    ycx21apec_665682/t1085197.shtml (date accessed 7 February 2017).

72 J. Vasagar, 'ASEAN show of unity over South China Sea collapses', *Financial Times*, 15 June
    2016.

73 Announcement by Defence Minister Datuk Seri Hishammuddin Tun Hussein and US Secretary of
    Defence Chuck Hagel on 19 January 2014.

74 World Population prospects; the 2015 revision, United Nations department of economic and social
    affairs, estimated population 2016: Brunei 428,874; Singapore 5,696,506.

75 UNCTADStat 2016.

76 Government of Singapore, Department of Statistics. Trade with major trading partners 2013.

77 Ibid. Singapore's direct investment abroad by country/region 2004–13 (S$ converted to US$ at May
    2015 rates).

78 Ibid. FDI in Singapore by country/region 2004–13.

79 See Chapter 4.

80 A. Yee, 'US deployment of littoral combat ships to Singapore', *East Asia Forum*, 21 July 2011.

81 SIPRI 2011 figures.

82 IMF WEO, 2015. GDP per capita, $ppp.

83 UNCTADStat 2016.

84 European Commission Directorate General for Trade, Brunei trade statistics, trade with world, 10 April 2015.

10

Turbulent seas

While its neighbours tried to keep the peace in the region, the Philippines enthusiastically threw itself behind Obama's new agenda in Asia, abrasively taking the offensive against China in the South China Sea. Aquino, then president of the Philippines, went so far as to claim that China was behaving like Nazi Germany in 1938 when it seized the Sudetenland from Czechoslovakia.[1]

But it was not just a matter of name-calling. The Philippines' interventions against China in the South China Sea from 2010 played a key role in turning the Sea into a global security hotspot where China has found itself staring down the barrels of US naval guns. The Philippines' 2013 decision to refer its dispute with China to the Arbitration Court at The Hague under the UN Convention on the Law of the Sea (UNCLOS) internationalised the conflict. This step abruptly broke with the combination of bilateral and ASEAN-brokered negotiations that had successfully regulated the situation in the Sea since the 1990s and provided a timely raison d'être for the involvement of the US navy as the alleged 'neutral' defender of a supranational quasi-legal interest in the issues.[2]

Given the public silence of other parties to the disputes – Malaysia, Indonesia and Brunei – the Philippines became the US's main agency in internationalising the disputes and justifying its heightened naval activity in the Sea. Even Vietnam, the only other claimant that has periodically openly contested China in the South China Sea, did not support the action in the Arbitration Court – although it was not above using the threat to do so to gain leverage over China.

Thus, it was entirely down to the Philippines that the US was able to strike a significant blow against China when in July 2016 the UN Arbitration Court ruled comprehensively against China's position on the South China Sea. The ruling was intended to be the launch pad for a campaign dubbing China an 'international outlaw', coupled with stepped-up US navy patrols in the South China Sea involving more regional partners. But instead, not only was the response to the UNCLOS ruling from countries in the region distinctly underwhelming, but almost immediately US relations with the Philippines itself began to disintegrate with the June 2016 inauguration of Duterte as the new Philippine president, signalling an unexpectedly sharp shift in foreign policy away from the US.[3]

This turn by the Philippines rather brutally underlined that even for a country with a history of ultra-dependence on the US market, China is an increasingly compelling partner. Having taken on the mantle of opposition to China in 2010, by mid-2016 even the Philippines was throwing it off in favour of a better accommodation with the PRC.

The US's semi-colony

The Philippines' dependent relationship with the US began when it was ceded to the US by Spain in 1898 for a payment of $20 million after defeat in the Spanish-American War. Once the US had finally subdued the Philippine independence movement in 1901, it became its only formal colony.[4] The Philippines' economy was reliant on the export of cash crops (hemp, sugar, tobacco, coconut) and some mined products; by 1934, 86 per cent of Philippine exports were to the US, and 66 per cent of its imports came from it.[5] But resistance to harsh working conditions in the countryside and pro-independence sentiment created constant problems for US rule, which was also controversial at home, and in 1934 it agreed to a ten-year transition to independence, delayed to 1946 by the Japanese occupation from 1942.

However, American interests remained protected. Treaties ensured the Philippines' economic subordination to its former colonial ruler. As part of the terms for American cash for post-war reconstruction the Bell Trade Act prohibited the Philippines from raising tariffs on US imports; the peso was pegged to the dollar at an inflated rate; and US citizens were given parity with Filipinos in access to raw materials and public services.[6]

It was entirely militarily dependent on the US, held together through the post-war period by a series of autocratic regimes that could only fight off repeated insurgencies and breakaway movements with the support of the US. Two major US bases – Clark air base and Subic Bay naval base – served as the centre for the US's regional presence and substituted for the Philippines' undeveloped armed forces. This was vital to the defeat of the widespread Huk rebellion led by former anti-Japanese resistance fighters in the 1950s; confronting later guerrilla and insurgent activities of the communist New Peoples' Army; and dealing with long-standing armed struggles by Muslim organisations in the south of the country (primarily Mindanao).[7]

These close relations with the US hit a blip in the mid-1980s, when US-backed strongman president Ferdinand Marcos was overthrown. Marcos, who was in power from 1965 to 1986, was one of the Cold War dictators that fell into the Americans' category of 'our son-of-a-bitch'.[8] Despite martial law from 1972 to 1981, Marcos was a major recipient of both US military and economic aid and World Bank support.[9] This period initially saw some improved growth in the Philippine economy but in the early 1980s this stalled. In both 1984 and 1985 GDP growth collapsed to −7.3 per cent.[10] Economic contraction combined with rampant corruption by Marcos and his cronies, in the context of grotesque inequality, abject poverty and political repression, created a powerful opposition movement led by Benigno Aquino Jnr.[11] Following his assassination in 1983, popular anger led to the ousting of Marcos in what was dubbed the Peoples' Power Revolution.[12] The US changed sides and, in 1986, elections brought Aquino's widow, Corazon, to the presidency.

The period of US-backed martial law had strengthened nationalist anti-American feeling, reinforced by accusations of rapes and other abuses by US marines stationed in the country. The end of the Cold War appeared to dissolve the need for US bases and in 1991 the Philippines' Congress voted not to renew the US leases on Clark and Subic Bay prohibiting all permanent foreign troop deployment on Philippine soil.[13] But this strike for independence from the US proved short-lived. Not only did the US continue to play a key role in the Philippines' economy, but the 1951 Mutual Defence Treaty was maintained and the Philippines still needed US support against its internal oppositions:

> The Philippines is less a country than a ramshackle empire ruled from Luzon. Indeed, the fact that despite being an archipelagic nation, the Philippine army is three times the size of its navy in manpower, proves just how internally insecure this country really is. Thus, ultimately … the Philippines has no choice … but to seek the patronage of the United States.[14]

Within a few years the Philippines was reaching out for help on security issues from the US. In 1999 a new agreement set a framework for US forces to temporarily station on the islands and for renewed defence cooperation. The Philippines became one of the first countries to sign up to Bush's post-9/11 'war on terror', supported the invasion of Afghanistan, and was one of only a handful of countries to endorse the 2003 invasion of Iraq, sending a small Filipino force and allowing the US to fly through its airspace and use Clark and Subic Bay for Iraq operations.[15] This reinvigoration of Philippines–US relations was partly driven by a new upsurge in Muslim insurgency for which it needed US support. Its endorsement of the 'war on terror' brought the Philippines another tranche of US military and economic aid, and the resumption of joint military exercises aimed at dealing with these internal oppositions.[16] In 2003 President Bush designated the Philippines as a 'major non-NATO ally'.

Announcing the 'pivot to Asia' in 2010, the US had made clear that the existing treaty allies of the US, including especially the Philippines, would be at its heart. In November 2011, the Manila Declaration, a statement of economic and military collaboration reinforcing the US–Philippines Mutual Defence Treaty on its 60th anniversary, was symbolically signed aboard the USS *Fitzgerald* in Manila Bay.

The price for US support was the Philippines role in buttressing a tough US strategy towards China on the disputes in the South China Sea, supporting US rhetoric against China and endorsing a stepped-up US presence in the Sea.

Internationalising the island disputes

The numerous atolls and rocky outcrops of the South China Sea, which are mainly semi- or uninhabited and some not even always above water, have become a storm centre between the US and China, with the US using the disputes as an excuse for a radical upscale in its naval presence and a variety of provocative actions aimed at China (see Map 7).

The US unveiled its intentions in the South China Sea in a 2010 speech by secretary of state Hillary Clinton at the annual ASEAN summit in Hanoi.[17] This speech declared that

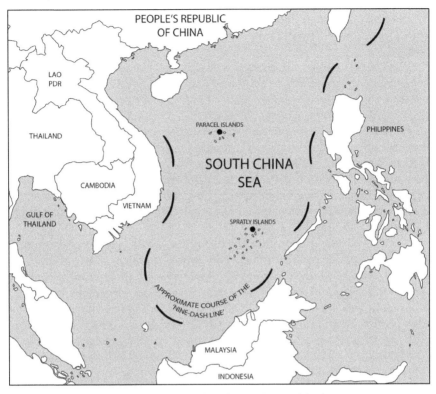

Map 7 *The South China Sea and 'nine-dash line'*

the South China Sea was in the US sphere of 'national interest' and proposed the US as 'mediator' for the sovereignty disputes in the Sea, which, until that point, had received very little attention outside the region.[18] The speech signalled that the issue of the islands would no longer be left in the hands of the actual protagonists, but become a tool in the US's campaign to align forces against China. China had no illusions on this point; the Chinese official media responded:

> The US … efforts to internationalise the disputes will only deal a blow to the peace prevailing in the South China Sea and run counter to the consensus reached among the disputing countries not to internationalise them … only Asians should lead the process to resolve regional issues.[19]

An article in *Xinhua* was even more blunt:

> In the 19th century, the British Empire adopted the tactics of 'divide and rule' … Nowadays, the United States is resorting to the same old trick … By claiming US national interests in the South China Sea, Washington intends to expand its involvement in an ocean area tens of thousands of miles away from America … to maintain America's 'long-held sway' in the western Pacific Ocean.[20]

The result of Clinton's intervention was seen almost immediately in a sequence of clashes with China over rights in the Sea, primarily involving the Philippines, but also Vietnam.

The conflicts turn on the disputed sovereignty over three main island groups – known in English as the Spratlys, Paracels and Scarborough Shoal – which are contested between China, Taiwan, the Philippines, Vietnam, Malaysia and Brunei.[21] They lie scattered across fertile fishing grounds, above a seabed containing fossil fuels and adjacent to the world's busiest sea lanes. Control of these islands may well turn out to yield economic riches, but they certainly offer maritime security; it is the latter that is China's predominant concern. Securing the safety of its merchant shipping across the Sea has been made more urgent by Pentagon discussions on how the US might blockade or close these routes in the event of conflict.[22] Such fears were deepened by Tillerson's confirmation hearing threat that the US navy might be deployed to cut China off from the islets that it occupies.[23]

China's claim to sovereignty over all three of these archipelagos fundamentally rests on historical evidence going back to the Han dynasty. But more recently its claim was accepted by the Allied powers in mid-1945 agreements with China about restitution of lands seized by Japan. However, in the event, China was not represented at the 1951 San Francisco peace conference that finalised the treaty with Japan, and the USSR withdrew from the negotiations for this among other reasons. As a result none of China's claims against Japan were included in the final treaty. Protesting this in the summer of 1951, Zhou Enlai, on behalf of the PRC, noted that following Japan's renunciation of all rights, title and claim to Spratlys, the treaty should have recognised that 'the Chinese government of the day had taken over those islands' and the PRC's rightful sovereignty should 'remain intact'.[24] The following year the treaty signed between Japan and the ROC government did refer to the fact that Japan surrendered Formosa (Taiwan), the Pescadores, the Paracels and Spratlys, without saying to whom.[25]

The area in the South China Sea that had been handed back to China by defeated Japan was summarised on what is known as the 'nine-dash line' map, drawn up by the GMD in 1947 to show where, as agreed with the Allied command, Japan had surrendered directly to China in 1945 (see Map 7).[26] Taipei thus makes its own claim to the disputed area based on the same evidence as Beijing. As with the Diaoyu, Taiwan's claim reinforces the PRC's position. Neither the map nor the extent of China's claimed jurisdiction in the South China Sea were seriously challenged until the 1970s, including by the US which was fully aware of the extent of China's claim in the Sea.[27] Indeed, throughout this period the US applied to the ROC government in Taiwan for permission to carry out mapping and nautical surveys off the islands.[28]

In 1956, in a somewhat comical episode, a Filipino adventurer named Cloma tried to claim the Spratlys with the aim of opening a guano farming and fish-canning operation, renaming them 'Freedomland' and attempting, unsuccessfully, to appeal to the UN against China. But the only significant permanent presence in the Spratlys before the 1970s was Taiwan, which had a garrison on the largest island, Taiping.[29]

From the 1970s various contesting claims to the islands began to be raised by countries bordering the sea, particularly after the signing of the UNCLOS rules in 1982 that extended the maritime rights that accrue to coastal or island territory. These various claims were subsequently advanced by attrition, primarily through garrisoning or building. By 2005, of the various features in the Spratlys, the PRC occupied or controlled eight, the ROC two, the Philippines ten, Vietnam twenty-six and Malaysia five plus one artificial island.[30]

After a series of clashes in the 1990s ASEAN took the initiative to engage all those with disputed claims in a mutual Declaration on the Conduct of Parties in the South China Sea.[31] The initial declaration, signed by ASEAN members and China in 2002, laid out a consensual framework on how to proceed on matters like seabed exploration and development of infrastructure pending future agreement on sovereignty.

This approach was in line with the policy Deng had set out in the 1980s on how China would handle the disputes. As with Japan on the Diaoyu, Deng proposed to shelf the sovereignty disputes for the 'wisdom of future generations', saying to president Corazon Aquino: 'we can set aside this issue for the time being and take the approach of pursuing joint development'; and not let 'this issue stand in the way of China's friendship with the Philippines and with other countries'.[32] This combination of China's policy of restraint and ASEAN's role in setting a compromise framework had kept conflicts in the Sea at bay for nearly 20 years.

In its actions on these disputed islands, China can with justice argue that it has done no more than others, and that others were first to breach the 2002 ASEAN Declaration – for example on seabed exploration – with China only following suit after extensive efforts to negotiate.[33] For example, in the media furore that met the news that China was building an airstrip on Fiery Cross Reef in May 2015, it was rarely mentioned that Taiwan had long had an airstrip on Taiping, Malaysia on Swallow Reef, Vietnam on Spratly Island and the Philippines on Thitu. As China said: 'We have simply repeated what everybody else was already doing.'[34]

While all the countries neighbouring the Sea – including China – objected to various steps others had taken, the issues had not become the overriding matter in their mutual relations. As Fu Ying, chair of the Foreign Affairs committee of the People's Congress put it: 'The disputes … spilled from those islands and reefs … but without spinning out of control.'[35]

The US's new policy for the region blew a hole in this carefully constructed balance. While the US continued to profess a neutral position on the disputed sovereignty of these reefs and islands, in reality it progressively hardened its opposition to China's claims.[36] From the 2010 ASEAN meeting onwards it attempted to create a US-led consortium of neighbouring countries – preferably with ASEAN itself – that formally declared the Chinese activity in the Sea a threat to regional stability and assenting to US naval and military initiatives 'countering' it.[37] In this context, progress towards a more detailed ASEAN-led agreement on conduct in the Sea stalled.

But it was the Philippines that took the decisive steps that escalated the disputes with China. There had been an earlier flare-up between China and the Philippines in 1995 over Mischief Reef in the Spratlys, but this had been rapidly calmed.[38] But, following Clinton's 2010 Hanoi speech, the Philippines went on the offensive, inviting foreign companies to bid for oil exploration rights in a disputed area, ending the de facto agreement to only take such steps on the basis of joint development agreements with any other claimants.[39] Chinese responded with augmented surveillance around the contested isles.

Then, in April 2012, in an act of inevitable escalation, the Philippines sent its navy to apprehend Chinese fishing vessels working in the Scarborough Shoal. Chinese coast-guards easily prevented this as the Philippines had only one recommissioned warship. But from then on the PRC maintained a garrison on the Shoal to protect its fishing fleet – this is what Aquino likened to the seizure of the Sudetenland. It was later the same year that the US and Philippines first announced in principle agreement for a semi-permanent return of the US navy to Filipino bases.[40] And the annual US and Philippines military exercises, rather than focusing as they usually did on counterinsurgency, took place close to the disputed Spratly Islands and involved mock beach landings.[41]

However the key step in internationalising the disputes was persuading the Philippines to break with the regime of ASEAN-led negotiations and bilateral agree-ments and instead refer its issues to the Arbitration Court at The Hague. This step, in 2013, decisively changed the nature of the conflict, allowing the US to present the issues in the Sea as a legitimate matter of international concern, providing a justification for the US naval build-up, with provocative patrols and flights around Chinese installations.[42] Having stirred up the conflicts by declaring its 'interest', the US now presented itself as crucial to maintaining stability through a more hefty US naval and diplomatic presence in the region.

Using UNCLOS against China

Agreed in 1982, UNCLOS had introduced a 'revolutionary change in the law of the sea'.[43] Previously maritime states had sovereign authority solely over their territorial waters, defined as 12 nautical miles (22 km) from their coasts; but UNCLOS additionally provided for extensive 'exclusive economic zones' (EEZs) giving rights to explore and exploit waters and seabed 200 nautical miles out from land, including from small islands. This new entitlement meant that, in the 1980s and 1990s, the atrophied island remnants of the old colonial empires allowed them to define vast tracts of the world's oceans as their 'exclusive economic zones'. For example, the combined EEZ of the Falklands, South Georgia and the Sandwich Islands delivers the UK rights over 2 million km^2 of the South Atlantic, almost three times the EEZ of the UK itself (774,000 km^2).[44] In the Pacific, excluding the US west coast, Alaska and the Aleutian Island chain, the US EEZ around its other island territories amounts to 5.8 million km^2. This is worth remembering when considering China's claims in the South China Sea, which is not a far-flung outpost of former empire, but its own backyard; and even if China's claims were accepted in full the area covered would be tiny compared to these.

UNCLOS itself does not include rules whereby to determine sovereignty over any land; but this was not what the Arbitration Court was asked to determine. Instead the Philippines case turned on whether the various disputed islets constitute 'land' as defined by UNCLOS at all; because if they were not 'land' then they were just 'sea features' that fell within the 200 nautical mile EEZs of the Philippines. Hillary Clinton first hinted at this approach to the issue in her game-changing Hanoi speech when she said: 'legitimate claims to maritime space in the South China Sea should be derived solely from legitimate claims to land features.' This was echoed in testimony to Congress by Danny Russel, assistant secretary of state: 'Any Chinese claim to maritime rights not based on claimed land features would be inconsistent with international law.'[45] Before this the various regional claimants had not questioned that the islets did indeed, in the main, constitute land and therefore sovereignty would deliver not just control of the islands but EEZs around them. The Philippines' case moved the goalposts.

From the moment that the Philippines submitted its case, the US began a sustained campaign that China must be bound by the outcome. Danny Russel spelled this out: 'We will come down forcefully when it comes to following the rules ... both China and the Philippines are obligated to follow the decision whether they like it or not.'[46] Obama echoed this saying China 'must adhere to the same rules as other nations'.[47] This was all somewhat ironic, given that the US remains one of a handful of nations that has not actually signed up to UNCLOS – while using its definitions to claim exclusive rights over vast areas of the Pacific Ocean. As with the International Criminal Court, the US welcomes rulings that apply to others while refusing to submit to such itself. China did sign up to UNCLOS in 1996, with a statement clarifying this was premised on acceptance of its claim in the South China Sea.[48]

China described the court case as 'a political provocation under the cloak of law' and suggested, with good reason, that it was entirely orchestrated by the US.[49] From the outset China rejected the authority of The Hague court to resolve the matter, and said it would not be bound by its findings; a position that was 'clear and explicit, and will not change'.[50] In this China was on strong legal grounds, because: 'All concede that China was within its legal rights under Article 298 of UNCLOS ... in explicitly exempting itself from compulsory dispute resolution of a wide swath of issues.'[51]

In July 2016 the Arbitration Court found in favour of virtually the entire Philippines' case: none of the islets were deemed 'land'; the key features disputed between the Philippines and China were declared within the Philippines' EEZ; and China was told to cease its building work and, for good measure, admonished for its damage to unique natural environments. The judgment was entirely rejected by China and a strong popular response within China declared that the Philippines was nothing more than the puppet of a bullying Uncle Sam.[52]

However, while the ruling may have gone against China, the international enthusiasm for it was muted to say the least. ASEAN failed even to agree that the ruling 'could be useful' and decided not to say anything; Singapore simply 'noted' it, as did South Korea. Vietnam more strongly called for the acceptance of international law, but steered round endorsing the ruling. The EU could only agree to note that the ruling had gone against China, while the statement from the Asia-Europe summit a few days after the ruling did not mention it at all. Taiwan rejected it in terms as strong as mainland China.[53] In the region only Japan and the Philippines itself gave full-throttled support to the outcome. While the ruling may have undermined the perceived status of China's claims in the Sea, China was far from isolated. The US on the other hand found itself facing a chorus of silence from the countries of the region that, having formally noted the ruling, clearly wanted to forget it as soon as possible, allow the situation to calm down and return to normal relations with China and in the region.

The Arbitration Court ruling was the sharpest blow the US had struck in its 'pivot', handing it a justification for its rhetoric against China in the South China Sea and legitimising its expanded naval presence. But this moment of triumph rapidly turned into a demonstration of declining US regional influence. And within weeks the Philippines' own insistence on the court ruling began to fade and by October its new president, Duterte, was in Beijing on a state visit at which he announced the Philippines' 'separation from the US', realignment with China and return to bilateral discussions on how to handle the disputed questions in the South China Sea.[54]

Militarising the South China Sea

In reality no serious commentator either before or after the July 2016 ruling thought the outcome would contribute to resolving the issues in the South China Sea, still less shift China from its position on the matter.[55] Thus it was evident that the US was not looking for a settlement but rather for a basis on which to brand China an international outlaw, justifying a further ratcheting up of the US military presence while blaming China for the increasing militarisation of the region.

Before the decision from The Hague, the US had accelerated its naval and other military activities in the Sea.[56] US navy surveillance in the Spratlys and surrounding waters intensified; US air sorties for close reconnaissance increased from about 260 in 2009 to over 1200 in 2014; from October 2015 US navy ships began making sailings within 12 nautical miles of Chinese installations on both the Spratlys and the Paracels. These were described as 'innocent passage' transits to defend 'freedom of navigation' in the Sea, and the US has sought to persuade its international allies – Japan, Australia and the UK in particular – to also participate in such sailings through the Sea.[57]

To justify this stepped up activity, the US exploited the asymmetry between China's growing global strength and the size of the Philippines to promote a narrative of 'plucky' little Philippines standing up to bully China, while presenting itself as the historic defender of 'freedom of navigation' against an alleged threat to free passage through the 'global commons'. This is, however, widely understood to be 'a legal cover for defending its maritime position and influence in Asia' and for the increased presence of the US 7th fleet in the region in a 'deterrent strategy indirectly directed at Beijing'.[58] Thus 'It is worth noting also that in addition to China, other states – including Malaysia, Indonesia, and India … and others – have also expressed their objection to what they see to be an expansive interpretation of what activities are included under "freedom of navigation" on the part of the US.'[59]

While the US may wish to present China's installations on the islets as a threat to free navigation, objective consideration must rather see them as aimed at shoring up the security of these sea lanes not closing them down – it is 'difficult to see China wanting to block [the sea passages] given its own reliance on critical sea lanes in the South China Sea and elsewhere'.[60] As the Pentagon has openly discussed the potential to impose a commercial blockade on China by closing the routes through the South China Sea, for China to adopt a strategy of making this more difficult is only sensible.[61] From this perspective, China building up its naval and air force presence in the Sea, expanding its Yalong submarine base on the south coast of Hainan and developing the capacities of its navy for 'open seas protection' have all been about guaranteeing it can keep these sea routes and straits open, the opposite of building the capacity to close them down.

But the narrative in the West does not discuss China's concerns for the security of its sea routes and the free passage of its commercial shipping. Instead, wide publicity has been given to contentious claims like Abe's that: 'increasingly, the South China Sea seems set to become a "Lake Beijing"', with 'the PLA navy's newly built aircraft carrier … a common sight.'[62] In reality the PLA navy will be a much less common sight in the South China Sea than the US navy for many years to come.

However, while the US has successfully inserted itself militarily in the South China Sea, it has so far failed to build up any united South East Asian bloc of countries behind its containment of China, still less recruit ASEAN as a grouping. Conflicting regional interests and more objective local perceptions about what has created tensions have rendered this illusory. China's neighbours in the region have had rather fewer problems with its activities in the Sea than the US has suggested to a Western audience. Malaysia, for example, has made it clear on several occasions that it has no problem with Chinese navy patrols in the contested areas, as long as 'their intention is not to go to war', and its defence minister told the Philippines: 'Just because you have enemies, doesn't mean your enemies are my enemies.'[63]

Philippines looks to end its China chill

Any euphoria in the US at the outcome of its tactics in the South China Sea was short-lived as, within weeks of the UNCLOS ruling, the Philippines had announced a change of course towards China. This shift followed hard on the heels of the election of Duterte as president of the Philippines in 2016, whose populist campaign won strong support among poorer Filipinos, defeating Aquino's candidate.

The long-standing orientation of the Philippines to the US, where it has preferential tariffs, meant traditional markets in the US and Japan had more weight than in the other seaboard states. But by 2015 China was the Philippines' second biggest trading partner with a 13.6 per cent share of total trade, behind Japan with 15.3 per cent, but ahead of the US with 12.9 per cent.[64] China is already the largest importer into the Philippines and growing as an export market.[65] In December 2015 the Philippines had said it would like to sign up to the AIIB and it supported China's 'one belt, one road' development initiative.[66]

Duterte made no secret of the fact that he saw more to gain for the Philippines economically from good relations with China than continuing a militarised confrontation to back up the US. Shortly after his election Duterte said: 'I will be chartering a [new] course [for the Philippines] on its own and will not be dependent on the United States.'[67] Despite strong growth for several years 25 per cent of Filipinos still live in internationally defined poverty, while a handful of elite families concentrate the country's wealth and power, in which the US is seen as deeply implicated. Duterte proceeded to deliberately scupper planned talks with Obama – by making personally insulting remarks – avoided meeting with the Americans at the summer 2016 ASEAN summit, and followed this up by cancelling joint patrols with the US in the South China Sea and announcing the end to joint military exercises – the latter was later reversed. At the same time he made it clear he was looking to stabilise Philippine relations with China, which led to an invitation for an early visit to Beijing in October 2016.[68] During this visit, he announced that the Philippines was reorienting to integration with 'ASEAN, China, Japan and South Korea' and that 'America had lost'. While China had previously responded to rising tensions by withholding promises of investment or joint projects, Duterte left Beijing having signed $13.5 billion in various deals.

The loud hurrah for the US policy in the South China Sea that the US hoped would flow from the Arbitration Court ruling had petered out within a few short months. Not only was it unable to whip up an international campaign against China, but its closest and most subordinate ally deserted it. Tillerson's pledge that Trump would deepen the naval campaign against China in the South China Sea was seen in the region as an untimely bid to restoke tensions when the atmosphere was just returning to a more economically propitious calm.

The US is back

Having stepped back militarily from the region after the Vietnam War and having lost its Philippine bases in the 1990s, the US navy is back in the South China Sea. But while most of the states in the region have welcomed the US navy – for reasons of their own internal security as much as for seeking a balance with China – they have not been enthusiastic towards attempts to turn this into a hostile campaign against China that would dominate relations in the region.

The US strategic position was reinforced by Australia's 2011 agreement to a base for up to 2500 US marines at Darwin, which may be expanded to include permanent docking facilities for the US navy, and a 2016 announcement suggested US B-1 bombers may also be based there.[69] However, even Australia is keen to balance its relations with China, and in October 2015 it agreed to China leasing disused port facilities in Darwin adjacent to the Royal Australian Air Force (RAAF) base and port currently used by the US.[70] And, despite his reorientation of Philippine foreign policy towards China, Duterte has committed to fulfilling previous pledges to host US navy assets semi-permanently in Philippine bases. But the US still does not have its own permanent bases in the Sea.[71]

Alongside augmenting its military position in the region, the US has advanced its diplomatic role in the South China Sea. Since announcing its 'interest' in 2010, the US has re-established itself as a regional player, in regular dialogue with governments and in multilateral forums like ASEAN. But it remains far from constructing a solid front of opposition to China in the region. China is increasingly central to the region's future prosperity and there is no applause for the US unnecessarily disrupting that.

Obama's offensive in the South China Sea made significant advances, but then ran into some definite limits. Trump will meet the same problems; the countries of the region do not perceive a threat from China of the type conjured by the US and are therefore not willing to risk the peace in order to contain it. Above all, without the support of the Philippines it is not clear for how long the US can maintain the South China Sea as a front line in a standoff over Asia's future.

Notes

1 K. Bradsheer, 'Philippines leader sounds alarm on China', *New York Times*, 4 February 2014.

2 'China says US involved in Philippines' South China Sea arbitration', *English.News.Cn*, 23 March 2016. Available at: http://news.xinhuanet.com/english/2016-03/23/c_135213624.htm (date accessed 24 March 2016).

3 P. Benich, 'Is the Philippines still a US ally?', *The Diplomat*, 14 September 2016. Available at: http://thediplomat.com/2016/09/is-the-philippines-still-a-us-ally/ (date accessed 23 February 2017).

4 S. Karnow, *In our image: America's empire in the Philippines*, Ballentine Books, New York, 1989, ch. 1.

5 P. A. Kramer, 'United States colonial rule in the Philippines', in T. Benjamin (ed.), *Encyclopaedia of Western Colonialism since 1450*, Vol. 3, Macmillan Reference, Detroit, 2007.

6 R. Jensen, J. Davidann and Y. Surgita (eds), *Trans-Pacific relations: America, Europe, and Asia in the twentieth century*, Praeger Publishers, Westport, CT, 2003, pp. 126–9.

7 Kolko, *Century of war*, pp. 389–94.

8 Widely attributed, inter alia, to Franklyn D. Roosevelt on Nicaraguan dictator Somoza: 'He may be a SOB, but he's our SOB'.

9 G. Katsiaficas, *Asia's unknown uprisings. Vol. 2: People power in the Philippines, Burma, Tibet, China, Taiwan, Bangladesh, Nepal, Thailand and Indonesia, 1947–2009*, Thomson Shore, Dexter, MI, 2013, p. 41.

10 World Bank indicators, 2016. Annual GDP % growth.

11 Karnow, *In our image*, ch. 12.

12 Katsiaficas, *Asia's unknown uprisings*, pp. 40–60.

13 Ibid., pp. 62–3.

14 Kaplan, *Asia's cauldron*, p. 126.

15 P. Bhattacharji, *Backgrounder: terrorism havens: Philippines*, Council on Foreign Relations, New York City, 1 June 2009.

16 J. A. Tyner, *Iraq, terror and the Philippines will to war*, Rowman and Littlefield, Lanham, MD, 2005, pp. 74–85.

17 H. R. Clinton, secretary of state, remarks at press availability, Hanoi, Vietnam, 23 July 2010, US Department of State.

18 N. Ottens, 'America's shadow over the South China Sea', *The Atlantic Sentinel*, 29 July 2010. Available at: http://atlanticsentinel.com/2010/07/americas-shadow-over-the-south-china-sea/ (date accessed 23 February 2017); H. R. Clinton, secretary of state, remarks at press availability, Hanoi, Vietnam, 23 July 2010, US Department of State.

19 Editorial, 'Regional lessons', *China Daily*, 30 October 2010.

20 L. M. Wu and Y. Chen, 'US involvement will only complicate South China Sea issue', *China Daily*, 27 July 2010.

21 The Spratlys are known as Nansha in Chinese; the Paracels as Xisha.

22 A. Etzioni, 'Who authorised preparations for war with China', *Yale Journal of International Affairs*, 8:2 (summer 2013), 37–51.

23 D. Brunnstrom and M. Spetalnick, 2017, 'Trump team struggles for cohesion on tougher China policy', *Reuters*, 14 January. Available at: http://www.reuters.com/article/us-usa-trump-china-analysis-idUSKB-N14X2LM (date accessed 19 February 2017).

24 Fu and Wu, 'South China Sea'.

25 Treaty of Taipei, 1952.

26 B. Hayton, *The South China Sea: the struggle for power in Asia*, Yale University Press, New Haven, CT, 2014, e-book location 1131–91.

27 M. J. Li, 'Reconciling assertiveness and cooperation? China's changing approach to the South China Sea dispute', *Security Challenges*, 6:4 (winter 2010), 54.

28 Fu and Wu, 'South China Sea'.

29 Hayton, *The South China Sea*, e-book location 1192–1358.

30 Digital gazetteer of the Spratly Islands, 2015. Available at: http://www.southchinasea.org/2011/08/19/digital-gazetteer-of-the-spratly-islands/ (date accessed 10 October 2016).

31 Declaration on the conduct of parties in the South China Sea, adopted by the foreign ministers of ASEAN and the PRC at the 8th ASEAN summit, Phnom Penh, Cambodia, 4 November 2002.

32 April 1988, as quoted in: 'Set aside dispute and pursue joint development', Ministry of Foreign Affairs of PRC. Available at: http://www.fmprc.gov.cn/mfa_eng/ziliao_665539/3602_665543/3604_665547/t18023.shtml (date accessed 7 February 2017).

33 Fu and Wu, 'South China Sea'.

34 T. Mitchell and G. Dyer, 'US military flight over South China Sea escalates tensions', *Financial Times*, 21 May 2015.

35 Fu and Wu, 'South China Sea'.

36 M. Taylor Fravel, *US policy towards the disputes in the South China Sea since 1995*, S. Rajaratnam School of International Studies, Nanyang Technological University, Singapore, 2014.

37 G. Dyer, 'US blames China for rising tensions in South China Sea', *Financial Times*, 9 February 2014.

38 Hayton, *The South China Sea*, e-book location 1621–91.

39 Agence France Presse, 'Philippines to seek more oil in South China Sea', *ABS-CBN News*, 29 June 2011. Available at: http://news.abs-cbn.com/business/06/29/11/philippines-seek-more-oil-south-china-sea (date accessed 23 February 2017).

40 J. Hardy, 'Back to the future: the US Navy returns to the Philippines', *The Diplomat*, 16 October 2012. Available at: http://thediplomat.com/2012/10/just-like-old-times-us-navy-returns-to-philippines/ (date accessed 19 February 2017).

41 For a full history of the disputes, see Fu and Wu, 'South China Sea'.

42 R. O'Rourke, 'Maritime territorial and exclusive economic zone (EEZ) disputes involving China: issues for Congress', Congressional Research Service report R42784, 22 December 2015.

43 P. Nolan, 'Imperial archipelagos', *New Left Review*, 80 (March–April 2013).

44 Ibid.

45 US Department of State, Maritime disputes in East Asia, Testimony before the House Committee on Foreign Affairs Subcommittee on Asia and the Pacific, Washington, DC, 5 February 2014.

46 P. Parameswaran, 'US not "neutral" in South China Sea disputes: top US diplomat', *The Diplomat*, 22 July 2015. Available at: http://thediplomat.com/2015/07/us-not-neutral-in-south-china-sea-disputes-top-us-diplomat/ (date accessed 23 February 2017).

47 Remarks by President Obama at Queensland University, The White House, Office of the press secretary, 15 November 2014.

48 China: declarations upon (1996) and after (2006) ratification of the UN Convention United Nations Convention on the Law of the Sea (1982).

49 Fu and Wu, 'South China Sea'.

50 Statement on the award on jurisdiction and admissibility of the South China Sea arbitration by the arbitral tribunal established at the request of the Republic of the Philippines, Ministry of Foreign Affairs PRC, 30 October 2015.

51 P. Gewirtz, *The limits of law in the South China Sea*, East Asia Policy Paper No. 8, Centre for East Asia Policy Studies at Brookings, Washington, DC, 2016.

52 X. H. Wang, 'S. China Sea arbitration: a US-led conspiracy behind the farce', China.org.cn, 12 July 2016. Available at: http://www.china.org.cn/opinion/2016-07/12/content_38864239.htm (date accessed 23 February 2017).

53 M. Mortago, M. Martina and B. Blanchard, 'ASEAN deadlocked on South China Sea', *Reuters*, 26 July 2016. Available at: http://www.reuters.com/article/us-southchinasea-ruling-asean-idUSKCN1050F6; Singapore Ministry of Foreign Affairs statement on Arbitral Court ruling, 12 July 2016;

H. Clark, 'Vietnam careful not jubilant after South China Sea ruling against China', *World Post*, 16 July 2016. Available at: http://www.huffingtonpost.com/helen_clark/vietnam-south-china-sea-ruling_b_11022864.html; R. Emmott, 'EU statement on South China Sea reflects divisions', *Reuters*, 15 July 2016. Available at: http://www.reuters.com/article/southchinasea-ruling-eu-idUSL8N1A130Y; S. Tiezzi, 'Taiwan: South China Seas ruling "completely unacceptable"', *The Diplomat*, 13 July 2016. Available at: http://thediplomat.com/2016/07/taiwan-south-china-sea-ruling-completely-unacceptable/ (all items last accessed 23 February 2017).

54 B. Blanchard, 'Duterte aligns with China, says "US has lost"', *Reuters*, 20 October 2016. Available at: http://www.reuters.com/article/us-china-philippines-idUSKCN12K0AS (date accessed 19 February 2017).

55 Gewirtz, 'The limits of law'.

56 J. Kurlantzick, 'Growing US role in South China Sea', *Council on Foreign Relations expert brief*, 11 October 2011.

57 G. Dyer and T. Mitchell, 'Hague ruling: US, China on collision course?', *Today*, 19 July 2016. Available at: http://www.todayonline.com/commentary/hague-ruling-us-china-collision-course (date accessed 23 February 2017).

58 C. Odeyemi, 'UNCLOS and maritime security: the "securitisation" of the South China Sea disputes', *Defence & Security Analysis*, 31:4 (2015), 297–8.

59 A. D. Ba, 'China and ASEAN: renavigating relations for a 21st-century Asia', *Asian Survey*, 43:4 (2003), 282.

60 Ibid.

61 Hammes, 'Offshore control'.

62 S. Abe, 'Asia's democratic security diamond', *Project Syndicate*, 27 December 2012. Available at: https://www.project-syndicate.org/commentary/a-strategic-alliance-for-japan-and-india-by-shinzo-abe?barrier=accessreg (date accessed 23 February 2017).

63 S. Chen, 'Malaysia splits with ASEAN claimants on China Sea threat', *Bloomberg*, 29 August 2013. Available at: https://www.bloomberg.com/news/articles/2013-08-28/malaysia-splits-with-other-asean-claimants-over-china-sea-threat (date accessed 23 February 2017).

64 CIA World Factbook, 2016.

65 K. Lester and M. Yapp, 'Philippines' Domingo says China may become biggest export market', *Bloomberg*, 7 October 2013. Available at: https://www.bloomberg.com/news/articles/2013-10-07/philippines-domingo-says-china-may-become-biggest-export-market (date accessed 19 February 2017).

66 S. Tiezzi, 'Philippines to (finally) join China's Asian Infrastructure Investment Bank', *The Diplomat*, 31 December 2015. Available at: http://thediplomat.com/2015/12/philippines-to-finally-join-chinas-asian-infrastructure-investment-bank/ (date accessed 23 February 2017).

67 R. J. Heydarian, 'Will Rodrigo Duterte revolutionise the Philippines' foreign policy', *The National Interest*, 14 August 2016. Available at: http://nationalinterest.org/feature/will-rodrigo-duterte-revolutionize-the-philippines-foreign-17353 (date accessed 19 February 2017).

68 S. Tiezzi, 'Duterte calls for end to US-Philippine military exercises', *The Diplomat*, 29 September 2016. Available at: http://thediplomat.com/2016/09/duterte-calls-for-end-to-us-philippine-military-exercises-part-of-tilt-toward-china/ (date accessed 19 February 2017).

69 AFP, 'US in talks to base long-range bombers in Australia', *Mail Online*, 8 March 2016. Available at: http://www.dailymail.co.uk/wires/afp/article-3483328/US-talks-base-long-range-bombers-Australia.html (date accessed 19 February 2017).

70 J. Perlez, 'US casts wary eye on Australian port leased by Chinese', *New York Times*, 20 March 2016.

71 Z. Keck, 'The Philippines is building a new naval base in South China Sea', *The Diplomat*, 8 October 2013. Available at: http://thediplomat.com/2013/10/the-philippines-is-building-a-new-naval-base-in-south-china-sea/ (date accessed 23 February 2017).

11

The courting of Vietnam

Contemporary Western ideas about the countries of the Mekong peninsula – Vietnam, Cambodia, Laos, Thailand and Myanmar – remain heavily influenced by the fallout from the 1964–75 Vietnam War, the epic and ultimately victorious struggle of the communist-led National Liberation Front (NLF) and North Vietnam over the US and its various stooge regimes in Saigon.[1]

The US defeat in Vietnam was of long-term global significance. Its costs, both in blood and in money, led to an unprecedented domestic and international anti-war movement that shook the US government and penetrated deeply into popular culture; its long political reverberations (the 'Vietnam syndrome') were powerful enough to prevent subsequent US governments launching any major military intervention until the first Gulf war of 1991.[2]

The Vietnam War – or American War as it is known in the region – affected the entire peninsula, engulfing it in a conflict originating in the fight to eject the French colonialists from Indochina after 1945. The attempts to liberate South Vietnam after the 1954 partition of the country led to the intervention of the US. The ensuing conflagration extended to Vietnam, Laos and Cambodia, while Thailand – a key post-war American ally – provided the airbases for many of the US operations in the war. After America's defeat in 1975 the post-shocks continued to play out in armed conflict on the peninsula until 1990. Only Myanmar kept out of it, which, despite its singular combination of conventional military dictatorship, 'socialist economics' and close relations with the USSR and China, was left undisturbed in its autarchic neutrality.

Today these countries constitute a buffer zone along China's vulnerable southern border (see Map 8). The US has been militarily excluded from the region since the end of the Vietnam War, apart from a small presence in Thailand, so, unlike in North East Asia, it has no forward bases close to the Chinese border. In the context of the US turn to China the allegiances of these countries are crucially fought over, none more so than Vietnam. While Thailand's status as a formal American ally is important, and political changes in Myanmar have created new openings for the West, Vietnam is the golden apple the US has hoped would fall in its lap.

This chapter considers how far the US has been able to progress down its path of engaging Vietnam in its project for Asia, as Vietnam faces a strategic choice between economic partnership with China and military partnership with the US.

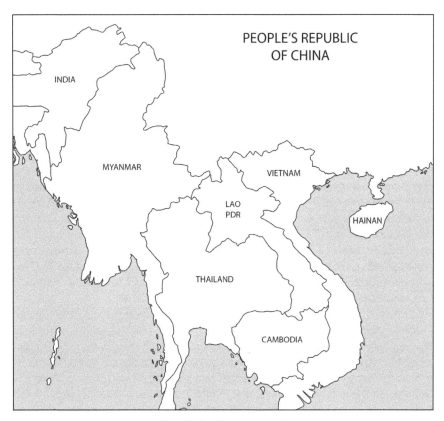

Map 8 The Mekong peninsula

The troubled history of China and Vietnam

If the US were able to 'triangulate' US–Vietnam–China relations in the way it did those between the USSR and China in the Cold War it would be a triumph for US strategic positioning in Asia, and place very significant pressure on China.

Given the 'American War'; China and Vietnam's shared history of struggle against colonialism and imperialism; their mutual distance from both American neoliberal economic ideology and its virulent anti-communism; the fraternal relations between their leading parties; their similar post-reform economic systems; and the potential for trade, the idea that Vietnam would willingly get sucked into an American strategy to isolate China appears counterintuitive.

The fact that this is a possibility is down to two factors. Firstly, as Robert D. Kaplan has pointed out, Vietnam has: 'no chips on the shoulder, no axes to grind, no face to lose regarding a future de facto military alliance with America. Vietnamese harbour relatively few sensitivities about the American War precisely because they won it.'[3]

Secondly, a long history of Vietnamese vassalage to China left a legacy of distrust, reinforced by China's invasion of Vietnam in 1979 and reawakened by current disputes in the South China Sea. Although it was colonial occupation by France from 1862 to

1945 that led to the national liberation movement and war with the US, this modern colonial history was preceded by 2000 years of frequent incursions by China; a long history that features strongly in Vietnamese national consciousness. The northern part of Vietnam was occupied by China for 1000 years until 938 CE. China's tenth-century ejection was followed by frequent attempts at reconquest until the conclusive defeat of the Ming dynasty armies in the fifteenth century. But this did not mark the end of on/off Chinese political interference.

The liberation war

This imperial history was superseded by the aid that revolutionary China extended to the Vietnamese liberation war after 1949, when Chinese support was crucial, especially in the early stages. Alongside the inspired leadership of General Vo Nguyen Giap, the defeat of the French at Dien Bien Phu in 1954 was partly due to the flow of arms and other support over the border from the newly established PRC. Ho Chi Minh had a particularly close relationship with the Chinese having been a member of the CPC for a time. He described the Chinese advisors who were integrated into the command structures of the war against the French as 'brotherly comrades'.[4]

However, some of the tensions to come began to emerge at the 1954 Geneva Peace negotiations that ended this phase of the war. The Vietnamese negotiators believed that Zhou Enlai, the Chinese representative, and Molotov, the Soviet representative, conceded more to the US, Britain and France than was necessary.[5] The liberation forces across Indochina had to accept separate settlements for Laos, Cambodia and Vietnam. Vietnam was divided at the 17th Parallel; in Laos most of the territory that had been taken by the liberation forces was handed back and a pro-Western monarchy re-established; and the rule of Prince Sihanouk was reaffirmed in Cambodia. Whether or not the Vietnamese were right that more could have been extracted from the West, China and the USSR both urged acceptance. China undoubtedly hoped this would buy peace on the peninsula, allowing it to focus on domestic development after the heavy toll of its commitments to the Korean and Vietnamese wars.[6]

But when ongoing resistance in the south began leading to increasing American military intervention, China came to the support of Vietnam despite the peace deal.[7] From the 1964 full launch of war by the US on North Vietnam – on the excuse of the 'Tonkin incident' when America falsely alleged that US navy ships had come under North Vietnamese fire (in fact the Americans fired first) – Chinese support stepped up.

> China's aid to Vietnam during 1965–69 was substantial. ... Over 320,000 Chinese engineering and anti-aircraft artillery forces (the peak year was 1967, when 170,000 Chinese troops were present in Vietnam) were directly engaged in the construction, maintenance and defence of North Vietnam's transport system and strategically important targets ... Such support allowed Hanoi to use its own manpower for more essential tasks, such as participating in battles in the South, and maintaining the transport and communication lines between the North and the South. Moreover, Beijing's support ... played a role in deterring further American expansion of war into the North. It is therefore fair to say that ... without the support, the history, even the outcome, of the Vietnam War might have been different.[8]

However, the Hanoi–Beijing relationship began to experience stress as the implications of the Sino-Soviet split started to work through.[9] Initially China believed that the Vietnamese would take its side as Ho Chi Minh was close to China and Khrushchev's policy of 'peaceful coexistence' meant Vietnam had been receiving little Soviet support. But after Khrushchev was removed in October 1964, the USSR's support to Vietnam stepped up. Alexei Kosygin visited Vietnam in February 1965 signing a defence treaty that guaranteed financial aid, military equipment and advisors.[10] Although China never withdrew its support nor obstructed the transit of Soviet supplies to Vietnam across its territory, its aid declined from 1969 following the death of Ho Chi Minh, reaching a low from 1970 to 1972.[11] At Hanoi's request it stepped up support in 1972–73 against renewed American bombing of the North, but close relations were not rebuilt.

As relations with the USSR deteriorated, China became increasingly concerned by the perceived threat of Soviet encirclement. With tensions high along its border with the USSR, it feared a victory for the NLF and its allies would extend these problems to its border with Indochina. In this context China stepped up its engagement with other liberation forces on the peninsula as a counterweight, especially with the Khmer Rouge in Cambodia.[12]

The 1979 Sino-Vietnam war

The liberation of Saigon and final defeat of the US in South Vietnam in April 1975 coincided with the victory of the Chinese-backed Khmer Rouge over the American-backed Lon Nol regime in Cambodia.[13] Support for the Khmer Rouge within Cambodia had grown exponentially in response to US carpet-bombing from 1965 to 1973, when it is estimated that American B-52 bombers dropped at least 500,000 tons of bombs on Cambodia, equalling or possibly exceeding what the US dropped in the entire Pacific theatre during the Second World War (500,000 tons), and three times that dropped on Japan, including Hiroshima and Nagasaki (160,000 tons).[14]

Pol Pot's Khmer Rouge regime visited further horrors on its already devastated people.[15] Deeply suspicious of Vietnam, which Pol Pot believed intended to subordinate Cambodia into some kind of vassal state, in 1977 the Khmer Rouge carried out a bloody purge of suspected Vietnamese sympathisers, and launched an assault across Vietnam's borders killing hundreds of Vietnamese villagers.[16] Eventually, in December 1978, Vietnam invaded Cambodia and threw out the Khmer Rouge.

In an attempt to come to the aid of its Cambodian allies, China launched an invasion of Vietnam in January 1979, but met battle-hardened, well-equipped Vietnamese regular and irregular troops.[17] Estimated casualties in the two weeks of the conflict range from 40,000 to 60,000.[18] China withdrew but both sides remained on a war footing throughout the 1980s, with occasional cross-border engagements.

In 1991 the collapse of the USSR and Vietnam's withdrawal from Cambodia created the conditions for normalising Sino-Vietnam relations. Both recognised the post-1991 government of Cambodia; in 2000 the disputed line of their land border was settled and maritime rights in the Gulf of Tonkin agreed.[19] But despite establishing regular high-level meetings and day-to-day communications, the tensions that had characterised Sino-Vietnamese relations from the 1970s remained near the surface, particularly infecting the hard-to-resolve disputes over the Paracels and Spratly islands. This combination of a legacy of bad feeling and intractable disputes is what the US has sought to exploit in relations with Vietnam.

Vietnam's economic reform

By 1975 Vietnam's economy had been utterly devastated by the war, particularly in the north, exacerbated by the mass exodus of technically and professionally skilled workers after the liberation of the south and Vietnam's international isolation (the US maintained a trade embargo against Vietnam until 1994). Its attempts to imitate the Soviet economic model failed to deliver substantial growth and for ten years after 1975 it became increasingly reliant on Soviet aid. This period did see advances in health and life expectancy, near universal literacy and other social gains; but this was no longer sustainable once Gorbachev's reforms in the USSR reduced the aid available.[20]

From the early 1980s Vietnam embarked on an economic reform close in model to China's. Officially adopted in 1986, Vietnam describes the Doi Moi, or renewal policy, as a 'socialist-oriented market economy', envisaging an expansion of the market while maintaining the primacy of the state in banking, infrastructure and key industries.[21] In description and content this policy was virtually identical to China's post-1978 'socialist market economy' and was a huge success, with growth rates rising steadily from the late 1980s to average 7.8 per cent a year from 1992 to 2007.[22] Similar policies were also followed in Cambodia and Laos, with similarly positive outcomes.[23]

As in China, Vietnam's reform was underpinned by a sharp increase in investment as a share of GDP – rising from 14 per cent in 1986 to 30 per cent by 2000, peaking at 40 per cent in 2007 – and opening up to the world market.[24] By the late 1990s its large pool of literate rural labour had allowed it to develop its export-oriented manufacturing sector, in particular beginning to compete in the production of textiles, garments, shoes and similar labour-intensive industries. Vietnam was well placed to attract such production from China as Chinese wage levels rose and it began to shift its production up the value chain. In the post-2008 crisis period Vietnam began to move towards technology assembly, as China had before it.

In current prices Vietnam's GDP was only $6.5 billion in 1990, but it had grown exponentially to $187 billion by 2014.[25] An estimated 30 million people were lifted out of poverty in the 20 years to 2010, with the poverty headcount falling from 60 per cent in 1990 to 21 per cent in 2010.[26] However, its GDP per capita is still low, at $2,016 in 2014, ahead of India's at $1,610, but well behind its South East Asian neighbours apart from Laos, Cambodia and Myanmar.[27] Maintaining an upward trend in living standards is crucial to Vietnam's domestic stability. This became more urgent with the contraction in world trade following the financial crisis, meaning growth in Vietnam slipped back to an average 5.9 per cent from 2008 to 2014.[28] Consideration of how to attract new sources of investment and expand export markets inevitably weighs in foreign policy choices.

Vietnam's economy between the US and China

Both China and the US played a crucial role in Vietnam's recent economic development. From the late 1990s growing trade and other economic links between China and

Vietnam helped put their relations on a more collaborative footing. Each supported the other's bid to join the WTO, while China's growing engagement in the APT created a regional framework for cooperation. Expanded transport links included a new cross-border railway. Chinese tourism to Vietnam grew year on year, contributing 25 per cent of all international visitors (nearly 2 million Chinese visited Vietnam in 2013).

Bilateral trade grew rapidly, expanding from only $4 billion in 1990 to $57.6 billion in 2014, with China becoming Vietnam's largest trading partner. But Vietnam has run a substantial trade deficit with China – $26.4 billion in 2014 – with the gap widening year on year.[29] This partly reflects the success of Vietnam's textile and garment industries, for which 90 per cent of the yarn is imported from China, but nonetheless the deficit causes concerns in Vietnam. Vietnam's exports to China remain mainly coal, crude oil, rubber, food, coffee and other primary products rather than manufactured goods where Vietnam cannot yet compete in China's home market.

On the other hand, once it had lifted trade sanctions on Vietnam in 1994, the US rapidly rose to become Vietnam's top export market. In 2014 Vietnam's exports to the US were valued at $30 billion, mainly footwear and clothing, while Vietnam's imports from the US were just $6 billion.[30] Although Vietnam's exports to China have been increasing at a faster rate than those to the US – which is a consideration for the future – at the current rate of increase China would not overtake the US as an export market for Vietnam until at least 2030.

In 2012 Japan had the largest stock of FDI in Vietnam at $8.4 billion, followed by Korea with $7.2 billion, Malaysia $2.8 billion and Singapore $2.6 billion; but China's stock of FDI in Vietnam, $1.6 billion, was higher than that from the US, $1.1 billion.[31] Overall China's FDI into Vietnam is growing steadily, while FDI from developed markets, including the US and Japan, is generally stalling.[32] To counter this, the US encouraged its companies to redirect their investment from China to Vietnam, so, for example, in 2010 Intel opened its biggest global factory, originally scoped for China, in Vietnam.

China's shift up the value chain offers an important opportunity for Vietnam. Taiwanese, Korean and Chinese companies that were successful in low-wage, low-skilled, labour-intensive production in the first three decades of China's industrial development have begun to relocate out of China as its wage levels rise; in 2015 the average factory worker in China earned $27.50 per day, compared with $8.60 in Indonesia and $6.70 in Vietnam.[33] A significant migration in global textile and garment production from China to Vietnam and Bangladesh has already occurred, and has begun in components and assembly. Hence there is a substantial synergy in the development curve of both China and Vietnam over the next decade if Vietnam chooses to take advantage of it – Japan's 'flying geese' model.

The US riposte was the TPP and its promise that tariff deals could secure and expand Vietnam's crucial export market in North America. Vietnam was an active partner in the TPP negotiations, and it helped tip Vietnam more strongly towards the US in regional politics. Its cancellation will be a particular setback to US influence in Vietnam.

Overall, Vietnam has strong economic interests in avoiding conflict with either the US or China. Vietnam needs stable international relations for its own 'peaceful rise'. This means weaving a careful path between the US's growing military presence in the region, collaboration with China, and its conflicts with China over the Paracels and Spratly islands.

China, Vietnam and the US in the South China Sea

One Vietnamese government official rather accurately described Vietnam 'as swinging on a tightrope in which China held one end and the United States held another'.[34] This analogy has been true of both Vietnam's economic orientation and its approach to its military security, particularly in relation to the South China Sea.

China's disputes in the South China Sea have on two occasions become actual armed confrontations and both involved Vietnam: in 1974 with South Vietnam over the Paracels and with unified Vietnam in 1988 in the Spratlys. Sovereignty over these islands had been moot from 1945, but seemed to be resolved when in 1958, in a formal note from Prime Minister Pham Van Dong to Chinese premier Zhou Enlai, North Vietnam accepted the Chinese claim to both the Paracels and Spratlys. Thus it was not controversial in the North when in 1974 a confrontation between the Chinese and South Vietnamese navies in the Paracels ended with the rout of the latter and China taking control of the island group.[35] But after the Vietnam War, in the context of deteriorating relations with China, the new Vietnamese government repudiated the 1958 position as purely a product of the conditions of war.

Vietnam's claims in the Spratlys are based on a combination of its own historical evidence of sovereignty, traditional fishing grounds, and rights it has sought under UNCLOS to an enlarged EEZ that extends to the edge of the continental shelf. The dispute with China has waxed and waned over the years, but in 1988 an armed confrontation between the Vietnamese and Chinese navies at Johnson's Reef – where China was building a UNESCO-commissioned oceanic observation post – resulted in the sinking of two Vietnamese vessels and a number of deaths. There are conflicting accounts of what exactly occurred, but both sides responded with a rapid expansion of their respective presences in the Spratlys, through fortifications and other structures. Vietnam developed 26 fortified holdings stretching from the south-west to the north-east of the Spratlys – the largest number of any claimant.[36]

From 1988 the thaw in relations between Vietnam and China saw these conflicts ease, but new tensions emerged from the mid-2000s as a number of factors made the issues more critical for both sides. The growing international trade of both China and Vietnam made the islands more strategically important in maintaining the security of important sea routes; the potential for exploitation of oil, gas and mineral deposits became more immediate for energy security; the depletion of fish stocks created pressure for expansion into disputed seas; and their strategic military significance was thrown into sharp relief as both sides developed their naval capacities.

Stoking the dispute

In 2009 clashes between Vietnamese fishing boats and Chinese coastguards indicated that the previous period of calm was faltering. While it was denied, the Vietnamese government may have tacitly encouraged discontented fishing communities to test China's response by unilaterally extending into disputed areas. At the same time as managing the dispute through high level meetings, both sides took steps to reinforce their claims: China by incorporating the disputed archipelagos in its development plan for Hainan

Island; and Vietnam by making a submission to the UN Commission on the Limits of the Continental Shelf.[37]

Further escalation, however, came on the heels of Hillary Clinton's speech at the July 2010 ASEAN meeting in Hanoi.[38] As outlined in Chapter 10, her intervention was both an undisguised rebuff to China, but also, by making it in Hanoi, signalled US backing for Vietnam's claims – US support for the Philippines was never really in doubt.[39]

In 2011 Vietnam began oil explorations breaking the de facto agreement with China that all such steps in the disputed areas would be bilaterally agreed. China increased its coastguard presence and other civilian shipping in the area. Tempers rose and in two incidents Vietnamese exploration ships' underwater cables were cut or snapped by Chinese craft.

At the 2012 meeting of ASEAN in Cambodia Clinton pushed for it to explicitly criticise China on the disputes. But this intervention compromised host, chair and close China-ally Cambodia, which, despite enormous US pressure, refused to go along with it. Cambodia is highly reliant on Chinese aid, trade and investment. Chinese investment in Cambodia between 1994 and 2013 totalled $9.1 billion. In 2011 alone Chinese investment was $1.2 billion – eight times that of the US at $0.15 billion.

With others also unhappy about escalating the conflict with China, this led to a debacle, with the ASEAN meeting for the first time breaking up without the traditional joint communiqué from participants.

The US–China–Vietnam triangle

Following these clashes both China and Vietnam took steps to ease tensions. In 2013, the first year of the new leadership in China, there were three high-level contacts between the two countries: Vietnam's president and prime minister both visited China, and Li Keqiang went to Hanoi. From this Hanoi meeting preliminary joint exploration programmes were announced in a disputed part of the Gulf of Tonkin, alongside commitments by China to step up trade and inward investment – leading to the jump in Chinese FDI to Vietnam in that year.

But Vietnam also pursued greater military engagement with the US. In 2011 it agreed a memorandum of understanding on areas for military cooperation, including senior-level defence dialogues on maritime security. In 2013 President Truong attended a bilateral summit meeting in the US, which produced a new 'comprehensive partnership' giving Vietnam's approval to American engagement in regional affairs. In December 2013, secretary of state John Kerry visited Vietnam to announce '$32.5m in new US assistance for maritime law enforcement in Southeast Asian states', of which $18 million was ear-marked for new coastguard patrol boats.[40]

Nonetheless Vietnam's main emphasis remained on improving relations with China. President Truong's 2013 visit to Beijing took place *before* his visit to the US, while the 'comprehensive partnership' announced with the US was one step down from its 'strategic partnership' with China. Above all, Vietnam did not follow the Philippines in referring its maritime disputes with China to UNCLOS adjudication.

The situation seemed to improve further when in July 2013 China agreed to participate in a process to consolidate the 2002 ASEAN-China Declaration on the Conduct of Parties in the South China Sea into a binding 'Code of Conduct'. A first meeting (held in Beijing in September 2013) agreed to seek 'gradual progress and consensus through consultations'.

Anti-China sentiment has dangers for Hanoi

However, these efforts fell apart dramatically in May 2014 when, in a step that ran counter to its careful conflict avoidance with Vietnam for the previous two years, China placed an exploratory oilrig in the disputed seas off the Paracels. Vietnam objected furiously and mass popular protests against China developed within the country. These led to the deaths of three Chinese nationals, the evacuation of 3000 Chinese from the country and a clash at sea resulting in the sinking of a Vietnamese fishing boat.[41]

Hanoi responded with a tilt towards the US. Premier Nguyen Tan Dung said: 'We expect the US to make more concrete, more effective contributions to regional peace and stability … The US is a global power and a power in the Asia-Pacific region.' Vietnam also announced it had a legal case ready to submit to UNCLOS at the 'appropriate' time, hinting at joint action with the Philippines.[42] China played down the conflict and quietly removed the rig earlier than planned; but it also pointed out that it was only doing what others had done before – Vietnam itself, Malaysia, the Philippines and Indonesia had all previously undertaken oil explorations in disputed areas of the South China Sea and it was only China that had not.

Although Hanoi could claim victory in the dispute, the events within Vietnam had demonstrated significant domestic risks in unleashing anti-China sentiment. The protests had rapidly become riots that ran out of control, with buildings torched, businesses ransacked and, in addition to the three Chinese killed, many were injured. Moreover the violence was by no means just directed against China. The *Financial Times* reported that up to 300 foreign businesses in more than a dozen industrial zones in the southern province of Binh Duong were damaged in the riots, but of these just 11 were from mainland China, while more than 150 were Taiwanese and 24 from Korea.[43] This level of violence suggests that it was giving expression to a more general malaise in the population than anger towards China; while the incapacity of the Vietnamese government to control the situation undermined foreign business confidence.

Additionally, the fact that the greatest violence was in the traditionally less pro-Hanoi south threw up warnings about the growing influence of political forces that not only favour the US over China, but have never supported the post-liberation government in Hanoi. Such currents are very influenced by the Vietnamese diaspora in the US, which is largely composed of those who fled Saigon after 1975 and which remains strongly anti-communist and hostile to both China and the government in Hanoi.[44] From the 1990s, after the normalisation of relations with the US, many began to return to Vietnam to visit (405,000 visited in 2004), revive or keep up family links, for business or even to resettle.[45] As a result the politics of the émigré community has increasing circulation within Vietnam, particularly in the south.

With legal constraints on the expression of outright opposition to the government, nationalist sentiment against China can be deployed to imply the government lacks patriotism. Thus diaspora-led campaigns for commemoration of the 1974 Paracels incident, the 1979 border war and the 1988 Spratly incident are inflected against China, but imply a critique of the government in Hanoi. Such campaigns also play a useful role for the US, which can support such anti-China sentiment in the diaspora without appearing to directly pressure Hanoi. A 2012 state department briefing remarked that 'anti-China sentiment' was behind the US's improved relations with Vietnam.[46]

Thus legitimising a nationalist sentiment inflected against China could set off a dangerous dynamic for Hanoi. Not only could such a domestic movement corner it politically into an escalation of conflict with China, but it could strengthen forces that have never accepted the legitimacy of the post-1975 government. Hence the events of 2014 also saw differences in Vietnam's leadership over the appropriate response, with premier Dung's pro-US line contrasting with a more conciliatory course from party general secretary Trong, leader of the more pro-China faction in the VCP.[47]

Vietnam's strategic choice

Vietnam occupies a powerful strategic position, dominating the west coast of the South China Sea. It is the largest of the Mekong countries (apart from China itself where the river rises) with a population of 90 million – 40 per cent of the whole peninsula – compared to Cambodia with 15 million, Laos 6.5 million, Thailand 66 million and Myanmar 53 million.[48] Its standing army, with 482,000 on active service, is the ninth largest in the world, plus it has a 3 million-strong reserve force.[49] It is well provided with tanks and combat aircraft in particular, and it has begun building up a submarine fleet with six Russian stealth subs ordered in 2009, armed with Russian land-attack missiles that are capable of reaching well into China. Its GDP is not yet half Thailand's – the most successful of these peninsula economies – but Vietnam's growth rate has been consistently faster and it is rapidly gaining.[50] Despite its close proximity to the mighty China, it has few reasons to feel insecure either economically or militarily.

Whatever their disagreements in the South China Sea, there is no evidence that Vietnam faces any security threat emanating from China. Their land borders are settled, the Gulf of Tonkin is agreed, none of China's military or naval build-up can be interpreted as directed at Vietnam and Chinese missiles point east not south. Above all, the fraternal party-to-party relations and ideological affinity between the Vietnamese and Chinese communist parties, their similar state-led economic systems and their shared history of long wars of liberation from nineteenth- and twentieth-century colonialism bind them together in ways that create a 'special relationship' that can reap economic and political dividends for both.

Although the US remains Vietnam's most important export market, on current trends, in less than 15 years it will have been eclipsed by China. And the US already has little to offer in investment, infrastructure development and the other underpinnings of growth. With most of the other less developed countries in the region queuing up to get into the Chinese market and to attract Chinese investment, Vietnam's advantages of proximity and similarity of political and economic systems can give it an edge.

While Vietnam has been keen to progress military relations with the US, this has limits. It also maintains close military ties with Russia, which remains its largest supplier of arms and military technology. Visiting American warships have not been given access to

Cam Ranh Bay where Russian warships can freely dock. It has avoided taking any action that would do irreversible damage to its relations with China.

This could shift if there was a fundamental change of direction by Vietnam itself. Part of the negotiations around the TPP clearly keyed into differences within the Vietnamese leadership as to how far it should look to greater integration with the West, including economically, by pushing further reform in the direction of large-scale privatisations and the other measures demanded by the neoliberal orthodoxy embodied in the framework of the TPP. Such debates inevitably overlapped with the strategic issue of whether Vietnam should orient more decisively to China or to the US. These differences led to a significant faction fight in the run-up to the 12th National Congress of the VCP in January 2016, which resulted in the removal of premier Nguyen Tan Dung, widely touted in the West as its favourite to become the all-important general secretary of the party, and the more pro-China wing consolidated its hold.[51] While Vietnam's policy-makers will continue to pursue a course of engaging the US as well as China, this outcome undoubtedly weakened the US's position.

The upshot is that while the US has gained some increased traction in Vietnam, this has been outweighed by the economic pulling power of China; the two countries' shared ideological outlook and economic synergies have trumped historic suspicions and disputes in the South China Sea. Vietnam has no intention of subordinating its foreign policy course to either China or the US; so while welcoming the increased leverage offered by a greater US military presence, Vietnam has given no sign it will endorse any kind of US bloc against China.

Notes

1 G. Kolko, *Anatomy of a war: the United States, Vietnam and the modern historical experience*, The New Press, New York, 1985.
2 G. C. Herring, 'America and Vietnam: the unending war', *Foreign Affairs*, 70:5, (winter 1991/92), 104–20.
3 Kaplan, *Asia's cauldron*, p. 58.
4 Kolko, *Anatomy of a war*.
5 W. Burchett, *The China, Cambodia, Vietnam Triangle*, Vanguard Books, Chicago, 1981, pp. 27–42.
6 Z. Qiang, 'China and the Geneva Conference of 1954', *The China Quarterly*, 129 (March 1992), 103–22.
7 M. B. Young, *The Vietnam Wars 1945–1990*, Harper Collins, New York, 1991.
8 J. Chen, 'China's involvement in the Vietnam War, 1964–69', *The China Quarterly*, 142 (June 1995), 356–87.
9 See Chapter 5.
10 Chen, *Mao's China*, pp. 230–2.
11 Chen, 'China's involvement', p. 379.
12 N. Khoo, *Collateral damage: Sino-Soviet rivalry and the termination of the Sino-Vietnamese alliance*, Columbia University Press, New York, 2011, ch. 6.
13 Khmer Rouge is the common name given to the Communist Party of Kampuchea.
14 B. Kiernan and T. Owen, 'Roots of US troubles in Afghanistan: civilian bombing casualties and the Cambodian precedent', *The Asia-Pacific Journal*, 8:26:4 (2010).
15 P. Short, *Pol Pot: The history of a nightmare*, Hodder & Stoughton, London, 2004, ch. 11.
16 Ibid., e-book location 7546.

17 China's *casus belli* was the mass exodus of Hoa (ethnic Chinese) owing to alleged anti-Chinese attacks.

18 Vogel, *Deng Xiaoping*, e-book location 10812–39.

19 C. G. Ang, 'Vietnam-China relations since the end of the Cold War', Institute of Defence and Strategic Studies, Working Paper no 98, Singapore, November 1998.

20 T. T. Bui, 'After the war: 25 years of economic development in Vietnam', *National Institute for Research Advancement Review*, 7:2 (2000).

21 B. Hayton, *Vietnam: rising dragon*, Yale University Press, New Haven, CT, 2011, e-book location 285.

22 UNCTADStat 2016, annual GDP growth rate.

23 J. Ross, 'China's socialist model outperforms capitalism', *Global Times*, 23 August 2016.

24 World Bank indicators, 2016. GFCF as % of GDP.

25 UNCTADStat 2016, GDP current $.

26 R. Badiani, B. Baulch, L. Brandt, V. H. Dat, N. T. Giang, J. Gibson, J. Giles, I. Hinsdale, P. Hung, V. Kozel, P. Lanjouw, M. Marra, V. V. Ngoc, N.T. Phuong, P. Schuler, N. Thang, H. X. Thanh, L. D. Trung, P. D. Tung, N. Viet Cuong, L. H. Vu and A. Wells-Dang, *2012 Vietnam poverty assessment: well begun, not yet done – Vietnam's remarkable progress on poverty reduction and the emerging challenges*, World Bank, Washington, DC, 2013.

27 UNCTADStat 2016, per capita GDP current $.

28 UNCTADStat 2016, annual GDP growth %.

29 CIA World Factbook 2016, Vietnam, economy, updated 6 April 2016.

30 Ibid.

31 UNCTADStat, Bilateral FDI statistics, 2014.

32 S. Donnan, 'Investment from emerging nations surges', *Financial Times*, 17 May 2015.

33 'A tightening grip', *The Economist*, 14 March 2015.

34 D. C. McCornac, 'Vietnam's relations with China: a delicate balancing act', *China Currents*, 10: 2, 2011. Available at: http://www.chinacenter.net/2011/china_currents/10-2/vietnams-relations-with-china-a-delicate-balancing-act/ (date accessed 1 March 2017).

35 N. M. Tri and K. S. L. Collin, 'Lessons from the battle of the Paracel Islands', *The Diplomat*, 23 January 2014. Available at: http://thediplomat.com/2014/01/lessons-from-the-battle-of-the-paracel-islands/ (date accessed 24 February 2017).

36 G. Torode, 'Spratly Islands dispute defines China-Vietnam relations 25 years after naval clash', *South China Morning Post*, 17 March 2013.

37 R. Amer, 'China, Vietnam and the South China Sea: disputes and dispute management', *Ocean Development and International Law*, 45:1 (2014), 17–40.

38 Clinton, remarks, Hanoi, 2010.

39 D. Ten Kate, 'South China Sea oil rush risks clashes as US emboldens Vietnam on claims', *NamViet News*, 27 May 2011. Available at: https://namvietnews.wordpress.com/2011/05/27/south-china-sea-oil-rush-risks-clashes-as-u-s-emboldens-vietnam/ (date accessed 24 February 2017).

40 S. Tiezzi, 'Vietnam, the US, and China: a love triangle?', *The Diplomat*, 18 December 2013. Available at: http://thediplomat.com/2013/12/vietnam-the-us-and-china-a-love-triangle/ (date accessed 24 February 2017).

41 V. Dicke and H. Holbig, 'Rising Sino-Vietnamese tensions in the South China Sea', *German Institute of Global and Area studies Focus*, 8 (2014), 5.

42 'Vietnam prepares suit against China in spat over oil rig', *Bloomberg*, 31 May 2014. Available at: http://www.thanhniennews.com/politics/vietnam-prepares-suit-against-china-in-spat-over-oil-rig-26795.html (date accessed 24 February 2017).

43 M. Peel and T. Mitchell, 'Thousands of Chinese evacuated from Vietnam', *Financial Times*, 18 May 2014.

44 A. T. Pham, 'The returning diaspora: analysing overseas Vietnamese (Viet Kieu) contributions toward Vietnam's economic growth', Depocen Working Paper, No. 2011/20, 27 November 2010, p. 10.

45 A. Lam, '35 years after war's end, Vietnamese diaspora finds its way home', *New American Media*, 19 September 2010. Available at: http://newamericamedia.org/2010/09/vietnamese-diaspora-slow-ing-returning-home.php (date accessed 24 February 2017).

46 US State Department Mobile, Background Briefing in Hanoi Vietnam, 10 July 2012.

47 S. W. Crispin, 'Is China interfering in Vietnam's politics with its South China Sea moves?', *The Diplomat*, 23 January 2016. Available at: http://thediplomat.com/2016/01/is-china-interfering-in-viet-nams-politics-with-its-south-china-sea-moves/ (date accessed 24 February 2017).

48 Vietnam, 2013 official government estimate, Cambodia 2013 UN estimate, Laos 2013 annual official government estimate, Thailand 2010 census, Myanmar 2013 UN estimate.

49 J. Hackett (ed.), *The military balance 2012*, International Institute for Strategic Studies, London, 2012, p. 287.

50 Vietnam average growth rate 2000–14: 6.4 per cent; Thailand: 3.8 per cent. Vietnam GDP current $ 2014: $187 billion; Thailand: $406 billion. UNCTADStat at April 2016.

51 Z. Abuza and N. N. Anh, 'Little fallout: Vietnam's security policy after the 12th Congress of the Vietnam Communist Party', Centre for International Maritime Security, 8 February 2016. Available at: http://cimsec.org/21720-2/21720 (date accessed 24 February 2017).

12

Thailand and Myanmar: shifting loyalties

For decades after 1945 the international alignment of Thailand and Myanmar respectively was unchanging; Thailand was closely allied to the US, while isolated Myanmar was often heavily reliant on China. In recent years this configuration has been shifting; while Thailand's governments since 2000 have leaned closer to China, Myanmar's moves to civilian government since 2010 have increased its orientation to the US.

This chapter considers the prospects for a tougher US policy on China in both these countries. This finds that despite the importance for the US in rebuilding its relations with Thailand, the country has continued drifting out of the US's tight orbit. Having intervened clumsily in Thai internal politics, the US alienated all sides, creating space for China to strengthen its position. In Myanmar, by contrast, the shift from Tatmadaw military rule to democracy has been accompanied by a turn to the West, with tensions emerging in its relations with China. But despite this opening, the US has lacked the economic tools to take real advantage of this to establish itself as Myanmar's main international partner, and after a bumpy few years, Myanmar's relations with China are once more improving. The chapter ends by surveying the success and failures in the US's policy across South East Asia, from the Philippines to Myanmar.

Thailand and the US – a relationship on the rocks

Thailand was a close Cold War ally of the US, a signatory to the 1954 Manila pact that founded the short-lived SEATO. This put in place a mutual defence treaty between all the SEATO countries and the US, which was reinforced by a Thailand–US bilateral defence agreement in 1962. Thailand played a crucial role in the Vietnam War with up to 50,000 US troops regularly stationed there, while U-Tapao, its military airbase, was the forward base for US B-52 bombing missions over the entire Indochinese theatre. After defeat in Vietnam, Thailand was the *only* US friend, let alone ally, in the huge geographical sweep of mainland southern Asia from Vietnam to India.

After the end of the Cold War, US relations with Thailand initially remained close. American warplanes en route to Afghanistan and Iraq used U-Tapao, Thailand sent a small contingent to join the UN peacekeeping forces in Iraq and was designated a 'major non-NATO ally', giving it preferential access to US aid and military assistance.[1] However, involvement in Iraq was not popular in Thailand, especially among Muslims in the south of the country.

American use of U-Tapao also proved controversial. The US withdrew its permanent personnel from the base in 1976, but still uses it for routine refuelling; however, any expanded US access to the base has been resisted. A 2012 proposal to establish a US regional humanitarian relief and disaster centre and allow NASA weather surveillance at U-Tapao had to be abandoned due to strong popular opposition. Even the military raised concerns this might disrupt relations with China.[2]

Thailand's good relations with China date from the mid-1970s, when – in the context of the Sino-Soviet split and the 1971 rapprochement between the US and China – they normalised relations. As elsewhere, following the deal with the US and the death of Mao, China backed away from support to anti-government and anti-US insurgencies, instead aligning with the opponents of alleged 'Soviet expansionism'.[3] In Thailand this meant persuading the pro-Chinese Communist Party of Thailand – which had made significant advances during the Vietnam War, but was disintegrating under the pressures of the change in Chinese policy towards the US – to abandon its armed struggle.[4] After 1978 China joined with Thailand in opposing 'Vietnamese expansionism' following its invasion of Cambodia. Through the 1980s the Thai military junta, undoubtedly with American agreement, allowed China to supply Khmer Rouge guerrillas based in Thailand against the Vietnamese-backed Cambodian government.

After the 1991 settlement in Cambodia, Thailand facilitated China's engagement with ASEAN and has remained an active agent in soothing tensions between China and ASEAN members over the South China Sea. In the new century Thailand moved even closer to China as it became increasingly important for the Thai economy.

The Asian financial crisis

The Asian financial crisis in 1997 deepened Thailand's shift away from the US. The negative impact of the IMF and World Bank's policies imposed in return for bail-out funding undermined the standing of the US and its international financial institutions not only in the eyes of the Thai population, but among its elites.

By the 1990s Thailand had become one of the Asian 'tiger economies'. Based on a steady increase in its investment as a share of GDP, from 26 per cent in 1985 to an average of over 41 per cent through the 1990s to 1996, it saw an average growth rate of 8.6 per cent per year from 1988 to 1996.[5] By the 1990s it had begun to attract growing foreign investment. To take advantage of this, and urged on by the IMF and World Bank, Thailand began deregulating foreign exchange controls and international capital accounts.[6] As Joseph Stiglitz has argued, this 'capital account liberalisation was the most important factor leading to the crisis', as rather than boosting long-term investment it led to a flood of speculative capital inflows.[7] Foreign money financed a frenzy of commercial building in Bangkok creating a real-estate 'bubble'.[8] By 1995 capital flows into the country reached 13 per cent of GDP, higher than any other emerging market, but 'since only a small portion of it consisted of long-term investment … Thailand was positively gorging on hot money'.[9]

When the bubble burst and these speculative inflows became a rush of capital out of the country in 1996–97, the baht collapsed unleashing a region-wide financial crisis.[10]

The IMF's medicine – high interest rates, tax increases, spending cuts and privatisations – in return for its support package (Thailand received a total of $17 billion from the IMF and G7 countries) simply deepened the economic contraction. High interest rates in particular wiped out large sections of indebted Thai business and nearly 50 per cent of Thai bank loans became non-performing. In 1998 unemployment increased three-fold and GDP fell by 10.8 per cent over two years. Three years later the economy had still not recovered to pre-crisis levels.[11]

The crisis rocked Thai politics. Apart from a short interval of civilian government from 1973 to 1976, post-war Thailand's constitutional monarchy was ruled by a series of military juntas, until a new constitution brought in a form of rigged 'democracy' from 1978. But this did not bring stability and there were further episodes of military rule in the 1980s and 1990s. Under the impetus of the financial crisis, in 1997 a new Thai constitution was approved that introduced compulsory voting, thereby ruling out the vote-buying that had characterised Thai politics, and opening elections to mass popular influence.

In 1998 telecommunications' mogul and politician Thaksin Shinawatra founded a new party, the Thai Rak Thai (Thai Loves Thai) that promised to restore economic growth. His party swept to power in 2001 in Thailand's first fully democratic elections, winning support from both business circles and the popular vote in the poor north of the country on a programme of ending the IMF privatisation programme and protecting distressed Thai businesses and the rural poor.[12]

Shinawatra particularly nurtured relations with China, which he saw as key to reviving the Thai economy. Part of his electoral support came from the well-integrated ethnic-Chinese community – 10–15 per cent of the population – that includes an influential business community closely linked to China through investment and trade. Shinawatra visited China five times from 2001 to 2006, while Hu Jintao's visit to Thailand in 2003 was his first visit to an ASEAN country as president of China.[13] In 2003 Thailand and China signed a bilateral agreement to immediately eliminate tariffs on a range of products identified in the 2002 ASEAN-China Free Trade Agreement (ACFTA).[14] Thailand's trade with China jumped from $4.22 billion in 1999 to $32 billion in 2007.[15] Military cooperation with China also increased, including some small-scale joint exercises.

However, Shinawatra also sought to improve Thailand's relations with the US, including through supporting the 'war on terror'. As a result Bush's administration was not uncomfortable with Shinawatra, which affected US policy towards the crisis that unfolded in Thai politics from 2006.[16]

The US mired in Thai domestic politics

From 2006 the democratic promise that had seemed to open up based on the 1997 constitution and the relatively corruption-free elections in 2001 and 2005 came to an abrupt end with a new military coup.

Shinawatra's policies from 2001 to 2006 had some success, with the GDP growth rate recovering to an average 5.8 per cent annually from 2002 to 2006.[17] But his increasingly populist orientation, particularly to the rural poor, alienated the Bangkok elites and the royalist faction of the army.[18] In September 2006 he was overthrown in a military coup – with the foreknowledge if not the actual support of the US.[19] From this point on US became increasingly mired in Thai domestic politics, seeming first to support one side and then the other, as it tried to both court the electorally successful Thaksinites and maintain its close relations with the Thai military and monarchical elites.

From 2006 there was no stable return to civilian rule as the deep divisions in Thai society, between the poverty-stricken areas north of the capital that supported Shinawatra and the affluent, westernised population of Bangkok, constantly blew up into new confrontations between the pro- and anti-Thaksinites. The Thaksinite movement became known as the 'red shirts', from their convention of wearing red shirts on protests; the anti-Thaksinites became the 'yellow-shirts'.[20] Despite widespread repression, the Thaksinites won the elections in 2007, only to be removed the following year through a judicial coup backed by the army, provoking sustained protests that reached a peak in 2010.

The US handled the situation badly. On the one hand in 2009 the US refused the exiled Shinawatra a visa in a gesture of support to the existing Thai government.[21] Then, as the protests heated up, in 2010 the US invited representatives of both sides to a US-convened meeting in Bangkok proposing to broker a compromise. The Thai government abruptly declined and sent an envoy to Washington to rebuke the US over political interference.[22] A few days later an army crackdown in Bangkok left 91 protesters dead. In elections held in 2011 the Thaksinites again won decisively and Yingluck Shinawatra, Thaksin's sister, became prime minister, but protests continued, this time coordinated by the Bangkok-based 'yellow-shirt' opposition. In the midst of these protests the US suddenly did a volte-face and granted Shinawatra a visa, leading to anti-US protests in Bangkok and online.[23] China, however, won favour for giving $16 million in emergency aid when floods devastated large parts of Thailand in 2011.

In May 2014 the Thai army used the excuse of the extensive disruption caused by the 'yellow-shirts' to organise a coup. The US was silent as the military takeover was prepared and when the army imposed martial law the State Department still insisted it was 'not a coup'.[24] When the Generals actually assumed power the US had no choice but to reverse this position. Under US law it therefore had to impose some sanctions, so it cut aid and reduced the scope of the annual Cobra Gold joint military exercises. Then, in 2015, Daniel Russel, the US assistant secretary of state for the region, not only publicly rebuked the junta for not holding elections, but also met with the leaders of the civilian political parties, including Yingluck Shinawatra. This provoked further irritation with the US, whose protests the junta ignored, postponing elections until had first introduced a new constitution institutionalising army control over the government.[25]

The upshot was that the US had alienated both sides, standing accused of nodding the army into power, while also reproaching the coup government, however ineffectually. This prompted a significant turn towards China by the junta.[26]

China's standing in Thailand

While the US meddled in Thai domestic politics, China stuck to its approach of non-interference in other countries' internal affairs and thereby succeeded in remaining close to the Thaksinites, while also developing good relations with the Thai army.[27]

In December 2014 Chinese premier Li Keqiang visited Thailand, the most prominent foreign leader to visit after the coup.

The key driver of Sino-Thai relations has been the potential for mutual economic benefit. Whatever the outcome on the political front, for Thailand to fully emerge from its recent crisis requires a return to steady growth, which in turn means inward investment, economic partnerships and export markets. In 2013 China, already Thailand's largest export market, inched ahead of Japan to become its largest trading partner. In 2014 Thai exports to China hit $24.7 billion and their bilateral trade in goods reached $58.6 billion, with Thai–Japan bilateral trade at $52.8 billion and Thai–US trade at $36.4 billion.[28] Chinese investments in Thailand have also increased; between 2007 and 2012 Chinese companies invested $3.6 billion in Thailand, in a similar range to investment by the US ($4 billion) and Singapore ($4.9 billion) though well behind Japan ($18 billion).[29] The ACFTA – which covered 90 per cent of goods and services traded between ASEAN and China by 2013 – boosted trade and encouraged an expansion in Chinese FDI. Many Chinese companies considering a move into Thailand or Vietnam plan to re-export their product back to China, so tariffs levels are crucial.

Growing numbers of Thai students study in China, drawn by the low costs, high educational standards and attractive scholarships.[30] Military exchanges have also stepped up, including scholarships for Thai officers to train and study in China. Within ASEAN Thailand has sought to ease the complicated relations over the South China Sea, playing a key role in drawing China into dialogue.

However, despite tensions, links with the US remain strong. Military-to-military ties in particular remain crucial and the annual US–Thai-led Cobra Gold military exercises, the largest multilateral exercises held in Asia, continue each year. But there is no doubt that since 1997 Thailand's relations with the US have become increasingly unfocused and even troubled, while its links with China have extended on all fronts. So far the US has failed to inject new life into this old alliance.

Contested Myanmar

Myanmar, in contrast, spent most of its post-independence history from 1948 in isolation from the West and subject to extensive US sanctions, particularly after the 1988 army crackdown on protests which first brought Aung San Suu Kyi, daughter of the leader of Burma's independence struggle, to prominence.[31] Her elevation to almost saintly prestige in the West has been in counterpoint to the pariah status accorded to the Burmese regime.[32] In 2005 Burma was included in Bush's register of outlaw regimes: 'in our world there remain outposts of tyranny … in Cuba, and Burma, and North Korea, and Iran, and Belarus, and Zimbabwe.'[33]

A combination of the US strategic shift to Asia and moves by the military junta to make concessions to the opposition movement began to change this. From 2010, when the military released Aung San Suu Kyi from house arrest and held partially democratic elections, Myanmar was suddenly and decisively brought in from the cold. In 2011 Hillary Clinton became the first senior US official to visit the country for 50 years; in 2012 Obama visited, the first US president ever to do so, followed by an unprecedented second visit in 2014. After decades when China and its other neighbours had pursued their relations with Myanmar without interference from the West, a battle had been unleashed to draw it into America's sphere of influence.

A textbook case of post-colonial underdevelopment

Myanmar's 50 years of isolation from the West began immediately upon the close of the Second World War.[34] After a prolonged anti-colonial struggle, Britain finally ceded Burma independence in 1948. With anti-British feeling running high, it became the only former British colony, apart from Aden, not to elect to join the Commonwealth upon liberation, for which it was rewarded by a British diplomatic cold-shoulder.[35] Relations between post-liberation Burma and the US foundered over US support for GMD forces that had fled China in 1949 and occupied parts of northern Burma. Burma refused to join SEATO and went on to join the non-aligned movement, which the US saw as no better than aligning with the USSR.

Its relations with the socialist countries were better but also troubled. The USSR was among the first to establish diplomatic relations with independent Burma, but initially even this was complicated by the fact the Burmese communists, who had played an important role in the independence struggle, were engaged in a civil war against the government. Burma was the first non-communist country to recognise the PRC and, after the Sino-Soviet split, its non-alignment reassured China that it would not facilitate Soviet encirclement. But again the insurgent activities of the Burmese Communist Party in the border provinces disrupted Sino-Burmese relations until the end of the Cultural Revolution.[36]

Burma had been the site of the longest and most destructive land battle of the Second World War, which left its main cities in ruins and famine looming, a devastation from which it took decades to recover.[37] Burma's GDP did not even reach its 1939 level until 1959–60, meaning that per capita consumption in 1959 was only 75 per cent of 1939 levels due to population growth.[38] From 1955 the USSR began providing some limited assistance to rebuilding the country and agreed preferential trade deals, but even this tailed off in the mid-1960s, as Burma was seen to lean to China in the Sino-Soviet split. As a result Japan was Burma's major source of aid, contributing an aggregated $2.2 billion up to 1988 – probably Japan's largest aid programme.[39] But this was nothing like enough to get the economy on track.

Splits in the parties emerging from the independence struggle and fears that this might bring the communists into government led the army to take power in 1962. It then proceeded down an economically disastrous course. Ne Win, whose army-led – Tatmadaw – government was in power until 1988, pursued his 'Burmese Road to Socialism' that was 'a strange blend of Buddhism, nationalism and command economics'.[40] Alongside this, almost constant ethnic and communist insurgencies in the north and east of the country meant the economy never functioned as an integrated whole and resources were sucked into attempts to quell these revolts.[41] After some stable growth from the mid-1970s, Burma's economy fell into recession in 1986, dropping to a devastating –10 per cent growth in 1988. This led to the eruption of a mass opposition movement in 1988 that looked close to overthrowing the military government. The army crushed the movement, and then conceded multiparty elections. In 1990 Aung

San Suu Kyi's National League for Democracy (NLD) – founded in the aftermath of the uprising – won the elections; but the army rejected the outcome and returned to military government.

The failure of the previous economic policies and the mass movement this had provoked led the new army government from 1988 to make a turn in both economic and domestic policy, liberalising the conditions for private business and foreign investment, while also negotiating ceasefires with many of its insurgent groups. Despite US and EU sanctions, this reaped economic benefit and the situation began to improve through the 1990s.[42] This eventually bore fruit in a growth rate averaging a stunning 11.3 per cent per year from 1999 to 2010; but this was from such an incredibly low base that in 2010 it was still among the world's poorest countries, with GDP per capita of only $391.[43]

Myanmar is rich in rich natural resources, including gemstones, rare wood, the world's 10th largest estimated gas reserves (2.54 trillion cubic metres) and the largest oil reserves in South East Asia (3.2 billion barrels), as well as significant river systems that could be exploited for hydroelectric power.[44] In the context of Western sanctions it was primarily Thailand, China and India that took up the opportunities this offered.

When the US began to turn towards the country from 2010, China's relations with Myanmar were already deeply entrenched.[45] China overtook Thailand as its leading trading partner in 2011, and by 2014 their total trade had hit $24.5 billion, nearly three times Myanmar's trade with Thailand, and ten-fold that with Singapore, India and Japan respectively. Trade with the US in 2014 still did not even reach $200 million.[46] Total accumulated FDI in Myanmar from 1988 to July 2013 was estimated at $43 billion of which China accounted for 32 per cent, Thailand 23 per cent, Hong Kong 14.6 per cent, and South Korea and the UK 7 per cent apiece.[47]

However, China's favoured position within Myanmar was to prove vulnerable as the Tatmadaw gradually stepped aside to allow civilian rule, bringing the pro-Western forces of Aung San Suu Kyi's NLD to effective power at the end of 2015.

Myanmar–China relations after 2010

Problems in Myanmar–China relations began to emerge very rapidly from the Tatmadaw's turn to reintegrate with the West. In 2011, against a background of some rise in anti-China sentiment, the government suspended several troubled Chinese-funded projects that had met strong local opposition due to environmental and other impacts.[48] These included the China Power Investment Company's £3.6 billion Myitsone hydroelectric dam on the Irrawaddy and the Letpadaung Copper Mine.

Between 2011 and 2013 relations deteriorated further when a 17-year ceasefire in the Kachin border province broke down, leading to renewed separatist insurgency. With refugees flooding across the border into China, China was caught between the two sides. The Kachin minorities demanded China intervene on their behalf, while the central government implied China was supporting the insurgents. Eventually China did get involved in negotiations, but the Tatmadaw distrusted China's role.[49]

The re-emergence of Kokang insurgency on another part of the border in 2015 brought further strain. Kokang has a mainly ethnically Chinese population of about 150,000 and for much of the post-war period was run semi-independently by the pro-Chinese Burmese Communist Party and its successor organisation. The Tatmadaw had taken control of the area in 2009, but in 2015 the opposition regrouped and attacked the army. China brokered a rapid ceasefire, but was nonetheless accused of aiding and abetting the rebels. In Myanmar anti-Chinese sentiment contributed to popular support for the army's action against the Kokang rebels, whereas in China there was equivalent popular sympathy for the rebels due to shared ethnicity.[50]

Reflecting these troubled relations, there were no visits by Chinese leaders between April 2011 and September 2012 – Myanmar's period of rapid political change, which also saw the historic visits of Clinton and Obama mentioned above. Chinese investments dropped sharply from $8.3 billion in 2010 to $4.3 billion in 2011 and down again to $0.5 billion in 2012.[51]

What posed the biggest question mark for China was the impact on Myanmar's foreign policy of the 2015 election of Aung San Suu Kyi and the NLD. China, ever careful not to interfere in internal affairs of other countries, had been signally neutral towards Suu Kyi and her movement, a coolness exacerbated by China's own sensitivities about 'democracy movements'. The West on the other hand built up her international profile during her house arrest in the 1990s; she was awarded the Nobel Peace Prize in 1991, was the subject of countless documentaries and popularised by the feature films *Beyond Rangoon* (1995) and *The Lady* (2011). Following her release from house arrest in 2010 she travelled to the US and Europe, receiving an ecstatic welcome.

The West has staked a great deal on Suu Kyi and the NLD. But even before assuming power, her image in the West had taken a knock from her failure to support the desperate plight of the Muslim Rohingya minority.[52] Such humanitarian concerns have made it difficult to present the situation in Myanmar as an untrammelled 'democratic' success.[53]

Seeking a reset

Following two bumpy years, in 2013 China took significant steps to improve its relations with Myanmar, particularly with proposals for infrastructure development that would integrate Myanmar's land and sea connections across South and South East Asia. Myanmar has a key role in China's 'Maritime Silk Road' proposals, which aim to improve port facilities along the east-west route from the Pacific to the Gulf and link these to improved land communications, including pipelines, railways and roads. In December 2013 the first four-country talks were convened on the 'BCIM economic corridor', a plan to improve overland trade and transport eventually continuously linking Kunming in South China to Kolkata in India.

At the same time, some of China's key investments in Myanmar bore fruit with the July 2013 opening of an overland pipeline linking gas reserves off Myanmar's coast via its deepwater port of Kyaukphyu to southern China. A similar oil pipeline was completed in August 2014, allowing China to transport crude oil from the Gulf, bypassing the vulnerable Malacca Strait. The pipeline is expected to deliver 12 million tons a year of crude oil to China as well as fuel oils to Myanmar itself.[54]

Despite the problems accompanying some Chinese projects – the Myitsone dam project remains on hold, for example – Myanmar desperately needs to develop its infrastructure for sustained growth. Analysts estimate that with the appropriate invest-ment Myanmar could grow its $45 billion GDP in 2010 to more than $200 billion by 2030.[55]

While the government in Myanmar may hope that the West will balance its reliance on China for trade and investment, the US is inhibited by slow growth and the problems in persuading risk-averse private companies to invest in a distant and still unstable South East Asian country. So far the US has delivered little beyond some limited investment in light manufacturing and consumer goods production. Japan proposed a Japan–Mekong initiative, providing $6.1 billion in aid to the whole region from 2015 to 2018, but only a small share will aid Myanmar.[56] Against this, China's state banks and construction companies offer investment in major infrastructure projects notwithstanding the 'risky' environment.[57]

China also took steps to reset relations with Suu Kyi, opening party-to-party rela-tions with the NLD before the 2015 elections. A 12-member NLD delegation visited China in 2013. Suu Kyi's first major foreign trip after becoming Myanmar's de facto leader was to China in August 2016 before visiting either the US or India.

The next five years will be crucial in how this previously closed and isolated country positions itself in the new global alignment. Alongside its internal changes, twenty-first-century political geography has moved Myanmar from the outer fringe of the old world to the epicentre of the new. Rich in natural resources, open to global trade and with a working-age population of 46 million, with the right policies it can become a new Asian success story. This considerably depends on whether it prioritises regional trade and development or instead is drawn into the web of anti-China power play that the US is weaving in the region.

After a sometimes rocky start with post-Tatmadaw Myanmar, China has worked to rebuild relations, deploying not just its own economic leverage, but playing to the advantages for Myanmar in integrating into the rising potential of Asia as a whole. The US on its side has sought to capitalise on its long-standing support for the NLD to build closer friends in the country, but as elsewhere in the region, beyond gunboats to protect against a chimerical Chinese threat, it has not been clear what else it has to offer.

Guns or butter?

The Obama administration invested considerable efforts in its relations with the coun-tries of the Mekong peninsula and across South East Asia, courting old enemies, reaching out to estranged friends and seeking new allies. To this end, the region saw a regular sequence of high-ranking US visits from the president downwards. US warships have become more frequent visitors to the region's ports. And the TPP was presented as the opportunity to take privileged advantage of the huge US market – precisely the reason that Trump cancelled it.

But, in the final analysis, while the US primarily offers a special relationship with the greatest armed force on the planet, China offers a close economic and trading relation-ship with the most dynamic global economy. The US argues that a strengthened China will disrupt the stability of Asia therefore America is needed to guarantee the peace. China counters that an integrated Asia based on mutual benefit can deliver economic development, growth and prosperity for all and it is the US that stirs up conflict.

In the recent past the US was the key market for almost all the countries of South East Asia, but since the 2008 financial crisis its imports have stagnated. By the end of 2013 world imports had risen by 9.8 per cent compared to the pre-crisis peak. Imports by developing Asian economies, of which China is the largest, rose by 34.3 per cent, but US imports were still 0.2 per cent below pre-crisis peaks. Even Japan's imports rose by 5.2 per cent.[58] Additionally, US annual FDI outflow is flat, whereas China's is taking off; the US needs international finance to cover its long-term trade deficit and the gap between savings and investment, whereas China can offer cheap loans, currency swaps and infrastructure investment. And if Trump really pursues an 'America first' trade policy, applying new elevated tariffs and penalties on US companies for outsourcing, then the US will have even less to offer the region economically.

In other words, as the US courts them to join a US-led bloc against China, these South East Asian countries find themselves facing the old 'guns or butter' choice: a US military umbrella or China's trade?

Most of these countries would like both. But the American umbrella comes with strings attached, including a high degree of US meddling between governments, oppositions and the military to secure a US role not just as external ally but domestic political patron. Until the end of the twentieth century such US fixing was largely seen as a necessary price for the Pax Americana – especially by what were essentially client regimes. But such de facto surrender of sovereignty has become unacceptable to stronger national governments. The outrage following the Snowden revelations of US phone tapping and email hacking of heads of state and senior politicians was near unanimous across the region. The US remains the world's pre-eminent military power, but this is not enough to buy compliant regimes.

Since announcing its foreign policy turn to Asia the US has advanced its military and naval presence in the South China Sea and rebuilt its relations with Vietnam and Myanmar. With the Philippines and Vietnam, backed by the US, pushing a hard line against China, an anti-China bandwagon in the South China Sea seemed on the cards.

But it has not played out like that just yet. Crucially, although Vietnam–China relations have seesawed, on balance Vietnam has chosen stability in its relations with China over a more aggressive policy in the South China Sea. As a result, with the other littoral states taking a determinedly neutral stance, rather than drawing the rest of ASEAN along in its wake, the Philippines and the US ended up looking rather isolated. And under Duterte even the Philippines has turned away from a confrontational course. Trump declared his administration's intention to make another try at using the South China Sea to draw a line against China, but for the time being the situation remains in uneasy balance.

At the same time, away from the flashpoint in the South China Sea, Thailand has moved closer to China and China has got its relations with Myanmar back on track.

All these countries may wish for American guns *and* Chinese butter, but the price they are willing to pay for American firepower depends to what degree they believe they face a real threat from China. As we have seen, neither China's behaviour nor its stated goals have so far given the US a convincing case that it has aggressive intent, and its neighbours have not been inclined to sign up to the US view that this is the main danger they confront. Whether they come to think so in the future depends to a large degree on how sensitively China treads and how gracefully it wears its new mantle of regional power.

Notes

1   E. Chanlett-Avery, 'Thailand: background and US relations', Congressional Research Service Report, RL32593, 29 July 2015.

2   J. Cole and S. Sciacchitano, 'Baseless controversy over Thailand's U-Tapao', Asia Times, 22 June 2012.

3   For the impact of the Sino-Soviet split on China's international policy, see Chapter 5.

4   Ba, 'China and ASEAN', p. 627.

5   World Bank world development indicators, 2015. GFCF % of GDP; UNCTADStat 2016, annual GDP % growth.

6   P. Blustein, The chastening: the crisis that rocked the global financial system and humbled the IMF, Public Affairs, New York, 2003, p. 59.

7   Stiglitz, Globalisation, p. 99.

8   Blustein, The chastening, pp. 54–61.

9   Ibid., p. 59.

10 Stiglitz, Globalisation, pp. 94–5.

11 Ibid., pp. 104–32.

12 P. Phongpaichit and C. Baker, '"Business" populism in Thailand', Journal of Democracy, 16:2 (2005), 58–72.

13 S. P. Limaye, Asia's China debate, Asia Pacific Centre for Security Studies, Honolulu, December 2003, ch. 14.

14 See ThaiFTA.com for details of all its free trade agreements.

15 Thailand China Links, Thailand China Economic Information, Statistics of bilateral trade, investment and tourism.

16 T. Pongsudhirak, 'An unaligned alliance: Thailand-US relations in the early 21st century', Asian Politics & Policy, 8:1 (2016), 63–74.

17 UNCTADStat 2016, Annual GDP growth rates.

18 Pongsudhirak, 'An unaligned alliance'.

19 'US embassy cables: Thai king's relaxed reaction to Thaksin Shinawatra's downfall', The Guardian, 14 December 2010. Available at: https://www.theguardian.com/world/us-embassy-cables-documents/79101 (date accessed 1 March 2017).

20 R. Bernstein, 'Thailand: beautiful and bitterly divided', The New York Review of Books, 20 November 2014.

21 'Thaksin ends visit, US on defensive', The Nation, Bangkok, 21 August 2012.

22 S. W. Crispin, 'US slips, China glides in Thai crisis', Asia Times, 20 July 2010.

23 'Thaksin ends visit'.

24 J. Schulberg, 'The military coup in Thailand is putting the US into an awkward position', New Republic, 24 May 2014. Available at: https://newrepublic.com/article/117894/thailand-coup-foreign-assistance-act-put-us-awkward-position (date accessed 28 February 2017).

25 Editorial, 'Thailand's power hungry generals', New York Times, 12 August 2016.

26 A. S. Lefevre, 'Thailand boosts military ties with China amid US spat', Reuters, 6 February 2015. Available at: http://uk.reuters.com/article/uk-thailand-china-idUKKBN0LA0LL20150206 (date accessed 28 February 2017).

27 P. Parameswaran, 'Thailand turns to China', The Diplomat, 20 December 2014. Available at: http://thediplomat.com/2014/12/thailand-turns-to-china/ (date accessed 28 February 2017).

28 CIA World Factbook, 2016.

29 UNCTADStat, Bilateral FDI statistics, 2014.

30 'Chinese benefits lure Thai students', Times Higher Education Supplement, 8 March 2002.

31 This chapter primarily uses 'Burma' as the name of the country when referring to the past and 'Myanmar' for the present.

32 D. I. Steinberg, 'Aung San Suu Kyi and US policy toward Burma/Myanmar', *Journal of Current Southeast Asian Affairs*, 29:3 (2010), 35–59.

33 Confirmation hearing of Condoleezza Rice, 18 January 2005.

34 For post-war Myanmar, see M. Callahan, *Making enemies: war and state building in Burma*, Cornell University Press, Ithaca, NY, and London, 2003.

35 M. Callahan, 'Myanmar's perpetual junta', *New Left Review*, 60 (November–December 2009), 38.

36 Ibid., p. 42.

37 Ibid., p. 37.

38 Maddison, *World economy*, Tables 5b and 5c.

39 D. I. Steinberg, 'Japanese economic assistance to Burma: aid in the "Tarenagashi" manner?', *Crossroads: An Interdisciplinary Journal of Southeast Asian Studies*, 5:2 (1990), 51.

40 Callahan, 'Myanmar's perpetual junta', p. 41.

41 Ibid., p. 42.

42 Ibid., pp. 46–8.

43 UNCTADStat 2016, GDP annual growth rates; GDP per capita constant prices.

44 C. Rask and C. Wong, 'Status quo revisited: the evolving ties between China and Myanmar', *Knowledge@Wharton*, 20 December 2013. Available at: http://knowledge.wharton.upenn.edu/article/status-quo-revisited-evolving-ties-china-myanmar/ (date accessed 10 June 2015).

45 M. Skidmore and T. Wilson (eds), *Dictatorship, disorder and decline in Myanmar*, Australian National University Press, Canberra, 2008, pp. 87–104.

46 IMF Direction of Trade statistics, 2016. Myanmar's trade figures are distorted by the vast scale of smuggled goods in and out of the country, including manufactured goods from China and Thailand and the illegal export of opium and jade.

47 *Myanmar Business Guide*, PriceWaterhouseCooper, London, February 2014.

48 M. A. Myoe, 'Myanmar's China policy since 2011: determinants and directions', *Journal of Current Southeast Asian Affairs*, 34:2 (2015), 21–54.

49 Ibid., pp. 40–2.

50 Ibid., pp. 42–5.

51 UNCTADStat 2016, Bilateral FDI Statistics 2014.

52 N. Syed, 'Where's Aung San Suu Kyi when Burma needs her?', *Foreign Policy*, 8 June 2015. Available at: http://foreignpolicy.com/2015/06/08/wheres-aung-san-suu-kyi-when-burma-needs-her/ (date accessed 28 February 2017).

53 B. Einhorn, 'Obama visits Myanmar, a success story that has soured', *Bloomberg*, 13 November 2014. Available at: https://www.bloomberg.com/news/articles/2014-11-13/obama-visits-myanmar-a-success-story-that-has-soured (date accessed 28 February 2017).

54 A. Anal, 'New China-Myanmar oil pipeline by-passes Malacca trap', *The Hindu*, 30 January 2015.

55 H. Chhor, R. Dobbs, D. N. Hansen, F. Thompson, N. Shah and L. Streiff, *Myanmar's moment: unique opportunities, major challenges*, McKinsey Global Institute, London, June 2013.

56 P. Parameswaran, 'The real importance of Japan's new strategy for the Mekong', *The Diplomat*, 7 July 2015. Available at: http://thediplomat.com/2015/07/the-real-importance-of-japans-new-strategy-for-the-mekong/ (date accessed 28 February 2017).

57 Rask and Wong, 'Status quo revisited'.

58 Calculated by John Ross from Centraal Planbureau, Netherlands Bureau for Economic Policy Analysis data.

Part V
Containment from south and west

13

Winning over India

Obama welcomed Manmohan Singh to Washington in 2009 by proclaiming that 'India is indispensable' and that US–India relations were 'one of the defining partnerships of the 21st century'.[1] What he meant was that India is the US's chief hope for a counterweight to China in Asia.

India was always going to be one of the top four players in Asia. Nuclear-armed and with a population of 1.25 billion, approaching and soon to overtake China's, by 2016 India was the seventh largest economy in the world (in PPPs India's economy was already third).[2] It is the cradle of three major religions (Hinduism, Sikhism and Buddhism) and has a globally influential historic and contemporary culture. It is a significant military and naval power, with the sixth largest defence budget in the world, at $51.3 billion and 2.3 per cent of GDP in 2015.[3]

Its growth rates have also been catching up on China's, growing at over 8 per cent from 2003 to a peak of 10.6 per cent in 2010 (apart from 2008 owing to the world financial crisis).[4] On the basis of its 2003 to 2007 record, a McKinsey study estimated it would be the fifth largest global consumer market by 2025.[5] In 2010 the *Economist* opined: 'Some economists think India will grow faster than any other large country over the next 25 years. Rapid growth in a country of 1.2 billion people is exciting, to put it mildly.'[6]

From the US perspective, a successful India has the potential to prevent China becoming the unchallenged leader in Asia and to ideologically push back against the encroaching authority of China's 'market socialism'. India has its own concerns about a resurgent China, focused primarily on unresolved border disputes, historic disagreements over relations with Pakistan, and China's increasing presence in the Indian Ocean. Thus the US has logged India as a strong candidate for recruitment to a policy of containing China.

But, as elsewhere in Asia, developments in India and its foreign relations have not gone exactly as the US expected. Firstly, India's advance has not been such to challenge China's economic position in Asia; India may have caught up with China in terms of growth rate but it is not even within range of the total size of the Chinese economy. Secondly, while both the Congress-led government of Manmohan Singh and, from 2014, Modi's Bharatiya Janata Party (BJP) government have sought to continue the warming in India's relations with the US that had begun in the 1990s, this has not meant

India privileging its relations with the US over all others. Rather India can be said to be pursuing a contemporary variant of its Cold War 'non-alignment'.[7]

Cold War estrangement from the US and China

Following independence in 1947, India rapidly became a champion of the Non-Aligned Movement, attempting to take a neutral stance in the global stand-off between the US and the USSR as the Cold War accelerated.[8] As the US cold warriors saw 'non-alignment' as nothing short of siding with the USSR, US post-war relations with India increasingly soured. Instead the US built close ties with Pakistan, which was at logger-heads with India over Kashmir. From 1954 the US supplied Pakistan with military aid; and Pakistan became a treaty ally through signing up to SEATO.[9]

India's Cold War estrangement from the US reached its nadir in 1971 when Nixon covertly armed Pakistan's military dictator, Yahya Khan, in a genocidal war against East Pakistan, which was to become Bangladesh. Pakistan, as created in 1947, was a geographically unwieldy two-part state, with its capital and military headquarters in the west, the majority of its population in the east, and a thousand miles of India in between.[10] With no rail or direct road link between East and West Pakistan and no passenger flights until 1955, it was held together by a series of military governments.[11] But in December 1970 Pakistan-wide elections saw the Bengali nationalist Awami League sweep the board in the east giving it an overall majority in the Pakistani National Assembly. Rather than convene the National Assembly, Yahya Khan, with implied American support, unleashed a reign of terror against the East Pakistani population, especially the large Hindu minority.[12] Literally millions of refugees flooded across the border into India.

Under overwhelming pressure to step in, Indira Gandhi's Congress government looked for international support, but when she visited the US at the height of the crisis, her meeting with Nixon became 'a cathartic brawl, propelled not just by totally opposite views of a brewing war, but … [by] hearty personal contempt'.[13] With Nixon covertly arming Pakistan despite a US embargo, Gandhi turned to the USSR and in August 1971 they signed a Treaty of Friendship and Cooperation.[14]

It was in the midst of this conflict that Kissinger and Nixon took the first steps in the thaw with China, with Kissinger's initial visit to China in 1971 brokered by Yahya Khan.[15] This unexpected rapprochement was eased by their similar views on the conflict in the subcontinent. China distrusted India, particularly due to the events that led up to their brief border war in 1962.[16] This was exacerbated by India's treaty with the USSR, which reinforced China's interpretation of the breakaway of Bangladesh as a step to further Soviet encirclement. When war finally came at the end of that year, the US and China both effectively supported Pakistan.

The 1971 conflict set the framework for India's foreign and diplomatic relations with both the US and China until the 1990s: China and the US in a de facto alliance and more or less enthusiastically backing Pakistan; and India increasingly close to the USSR.

Turn to the West

The end of the Cold War broke this apart and the 1990s saw India seek to reconfigure relations with the US and adopt a stronger orientation to its neighbours in Asia.

Although begun under the Congress government in the first half of the decade, rapprochement with the US moved forward most rapidly under the BJP government elected in 1998, paradoxically accelerated by India's nuclear weapon's test in that year. The Vajpayee government was dangling the possibility of a much closer India–US relationship, in which India's nuclear weapons would even the playing field with China and Russia.[17] While Clinton had to impose sanctions, he nonetheless visited India in 2000, the first visit by a US president for over 20 years. And in 2002, George W. Bush's National Security Strategy described India as 'as a growing world power with which we have common strategic interests'.[18]

The high point of this post-Cold War thaw was the 2005 agreement between Bush and Manmohan Singh to legitimise India's civil nuclear power programme and lift sanctions, aided by India's previous endorsement of the 'war on terror'. This removed the nuclear issue from US–India relations. India had been banned from participation in civilian nuclear power programmes since refusing to sign the NPT in 1968. India refused because the treaty meant only the existing five nuclear states could develop nuclear weapons. Apart from India the only states that have openly tested a bomb against the terms of the NPT are Pakistan and North Korea (although Israel is known to have clandestinely developed nuclear weapons). After 2005 de facto the NPT did not apply to India.[19]

India's annual arms spending has risen rapidly, from $11.04 billion in 2001 to $38.35 billion in 2015.[20] In 2010 India became the largest global importer of arms; in 2013 the US's $1.9 billion sales to India were its largest to any country, and in 2014 it displaced Russia as India's biggest arms supplier.[21] The US also began to hold more military exercises with India than any other country – around 80 joint combat exercises over the decade to 2014.

But despite this orientation to the West from the 1990s, India did not simply move into the US camp. It refused to support the invasion of Iraq and never fully agreed to the sanctions on Iran.[22] India also stayed out of the TPP – the attractions of a free trade area with the US did not outweigh the deregulatory adjustments India would have had to make to participate.[23] And India has never abandoned its close ties with Russia, evidenced for example by India's abstention on the 2014 UN vote condemning Russia over the Crimea. Moreover, Russia still plays a vital role in providing technology for India's nuclear power programme, as a major arms supplier and as a source of energy imports.

Overall post-Cold War India has pursued a position of 'strategic autonomy', a recasting of 'non-alignment' for the twenty-first century. India has sought closer relations with the US, but also has shored up its own independent position through ties with Russia; improving links with other Asian neighbours, especially Japan; and stable relations with China.[24]

From the high point of 2005, apart from in military collaboration, further progress in US–Indian relations ran into the sand. In the aftermath of the 2008 financial crisis, when China was courted for loans and referred to as half a 'G2', India seemed to drop off the US radar. Things did not improve when president-elect Obama proposed to interfere in India's sovereign affairs by declaring that sorting out the 'tar-pit' of relations between India and Pakistan over Kashmir would be a 'critical task' for his administration, proposing to 'get a special envoy in there to figure out a plausible approach'.[25] Insult was added to injury when Obama's first trip to Asia in November 2009 not only bypassed India, but in his keynote speech in Japan setting out his vision for US policy in Asia-Pacific he did not mention India.[26] An attempted reset in 2010, through a glitzy welcome to Manmohan Singh in Washington, followed by a state visit to India in November when Obama supported India's case for a permanent seat on the Security Council, failed to kick off any compelling new initiatives. As a Carnegie Foundation report put it, India's policy elites felt Washington viewed India 'more as the object of American problem solving than as a full strategic partner'. [27] The 2013 debacle of the treatment of Devyani Khobragade, an Indian diplomat in the US who was arrested and strip searched for alleged visa fraud, seemed to confirm Indian suspicions that the US harbours a contemptuous, indeed racist, attitude towards it.[28]

Modi: resetting the foreign policy agenda

For the US foreign policy establishment, this stall in relations with India was disastrous: 'the challenge of restoring strong ties with India should lie at the top of the Asia agenda. No amount of pivoting will matter much if US ties to the world's largest democracy … lie in tatters.'[29] The election of Modi's BJP in 2014 was widely greeted as an opening for a reset, despite the US having denied him a visa in 2005 due to his alleged role in the 2002 Gujarat sectarian riots.[30]

The BJP's 2014 electoral success followed several years of increasing problems for both Manmohan Singh's government and the Congress Party. Euphoria about India's growth rate had been pricked from 2011 when it slowed to 6.4 per cent, fell sharply to 4.7 per cent in 2012 and recovered to only 5.4 per cent in 2014.[31] Growth in income per head, which had almost doubled between 2000 and 2010, also slowed. In 2014 per capita GDP was still only $1610 per year.[32] Inflation averaging over 10 per cent from 2008 to 2013 exacerbated the pressure on living standards.[33]

At the same time the Congress-led coalition government became paralysed by a series of corruption scandals and internal divisions.[34] Other domestic problems deepened the sense of crisis: a new wave of Naxalite insurgency in the east;[35] massive power cuts in 2012 affecting half the population;[36] and deadly communal violence. The upshot was that in the 2014 elections the Congress Party reaped its worst result since 1947, reduced to 19 per cent of the vote and 44 seats in the 543-strong Lok Sabha, while Modi and his Hindu nationalist BJP won a landslide in seats – though not in votes.[37]

Modi is a controversial figure due to his well-documented Hindu sectarian politics, which can unleash communal violence towards Muslims and other non-Hindus, justify the oppression of women, reinforce the caste system, exclude non-caste dalits from full rights and disrupt the path towards integration of India's diverse society.[38] But analysis of that and its consequences are beyond the scope of this book.

What is clear is that electoral analysis suggests that Modi's pledge to turn around India's slowing economy was decisive in the BJP's success; this had to be Modi's priority, with underdeveloped infrastructure and a weak manufacturing sector the key challenges.[39] India's national grid is beset by failures; its roads are poor and the network inadequate; its railway is extensive but out of date; and slums, shoddy construction and inadequate sewage plague its cities. An estimated $200 billion a year in investment is needed to update India's power and transport infrastructure.[40]

However, while domestic economic policy was Modi's first concern, he also energetically set about boosting India's profile abroad – primarily directed at driving up foreign trade and investment, but also 'balancing' the growing influence of China.[41] In general these two goals meshed. Under the rubric of 'Act East' Modi announced a policy of pursuing stronger Indian cooperation with ASEAN in particular, but also Japan and Australia. While driven by economic priorities, this also met US needs in Asia. It was Hillary Clinton in a 2011 speech in India, who first proposed an Indian 'Act East' policy, urging that India place a stronger focus on the Asia-Pacific to back up the US 'pivot'.[42] Modi's decision to make Japan, the US and Australia the first three countries he visited outside South Asia pointed to further alignment with US priorities.[43]

However, despite Modi's investment of diplomatic energy, there were no significant new bilateral initiatives with the US or its allies.[44] The US has little to put on the table to aid Modi's trade and investment agenda, and Modi has not been prepared to sign India up as a second fiddle in a US strategy framed by its relations with China.

Trump flagged that he would seek to reboot US–India relations. After inauguration, Trump put in a formal call to Modi ahead of any European leader, inviting him to visit the US in 2017.[45] But while there are affinities between Modi and Trump in their rightwing populist politics and ultra hardline line against Islamist terrorism, Trump's protectionist trade policies, anti-immigration stance and 'America first' rhetoric will not fit well with Modi's other priorities.

The Japan–India axis

While US–India relations failed to find ongoing warmth, India's relations with the US's closest Asian ally – Japan – proceeded apace. In the 1990s Indian governments had stepped up an orientation to Japan.[46] But the most substantive progress began during Abe's 2006–07 administration, when Japan and India agreed a 'strategic and global partnership' to boost economic and military ties.[47] In 2009 annual bilateral strategic dialogues were established, putting India–Japan security relations on a par with its relations with Russia.[48]

Abe always understood the importance of a strategic orientation to India to counter the rise of China in Asia.[49] His 2006 book – and political manifesto – *Toward a beautiful country* argued: 'It is of crucial importance to Japan's national interest that it further strengthen ties with India ... It would not be a surprise if in another 10 years, Japan-India relations overtake Japan–US and Japan–China relations.'[50]

Abe's variant of Japanese nationalism does not raise the same alarm in India as elsewhere in Asia, not just because of geographical distance, but because India has no history of invasion or colonisation by Japan. Indeed, during the Second World War, many pro-independence Indians joined Bose's 'Indian National Army', which fought alongside Japan against the British in some arenas.[51] Japan is thus well placed to provide India with a counterweight to China – and the US with a useful proxy.

Modi's election gave relations a further boost, reinforced by the affinities between Abe and Modi's shared right-wing nationalist politics. When Modi visited Japan in August 2014, Abe spent more time with him than he had with any other official guest.

In 2014 Japan joined the annual US-Indian Malabar naval exercises – it had participated in 2007 and 2009 but not been invited since due to formal remonstrations from China. In 2015 the annual exercises were formally redesignated as trilateral.[52] Also that year the first India–Japan–US trilateral ministerial meeting took place in New York, and the first high-level India–Japan–Australia trilateral in New Delhi. These were followed by strong hints from the US that the abandoned 2007 Quadrilateral Security Dialogue with Japan, Australia and India would soon be revived.[53]

But collaboration on security is one thing: the critical issue is what Japan can deliver economically. Modi's premiership will stand or fall on growth in the Indian economy.

'Make in India'

Modi's economic reforms were launched under the slogan 'Make in India', primarily directed at addressing India's manufacturing weakness, thereby de facto abandoning the unrealistic suggestion of the World Bank and others that India could leap directly to becoming a service sector-led economy.[54] This requires boosting and sustaining investment levels in manufacturing and infrastructure, to lift productivity and attract overseas manufacturers to India.

Modi had some initial success, with growth on reported figures back to over 7 per cent in 2015, for the first time outperforming China's growth of 6.9 per cent.[55] While this was mainly down to the dramatic fall in world oil prices in 2014–15, which benefited India as a major oil importer, India had also seen a boost to investment (GFCF), which began to edge up again as a share of GDP in 2014 after falling every year from its peak at 33 per cent of GDP in 2007 to 28.4 per cent in 2013.[56] The key element in this was a very significant increase in public investment as a share of GFCF, which increased by 21 per cent in 2015–16, while private investment fell 4 per cent.[57]

India's FDI inflows, which had only reached $23.5 billion at their 2011 peak compared to China's $124 billion, also looked likely to overtake China in 2016. However, with China's FDI stock standing at $1.34 trillion compared to India's $218 billion, catching up with China in inward investment impact is still a long way in the future.[58]

Japan's investment in India had risen from a paltry $86 million in 2006 to $1.3 billion in 2012.[59] During his 2014 visit Modi secured a promise of $35 billion infrastructure investment and agreed to create a fast track for Japanese investment in India – 'Japan Plus'. In 2015 a further agreement set a target of doubling Japan's FDI in India over five years. Japan is also the largest donor of international aid to India.[60] But while India may be more comfortable with Japan investing in its strategic infrastructure rather than China, the Japanese economy is simply not dynamic enough to substitute for trade and investment relations with China.[61]

Bilateral trade with Japan, for example, has not taken off like FDI. Already low, it stagnated from 2011 and actually fell to 2.1 per cent or $16.3 billion of India's total trade in 2013–14.[62] This contrasts with India's volume of trade with China, which hit a new high of $68 billion in 2013.[63] Thus 'the economic content of India-Japan bilateral relation so far is not commensurate with the diplomatic energy'.[64] With this even more true of the US, economic relations with China remain crucial for the long term.

China and India – a delicate relationship

Despite international pressures and domestic wariness, India has been careful to guard its relations with China. In any case, whatever the plans of Indian policy-makers, economic relations between India and China have galloped ahead. In 2014 China was India's top trading partner, although the US and the UAE remained its lead export markets.[65] But, with the US import market stagnant, even falling by $8 billion between 2012 and 2013, India cannot turn its back on China.[66]

While a ballooning trade deficit with China is a point of friction, for India's myriad small retailers access to cheap Chinese goods remains vital to survival. In 2013 an estimated 360,000 Indian retailers visited Yiwu – China's small commodities wholesale centre.[67] And India's strong IT and pharmaceuticals companies are simply not competitive within the US and Europe; the big Western pharmaceuticals and software companies are much bigger and reinforced by extensive intellectual property protection (IPP). For these Indian industries, the sensible strategy is to target developing markets, particularly China.

These considerations have driven Modi's approach to China, balancing suggestions of a looming India–Japan–US axis with positive steps towards Beijing. In May 2015 Modi visited China. In his most significant speech, as the context for an invitation to Chinese companies to invest in India, he made a point of drawing out the affinities between Chinese and Indian narratives of emergence after the painful detour of colonialism; their shared vision that 'this century belongs to Asia'; and their common agenda on growth and poverty.[68] Modi took away deals worth $22 billion in Chinese investment, which, on top of $20 billion in infrastructure investment promised during Xi's India visit the previous year, would put China's current investment in India on a par with Japan's.[69] But much depends on whether these deals are brought to fruition, and whether other Chinese companies decide to move into India.

Modi also continued India's embrace of Chinese-led efforts to develop an international financial and investment architecture independent of the IMF and World Bank. India agreed to head up the New Development (or BRICS) Bank based in Shanghai, with Modi appointing the highly regarded Indian banker K. V. Kamath, former head of ICICI, India's largest private bank, as its first president. India was also a founding signatory to the AIIB and provided its first vice president. If China and India were able to establish a collaborative framework at the head of these institutions, steering major investment in the development in Asia over the next decade, this could shift Asian leadership away from the old US–Japan axis.

But despite these friendly moves, a number of issues remain substantial sticking points, which militate against the emergence of an agenda-setting China–India Asian axis. The long-rumbling Sino-Indian border disputes, China's relations with Pakistan and China's new presence in the Indian Ocean all create wariness.

In the Indian Ocean China has invested in a series of ports that include Karachi and Gwador in Pakistan, Colombo in Sri Lanka, Chittagong in Bangladesh, Kyaukpyu in

Myanmar, Kuantan in Malaysia and others stretching to Lame in Kenya, Piraeus in Greece and beyond. Dubbed the 'string of pearls', this has been presented as evidence of an expansionist Chinese naval strategy across the Indian Ocean.[70] Undoubtedly one goal is to support the increased presence of the PLA navy along these sensitive sea routes. But this development of ports and their overland transport and pipeline links is primarily projected as a new 'maritime silk road' from the South China Sea to the Mediterranean, with advantages for all the economies bordering these oceans; the oceangoing counterpoint to the 'belt' of similar linkages China proposes across Asia north of the Himalaya, together forming its 'one belt, one road' vision for the twenty-first-century integration of Asia.[71]

India has long – and unrealistically – opposed any naval presence by non-littoral powers in the Indian Ocean; from Britain's 1967 withdrawal 'east of Suez' it argued that the Indian Ocean should become a 'zone of peace'. The US saw this as serving the interests of the USSR, not least as it implied the US should leave Diego Garcia; while neighbours such as Pakistan viewed it as an attempt to turn the Indian Ocean into 'India's ocean'. China's presence has renewed such arguments, alongside rhetorical warnings of a threatened naval encirclement. But India's more judicious advisors have argued that it should 'find a way to deal with the reality of American and Chinese interests and presence in the Indian Ocean' rather than 'proclaiming a Monroe Doctrine that it can't enforce'.[72] This is the course India has largely pursued, shoring up its own Indian Ocean partnerships and investing in its own navy.

The almost allies: China and Pakistan

Pakistan remains a significant irritant in Sino-Indian relations. As discussed above, China's relations with Pakistan drew closer after the 1971 treaty between India and the USSR; through the 1970s and 1980s China armed and aided Pakistan, helped it with nuclear technology and supported it diplomatically, though never militarily, over Kashmir. However, from the end of the Cold War, China became less partisan, remaining more or less neutral when Pakistan launched an offensive across the border at Kargil in 1999.

China's contemporary orientation to Pakistan is driven by a combination of geostrategic and domestic political and economic concerns. With the rise of violent Islamic fundamentalism in Afghanistan and elsewhere, China became concerned about potential eastward spillage into its own primarily Muslim autonomous region of Xinjiang, where some of the ethnically Turkic, Uyghur population already espouse separatist demands. Some of Pakistan's border areas provide a haven for terrorist groups operating in neighbouring countries, including small numbers of Chinese Uyghur extremists. China therefore has an interest in border security, counter-terrorism and in generally improving long-term stability in the country.[73]

This gels with China's main geostrategic concern: its vulnerable sea routes from the Gulf. China has invested in Pakistan's deepwater port at Gwadar as the nexus of the China–Pakistan Economic Corridor (CPEC), a proposed network of roads, railways and pipelines linking refineries at Gwadar to China.[74] With a proposed Iranian oil pipeline into Gwadar, this $46 billion project could eventually allow China to transport at least some oil from the Gulf overland, avoiding the 16,000 km sea route to Shanghai. China has also invested in power, mining and urban development, while China Mobile won the licence to develop Pakistan's first 4G mobile-phone network. China–Pakistan bilateral trade has grown rapidly, with China responsible for 18.5 per cent of Pakistan's total trade by 2015.[75]

China–Pakistan military-to-military relationship has remained strong; China is Pakistan's chief arms supplier and their cooperation includes joint development of the JF-17 fighter jet. If anything their military relations have become closer as Pakistan's long-standing relations with the US came under strain, primarily due to US counter-terrorism operations on Pakistani soil, including thousands of drone strikes, many of which have led to civilian or Pakistani army deaths.

China's role in Pakistan ruffles Indian sensitivities, but objections have been muted by India's own interest in stability in Pakistan.[76] And China has stayed away from Pakistan's disputes with India – and certainly not making Obama's mistake of offering to 'mediate' over Kashmir. Moreover, it has not gone unnoticed in India that in the pecking order of high-profile Chinese state visits, going to India now comes first, followed by emollient trips to Pakistan rather than the other way around.[77] But with Modi increasing his rhetoric against Pakistan in a renewed offensive against Islamic terrorism in India, China and India's different relations to Pakistan will remain a major point of issue between them.

However, as we will see in the next chapter, India's Himalayan borders with China present even more difficult problems to resolve, as they impinge not just on Sino-Indian relations but some knotty internal difficulties for both countries.

Notes

1   Remarks by President Obama, 24 November 2009, The White House, Office of the press secretary.
2   IMF WEO 2016. India GDP (2015) $2091 billion current $; $7965 billion $PPP.
3   SIPRI 2016.
4   UNCTADStat 2016. Annual GDP % growth rates.
5   J. Ablett, A. Baijal, E. Beinhocker, A. Bose, D. Farrell, U. Gersch, E. Greenberg, Sh. Gupta and Su. Gupta, The 'bird of gold': the rise of India's consumer market, McKinsey Global Institute, London, May 2007.
6   'India's surprising economic miracle', The Economist, 30 September 2010.
7   S. Khilnani, R. Kumar, P. B. Mehta, Lt. Gen. (Retd.) P. Menon, N. Nilekani, S. Raghavan, S. Saran and S. Varadarajan, Nonalignment 2.0: a foreign and strategic policy for India in the twenty first century, Penguin, London, 2014.
8   J. Chiriyankandath, 'Realigning India: Indian foreign policy after the Cold War', The Round Table, 93:374 (2004), 199–211.
9   G. J. Bass, The blood telegram: Nixon, Kissinger and a forgotten genocide, C. Hurst & Co. London, 2014, ch. 1.
10 A. Jalal, The sole spokesman: Jinnah, the Muslim League and the demand for Pakistan, Cambridge University Press, Cambridge, 1985.
11 W. van Schendel, A history of Bangladesh, Cambridge University Press, Cambridge, Delhi and New York, 2009, ch. 11.
12 Bass, Blood telegram, pp. 49–87.
13 Ibid., p. 253.
14 Ibid., pp. 217–24.

15 Ibid., pp. 171–5.
16 See Chapter 14.
17 Chiriyankandath, 'Realigning India'.
18 National Security Strategy of the USA, President of the United States, Washington, DC, September 2002, p. 27.
19 T. C. Schaffer, *India and the United States in the 21st century: reinventing partnership*, The Centre for Strategic and International Studies Press, Washington, DC, 2009, ch. 5.
20 SIPRI 2016.
21 G. Plimmer and V. Mallet, 'India becomes biggest foreign buyer of US weapons', *Financial Times*, 24 February 2014.
22 C. R. Mohan, *Crossing the Rubicon: the shaping of India's new foreign policy*, Palgrave Macmillan, London, 2003.
23 G. Nataraj, 'India's TPP dilemma', *East Asia Forum*, 31 October 2015. Available at: http://www.eastasiaforum.org/2015/10/31/indias-tpp-dilemma/ (date accessed 28 February 2017).
24 Khilnani et al., *Nonalignment 2.0*.
25 Editorial, 'Kashmir issue leading Obama into first "tar pit"', *Washington Times*, 6 January 2009.
26 Remarks by President Barack Obama at Suntory Hall, Tokyo, 14 November 2009.
27 G. Perkovich, 'Obama in India', *Carnegie Endowment for International Peace*, 28 October 2010. Available at: http://carnegieendowment.org/publications/?fa=41876 (date accessed 28 February 2017).
28 'Devyani Khobragade: Indian diplomat reindicted in US', *BBC News*, 15 March 2014. Available at: http://www.bbc.co.uk/news/world-us-canada-26587333 (date accessed 28 February 2017).
29 K. A. Lees, 'A Modi win: a loss for US-Indian ties?', *The National Interest*, 16 May 2014. Available at: http://nationalinterest.org/feature/modi-win-loss-us-indian-ties-10475 (date accessed 28 February 2017).
30 A. J. Tellis, 'Productive but joyless: Narendra Modi and US-India relations?', *Carnegie Endowment for Peace*, 12 May 2014. Available at: http://carnegieendowment.org/2014/05/12/productive-but-joyless-narendra-modi-and-u.s.-india-relations-pub-55576 (date accessed 28 February 2017).
31 UNCTADStat 2016, Annual GDP growth rates.
32 UNCTADStat 2016, GDP per capita, current prices.
33 UNCTADStat 2016, Consumer price indices.
34 M. Torri, 'The "Modi wave": Behind the results of the 2014 general elections in India', *The International Spectator*, 50:2 (2015).
35 A. Roy, *Walking with the comrades*, Penguin Books, London, 2011.
36 H. Pidd, 'India blackouts leave 700 million without power', *The Guardian*, 31 July 2012.
37 E. Sridharan, 'Behind Modi's victory', *Journal of Democracy*, 25:4 (2014), 20–33.
38 R. Desai, 'India's saffron capitalism', *Counterpunch*, 27 June 2014. Available at: http://www.counterpunch.org/2014/06/27/indias-saffron-capitalism/ (date accessed 28 February 2017).
39 Torri, '"Modi wave"'.
40 B. Xu and E. Albert, 'Governance in India: infrastructure', Backgrounder, Council on Foreign Relations, New York City, October 2014. Available at: http://www.cfr.org/india/governance-india-infrastructure/p32638 (date accessed 28 February 2017).
41 T. Madan, 'Indian prime minister Modi's foreign policy: the first 100 days', *Brookings*, 29 August 2014. Available at: https://www.brookings.edu/opinions/indian-prime-minister-modis-foreign-policy/ (date accessed 28 February 2017).
42 M. Kugelman, 'India acts east', *Foreign Policy*, 17 May 2016. Available at: http://foreignpolicy.com/2016/05/17/india-acts-east/ (date accessed 28 February 2017).
43 H. V. Pant and Y. Joshi, *The US pivot and Indian foreign policy: Asia's evolving balance of power*, Palgrave Macmillan, Basingstoke, 2016, ch. 5.

44 A. Pillalamarri, 'What did Modi's US trip accomplish?', *The Diplomat*, 2 October 2014. Available at: http://thediplomat.com/2014/10/what-did-narendra-modis-us-trip-accomplish/ (date accessed 28 February 2017).

45 Trump called Modi 5th after Trudeau (Canada), Nieto (Mexico), Netanyahu (Israel) and Sisi (Egypt).

46 D. Brewster, *India as an Asia Pacific power*, Routledge, Abingdon, 2012, p. 64.

47 Prime Minister of Republic of India and Prime Minister of Japan, Joint statement towards Japan-India strategic and global partnership, 15 December 2006.

48 K. Koga and Y. Joshi, 'Japan-India security cooperation', *The Diplomat*, 17 July 2013. Available at: http://thediplomat.com/2013/07/japan-india-security-cooperation/ (date accessed 28 February 2017).

49 S. Smith, 'Japan's pivot to India', *Forbes*, 9 February 2014. Available at: https://www.forbes.com/sites/sheilaasmith/2014/09/02/japans-pivot-to-india/#1a1bbae86dca (date accessed 28 February 2017).

50 S. Abe, *Towards a beautiful country: my vision for Japan*, Vertical, New York, 2007.

51 Subhas Chandra Bose declared the Provisional Government of Free India in 1943 and its Indian National Army fought alongside Japan, particularly in Burma.

52 F.-S. Gady, 'Confirmed: Japan will permanently join US-India naval exercises', *The Diplomat*, 13 October 2015. Available at: http://thediplomat.com/2015/10/confirmed-japan-will-permanently-join-us-india-naval-exercises/ (date accessed 28 February 2017).

53 P. Parameswaran, 'Return of Asia's quad "natural": US defence chief', *The Diplomat*, 9 April 2016. Available at: http://thediplomat.com/2016/04/return-of-asias-quad-natural-us-defense-chief/ (date accessed 28 February 2017).

54 E. Ghani, *The service revolution in South Asia*, The World Bank, Washington, DC, June 2009; R. Banga, 'Critical issues in India's service-led growth', *India Resident Mission Policy Brief* No. 2, Asian Development Bank, New Delhi, 2006.

55 The reliability of India's adjusted growth figures is questioned. See C. Furtado, 'Fresh wave of doubts arises over India's growth rates', *exchange4media*, 8 June 2015. Available at: http://www.exchange4media.com/marketing/fresh-wave-of-doubts-arises-over-indias-growth-rate_60310.html (date accessed 20 October 2016).

56 M. Kumar, 'Falling oil prices pull India's budget out of the fire', *Reuters*, 5 February 2015. Available at: http://in.reuters.com/article/india-budget-idINKBN0L905J20150205 (date accessed 28 February 2017).

57 J. Ross, 'Why are China and India growing so fast?', *Huffington Post*, 29 August 2016. Available at: http://www.huffingtonpost.com/john_ross-/china-india-growth_b_11655472.html (date accessed 28 February 2017).

58 UNCTADStat, Bilateral FDI statistics 2014.

59 Ibid.

60 A. Mohan, 'India-Japan relations: a fillip on the cards?', *The Diplomat*, 23 April 2014. Available at: http://thediplomat.com/2014/04/india-japan-relations-a-fillip-on-the-cards/ (date accessed 28 February 2017).

61 Pant and Joshi, *US pivot and Indian foreign policy*.

62 Government of India, Department of Commerce, Import Export Data bank, 2014.

63 CIA World Factbook 2016, India economy, 2015.

64 T. Basu, 'India-Japan relations: new times, renewed expectations', comment, Institute for Defence Studies and Analyses, 4 September 2014. Available at: http://www.idsa.in/idsacomments/IndiaJapanRelations_tbasu_040914 (date accessed 28 February 2017).

65 CIA World Factbook 2016. China 10.6 per cent, US 9 per cent, UAE 8.2 per cent total trade 2014.

66 J. Ross, 'China is now the world's main trade locomotive', *Key Trends in Globalisation*, 12 April 2014. Available at: http://ablog.typepad.com/keytrendsinglobalisation/2014/04/china-is-now-the-worlds-trade-locomotive.html (date accessed 20 October 2016).

67 PTI, 'India's traders swarming China's trade hub for cheap goods', *The Economic Times*, 3 May 2014. Available at: http://articles.economictimes.indiatimes.com/2014–04–30/news/49523702_1_yiwu-and-india-deepak-raheja-traders (date accessed 20 October 2016).

68 Narendra Modi, Speech at the India-China Business Forum, Shanghai, 16 May 2015.

69 V. Mallett and L. Hornby, 'India and China sign $22bn in deals during Modi visit', *Financial Times*, 17 May 2015.

70 'China's foreign ports: the new Masters and Commanders', *The Economist*, 8 June 2013.

71 D. Dollar, 'China's rise as a regional and global power: the AIIB and the "one belt, one road"', *Horizons*, 4 (summer 2015), 162–72.

72 C. R. Mohan, 'India's new role in the Indian Ocean', *Seminar: the monthly symposium*, 617, New Delhi, January 2011.

73 R. Kabraji, 'The China-Pakistan alliance: rhetoric and limitations', Chatham House, Asia Programme Paper 2012/01, London, December 2012.

74 G. Bowring, 'How will China's regional development bank work?', *Financial Times*, 7 May 2014.

75 CIA World Factbook 2016.

76 PTI, 'India not worried over Pakistan-China economic corridor: High Commissioner TCA Raghavan', *The Economic Times*, 22 April 2015.

77 A. Krishnan, 'China announces Premier Li Keqiang's visits to India, Pakistan', *The Hindu*, 14 May 2013.

14

Tibet and the Sino-Indian borders

The long-standing Sino-Indian border disputes over Arunachal Pradesh and Aksai Chin have defied settlement and frequently disrupted their relations. This chapter considers the background to these disagreements and how they intersect with the sensitive issue of Tibet, which the US has exploited in creating problems for China. It concludes that the disputed borders, while provoking frequent minor tensions, is not a substantial threat to China–India relations today. On this, as on most other issues that are flagged to lead to hostilities between India and China, both sides prefer collaboration to conflict, and none has led India to throw its weight behind the US's new Cold War strategies towards China.

The borders and Tibet

To the east the disputed border runs through the historic region of Tibet, which originally included most of the Indian province of Arunachal Pradesh. How it came to be in India relates closely to the issues surrounding the status of Tibet as part of China. The present border originated at a 1913–14 conference in Simla convened by Britain (British India) with representatives of the Chinese government and the Dalai Lama. Britain had invaded Tibet in 1904 and wanted to give its de facto occupation some legitimacy in order to keep out potential rivals, especially Russia. Prior international treaties had recognised that Tibet fell under China's sovereignty, so Britain wanted the Chinese representatives at Simla to grant it similar rights in Tibet as it had in the Chinese 'treaty ports', that is British sovereignty in all but name. The British also proposed China cede territory from Tibet to British India – the area that is now Arunachal Pradesh. The Chinese refused to sign, so Britain simply persuaded the Tibetan representative to sign anyway. This was not only blatantly illegal, but subsequently repudiated by the Dalai Lama. Not even London believed the Simla Accord had legitimacy: it was not published; international recognition of it was neither sought nor gained; and the British Indian government did not amend its maps to include the new territory. But Britain did not pull back from Tibet, which 'for all intents and purposes, became a British protectorate. China and Russia were effectively forced out of the area'.[1]

After 1937, when central Chinese authority collapsed, Britain resurrected the Simla Accord and included the Tibetan territory claimed in 1914 within the North-East

Frontier Agency of British India. But the annexed territories remained a semi-no-man's land, run by tribal groups and a weak Tibetan administration tied loosely to Lhasa, until in 1951 Nehru's newly independent India summarily ousted the Tibetans and set up its own administration over what became Arunachal Pradesh.[2]

To the west, the disputed border between China, India and Pakistan adjacent to sensitive Kashmir mainly concerns the region known as Aksai Chin. Again the British in India had at one point claimed it, but in this case there was not even the figleaf of a pseudo-treaty and Britain had never sought to legitimise it. Nehru claimed this territory for India but, unlike in Arunachal Pradesh, China rather than India had actual control. The bulk of the disputed region lies on the Chinese side of the Karakoram Mountains, is not so easily accessible from the south and includes the most direct overland route between southern Xinjiang and Tibet.[3]

All attempts to negotiate in the post-war years foundered on Nehru's intransigence on what he claimed were India's historical borders. In 1961–62 there were constant border clashes as India attempted to establish a presence in Aksai Chin (all of which failed). In 1962 Nehru's 'forward policy', pushing India's claims even beyond the 'Simla' border in the east, led to a brief war between China and India. China invaded and crushed the Indian army within a few days, later declaring a unilateral ceasefire and withdrawing to the status quo ante, leaving Arunachal Pradesh in India and Aksai Chin within China. This 'Line of Actual Control' has remained the effective border for the last 70 years and, while not formally accepted, it has been the basis for several Sino-Indian agreements on management of the border in 1993, 1996 and most recently in 2013.[4] The absence of any settlement of the border is primarily due to Indian intransigence over Aksai Chin, as from the 1950s China has been prepared to surrender Arunachal Pradesh.[5]

Nonetheless these borders remain highly sensitive for China as to both east and west they impinge on the security of Tibet.

The strategic importance of Tibet

Evidently China rejects the history of imperialist manipulation of Tibet's status by Britain. But this is amplified by the unimaginable military, political and economic consequences if it were to lose Tibet. China is a vast country with no shortage of vulnerabilities along its extensive frontiers. Tibet sits on the Chinese side of the high Himalayan passes, creating a vast natural barrier that protects the heart of China from any incursion from the south. Tibet's continued integration within a single Chinese state is non-negotiable on profound security and military grounds.[6]

Of course, China also considers that Tibet has been part of historic China for centuries, although with a high degree of autonomy. The Dalai Lamas became de facto rulers of Tibet in the seventeenth century when their Mongol-supported Gelugpa sect crushed the other lamas and the 5th Dalai Lama effectively assumed secular as well as religious power over the territory. The 5th Dalai Lama visited the Chinese emperor and knelt before him – part of China's evidence that the Dalai Lamas accepted that they were protégés of the Chinese state. All this is well documented historically on China's side, although disputed today by the Dalai Lama.[7]

Map 9 *India, Nepal, Bhutan, Tibet, Xinjiang and the Central Asian republics*

What is clear is that the claim that Tibet was an independent theocracy not subject to the Chinese imperial state only has definite substance for the short period from 1937 to 1950 when central Chinese authority had broken down. But in truth this Tibetan 'independence' was a British fiction justifying its colonial control over Tibet and annexation of Chinese territory.[8]

Today's Tibet Autonomous Region (TAR) is home to less than half the ethnically Tibetan population of China. The rest are mainly concentrated in what are now neighbouring provinces, but were historically part of Tibet (see Map 9). Thus supporters of the Dalai Lama have claimed specific territory in the adjoining Chinese provinces of Yunnan, Sichuan, Gansu and Qinghai, in total amounting to about 25 per cent of present-day China.

Any attempt to carve out the TAR from China, let alone this more extensive territory, would mean China lost control over its southern borders, its water supplies – both the Yangtze and the Yellow rivers rise on the Tibetan plateau – significant hydroelectric power and important mineral reserves. But above all, it would amount to a new dismemberment of China. An equivalent in relative scale would be if North America had to return California and Texas to Mexico.

American intervention in Tibet and the Dalai Lama

A fundamental strategic concern is that an independent Tibet could allow the advance of hostile American political influence and even potentially a military presence into central China. This is reinforced by the history of American intervention in Tibet.

The CIA was covertly active in Tibet before 1949, but this stepped up in earnest from 1955 as part of its destabilisation campaign against the PRC.[9] Exploiting fears among the monastic ruling elites that their lands would be expropriated and monasteries destroyed by the advancing PLA, the CIA helped organise anti-communist 'resistance' forces. The overwhelmingly illiterate and superstitious local population venerated the Lamas and suggestions they were threatened by the PLA undoubtedly created support for the opposition. The CIA trained Tibetan guerrilla fighters in Nepal and northern India, dropped in arms and radio equipment and helped stir up what became the 1959 revolt in Lhasa.

For its part, after 1949, the CPC postponed radical measures such as land redistribution in Tibet and some adjacent regions, recognising the expropriations of the landlords that had taken place in the rest of China did not yet command popular support in more backward regions, including semi-feudal Tibet. Mao's strategy was to draw the monastic elites over to gradual reform, including the young 14th Dalai Lama himself, while winning the mass of the population to support more fundamental change over time.[10] But this strategy was interrupted by the events of 1959 when, amid wild rumours that Beijing was planning to abduct the Dalai Lama, mass protests erupted in Lhasa and the Dalai Lama and his core supporters secretly fled to India.[11]

After the failed revolt the CIA continued to arm and train Tibetan guerrilla fighters at its specialist high-altitude training centre at Camp Hale in Colorado until 1964, and funded a base in northern Nepal until 1974.[12] The CIA also funded the Dalai Lama personally to the tune of $180,000 a year until 1974.[13] US support declined in the 1970s and 1980s following rapprochement with China, but from the 1990s the US again began to make an issue of Tibet, encouraging the 'Free Tibet' campaign, which won widespread popular support in the US.

However, even in the 1950s and 1960s US intervention in Tibet was only at a level to create irritation for the PRC. Moreover, neither the US, India, Britain nor any other major state endorsed the view that Tibet was an independent country. The furthest that the US would go was with the ambiguous formulation that Tibet was 'an autonomous country under the suzerainty of China' and that it supported self-determination.[14]

Alongside creating difficulties for China in Tibet itself, the activities of the Dalai Lama amplified by American support have been used to discredit China's image in the West. In the fable peddled in the US, taken up by a range of pop stars and celebrities, the Dalai Lama is a purely spiritual Buddhist guru, a man of 'peace' and wisdom, rather than the figurehead of a political campaign to break Tibet away from China – although since 1987 he has personally called for greater autonomy for Tibet, rather than independence.[15] The fact that up to 1959 he was the head of a feudal theocracy that exacted tithe for its monastic palaces from its subject population who lived in servility, illiteracy and abject poverty is pushed aside in favour of a romance that Tibet under the Lamas was close to the Buddhist 'pure, perfected land'.

Within Tibet

The Dalai Lama certainly has had support within Tibet, especially among the traditional Tibetan monks and monasteries. But the future is unclear, as only the Dalai Lama among the Tibetan exile community has any real purchase in Tibet itself – as well as being the only Tibetan known in the West. It is unlikely any successive Dalai Lama could have the same unquestioned authority, especially as any eventual designation is almost certain to be disputed. The child candidates would normally be identified following a search by the Tibetan monasteries, but this would deprive the exiled supporters of the current Dalai Lama of any control. A choice conducted among candidates outside the country would have little legitimacy.

Economic grievances have been behind most of the more recent disturbances in the region. The TAR has only 3.2 million inhabitants (of whom around 90 per cent are ethnic Tibetans), the terrain is inhospitable, and traditional animal farming and agriculture remain dominant in its economy. Initially Tibet did not greatly benefit from China's economic take-off and its GDP per capita fell behind China's average, contributing to disturbances in Tibet in the late 1980s. The government responded with measures to boost growth in the Tibetan economy.

From 1995 growth picked up and from 2006 Tibet's GDP growth averaged over 12 per cent a year. But still by 2013 its $6,131 per capita GDP, while not the lowest of any Chinese region, had not caught up with the Chinese average of $9,868.[16] Tourism, retail and related service sectors were the largest contributors to growth, as transport infrastructure remains limited and industry underdeveloped due to its isolation and altitude. In 2011 its GDP stood at 60 billion RMB ($9.7 billion), the smallest of any of China's regions, but this is not a surprise given how thinly populated it is.[17]

The last major disturbances in 2008 began with coordinated demonstrations by monks calling for Tibetan independence, followed by a highly organised international campaign to disrupt the Torch Relay for the 2008 Beijing Olympics as it went through several countries. Popular protests were triggered within Tibet, but these were primarily focused on economic issues, particularly that the benefits of growth had disproportionately advantaged Han and other inward migrants who dominate the growing retail and service sector. Since 2008 occasional individual protests – including dramatic self-immolations – have not spilled into more generalised unrest.

India, China and Tibet

Tibet was often a troublesome issue between India and China, although it had never caused a decisive breach. Before the flight of the Dalai Lama, Nehru had advocated neutrality over Tibet, not allowing the CIA to use Indian resources or airspace in aid of the rebels and signing an agreement with China in 1954 that recognised Tibet as integral to China. But despite this, Nehru was almost certainly implicated in the Dalai Lama covertly leaving Tibet in 1959, and subsequently allowed him to make his base at Dharamshala in northern India, where it remains to this day. After the 1962 Sino-Indian border war Nehru's position shifted openly against China and India supported Tibetan separatists within its borders, adding to Cold War tensions between India and China.[18]

By the late 1970s, however, and particularly following an agreement between China and Nepal to drive Tibetan separatists out of the Himalayan kingdom, any meaningful cross-border actions by Tibetan separatists had ceased. Ongoing Cold War estrangement between India and China no longer turned on Tibet.

The eventual thaw marked by Rajiv Gandhi's visit to China in 1988, included agreement by India to recognise Tibet as 'an autonomous region of China' and that 'anti-Chinese' political activities would not be permitted on Indian soil. In 2003 the BJP-led government of Vajpayee for the first time used China's terminology in recognising the 'Tibet Autonomous Region' as a part of China – echoed by a similar statement from China recognising India's sovereignty over Sikkim.[19]

This led to agreement to reopen three cross-border passes between India and the TAR. The most important of these, at Nathu La in Sikkim province, reopened in 2006 for the first time since 1962. Although only open in the summer months due to their high altitude, these passes allow direct cross-border trade.

With these developments Tibet largely disappeared from the list of problematic issues between India and China, contributing to a reboot in Sino-Indian relations. Despite its new friendship with the US, India has not shifted its position on Tibet as part of China.

Nepal and Bhutan

China's other Tibetan neighbours – Nepal and Bhutan – are too small and isolated to be significant players on their own; but are geostrategically placed between India and China.

Throughout the Cold War, India used tiny Nepal's dependence on Indian trade and aid to discourage relations with China across their 1236 km border, while China closed the traditional foot passes from Tibet as part of its security operations against separatists based in Nepal. Nepal and China had no overland transport links until, in the 1960s, King Mahendra, against Indian objections, agreed to China building a cross-border highway; in return Nepal agreed to drive out the remnants of armed Tibetan separatists.

From 1996 to 2006 the country was rent by civil war. After a peace agreement in 2006, elections to a constituent assembly elections resulted in a 2008 decision to abolish the monarchy and declare a federal republic. Self-described Maoist parties have been in each government since.[20]

While India remains Nepal's main trading partner, its relations with China have developed rapidly. India still accounts for nearly 60 per cent of all Nepal's trade, but imports from China are catching up.[21] In 2014 China overtook India as Nepal's biggest foreign investor, investing in both manufacturing and infrastructure, and in April 2015 plans were approved for a $1.6 billion hydropower project.[22] China also plans to extend the Qinghai-Tibet railway from Lhasa to the Nepal border. It has funded the development of Lumbini, the birthplace of Buddha, as a pilgrimage and tourist centre; promoted the teaching of Chinese in Nepalese schools; and set up Confucius Institutes (Chinese cultural centres) in Nepalese centres.[23] Military cooperation has increased, including a 2013 $8 million assistance package to the Nepali army focused on border security, aimed at preventing any flow of anti-China activity into Tibet.

India has shown signs of irritation at Nepal's growing ties with China, but recent problems in India's relations with Nepal have not been attributable to this. For example, in 2015 a campaign for greater regional autonomy by the Madhesi people in Nepal led to a several-month-long blockade of the border with India. Modi called on the Nepali government to address Madhesi demands, while Kathmandu accused New Delhi of aiding the blockade, which created major fuel shortages and delayed reconstruction work after the April 2015 earthquake. When Nepal turned to China for help the blockade was soon over.[24]

Hence, rather than Nepal caught in a tug of war between India and China, a more accurate view is that its growing links with China have given Nepal greater leverage in its bilateral relationship with India.

Bhutan

Tiny, semi-closed Bhutan has been more cautious about China. A history of unresolved disputes along their 470 km border meant that by 2015 they still did not have formal diplomatic relations.

India has effectively blocked its protégé state from negotiating its own border settlement with China. The India–Bhutan 1949 Treaty of Friendship agreed that the Bhutan government would 'be guided by the advice of the Government of India in regard to its external relations'. In 2007 this was amended to 'cooperate closely with each other on issues relating to their national interests', but included India's right to a voice on contentious matters. The border is contentious for India as it fears Bhutan might concede disputed territory on the Doklam plateau in eastern Bhutan, bringing the Chinese border closer to the strategically vulnerable narrow neck of land between Bhutan and Bangladesh that links India to its north-eastern provinces.[25]

However, while Bhutan has been at great pains to reassure India, it has also much to gain from good relations with its northern neighbour. China can give Bhutan greater leverage with India in addition to the well-rehearsed economic advantages. As a result Bhutan's relations with China have grown warmer, despite no formal diplomatic ties.

Both Nepal and Bhutan have affirmed support for 'one China', accepting that both Taiwan and Tibet are part of China and banning Tibetan separatist activities from their territories.

The India–China border conflict

The border issues between India and China discussed in this chapter may chafe with India's extreme nationalists, but in reality they could be settled if India would compromise on Aksai Chin, especially as it is questionable whether 'India' ever controlled it, and China has offered to compromise on Arunachal Pradesh, which certainly was part of Chinese Tibet. If this were settled, it would be clearer that most of the other issues flagged for conflict between India and China have been more imaginary than real.

India does not like the increased presence of China in the Indian Ocean, but China stresses this is about trade not war. And India's more serious foreign policy experts point out that while 'an enduring feature of Indian maritime thinking has been the opposition to the presence of extra-regional powers in the Indian Ocean', this has always been unrealistic and it would be better for India to work with Washington and Beijing on protocols for activities in the Ocean.[26] India might prefer China did not invest in Pakistan, but China has not interfered over Kashmir, and India and China share a concern for greater stability in that volatile country to reduce the danger of spillover activity by Pakistan-based extremist terrorist groups. India would prefer to reduce its trade deficit with China, but the best route to that is closer economic collaboration to improve the ground for Indian exports, not stirring up conflicts.

The pitfalls in having militarised borders have been demonstrated on many occasions. For example, in what was later described as an 'accidental' incursion, in April 2013, about 50 Chinese soldiers made camp some dozen miles into Indian-held territory in the west and a tense border stand-off lasted 20 days.[27] Eventually both sides withdrew without any shots fired and a new border defence cooperation agreement was put in place aimed at avoiding such unintended confrontations.[28]

The run-up to the 2014 Indian elections was the occasion for predictable nationalist grandstanding from Modi over the borders. 'No power on earth can take away even an inch from India', Modi said at one rally, accusing China of an 'expansionist attitude'.[29] China responded: 'China has never waged a war of aggression to occupy an inch of land of other countries'; and urged keeping the peace.[30] But despite strong words on the election stump, Modi's approach afterwards was to nurture relations with China.

It is true little progress has been made in settling the border issues. But in reality, whatever Indian governments may say, both sides de facto accept the Line of Actual Control, and these borders have not been decisive in India's geostrategic orientation.

India and the Asian century

The direction that India takes in foreign policy over the next five years will be decisive in shaping the future of Asia.

The future that the US foreign policy establishment wishes to engineer would see India within a US–Japan–India bloc, containing China and weakening Russia. In this scenario India plays something like the role of China after Vietnam, guaranteeing a voice for the US in the new Asian century and prolonging its global influence as its economic pulling power declines.[31] But while India now collaborates more closely on the military field with the US and Japan, and relations with the West have improved, it has refused to tie itself to wider US foreign policy objectives. The strongly nationalist government in New Delhi may look askance at the increased weight of China and has sought out Japan as a counterweight, but it does not have any special warmth for an overbearing and ingracious West.

An alternative axis – of India with China and Russia – is America's Asian nightmare. Comprising three-fifths of the BRICS, most of the landmass of Asia and 40 per cent of the earth's population; rich in natural resources; and including the world's contemporary manufacturing powerhouse, such an axis would not only dominate Asia, but be a global force to reckon with. The potential of such a bloc clearly has some persuasive power for India – reflected in Singh saying that 'when China and India shake hands, the world watches' or Modi's comments on the 'new Asian century'.[32] But for such a bloc to cohere India would not accept anything less than equal status with Russia and China, including a permanent seat on the UN Security Council. This will remain problematic, as neither China nor Russia is keen to upset the existing architecture of the Security Council. India is not the only candidate for permanent status and to open up the issue would lead to uncertain outcomes.

So while India has strengthened its strategic collaboration with both China and Russia, particularly in the framework of the annual BRICS summits, the BRICS bank, the Shanghai Cooperation Organisation and other multilateral initiatives, it is not moving into a three-way bloc with them either.

Overall India looks set to maintain its course of 'strategic autonomy' in foreign policy. The 2014 BJP manifesto promised a multilateral approach developing a 'web of allies' based on mutual interest, with India remaining independent of 'big power interests', seeking stronger relationships with its neighbours and a more developed regional and international leadership role. As one Indian analyst put it: 'Standing with Chinese leaders, we talk about the promotion of a multi-polar world; shaking hands with the Americans, we proclaim a natural alliance with the United States.'[33]

Notes

1 A. T. Grunfeld, *The making of modern Tibet*, Zed Press, London, 1987, pp. 62–6.

2 Maxwell, 'Sino-Indian border reconsidered', p. 908.

3 Ibid.

4 Ibid.

5 Ibid.

6 Nathan and Scobell, *Search for security*, pp. 198–9.

7 Grunfeld, *Making modern Tibet*, pp. 39–45.

8 Ibid., pp. 62–78.

9 Ibid., p. 97.

10 M. C. Goldstein, *A history of modern Tibet, Volume 3: The storm clouds descend, 1955–57*, University of California Press, Berkeley, 2014, pp. 4–16.

11 Grunfeld, *Making modern Tibet*, pp. 129–34.

12 Ibid., pp. 147–60.

13 J. Mirsky, 'Tibet: The CIA's cancelled war', *New York Review of Books*, 9 April 2013.

14 Grunfeld, *Making modern Tibet*, p. 135.

15 'Dalai Lama: Tibet wants autonomy not independence', *Time Magazine*, 15 April 2006.

16 Pre-estimate of the 2012 Statistical Communiqué of the provinces on National Economic and Social Development; PPPs calculated according to IMF April 2013 data.

17 The China Perspective, US$ at May 2015 exchange rates. Available at: http://www.thechinaper spective.com/topics/province/tibet/ (date accessed 17 February 2017).

18 Grunfeld, *Making modern Tibet*, pp. 153–60.

19 R. S. Kalha, 'Tibet as a factor in Sino-Indian relations past and present', *Journal of Defence Studies*, 6:4 (2012), 7–26.

20 The Unified Communist Party of Nepal (Maoist) won a majority in 2008. In the 2013 elections the Communist Party of Nepal (Unified Marxist-Leninist) (CPN) came second to the Nepali Congress and formed a coalition. In 2015 the parliament elected Osi of the CPN as prime minister.

21 IMF Direction of Trade Statistics, 2016.

22 K. R. Koirala, 'Nepal and its neighbors', *The Diplomat*, May 2016. Available at: http://thediplomat.com/2016/04/nepal-and-its-neighbors/ (date accessed 17 February 2017).

23 S. Sehgal, 'China expands into Himalayan neighbour Nepal', *Defence Review Asia*, 7:8 (December 2013–January 2014), 22–6.

24 Koirala, 'Nepal and its neighbors'.

25 B. Benedictus, 'Bhutan and the Great Power tussle', *The Diplomat*, 2 August 2014. Available at: http://thediplomat.com/2014/08/bhutan-and-the-great-power-tussle/ (date accessed 17 February 2017).

26 Mohan, 'India's new role'.

27 I. Bagchi, 'Depsang Bulge incursion accidental, Chinese military think tank says', *Times of India*, 15 July 2013.

28 Agreement between India and the PRC on border defence cooperation, 23 October 2013.

29 A. Panda, 'Narendra Modi gets tough on China', *The Diplomat*, 25 February 2014. Available at: http://thediplomat.com/2014/02/narendra-modi-gets-tough-on-china/ (date accessed 17 February 2017).

30 'China refutes Narendra Modi's "expansionist mindset" remark', *The Economic Times*, 24 February 2014.

31 P. J. Leaf, 'With China on the rise, America must woo India', *The National Interest*, 15 September 2014. Available at: http://nationalinterest.org/feature/china-the-rise-america-must-woo-india-11275 (date accessed 17 February 2017).

32 See Chapter 13.

33 Mohan, 'India's new role'.

15

Losing Central Asia

To the north, east and west, the Central Asian republics – Kazakhstan, Kyrgyzstan, Tajikistan, Turkmenistan and Uzbekistan – are enclosed by Russia, China and the Caspian Sea. To the south they are landlocked behind the swirling problems of Afghanistan and Pakistan and the wild lands of the Hindu Kush. Together with Iran, they buffer northern and eastern Asia from encroaching chaos (see Map 9). Stable and in alliance with Russia and China the Central Asian republics form an effective backdoor security system for the distant and insecure border territories of both. If unstable, particularly if due to the growth of Islamic extremist currents, or open to a Western military presence they could become a dangerous weakness in China and Russia's most remote defences. China's concerns are exacerbated by one of its most sensitive internal problems – the allegiances and orientation of the Muslim Uyghur people in its thinly populated, expansive autonomous region of Xinjiang. The border states in Central Asia can either be a conduit for Islamist extremist politics to flow over the border radicalising separatist sentiments in China's far west or be a means to hold such dangerous developments at bay.

Prolonged war in Afghanistan and beyond has created waves of insurgent Islamic extremism that have threatened to spill over its borders in all directions. With no stability immediately in sight, both Russia and China have increased their priority to containing the chaos with Afghanistan's borders, while also seeking to improve the collapsing internal situation through increased economic, political and military support. Ensuring the chaos is contained means paying particular attention to the Central Asian republics.[1] Both China and Russia have stepped up their engagement in Central Asia over the last two decades, increasing their military collaboration with and support to the republics.

The US has also had its eyes on Central Asia. It saw the collapse of the USSR as the opportunity to advance strategically from its foothold in Afghanistan where it had been funding and arming the Mujahedeen against the Soviet-supported government.[2] From the 1990s the US attempted to nurture pro-Western political forces and, especially after 9/11, to negotiate agreements for US bases in the former Soviet republics. The US expected to be aided by Sino-Russian rivalry for influence in the region, allowing it to 'triangulate' relations to advance its own strategic position in Central Asia.[3] Issues in the region had certainly led to conflict between China and the former USSR in the past, but today their shared interests in combating Islamic fundamentalism and ensuring the

US does not form its own military alliances among these states have proved much more powerful considerations than old-style Sino-Russian rivalries.[4]

Geographically, Central Asia also lies at a strategic junction for India, which shares Russian and Chinese security concerns about spillover from conflict in Afghanistan, particularly its destabilising impact on Pakistan. But India is also interested in tapping into the rich energy resources of the region. As elsewhere the US has tried to deploy its improved relations with India to further an alternative American-led axis for the region. But India has rather pursued its own diplomacy and economic agreements in Central Asia and increasingly engaged with the Shanghai Cooperation Organisation (SCO), the joint Chinese and Russian-led security framework with Central Asia.[5]

This chapter considers the strategic interrelation of the US, China and Russia in Central Asia from the perspective of China's concerns for the stability of its sensitive western province of Xinjiang, and the prospects for a US military and strategic advance in the region applying pressure on China from the west. It concludes that after progress into the region following the fall of the USSR, accelerated by US and NATO intervention in Afghanistan from 2001, the US is now in retreat from Central Asia, while Russian and Chinese influence has grown.

Vulnerable Xinjiang

Xinjiang, sprawled across China's western and north-western frontiers, is largely uninhabitable desert, mountains and arid scrub with huge extremes of temperature. Its 21.5 million-strong population is thinly spread over less than 5 per cent of the territory.[6] But though inhospitable, Xinjiang is rich in gas, oil and other natural resources and profoundly important to China's security.

The region has a chequered history. Broadly speaking, whenever China was unified in a single dynastic state, the areas that now compose Xinjiang were part of it to one degree or another. Whenever China went through one of its historic periods of central disintegration and warring factions, the inaccessibility and remoteness of the region meant it would tend – in part or in whole – to fall out of central control. In these periods the region would suffer a range of fates, from reverting to fragmented tribal control to being run by a changing patchwork of Mongol or Turkic khanates, conquered from the west or north or marched over by invading armies looking to raid a weakened China. Stability in the region depended upon its integration into a unified Chinese state, as it was in the modern period under the Qing. The components that now administratively form Xinjiang were first organised into a single province of that name in 1884. Its diverse population was composed of settled Turkic Muslim tribes (the Uyghurs) living around the desert oases of the south; mainly Mongol nomads and later Han and Hui peoples in the north; with Kazakhs in the far north. It was the USSR that first used the term 'Uyghur' to distinguish the Turkic sedentary populations of Central Asia. Adopted from the name of a sixteenth-century khanate, it was subsequently taken on by the Uyghur people themselves within China and beyond.

With the instability in China in the 1930s, the USSR began to intervene across its borders into the province, encouraging regional separatism and nationalism, initially with the aim of drawing it into its own sphere of influence or even part of it joining the

Central Asian Soviet republics. But a Soviet-backed attempt to set up an independent republic in Xinjiang in 1933 was short-lived and the region soon returned to China.[7] In 1944, with Chinese central authority even further disintegrated in the context of war, the USSR backed a new declaration of an independent East Turkestan Republic. However, when the victorious PLA entered the region in 1949 the USSR backed down and helped negotiate a peace deal that meant the region rejoined China. In 1955 the region was reorganised as the Xinjiang Uyghur Autonomous Region of China.

With the onset of the Sino-Soviet split in the 1960s Xinjiang again became a flash-point for tensions between China and the USSR. From 1962 the USSR returned to encouraging separatist tendencies, setting up radio stations and other media to spread propaganda into Xinjiang. It funded and aided the establishment of the pro-Soviet East Turkestan People's Revolutionary Party and other separatist organisations and provided a haven for armed separatists, sponsoring their periodic attacks into China. Chinese and Soviet forces directly fought along the Xinjiang-Soviet border in 1969. It remained a focus of Sino-Soviet conflict until relations began to improve in the mid-1980s, when the disputed borders were settled and Russia stopped funding and inciting anti-China forces.[8]

Denied this external prop separatist currents virtually disappeared from the region in the 1980s until 2006. Bus bombings by terrorist separatists in 1992 and 1997 showed that the issue had not entirely gone away, but the region was generally calm.

Uneven development and separatism

This was a period of dramatic change in China and Xinjiang, when China's economic success led to a growth of jobs and opportunities in the northern Xinjiang cities, including Urumqi, the capital of the region.

From 2000 to 2005 the population of Xinjiang grew by 1.62 million, or 8.8 per cent in just five years.[9] This changed the balance of the population in the region as a whole and in the north in particular, as both Han people from the east and Uyghur people from the south migrated into the more industrial north of the province. In 1955 around 73 per cent of the 5 million population of Xinjiang was Uyghur, almost entirely concentrated in the more inaccessible south. By 2010 the population had risen to 22 million, but the Uyghur share had declined to 46 per cent, although up in absolute numbers to around 10 million, with Han making 39 per cent, Muslim Hui 4.5 per cent and Kazakhs 7 per cent.[10]

Behind this migration from south to north lies the uneven economic development of Xinjiang. One study found that while Xinjiang's economic performance overall was around the national average for China (18th out of 31 regions) this hid enormous regional variation. The southern, 90 per cent Uyghur, areas, such as Kashgar, had lower GDP per capita than Guizhou province, officially China's poorest. Only 10 per cent of the southern population is urbanised, and agriculture in the archipelago of isolated oases in the Taklamakan (Western Gobi) desert is largely subsistence. On the other hand, northern Xinjiang's most wealthy prefecture, Karamay, had higher GDP per capita than the eastern coastal municipality of Tianjin. Northern Xinjiang has only a third of the land area but 54 per cent of its population, 76 per cent of its GDP, 78.8 per cent of industrial production and 74.8 per cent of fixed investment.[11] Uyghur people migrating from the south have faced employment discrimination, not just in wider China, but in Urumqi and the prosperous north of the region.

These economic inequalities, together with the global rise of Islamic activism, contributed to a new wave of Uyghur separatist activity beginning in 2006. Serious terrorist attacks occurred in Xinjiang and even outside the province, including a knife attack that left 29 dead in Kunming railway station in March 2014.

This fed justifiable Chinese anxiety that al-Qaeda-type terrorist groups were active inside the province. Uyghur militants are known to have been at Islamist training camps in Pakistan.[12] Moreover, China is convinced separatist groups have had tacit US support aimed at destabilising China's western borders.[13] The US has undeniably fanned the problem. For example, it has supported the exiled Uyghur separatist Rabiya Kadeer, president of the World Uyghur Congress, which is accused of organising riots in Xinjiang in 2009 and is allegedly linked to the East Turkestan Islamic Movement, which has been branded a terrorist organisation by the UN.[14] Whatever the truth of these allegations, the US endorsement of Kadeer's case has implied encouragement of Uyghur separatism.

China's response has been a mixture of speeding up development in the region, addressing ethnic inequalities and stepping up security.[15] From around 2010 increased investment in transport infrastructure, oil and gas extraction and manufacturing in particular, delivered growth rates sharply ahead of the national average, hitting 12 per cent in 2011 and 2012, and staying at 8.5 per cent in 2015, when national growth fell to 6.5 per cent.[16] Xinjiang has been integrated into China's economic initiatives with the Central Asian republics, particularly the 'One Belt' mega-development project for the region discussed below.

But these steps have contained rather than eliminated the problems and the security situation in the region has remained on alert. This outlook in Xinjiang has made security beyond China's western borders even more sensitive. Keeping both Islamic fundamentalism and US influence at a distance is crucial in maintaining internal stability.

Afghanistan and US bases

Central Asia moved up the agenda for both Russia and China after the US sent forces to Afghanistan in 2001. To support the intervention the US was granted access to Manas airbase in Kyrgyzstan and Karshi-Khanabad in southern Uzbekistan; an extensive NATO regional presence to secure supply chains and logistical support to the Afghanistan theatre followed. At a stroke, the US was a military presence on Russia's southern border and China's sensitive western flank.

Since the break-up of the USSR, American policy-makers had stressed the region's importance in securing their vision of US pre-eminence in the twenty-first century. Carter's national security advisor, Zbigniew Brzezinski, argued that Central Asia was the lynchpin of a Eurasian 'grand chessboard', which the US had to control to prevent the emergence of a rival superpower.[17] Kissinger called for it to become a pro-Western 'buffer zone'.[18] But until the intervention in Afghanistan the US made limited progress beyond discussions about possible gas and oil pipelines through Georgia and Turkey aimed at breaking the Russian monopoly over the region's reserves. From 2001 the US was suddenly in Central Asia with a vengeance.[19]

Although Russia had agreed to the use of the bases against the Taliban, both Russia and China were deeply wary of this influx of NATO and US troops so close to their borders. China viewed 'US bases in Central Asia as constituting a potential source of its strategic encirclement' and as 'an ideal breeding ground for US intelligence agencies and for the Pentagon to run covert destabilising operations into … Xinjiang'.[20]

From the outset Russia and China worked together to ensure this did not become a permanent US/NATO presence and that it should not outlast the US drawdown from Afghanistan.[21]

In February 2009, the Kyrgyz government announced that it would close the US airbase at Manas – a quid pro quo for a $1 billion plus Russian aid package. The Pentagon negotiated to stay for a few years, but eventually in October 2013 the US quietly announced it would be leaving the following year. This came on top of the US's 2005 eviction from the Karshi-Khanabad base in Uzbekistan over disputed rent payments and anger at US criticism of the response to anti-government protests earlier that year.[22]

The US tried to prolong its regional engagement by proposing to sell its Afghanistan-based equipment to Central Asian countries at cut prices, rather than bear the costs of transport home, which would have created an ongoing reliance on the US to repair and update the equipment. But Russia rapidly countered with its own offer of $1.2 billion in second-hand Russian equipment as long as the US proposal was rejected.[23] This was agreed. In 2014, the year the US left, Russia secured a long-term extension for its military bases in Kyrgyzstan and Tajikistan.

Thus 2014 saw the US not just scaling back from Afghanistan, but entirely pulling out of Central Asia militarily; leaving China and Russia's backyard once more free of US or NATO military presence. This was not the outcome that the US had hoped for. As the *New York Times* put it, the withdrawal from Kyrgyzstan marked 'the end of a brief experiment to extend American power and influence into the distant strategic arena of Central Asia'.[24]

But although the threat of US encroachment into Central Asia had been blocked, this had not dealt with the ongoing menaces to stability in the region. The aftermath of NATO intervention in Afghanistan left major questions over the effective authority of the Kabul regime and the extraterritorial impact of ongoing insurgency.

The Shanghai Cooperation Organisation

With NATO and the US gone, the Russian-led Collective Security Treaty Organisation (CSTO) – the mutual defence alliance established in 1992 to coordinate the military and security policy of the ex-Soviet republics – once again dominated the security relations in the region. Kazakhstan, Kyrgyzstan and Tajikistan are all members of the CSTO.[25] However, the SCO, involving China and Russia, is gradually surpassing this in importance.

The SCO originated in multilateral negotiations between Russia, China and the countries of Central Asia in the 1990s to resolve outstanding border issues after the dissolution of the USSR. An ongoing consultation grouping comprising China, Russia, Kazakhstan, Kyrgyzstan and Tajikistan – known as the 'Shanghai Five' – was formally reconstituted as the SCO when Uzbekistan joined in 2001. India, Pakistan, Afghanistan, Iran and Mongolia have been observers since 2005, with India and Pakistan agreed as full members in 2015. Only Turkmenistan is not a member or observer, due to its 1995 adoption of 'permanent neutrality' in international affairs, but it attends the main SCO meetings without a definite status.

The SCO as an organisation could not be more emblematic of the changing centre of gravity in world affairs. Together with its observer nations it represents over half of humanity, about 85 per cent of the Asia-Europe land mass and 30 per cent of the world economy.[26] Its scope tends to cast Europe as a mere subcontinental extrusion of western Asia.

Initially primarily concerned with counter-terrorism and border security the SCO's activities have broadened to include more extensive military cooperation.[27] There have been a number of SCO joint military exercises and large-scale war games since the first in 2003. In 2007 the SCO signed a wide ranging agreement with the CSTO, engaging China comprehensively in Russian military planning with the Central Asian republics.

A key security concern has been the situation in post-NATO Afghanistan. Although some 10,000 NATO troops looked set to remain in Afghanistan for the time being, the Kabul government has sought other regional support. This has partly been the spur to increasing engagement from China, Russia and India in Afghanistan individually and via the SCO. Russia has stepped up arms supplies and military training to the region, including to Afghanistan.

At the same time, volatility in and between some of the Central Asian republics also has the potential to flare up into destructive local conflicts rather than see off instability from the south. The increasing collaboration through the SCO is aimed at mitigating these risks. And China's 'Belt and Road' proposals for the mega-expansion of the connectivity between Central Asia and both east and west of the continent to end the region's semi-isolation and fast track its development also address these concerns.

Economic success

In the 1990s, Russia's western facing 'reformers' had been only too keen to shed what were generally seen as the embarrassing basket-case republics from the former USSR.[28] But after the disasters of shock therapy that saw them teeter on the brink of becoming failed states, in the twenty-first century they enjoyed robust growth, ironically stronger than that of Russia itself. Compared to Russia's average 4.07 per cent annual growth from 2000 to 2015, Uzbekistan, Kazakhstan, Tajikistan and Turkmenistan averaged 7–8.5 per cent annual growth; and even Kyrgyzstan clocked up a healthy 4.4 per cent.[29] All except Uzbekistan saw some slowing as a result of the fall in world commodity prices, with oil-dependent Kazakhstan suffering the most, falling to 1.2 per cent growth in 2015.[30] But there has been no catastrophe.

Before the collapse of the USSR, these states were largely agricultural and raw material suppliers to Russia: Turkmenistan and Kazakhstan have major hydrocarbon reserves; and Uzbekistan, Turkmenistan and Tajikistan produce agricultural exports, mainly cotton, fruits and grain. Since the 1990s all have diversified: Kazakhstan has used its hydrocarbon resource to launch other industries; Turkmenistan is pursuing a similar route with gas-related projects; Tajikistan is broadening its agricultural base; Kyrgyzstan has become an entrepôt for the region's trade with China; and Uzbekistan is developing as a communications hub.[31] Increasingly therefore these Central Asian republics have become not just important defensively but vied over for commerce, their stocks of oil, gas and other minerals and investment opportunities.

China's expanding network of gas and oil pipelines and multiple trade deals have underpinned its presence in the region. A 3000 km oil and gas pipeline from Kazakhstan to China was agreed in 2006, and in 2013 it was agreed to double its capacity.[32] In 2009 a 1840 km Turkmenistan–China pipeline was concluded. By 2012 Turkmenistan was providing over 50 per cent of China's natural gas imports. Additionally Iran already has a pipeline to Turkmenistan, which could be linked to the Turkmenistan–China pipeline, providing a land link for Iranian oil to China via Central Asia.

'One Belt, One Road'

The centrality of the region to both Chinese military and energy security was underlined by Xi Jinping's 2013 visits to Kazakhstan, Kyrgyzstan, Turkmenistan and Uzbekistan early in his presidency. The visits saw the announcement of a raft of new deals, including $30 billion of investment in energy, mining, infrastructure, science and education with Kazakhstan, 22 deals worth $15 billion with Uzbekistan and a $3 billion soft loan for infrastructure to Kyrgyzstan.[33]

But even more significant than these individual deals is China's vastly ambitious proposal for a 'Eurasian land bridge', an intercontinental corridor of continuous, modern, secure transport infrastructure linking eastern China through the Central Asian republics to Europe.[34] This is projected as one part of its 'One Belt, One Road' (OBOR) proposal, a comprehensive blueprint for the integrated development of the whole Asian continent linking it to Europe by land and sea. The whole proposal is breath-taking in its scope:

> The Silk Road economic belt focuses on bringing together China, Central Asia, Russia and Europe (the Baltic); linking China with the Persian Gulf and the Mediterranean Sea through Central Asia and West Asia; and connecting China with Southeast Asia, South Asia and the Indian Ocean. The 21st century Maritime Silk Road is designed to go from China's coast to Europe through the South China Sea and the Indian Ocean in one route, and from China's coast through the South China Sea to the South Pacific in the other.
>
> On land, the initiative will focus on jointly building a new Eurasian land bridge and developing China-Mongolia-Russia, China-Central Asia-West Asia and China-Indochina peninsula economic corridors … The China-Pakistan Economic Corridor and the Bangladesh-China-India-Myanmar Economic Corridor are closely related.[35]

Since 2013 Xi Jinping has made this a priority for China's economic foreign policy.[36] Engaging approximately 60 countries, it comes with a promise that China will eventually invest a cumulative $4 trillion. In 2015 this was kick-started with $82 billion identified by the Chinese state bank for OBOR projects, added to a $40 billion Silk Road sovereign fund established for the Xinjiang-Central Asian component, with further investment to come from the AIIB and New Development (BRICS) Bank among others.[37]

It is far more than a massive infrastructure investment programme. As the *Economist* put it:

> OBOR ... is a challenge to the United States and its traditional way of thinking about world trade. In that view, there are two main trading blocs, the trans-Atlantic one and the trans-Pacific one, with Europe in the first, Asia in the second and America the focal point of each ... But OBOR treats Asia and Europe as a single space, and China, not the United States, is its focal point.[38]

Central Asia will be the nexus of these east-west land routes. One of the first projects is to link China's domestic long distance rail network to a continuous route via Xinjiang through the Central Asian republics to freight hubs in Russia and Germany. Alongside economic benefits, China clearly hopes this will foster regional stability.

Against this formidable geo-economic strategy encompassing the whole of Asia, the US has been able to offer very little. It would like to see an alternative Indian-led axis into Central Asia, and in 2011 the US launched its own 'New Silk Road' initiative described by Hillary Clinton, then secretary of state, in a speech in Chennai, as 'an international web and network of economic and transit connections' from Central Asia via Afghanistan and Pakistan to India.[39] However, her explanation that this would mean trade between India and Central Asia could thereby avoid 'China or Iran' reinforced the perception that the US proposal was driven more by geopolitics than economics. Given it was anyway thin on concrete initiatives, without any dedicated finance or investment deals, unsurprisingly it gained little traction.

Poor relations with Pakistan, which lies geographically between them, have obstructed India's orientation to Central Asia. A project for a direct pipeline from the republics to India, the Turkmenistan–Afghanistan–Pakistan–India (TAPI) pipeline, was delayed for years and even after the first ground was broken on the project in December 2015 sceptics remained unconvinced that it will ever be completed.[40]

Nonetheless India remains interested both in stability in Afghanistan and in access to Central Asia's gas and oil. In this India has increasingly found collaboration with the SCO, that is Russia and China, more fruitful for its interests in Central Asia than working with the US.

The US pushed back from Central Asia

Overall the US has suffered a considerable setback in Central Asia. Despite, at immense cost, having fought two wars in Afghanistan – one by proxy in the 1980s and then from 2001 the US's longest ever war – the US was forced to retreat with no firm advantages on the ground. Afghanistan itself remained unstable and looks to become increasingly reliant on India and China for its ongoing security and on Russia for arms. The Central Asian republics were even more firmly locked into their primary relations with Russia and increasingly China. Rather than India emerging as a pro-US counterweight to the advance of the SCO, it has rather become more deeply engaged in it.

Fourteen years after the launch of Operation Enduring Freedom, intended to mark the beginning of a new era of US interventionist foreign policy and expansion of its global military operations to ensure a new 'American century', the US's regional influence and military clout instead saw full-scale retreat.

The cost of losing Central Asia

The coordination of Chinese and Russian and to a certain extent Indian policy goals in Central Asia has rendered the US virtually unnecessary in the region. Increased military cooperation, securing vulnerable borders for both China and Russia, has strengthened multilateral relations not just on military, but economic, trade and development issues. China has advanced its interests in Central Asia partly by staying out of the internal affairs of these volatile republics, steering clear of the partialities, criticisms and attempted interference that have contributed to the US's lack of welcome in the region.

But above all, Central Asia is the part of the world where the confrontation between China's win-win geo-economics and the US's old style geopolitics are playing themselves out with the starkest contrast.

Rather than just secure its vulnerable 'backdoor', China has proposed that Central Asia should be at the crossroads of a reimagined Eurasia connected by oil and gas pipelines, high speed trains and continuous carriageways, with stability underpinned by growth and fuelled by trade. China offers a vision of a world turned on its axis, placing not the 'middle kingdom' but the entire Asian continent at the centre of the next phase of human development. This is the challenge to which the US has no answer in Central Asia.

The US's retreat from Central Asia may come to be seen as the peripheral wound through which its claims to global leadership seeped away.

Notes

1 D. B. H. Denoon (ed.), *China, the United States and the future of Central Asia, US-China relations, Vol. 1*, New York University Press, New York, 2015, ch. 6.

2 M. Bearden, 'Afghanistan: graveyard of empires', *Foreign Affairs*, 80:6 (November–December 2001), 17–30.

3 V. Marantidou and R. A. Cossa, 'China and Russia's great game in Central Asia', *The National Interest*, 1 October 2014. Available at: http://nationalinterest.org/blog/the-buzz/china-russias-great-game-central-asia-11385 (date accessed 15 February 2017).

4 Denoon, *Future of Central Asia*.

5 Ibid., ch. 10.

6 Xinjiang Population Statistics, 2010 Statistical Yearbook cited in: 'Xinjiang', The China story, Australian Centre on China in the World, 2 August 2012. Available at: https://www.thechinastory.org/lexicon/xinjiang/ (date accessed 15 February 2017).

7 For background on Xinjiang, see S. F. Starr (ed.), *Xinjiang: China's Muslim borderland*, M. E. Sharpe Inc., New York, 2004 (for the USSR in Xinjiang, see chs 3 and 8 in particular).

8 See Chapter 5.

9 'Population in Xinjiang reaches 20.10m', *Xinhua*, 8 April 2006. Available at: http://news.xinhuanet.com/english/2006-04/07/content_4396564.htm (date accessed 15 February 2017).

10 Xinjiang Population Statistics, 2010 Statistical Yearbook.

11 R. Lee, 'Report: Unrest in Xinjiang, Uyghur province in China', *Al-Jazeera Centre for Studies*, 20 February 2014.

12 B. Blanchard, 'China official sees militant links in Pakistan', *Reuters*, 7 March 2013. Available at: http://www.reuters.com/article/us-china-xinjiang-pakistan-idUSTRE8260BZ20120307 (date accessed 15 February 2017).

13 M. FlorCruz, 'Beijing cracks down on Uyghur unrest in Xinjiang province, blames US for encouraging "terrorists"', *International Business Times*, 1 July 2013.

14 'Civilians and police officer killed in NW China violence', *Xinhua*, 5 July 2009 Available at: http://news.xinhuanet.com/english/2009-07/06/content_11658819.htm (date accessed 15 February 2017).

15 PRC state council information office, 'Ethnic equality, unity and development in Xinjiang', published in *China Daily*, 25 September 2015.

16 Xinjiang province, *Deutsche Bank Research*, July 2016. Available at: https://www.dbresearch.com/servlet/reweb2.ReWEB?document=PROD0000000000247542&rwnode=DBR_INTERNET_EN-PROD$RMLCHPM&rwobj=ReDisplay.Start.class&rwsite=DBR_INTERNET_en-PROD# (date accessed 15 February 2017).

17 Brzezinski, *The grand chessboard*.

18 J. Kucera, 'US checked in Central Asia', *New York Times*, 4 November 2013.

19 B. Rumer, 'The powers in Central Asia', *Survival*, 44:3 (2002), 57–68.

20 Y. Kim and F. Indeo, 'The new great game in Central Asia post 2014: The US "New Silk Road" strategy and Sino-Russian rivalry', *Communist and Post-Communist Studies*, 46: 2 (2013), 275–86.

21 S. Blank, 'US interests in Central Asia and their challenges', *Demokratizatsiya*, 15:3 (summer 2007), 315.

22 E. Rumer, 'The US interests and role in central Asia after K2', *The Washington Quarterly*, 29:3 (2006), 141–54.

23 F. Mashrab, 'Russian arms nudge Central Asia to edge', *Asian Times*, 8 January 2014.

24 Kucera, 'US checked in Central Asia'.

25 CSTO official site in English. Available at: http://www.odkb.gov.ru/start/index_aengl.htm (date accessed 14 February 2017).

26 Refers to China, India, Russia, Uzbekistan, Tajikistan, Kirghizstan, Kazakhstan, Mongolia, Pakistan, Iran and Afghanistan.

27 E. Albert, 'The Shanghai Cooperation Organisation', Council on Foreign Relations Backgrounder, 14 October 2015. Available at: http://www.cfr.org/china/shanghai-cooperation-organization/p10883 (date accessed 14 February 2017).

28 Denoon, *Future of Central Asia*, ch. 7.

29 Average GDP growth calculated from UNCTADStat for 2000–14 and IMF WEO for 2015: Uzbekistan 7.1 per cent, Kazakhstan 7.3 per cent, Tajikistan 7.3 per cent, Turkmenistan 8.5 per cent.

30 IMF WEO 2016.

31 Denoon, *Future of Central Asia*, Introduction.

32 B. Kurmanov, 'China goes west, to Kazakhstan's benefit', *East Asia Forum*, 27 September 2013. Available at: http://www.eastasiaforum.org/2013/09/27/china-goes-west-to-kazakhstans-benefit/ (date accessed 14 February 2017).

33 L. Horta, 'Central Asia's new silk road, paved by China', *East Asia Forum*, 26 October 2013. Available at: http://www.eastasiaforum.org/2013/10/26/central-asias-new-silk-road-paved-by-china/ (date accessed 14 February 2017).

34 S. Tiezzi, 'China's "New Silk Road" vision revealed', *The Diplomat*, 9 May 2014. Available at: http://thediplomat.com/2014/05/chinas-new-silk-road-vision-revealed/ (date accessed 14 February 2017).

35 Ministry of Foreign Affairs, and Ministry of Commerce of the PRC, with State Council authorisation, Vision and actions on jointly building Silk Road economic belt and 21st-century maritime Silk Road; National Development and Reform Commission, March 2015.

36 C. K. Johnson, *President Xi Jinping's "Belt and Road" initiative*, A report of the CSIS Freeman chair in China studies, Center for Strategic and International Studies, Washington, DC, 28 March 2016.

37 J. Anderlini, 'China expands plans for World Bank rival', *Financial Times*, 24 June 2014.

38 'Our bulldozers, our rules', *The Economist*, 2 July 2016.

39 Hillary Rodham Clinton, Secretary of State, 'Remarks on India and the United States: a vision for the 21st Century', Chennai, India, 20 July 2011.

40 M. Reyaz, 'TAPI pipeline: a new silk route or a pipe dream?', *Al Jazeera*, 16 December 2015. Available at: http://www.aljazeera.com/news/2015/12/tapi-pipeline-silk-route-pipe-dream-151215211343976.html (date accessed 14 February 2017).

16

Conclusion: the sword or the spirit?

Since 2010 the US has been engaged upon an ambitious project to shift the focus of its entire post-1945 foreign policy towards China and Asia. In proclaiming the launch of 'America's Pacific century', its aim was straightforward: to secure the future of American global leadership by preventing China emerging as the leading nation of Asia, in the way that its Atlantic alliances had halted the advancing influence of the USSR in Europe after the Second World War. But, as this book has shown, rather than a triumphant reassertion of its 'indispensible' position, the US's efforts have drawn attention to the gradual, continuing eclipse of the its 'leading' role in Asia as it failed to galvanise partners and allies behind a project to contain China. And instead it has been China that is increasingly drawing up the roadmap for the continent's own 'common destiny'.[1]

At the heart of this is China's extensive proposal to develop a continuous transport and trade network linking Asia over land and sea from east to west and on to Europe (One Belt, One Road). This is a vision of continental integration on a historic scale, even dwarfing that which drove the westward expansion of nineteenth-century North America – and without the element of conquest.

At the level of world leadership, in response to Obama's 'pivot' China proposed a recasting of the conduct of global relations to replace the outdated US blueprint for a post-1992 unipolar world with a 'new type of great power relations' based on equality and mutual benefit.[2] What that might mean began to be seen with the establishment of the AIIB and the 'BRICS' bank, which limit the ability of the US-led international financial institutions, particularly the IMF and World Bank, to impose one-size-fits-all neoliberal economic solutions on the rest of the world.

Then, in response to Donald Trump's excoriation of free trade and globalisation as having been somehow unfair to the US, it fell to Xi Jinping, making the first speech by a Chinese leader at the Davos forum, to argue for the advantages of open-door policies and global trade. *Newsweek* was not alone in pointing out that the world seemed turned upside down and that increasingly 'Trump's America seems more like the irresponsible and bystander state and China appears more like the guarantor and bulwark of global economic stability through a shared vision of increased economic cooperation and commitment to inclusive growth'.[3]

In sum, rather than 'a new American century', the coming decades are more likely to see the beginning of what is quite simply an 'Asian century' with China and India at its centre.

This book started by showing how China's current rise has been greeted with alarm by the entire US foreign policy establishment, which insists on the indispensable leading role of the US in maintaining and determining the parameters of a stable world order. As an influential CFR special report on China argued: 'preserving US primacy in the global system ought to remain the central objective of US grand strategy in the twenty-first century', because the security of the US and its allies depends on 'the US position at the apex of the global hierarchy, and the strength of the liberal international order, which is owed ultimately to the robustness of American relative power'.[4] On this the debate between the liberal and the neocon wings in US strategic circles, with some honourable exceptions, has been primarily whether a strong China can be persuaded to remain a subordinate partner within an American-led world – as are the UK, Japan or Germany – or whether it will have to be forced to.[5]

In other words, while the US is certainly opposed to China's communist system, fundamentally the US sets itself against any other state developing what the Chinese call 'comprehensive national power' to a level that means it can refuse to go along with the demands of the US, irrespective of ideological outlook, economic system or form of government.[6] This can be seen in the US's relentless offensive to weaken Russian power long after it had restored capitalism in the 1990s. As the US defence department set out at the end of the Cold War:

> Our first objective is to prevent the re-emergence of a new rival, either on the territory of the former Soviet Union, or elsewhere, that poses a threat on the order of that posed formerly by the Soviet Union. This is a dominant consideration ... and requires that we endeavour to prevent any hostile power from dominating a region whose resources would, under consolidated control, be sufficient to generate global power. These regions include Western Europe, East Asia, the territory of the former Soviet Union, and Southwest Asia.[7]

If China continues to grow at around 6.5 per cent a year and with US growth projected at only around 2–2.5 per cent a year, then it is only a relatively short time before its economy overtakes the US at market prices, as it has already in PPP terms.[8] And it will then go on pulling further ahead. Unless the US can prevent this – which means slowing China's growth as there are no measures it can realistically take to significantly accelerate its own that are also acceptable to the US establishment – the global power of the US economy will gradually wane and its capacity to impose its leadership will falter. The CFR report quoted above put the problem succinctly: 'China's rise thus far has already bred geopolitical, military, economic, and ideological challenges to US power, US allies, and the US-dominated international order. Its continued, even if uneven, success in the future would further undermine US national interests.'[9]

The US's fear is not that countries are going to do what China wants, but simply that they will no longer feel obliged to do what the US wants. The goal of the US defence and foreign policy establishment is to stop this. However, that is not so easy. As the CFR report laments, even 'a modest Chinese stumble would not eliminate the dangers presented to the United States in Asia and beyond' and only 'a fundamental collapse of the Chinese state would free Washington from the obligation of systematically balancing Beijing'.[10] We have seen what such 'a fundamental collapse' would look like in the economic catastrophe and political dismemberment that Russia experienced in the 1990s. However, even the most hyperbolic of neocon policy-makers do not believe that a 'fundamental collapse' of China can be easily achieved. They know that the Chinese economy is not about to fatally disintegrate – although we have seen how the school of commentators on China's 'imminent crash' is promoted as purveyor of wish fulfilment in the West.[11]

Nor is there any sign of the emergence of a 'Chinese Gorbachev' who would solve the problem by collapsing the CPC and subordinating China to the West – although the Western media spent a long time declaring one was about to emerge. This was the initial hope vested in Xi Jinping (as it was in Hu Jintao and Jiang Zemin before him).[12] Instead, Xi Jinping has reinforced the leading role of the Communist Party in China and made clear that 'socialism with Chinese characteristics', including the central role of the state, is non-negotiable.[13] Thus the *Financial Times*, noting a new upsurge in the popularity of Mao in China, said that it was Xi who 'has done possibly more than anyone to foster the current Maoist revival'.[14]

If a self-inflicted Chinese collapse is ruled out, the only way that the US can guarantee the preservation of its global primacy is to polarise the rest of the world against China, with the aim that it is slowed by trade and military pressures, squeezed by international and especially regional isolation, and eventually turned inward by domestic divisions created by these stresses.

The only parallel for such an attempt is the Cold War, which mobilised much of the world against the former USSR. The tactics against China evidently cannot be exactly the same, but the projected endgame is entirely similar: to isolate, delegitimise, surround, economically exclude and militarily pressure China until this provokes an internal crisis, forcing it into the camp of the US or face its own destruction.

An inverted balance of forces

However, in such a strategy against China the US confronts an inversion of the military and economic relation of forces it faced with the USSR 70 years ago.

When it embarked on the Cold War the US was at the height of its economic power, American companies from Ford to Coca-Cola had been the world's fastest growing, its commodities were the most desirable and its economy was the most dynamic. The Soviet economy on the other hand, having grown much faster than the US in the period to 1939 when the Western economies were grappling with the Great Depression, then suffered devastation in the war. After a new phase of faster growth than the US in the 1950s and 1960s, by the early 1970s the Soviet economy entered a period of stagnation, falling steadily behind. From 20 per cent the size of the US economy in 1944, its economy peaked at 44 per cent that of the US by 1970 ($1,352 billion to $3,082 billion) but had fallen back to 36 per cent of the US by 1989 ($2,037 billion to $5,704 billion).[15] It never came near challenging the economic weight of the US.

On the other hand, the USSR certainly did have the capacity to challenge the US militarily, keeping pace in developing long-range nuclear weapons, missile and space technology, stealthy nuclear submarines, fighter aircraft, tanks, a prodigal supply of

Kalashnikovs, as well as a large, well-trained and well-equipped army. At the onset of the Cold War in the 1950s both the US and the Red Army had been through the fire of the Second World War, with the latter having taken the full brunt of the Nazi eastern offensive. Both therefore had well-seasoned officers and troops. Nuclear war – indeed any direct confrontation – was avoided by the shared doctrine of Mutually Assured Destruction, a reflection of the nuclear military balance between the two.

It was the US's economic superiority, not its military threat, which eventually created the conditions for the defeat of the USSR. By the 1980s the USSR's economic problems meant it was impossibly squeezed by Reagan's new arms race. Rather than carry out a fundamental economic reform – as China had been doing for a decade – Gorbachev and then Yeltsin capitulated to the West, dissolved the Communist Party, accepted shock therapy and the break-up of the USSR.

Today, in setting out to contain China, this balance is inverted. The US may be by far the most militarily powerful state on the planet and China cannot match that, but the US is no longer the most dynamic major economy. And while military power can achieve some objectives, it cannot compensate for lack of economic power. The US still wears the giant's robe, but it hangs increasingly loose as its economic capacities shrink.

The US has far from given up on exercising global economic leadership, but its sluggish growth, budget squeezes, trade deficit and stagnant imports limit what it has to offer. In the post-1945 world the US economic powerhouse towered over the war devastated global economy; Marshall Aid contributed to the reinvigoration of Europe;[16] reconstruction in Japan was considerably driven by trade with the US; and the US and its markets constituted a powerful pole of attraction to every newly emerging economy. In contrast, after the 2008 financial crash the US had to look to China to power up the world economy.

Trump presented his own solution to these problems: on the one hand, to insist that US allies pay more towards the cost of the US global military role, and on the other, to try to reboot the US economy by ensuring that these same allies only have access to the US market on terms favourable to US business. The first explains his attacks on NATO countries for failing to meet their budget commitments and on Japan and South Korea for not meeting a greater share of the costs of the US military presence in the region. The second has meant tearing up multilateral trade deals and aiming to replace them with new bilateral deals where the US can negotiate 'America first' terms from a position of strength. As that adds up to a lose-lose equation for US allies, it will not prove very attractive, except for those who have little choice – a UK out of the EU for example?

Such policies may well force an increase in military spending in Europe, Japan and South Korea, but they will not win the US friends, will not crush China and will not solve the US balance of payments deficit, which rose to $463 billion in 2015 – and which will require those same allies to purchase US Treasury bonds to bail it out.

In contrast to this, when the US embarked on its cold confrontation with the USSR it was at the height of its power, the earthly representative of the interests of global capital, exercising a hegemony that is different from sheer domination: 'the capacity of dominant groups to present their rule as credibly serving not just their interests but those of subordinate groups as well.'[17] Today, as it gears its forces towards an attempted containment of China, the allure of the US is waning.

US policy-makers understand the decline of the US's 'asymmetric economic advantages over others' is a major problem. As the CFR put it: 'Nothing would better promote the United States' strategic future and grand strategy toward China than robust economic growth.'[18] But there is no of sign this. After 2008 the advanced economies of the West grew extremely slowly. Between 2007 and 2015 the US grew an average 1.3 per cent, while the EU hardly scraped above zero, registering 0.5 per cent average growth.[19] Short-term growth in the US was likely to improve from 2017, fortuitously coinciding with Trump first year in office – but not because of it – as pre-crisis trends in growth slowly resumed.[20] But this still means average US growth will remain below 3 per cent per year.

This inevitably means that in attempting an offensive against China the US faces a significantly worse relationship of forces than it did when it stood in opposition to the USSR. Rather than being able to offer a dynamic domestic economy *as well as* a military umbrella it has been increasingly reduced to trading on the latter alone.

The US's 'return to Asia'

The US under Obama made some progress in its reorientation to Asia, but its lopsided strengths determined the pattern of its advance. By 2013 60 per cent of US naval resources were stationed in the Pacific rather than the Atlantic for the first time since 1945 and the US had reinserted itself as an actor in key strategic issues in the region.

The US's most powerful Asian ally, Japan, stepped up to the plate, increasing its rhetoric against China both domestically and in international arenas. Japan has reoriented its military policy to focus on China; was prepared to drive through agreement to the TPP; and agreed to participate in the 'defence' of Taiwan. It has presented itself as an alternative regional economic and strategic partner, particularly where hostility to or suspicion of the US has inhibited smooth relations, as in India, the Mekong peninsula and parts of South East Asia.

Other key regional US allies have been supportive of an expanded US military presence, with the Philippines agreeing to host US forces in its bases, Australia leasing the US a new base in Darwin, and South Korea and Singapore welcoming an expanded US military presence, with South Korea also agreeing to the stationing of the THAAD missile defence system. The US opening to Myanmar initially seriously wrong-footed China, creating a US challenge in an area that China once considered safe. In India the US has replaced Russia as its main supplier of arms, while Japan has proposed itself as India's key Asian partner. The increased US collaboration with Vietnam was a significant breakthrough, although this has proved to have greater limits than the hyperbole of some commentators' speculations.

The US deepened its engagement with ASEAN. Following Clinton's Hanoi speech in 2010, the US appointed its first resident ambassador to ASEAN in Jakarta. From 2011 it began participating in the East Asia Summit, the ASEAN-led security, finance and education forum.

Above all, the US successfully used the agency of the Philippines under Aquino to internationalise the South China Sea disputes, thereby justifying its increased military presence and diplomatic engagement on the issues in the Sea, particularly striking a blow with the July 2016 UNCLOS ruling against China.

But although the US has made progress it is a long way from enough to achieve its aim of stalling China's rise. China has remained far from the international isolation that faced the USSR during the Cold War. While the former USSR was never without friends, including some major countries such as India, these were primarily among the relatively weak mainly former colonies of the Third World, for which Soviet aid and arms had often been crucial. The breakneck economic rise of China is proving attractive to a far wider range of countries than that. Rather developed neighbours such as South Korea or Taiwan are deeply economically engaged with China and do not want this derailed. South Korea for example 'wants a rock-solid US commitment with respect to the North Korean threat, but does not want to be explicitly asked to support US strategies vis-à-vis China. Thus, while polling has found that 94 per cent of South Koreans view the alliance with the United States as a necessity, only 54 per cent say they support the rebalance [pivot].'[21]

Chinese trade and investment are making – or keeping – friends of countries as diverse as Indonesia, Pakistan, Thailand and Cambodia. Even most of those that for a variety of reasons have been cooler towards China – Malaysia, Singapore, Vietnam, India, Australia – would rather face both ways. Thus Singapore tempers its enthusiasm for 'a long-term, implacable, inexorable presence' from the US with its preference that US-China relations are stable so that 'we don't have to choose sides'.[22] Myanmar, India and Vietnam have echoed this approach, as have all the US's treaty allies in the region apart from Japan and Philippines. And even in Japan, not all is smooth sailing. Opposition to the US base in Okinawa refuses to go away, with a plan to relocate it to a less heavily populated part of the island meeting intractable local opposition.[23]

Even America's European allies, notably Germany, France and Britain, were prepared to ignore US opinion on China when they signed up to the AIIB.

Finally, rather than a renewed Cold War 'triangulation' of relations between China, Russia and the US, it is America that has been in the cold as Russia and China moved closer together.

Stuck in old problems

Obama's administration was held back from putting more focus on a turn to Asia and China by its inability to extricate itself from its extensive commitments to the Middle East on the one hand, and because it became embroiled in new confrontations with Russia in Eastern Europe over Ukraine on the other.

Since the end of the Cold War, holding on to its position in the Middle East has involved the US in three wars in Iraq, an invasion of Afghanistan, the bombing of Libya, the 2013 coup in Egypt and the civil war in Syria. A toxic combination of despair, dispossession, dislocation and anger coupled with a sea of weaponry has fostered a swirling extension of chaos and bitter struggle across the Middle East. This has shattered Syria, Iraq and Yemen; swept up through Afghanistan to Pakistan; destabilised the Maghreb with chaos in Libya, terrorism in Tunisia and extremism rising in the Western Sahara; and violence and instability have also spread south into sub-Saharan Africa hitting Mali, northern Nigeria, Somalia, Sudan and affecting Kenya and beyond. As a result, despite pulling out of Iraq, planning to leave Afghanistan, taking a backseat role in the assault on

Libya and refusing to contemplate a 'boots on the ground' operation in Syria, the US has been constantly drawn back in.

Compared to the Middle East, scaling back in Europe looked less problematic until Ukraine exploded early in 2014. The US had steadily reduced its troops in Europe from the Cold War force of 350,000 to about 50,000 in 2015.[24] But in the wake of events in Ukraine there was pressure for larger and more combat-ready US deployments. In 2016 the US announced it would quadruple its military spending in Europe to $3.4 billion. At its 2016 summit NATO agreed to a 'rotational' stationing of 4500 troops, the core being from the US, in the Baltics and Poland, together with a permanent shift of tanks and other materiel to these locations.[25] Additionally NATO and the US have stepped up European military exercises, increased its naval presence in the Black Sea and the Baltic and further expanded missile defence – to which Russia promised an 'asymmetrical response'.[26]

A dynamic of militarisation and continuous tensions was unleashed in Eastern Europe that diverted the White House and the Pentagon from Asia.[27] It also pushed Putin even closer to China, with no sign of any decline in his popularity in Russia – rather the reverse.[28] The fact that the US was seen to have played a key role in pushing the situation in Ukraine to a crisis point – by blocking a compromise brokered by the EU and forcing the issue of NATO expansion – added to mounting concern among its Asian allies that it was not really serious about a fundamental shift from its old Atlanticist priorities and perspective.[29]

Carrying out an effective turn to Asia and China does not just require a shift in military priorities but the devotion of forensic diplomatic and political attention; the constant application of the top resources of the Pentagon and the White House to seek ways through the conflicting interests, histories and interrelationships of the diverse countries involved to tie them into a new relationship with the US. This was the kind of complex tactical and strategic operation that the US excelled at in the Cold War itself. Its biggest coup was in playing China off against the USSR, but it also had many other successes, covertly bringing pro-American regimes to power and isolating the USSR in public opinion.

To carry out an operation on such a scale against China the US has to do more than shift warships to the Pacific. It has to shore up its allies, court new friends and get close to developments on the ground in order to see the moments it can swing events in its favour. Its allies and friends have to be entirely convinced that if they join with the US and risk relations with China deteriorating that they will not be left high and dry. Obama's inability to disengage from the Middle East and new conflicts like the Ukraine did not give the greatest confidence to those it needs to court that the US was fully committed to the Asian theatre. Trump's withdrawal from the TPP was a further huge blow to US strategic credibility in the Pacific.

This has led US foreign policy strategists to despair, warning that US responses to chaos in Syria, Iraq, and Ukraine had 'elicited concern that Washington might either "pivot" away from Asia, or somehow be shown to lack the underlying willpower or resources to manage new security challenges in the Asia–Pacific region'.[30] Or as Fukuyama argued: 'ISIS risks distracting US from more menacing foes' and while 'Russia's power is based … on a flawed economic model that in time will weaken its power. Not so with China: it already has the world's second-largest economy, and may overtake the US in the coming years.'[31]

Trump's proposal for a new US deal with Russia was partly motivated by addressing such concerns: to construct a US–Russia axis which would allow the US to pull out of the Middle East, draw down from Eastern Europe and concentrate its fire on China. But this immediately met massive US establishment opposition. While there are serious forces in the US that favour such a reset with Russia, chiefly in order to better deal with China, they have long been outside the main centres of power in US foreign policy. Even if Trump succeeded in bringing such opinion more centrally into his administration – and losing his security advisor and leading pro-Russian, Michael Flynn, within weeks of taking office was not a good omen – the self-styled great 'deal-maker' would still find it difficult to broker a stable settlement. A lasting deal would have to deliver some concessions that made it worthwhile for Russia; lifting sanctions would be a minimum, but Russia would also have to be offered something meaningful on Ukraine. The sticking point here would almost certainly be the Crimea; Trump reaffirmed that the US position is that Crimea has to be returned, while Russia has made it clear that is not on the table. Moreover, unless Trump was prepared to ignore profound objections from the US's Middle East allies, any deal would have to be acceptable to the Gulf States and Israel; and that appears impossible to achieve unless Russia were prepared to totally abandon Syria and Iran.

How this triangular relationship between the US, Russia and China plays out will be the single most decisive factor in shaping international relations and global politics in the coming years. If a US administration succeeded in reconfiguring the relations between the US and Russia to the detriment of China, then the shape of the world in the next two decades would look entirely different. A new Cold War would become an immediate reality and the threats against China would escalate rapidly. As it is, the US faces a strengthening Sino-Russian de facto alliance that ties US hands in East Asia and allows space for China to continue to develop.

A faltering US turn to China

During the Vietnam War Che Guevara famously said that true solidarity lay in creating 'two, three or many Vietnams' to force the US to divert resources from Vietnam to other challenges.[32] Fifty years later, it is not the deliberate plans of anti-imperialists like Che, but the increasing incapacity of the US and its allies to maintain order in the capitalist world that has led to the US's inability to concentrate its resources on its China problem.

Concretely, Obama's 2010 announcement of the 'pivot' to China was followed by the 2011 Arab Spring and war in Libya; in 2012 stepped up pressure on China by Japan and the Philippines received less US attention than the crisis in Syria, the temporary advance of the Muslim Brotherhood in Egypt and attempts to isolate Iran; in 2013 Obama cancelled his trip to the ASEAN summit because of the 'fiscal cliff'; and his visit in 2014 was overshadowed by a new conflict in Ukraine.

Ankit Panda, writing in *The Diplomat* tried to give these problems a positive spin. 'US sluggishness and lethargy towards the pivot has had some benefits … the United States may have found a way to remain influential in Asia without allowing its friends and allies in the region to slump into the moral hazard of relying on the United States for the ultimate guarantee of maintaining the status quo in the Asia-Pacific.'[33]

But precisely the point was to convince the US's friends and allies that the US can, indeed must, be relied on to maintain the status quo in the region; that the 'United States is and remains the one indispensable nation'.[34]

'If you come or do not come, we will be here.'

It may be the case that the US's sluggishness toward Asia encouraged an independent military build-up in the region, but it also reinforced the view that it might well be unwise to burn bridges to China. The inescapable fact for the US, and the reality for the other countries of the region, is that while America may get distracted elsewhere or just get domestically bogged down, China stays exactly where it is, not nearly 10,000 km away on the other side of the world's largest ocean. To put this in perspective, the distance from San Francisco to Shanghai is nearly three times the distance from New York to Europe; the Atlantic really is a 'pond' compared to the scale of the Pacific.[35]

This is a reality that must be weighed by the US's friends and allies in Asia. While the US's long-distance friendship could in the end prove ephemeral, China will always be at the heart of Asia. As one Chinese spokesperson put it, responding to a cancelled Obama trip: 'If you come or do not come, we will be here.'[36] Less than a century ago the Portuguese, Dutch, British and French were all too present in East Asia, but where are they today? Countries of the region must consider the possibility that America's global long-range operations may also eventually contract – indeed may be doing so already – and that the future belongs to Asia itself. In that scenario what is the point of whipping up conflict with China?

In an attempt to reassure allies and friends of the US's commitment to the region under Obama there were constant high-level visits, and Trump repeatedly stressed his hardline China credentials on the election stump.[37] But as Asia security specialist Rory Medcalf pointed out, 'it will take more than another speech to manage the quiet misgivings in Asia about America's willingness to take risks in support of partners or even allies'.[38] As a result 'its friends and allies in the region' have certainly not slumped into the 'moral hazard' of relying on the US and have rather sought to build their own independent relations with their regional neighbours including particularly China.

As we have seen, in the East China Sea, South Korea and Taiwan rather determinedly stayed out of Japan's attempts to paint China an aggressor, and even implied some sympathy with China over the Diaoyu/Senkaku Islands.

To the south, the other ASEAN countries refused to get drawn into the Philippines' attempts under Aquino to drive a line against China in the South China Sea. Indonesia in particular has ploughed an independent approach. Malaysia has been careful not to provoke confrontation. And despite a few crises, China's rocky relationship with Vietnam has not tipped over into outright confrontation.

On the Mekong peninsula, post-coup Thailand has been keen to reassure China of friendly relations. And in Myanmar, despite the victory of Aung San Suu Kyi's party in the 2015 elections, a regime that the US can rely on is still some way off.[39] Not only does the army continue to exercise considerable power, but a rise of extreme Buddhist nationalism has led to a virtual attempted genocide of the Rohingya Muslims; a civil war in the Kachin Christian border areas continues; and powerful ethnic rebel armies across the north of the country still refuse to treat with the government.[40]

Even Modi's India has proved keen to cultivate closer economic relations with China, refusing to go along with US pressure to chide or disparage it, instead insisting that: 'Today's era once again belongs to Asia. India and China are both growing rapidly together.'[41]

In sum, after six years of reprioritising China in US foreign policy, the only major Asian country the US can rely on is Japan. Even its previous cheerleader, the Philippines under Duterte, has virtually deserted the US ship. That is not a huge amount to show for the efforts of the world's 'indispensable nation' in its reassertion of Asian leadership.

US bombs vs China's banks?

The problems confronting the US in dealing with China in the end come down to a straightforward question: which will prove more effective, US allegations that China poses a military threat to other Asian countries or the potential economic advantage offered by closer relations with China?

The US indeed offers a powerful military alliance that can dominate the situation in Asia for a considerable period. As Obama put it in his final State of the Union address:

> The United States of America is the most powerful nation on Earth. Period. … We spend more on our military than the next eight nations combined. Our troops are the finest fighting force in the history of the world. No nation attacks us directly, or our allies, because they know that's the path to ruin. … when it comes to every important international issue, people of the world do not look to Beijing or Moscow to lead – they call us.[42]

Against this, China offers investment, trade and economic collaboration that can deliver win-win growth and stability for a similarly long-term perspective. While China strongly disavows any proposal to substitute itself for the US in claiming global leadership, and rejects the allegation it is attempting to achieve regional hegemony, it does propose a reconsideration of the 'international order and global governance', and is increasingly critical of the US's obsession with how it can remain the world's preponderant power.[43]

Thus China does indeed reject the US's claim to a unique sway over global institutions like the IMF or that the US should be the critical arbiter of whether regimes are deemed 'responsible stakeholders' or ripe for intervention – as do many other countries. But China's alternative to American leadership is not Chinese domination – it does not want to 'rule the world'.[44] Nor does this possibility exist objectively. The post-1945 predominant influence of the US was only possible due to the huge disparity between the scale of the US economy created during the war, which had grown at an unprecedented rate between 1939 and 1944, compared to those of its real or imagined rivals.[45] Against this, apart from the UK, all the other developed capitalist countries and the USSR had suffered huge destruction of their economies by the end of the war.[46] Emerging from the Second World War, by 1944–45 the US economy alone accounted for an unprecedented 35 per cent share of world GDP, while its nearest rivals in the West – the UK and Germany – had an estimated less than 8 per cent apiece, and the USSR less than 10 per cent.[47] China's rise is not set to place it in that kind of preponderant position.

In line with this China proposes a vision of Asia's future as an economically integrated continent whose growth can power a new era of human development, as North America and Europe did for the last 150 years. This perspective is not *against* any other country including the US. On the contrary it is premised on the idea that relations between states can be organised to their mutual benefit and that the way to secure peace and stability is precisely to build on such win-win relations. China proposes to look for the material shared interests between itself and its neighbours and build its diplomatic relations on such a base. It does not suggest that every problem can be solved immediately – imbalances of trade will exist, not all economies will be equally competitive all the time, intractable border disputes may just have to be managed rather than settled – but identifying and addressing fundamental interests make mutually beneficial agreements and relations possible and avoid conflict. China's own economic success means that it has a great deal to bring to such a table if others are prepared to sit at it.

While the US has not abandoned the economic terrain to China, the truth is that only in military competition with China does the US still have an unchallenged lead. According to the Forbes Global 2000 rankings in 2015 the top four largest companies in the world were four Chinese banks (whereas in 2008 the largest Chinese company had been PetroChina ranked at number 30). Increasingly therefore the choice confronting China's neighbours could be characterised as that between American bombs or Chinese banks.

The US may be able to send more warships to the region's oceans, but ports they visit increasingly rely on Chinese investment. While China sends its diplomats and government representatives throughout the region to discuss trade, investment deals and improving infrastructure, the US's equivalents have been discussing arms deals, military exercises and missile shields. It is because of the economic dynamism of Asia, and China in particular, that the facts of trade are increasingly fulfilling Karl Marx's anticipation that the Pacific Ocean would come to 'perform the same role as the Atlantic does now and the Mediterranean did in antiquity and the Middle Ages – the great sea-route for international traffic – and the Atlantic Ocean will decline to a mere inland lake such as the Mediterranean is today'.[48] US trade across the Pacific is now double that of its Atlantic trade.[49]

So far, despite raising the temperature in the South and East China Seas, warning of China's alleged ambitions in Asia, encouraging great power competition for Asian leadership by India and Russia, sounding the alarm at China's military and naval advances, and urging a common front to contain China, the US has signally failed to convince the nations of Asia that they face an imminent threat. It has led to elements of an arms race in Asia – not all directed against China – but the US has not proved able to set an Asian agenda where defensive concerns about the strengthening of China trump the attraction of collaboration with China for trade and investment. China's proposed vision of

Asia's future as 'a community of common destiny' is more appealing than the prospects of a continent increasingly wracked by conflict and bristling with weaponry.[50]

This struggle is far from over, but in the first few rounds it is China that has continued to advance, while the US has hit a range of problems. China had a diplomatic and strategic coup with the AIIB; Japan, the US's closest Asian ally, has become rather estranged from many of its regional neighbours especially South Korea; Russia is more closely oriented to China than before the 'pivot' began; the US has been pushed out of Central Asia; and China's relations with Modi's India have been carefully nurtured despite a history of conflict. Even the Philippines is deserting the US. The US has abandoned the TPP; failed to drive a decisive wedge between China and any of its major neighbours apart from Japan; and has not been able to inflect tensions between Vietnam and China into a more substantive advantage. There is an increasing risk for the US that if it cannot turn this around quite soon, it may all become too late.

Rather than reinforcing America's global power projection, the US turn to reassert itself in Asia has tended to chiefly underline its ongoing relative economic weakening and expose the growing challenges to its continued claim to global leadership. Moreover, however it fares against China, the challenges to its leading position are only beginning; while China is already on the verge of overtaking it, before the end of this century India undoubtedly will do too.

Napoleon Bonaparte reputedly said: 'There are only two forces in the world, the sword and the spirit. In the long run the sword will always be conquered by the spirit.' This is the lesson that the US looks set to learn in its struggle in Asia; in the end the sword cannot win against the desire of human beings to go forward and improve their lives if they can see a way to do so.

Notes

1   Xi, 'Towards a community of common destiny'.
2   See Chapters 1 and 3.
3   B. Momani, 'Xi Jinping's Davos speech showed the world has turned upside down', *Newsweek*, 18 January 2017.
4   Blackwill and Tellis, 'Revising US grand strategy'.
5   See Chapter 4.
6   'Comprehensive power' describes impact of a nation's combined economic, military and other strengths, including technological level, culture and image.
7   Excerpts from the Pentagon's Defence Planning Guidance 1994–99 quoted in: 'Prevent the emergence of a new rival', *New York Times*, 8 March 1992.
8   See Chapter 2.
9   Blackwill and Tellis, 'Revising US grand strategy', p. 5.
10 Ibid., p. 4.
11 See Chapter 2.
12 'Albright says Jiang is a reformer', *CNN*, 26 October 1997. Available at: http://edition.cnn.com/WORLD/9710/26/albright.china/ (date accessed 16 February 2017); B. Gwertzman, 'China's new leader could prove a political reformer, says Council's Asia studies director, Elizabeth Economy', Council on Foreign Relations, 15 November 2002. Available at: http://www.cfr.org/china/chinas-new-leader-could-prove-political-reformer-says-councils-asia-studies-director-elizabeth-economy/

p5206 (date accessed 16 February 2017); M. Schiavenza, 'Where is China's Gorbachev', *The Atlantic*, 14 August 2013.

13 L. Homby, 'Xi Jinping pledges return to Marxist roots for China's communists', *Financal Times*, 1 July 2016.

14 J. Anderlini, 'The return of Mao: a new threat to China's politics', *Financial Times*, 29 September 2016.

15 Maddison, *World economy*, Tables 2b and 3b. Values in 1990 Geary-Khamis dollars.

16 A. S. Milward, *The reconstruction of Western Europe, 1945–51*, University of California Press, Berkeley, 1984.

17 Arrighi, *Adam Smith*, p. 150.

18 Blackwill and Tellis, 'Revising US grand strategy', p. 23.

19 Calculated from UNCTADStat 2017, GDP growth rates.

20 J. Ross, 'Trump's consequences for the US economy explained in 3 charts', *Key Trends in Globalisation*, 26 January 2017. Available at: http://ablog.typepad.com/keytrendsinglobalisation/2017/01/trumps-effects-on-the-us-economy-explained-in-3-charts.html (date accessed 16 February 2017).

21 M. J. Green and Z. Cooper, 'Revitalising the balance: how to keep the US focus on Asia', *The Washington Quarterly*, 37:3 (fall 2014), 25–46.

22 L. Weymouth, 'We can't be the nanny: an interview with Singapore's prime minister, Lee Hsien Loong', *Slate*, 15 March 2013. Available at: http://www.slate.com/articles/news_and_politics/foreigners/2013/03/lee_hsien_loong_interview_singapore_s_prime_minister_must_navigate_the_challenges.html (date accessed 16 February 2017).

23 M. Fackler, 'In a city on Okinawa, Mayor's re-election deals a blow to marine base relocation plan', *New York Times*, 19 January 2014.

24 A. Tilghman, 'Spotlight back on US European Command', *Military Times*, 27 March 2014.

25 A. Rettman, 'US military plans for Europe prompt Russia warning', *Euobserver*, 7 July 2016.

26 P. Stewart and D. Mardiste, 'US to pre-position tanks, artillery in Baltics, Eastern Europe', *Reuters*, 23 June 2015. Available at: http://www.reuters.com/article/us-usa-europe-defense-idUSKBN0P315620150623 (date accessed 16 February 2017).

27 See Chapter 5.

28 D. Sharkov, 'Putin scores highest ever poll rating', *Newsweek*, 25 June 2015.

29 See Chapter 5.

30 Green and Cooper, *Revitalising the balance*.

31 F. Fukuyama, 'ISIS risks distracting US from more menacing foes', *Financial Times*, 25 June 2014.

32 Che Guevara, Message to the Tricontinental, Havana, 16 April 1967. Available at: https://www.marxists.org/archive/guevara/1967/04/16.htm (date accessed 18 February 2017).

33 A. Panda, 'The benefits of a sluggish pivot to Asia', *The Diplomat*, 11 June 2014. Available at: http://thediplomat.com/2014/06/the-benefits-of-a-sluggish-pivot-to-asia/ (date accessed 16 February 2017).

34 Remarks by the president, US Military Academy, 2014.

35 San Francisco to Shanghai 9873 km; New York to Lisbon 3367 km.

36 M. Spetalnick and M. Felsenthal, 'Obama reassures allies, but doubts over "pivot" to Asia persist', *Reuters*, 29 April 2014. Available at: http://www.reuters.com/article/us-obama-asia-idUSBREA3S03920140429 (date accessed 16 February 2017).

37 Z. Keck, 'US swears Asia pivot isn't dead', *The Diplomat*, 2 April 2014. Available at: http://thediplomat.com/2014/04/us-swears-asia-pivot-isnt-dead/ (date accessed 16 February 2017).

38 T. Shi and S. Chen, 'US promise of Asia focus faces questions as China rises', *Bloomberg*, 30 May 2014. Available at: https://www.bloomberg.com/news/articles/2014-05-29/pivot-pledge-seen-wearing-thin-on-hagel-trip-as-china-sway-rises (date accessed 16 February 2017).

39 H. Clinton, *Hard Choices*, Simon & Schuster, New York, 2014, ch. 6.

40 A. Gowen and D. Nakamura, 'US wanted Burma to model democratic change, but it's not turning out that way', *Washington Post*, 6 July 2014.

41   F. Zakaria, Interview with Narendra Modi, *CNN*, transcripts, aired 21 September 2014. Available at: http://transcripts.cnn.com/TRANSCRIPTS/1409/21/fzgps.01.html (date accessed 16 February 2017).

42   President Obama, State of the Union address, The White House, Office of the press secretary, 13 January 2016.

43   Fu, 'Under the same roof'.

44   M. Jacques, *When China rules the world*, Penguin, London, 2012.

45   Desai, *Geopolitical economy*, ch. 3.

46   Maddison, *World economy*.

47   Maddison, ibid., 1944 shares (1990 Geary-Khamis dollars).

48   K. Marx, *The revolutions of 1848*, Verso, London, 2010, p. 276, reviews from the *Neue Rheinische Zeitung* revue, January–February 1850.

49   US Census Bureau 2016. US, trade in goods by country. 2015 total US trade with Europe and Africa compared to with Asia and Australia/Oceania.

50   Xi, 'Towards a community of common destiny'.

Select bibliography

Note: Only articles, papers and speeches central to the argument of the book or referred to several times are listed here; others are referenced in the notes to each chapter.

This book relied on articles from many sources, particularly: *The Atlantic, Atlantic Sentinel, BBC News,* Bloomberg, Brookings Institute, *China Daily, China.org.cn,* Centre for Policy Research, Council on Foreign Relations, *The Diplomat, Economist, Financial Times, Foreign Affairs, Foreign Policy,* The Heritage Foundation, *Huffington Post,* McKinsey Global Institute, *The Nation, The National Interest, New York Times, Reuters, Wall Street Journal, Washington Times, Xinhua News Agency* as well as a wide range of academic journals, the Congressional Research Service and archival sources.

Economic material was drawn primarily from:

UNCTADStat economic trends, (http://unctadstat.unctad.org/wds/ReportFolders/reportFolders.aspx ?sCS_ChosenLang=en), UNCTADStat world investment reports (http://unctad.org/en/Pages/DIAE/ World%20Investment%20Report/World_Investment_Report.aspx), and UNCTADStat bilateral FDI statistics (http://unctad.org/en/Pages/DIAE/FDI%20Statistics/FDI-Statistics-Bilateral.aspx); IMF world economic outlook (http://www.imf.org/external/pubs/ft/weo/2016/01/weodata/index.aspx); the World Bank world development indicators databank (http://databank.worldbank.org/data/reports.aspx?- source=world-development-indicators); Maddison, 2006, *The world economy,* vol. 2, Historical statistics; CIA World Factbook country information (https://www.cia.gov/library/publications/the-world-factbook/); Trading Economics (http://www.tradingeconomics.com/); US Census Bureau (https://www.census.gov/ foreign-trade/data/index.html); Japan External Trade Organisation (https://www.jetro.go.jp/en/reports/ statistics); And a variety of national economic, trade and investment data sources as per relevant notes.

Abe, S., *Towards a beautiful country: my vision for Japan,* Vertical, New York, 2007

Anderson, P., 'Imperium and Consilium', *New Left Review,* 83 (September–October 2013), 5–167

Angell, N., *The great illusion,* William Heinemann, London, 1909

Armstrong, C. K., *The North Korean revolution, 1945–50,* Cornell University Press, Ithaca, NY, 2003

Armstrong, C. K., *The tyranny of the weak: North Korea and the world, 1950–1992,* Cornell University Press, Ithaca, NY, and London, 2013

Armstrong, S., 'Sino-Japanese economic embrace is warm enough to thaw the politics', *East Asia Forum,* 27 September 2015. Available at: http://www.eastasiaforum.org/2015/09/27/sino-japanese -economic-embrace-is-warm-enough-to-thaw-the-politics/

Arrighi, G., *Adam Smith in Beijing,* Verso, London, 2007

Ba, A. D., 'China and ASEAN: renavigating relations for a 21st-century Asia', *Asian Survey,* 43:4 (2003), 622–47

Bacevich, A. J., *American empire: the realities and consequences of US diplomacy*, Harvard University Press, Cambridge, MA, 2002

Bacevich, A. J., *The limits of power: the end of American exceptionalism*, Henry Holt & Co., New York, 2008

Bass, G. J., *The blood telegram: Nixon, Kissinger and a forgotten genocide*, C. Hurst & Co., London, 2014

Beal, T., *Crisis in Korea: America, China and the risk of war*, Pluto Press, London, 2014

Berger, T. U., *Abe's perilous patriotism: why Japan's new nationalism still creates problems for the region and the US-Japanese alliance*, Centre for Strategic and International Studies, Washington, DC, 2014

Bernkopf Tucker, N. and Glaser, B., 'Should the US abandon Taiwan?', *The Washington Quarterly*, 34:4 (2011), 23–37

Blackwill, R. D. and Tellis, A. J., *Revising US grand strategy towards China*, Council on Foreign Relations, New York City, Special report no. 72, March 2015

Blustein, P., *The chastening: the crisis that rocked the global financial system and humbled the IMF*, Public Affairs, New York, 2003

Bowring, G., 'How will China's regional development bank work?', *Financial Times*, 7 May 2014

Brazinsky, G., *Nation building in South Korea: Koreans, Americans and the making of a democracy*, University of North Carolina Press, Chapel Hill, NC, 2007

Brenner, R., *The economics of global turbulence: the advanced capitalist economies from long boom to long downturn, 1945–2005*, Verso, London, 2006

Brewster, D., *India as an Asia Pacific power*, Routledge, Abingdon, 2012

Breznitz, D. and Murphree, M., *Run of the Red Queen: government, innovation, globalisation, and economic growth in China*, Yale University Press, New Haven, CT, 2011

Brown, J. D. J., 'Ukraine and the Russia-China axis', *The Diplomat*, 2 April 2015. Available at http://thedip lomat.com/2015/04/ukraine-and-the-russia-china-axis/

Brzezinski, Z., *The grand chessboard: American primacy and its geostrategic imperatives*, Basic Books, New York, 1997

Burchett, W., *The China, Cambodia, Vietnam triangle*, Vanguard Books, Chicago, 1981

Bush, R. C., *Uncharted Strait: the future of China-Taiwan relations*, The Brookings Institution, Washington, DC, 2013

Bush, R. C., *Taiwan's January 2016 elections and their implications for relations with China and the United States*, Asia Working Group, Paper 1, Brookings Institution Press, Washington, DC, 2015

Buszynski, L., *Negotiating with North Korea: the six-party talks and the nuclear issue*, Routledge, Abingdon and New York, 2013

Callahan, M., *Making enemies: war and state building in Burma*, Cornell University Press, Ithaca, NY, and London, 2003

Callahan, M., 'Myanmar's perpetual junta', *New Left Review*, 60 (November–December 2009), 26–63

Chang, G. C., *The coming collapse of China*, Random House, New York, 2001

Chao, C. M. and Dickson, B., *Remaking the Chinese state: strategies, society, and security*, Routledge, London, 2003

Chari, C. ed., *War, peace and hegemony in a globalised world*, Routledge, Abingdon, 2008

Chen, J., 'China's involvement in the Vietnam War, 1964–69', *The China Quarterly*, 142 (June 1995), 356–87

Chen, J., *Mao's China and the Cold War*, University of North Carolina, Chapel Hill, NC, 2001

Cheng, D. and Cohen, A., *How Washington should manage US-Russia-China relations*, The Heritage Foundation, Washington, DC, 2013

Chiriyankandath, J., 'Realigning India: Indian foreign policy after the Cold War', *The Round Table*, 93:374 (2004), 199–211

Chomsky, N., *Towards a new Cold War*, Pantheon, New York 1982

Chomsky, N., *Hegemony or survival: America's quest for global dominance*, Penguin, London, 2003

Clark, C., *The sleepwalkers: how Europe went to war in 1914*, Penguin, London, 2012

Clegg, J., *China's global strategy*, Pluto, London, 2009

Cliff, R., *China's military power: assessing current and future capabilities*, Cambridge University Press, New York, 2015

Clinton, H. R., Secretary of state's remarks at press availability, Hanoi, Vietnam, 23 July 2010, US Department of State

Clinton, H. R., 'America's Pacific century', *Foreign Policy*, 189 (October 2011), 56–63

Clinton, H. R., *Hard choices*, Simon & Schuster, New York, 2014

Cohen, I. C., *America's response to China: a history of Sino-American relations*, 5th edition, Columbia University Press, New York, 2010

Cumings, B., *The Korean War: a history*, The Modern Library, New York, 2006

Davis, M., *Planet of slums*, Verso, London, 2010

De Burgh, H., *China friend or foe?*, Icon Books, Thriplow, 2006

De Haas, M., *Russia's foreign security policy in the 21st century: Putin, Medvedev and beyond*, Contemporary Security Studies, Routledge, Abingdon, 2010

Deng, R., *Deng Xiaoping and the Cultural Revolution*, Foreign Language Press, Beijing, 2002

Denoon, D. B. H. ed., *China, the United States and the future of Central Asia, US-China relations Vol 1*, New York University Press, New York, 2015

Desai, R., *Geopolitical economy: beyond hegemony, globalisation and empire*, Pluto, London, 2013

Destler, I. M., *American trade politics*, Institute for International Economics, Washington, DC, 1995

Dijk, R. van, Gray, W. G., Savranskaya, S., Suri, J. and Zhai, Q. (eds), *Encyclopedia of the Cold War, Vol 1*, Taylor and Francis, New York, 2008

Dumbaugh, K. B., 'Taiwan: recent developments and US policy choices', Congressional Research Service Issue Brief, IB98034, 24 January 2006

Dyer, G., 'The US v China: is this the new Cold War?', *Financial Times*, 20 February 2014

Easter, D., *Britain and the confrontation with Indonesia, 1960–66*, New York, I.B.Tauris, 2004

Emmott, B., *Rivals: how the power struggle between China, India and Japan will shape our next decade*, Penguin, London, 2009

Fenby, J., *Tiger head, snake tails: China today, how it got there and where it is heading*, Simon & Schuster, New York, 2012

Ferguson, N., *Colossus: The rise and fall of the American empire*, Penguin, London, 2009

Flath, D., *The Japanese economy*, 3rd edition, Oxford University Press, Oxford, 2014

Frank C. R. Jr., Kim, K. S. and Westphal, L. E., *Foreign trade regimes and economic development: South Korea*, National Bureau of Economic Research, Cambridge, MA, 1975

Friedberg, A. L., *A contest for supremacy. China, America and the struggle for mastery in Asia*, W.W. Norton & Co., New York, 2012

Friedman, J., *Shadow Cold War: the Sino-Soviet competition for the Third World*, University of North Carolina Press, Chapel Hill, NC, 2015

Fromkin, D., *Europe's last summer: who started the Great War in 1914?*, Vintage Books, New York, 2005

Fu, Y., 'Under the same roof: China's concept of international order', *New Perspectives Quarterly*, 33:1 (January 2016), 45–50

Fu, Y. and Wu, S. C., 'South China Sea: how we got to this stage', *The National Interest*, 9 May 2016. Available at: http://nationalinterest.org/feature/south-china-sea-how-we-got-stage-16118

Gewirtz, P., *The limits of law in the South China Sea*, East Asia policy paper 8, Brookings Institution Press, Washington, DC, May 2016

Glaser, B. and Mark, A., 'Taiwan's defence spending: the security consequences of choosing butter over guns', *Asia Maritime Transparency Initiative*, Centre for Strategic and International Studies, Washington, DC, 18 March 2015. Available at: https://amti.csis.org/taiwans-defense-spending-the-security-consequences-of-choosing-butter-over-guns/

Goh, E., *The struggle for order: hegemony, hierarchy, and transition in post-Cold War East Asia*, Oxford University Press, Oxford, 2013

Goldgeier, J. M., *Not whether but when: the US decision to enlarge NATO*, Brookings Institution Press, Washington, DC, 2010

Goldstein, M. C., *A history of modern Tibet, volume 3: The storm clouds descend, 1955–57*, University of California Press, Berkeley, 2014

Green, M. J. and Cooper, Z., 'Revitalising the balance: how to keep the US focus on Asia', *The Washington Quarterly*, 37:3 (fall 2014), 25–46

Grunfeld, A. T., *The making of modern Tibet*, Zed Press, London, 1987

Hammes, T. X., 'Offshore control is the answer', *Proceedings*, 138:12 (2012), 22–6

Hayton, B., *Vietnam: rising dragon*, Yale University Press, New Haven, CT, 2011

Hayton, B., *The South China Sea: the struggle for power in Asia*, Yale University Press, New Haven, CT, 2014

Heo, U. and Roehrig T., *South Korea since 1980*, Cambridge University Press, New York, 2010

Holslag, J., *China's coming war with Asia*, Polity Press, Cambridge, 2015

Holst, H., 'Blue means blue: China's naval ambitions', *The Diplomat*, 7 January 2014. Available at: http://thediplomat.com/2014/01/blue-means-blue-chinas-naval-ambitions/

Horsburgh, N., *China and global nuclear order: from estrangement to active engagement*, Oxford University Press, Oxford, 2015

Hsu, R. C., *Economic theories in China 1979–1988*, Cambridge University Press, Cambridge, 1991

Hung, H. F., 'America's head servant', *New Left Review*, 60 (November–December 2009), 5–25

Huntington, S. P., *The clash of civilisations and the remaking of world order*, Simon & Schuster, New York, 1997

Hutton, W., *The writing on the wall: China and the West in the 21st century*, Hachette Digital, London, 2007

Jacques, M., *When China rules the world*, Penguin, London, 2012

Jager, S. M., *Brothers at war: the unending conflict in Korea*, W.W. Norton & Co., New York, 2013

Jalal, A., *The sole spokesman: Jinnah, the Muslim League and the demand for Pakistan*, Cambridge University Press, Cambridge, 1985

Jensen, R., Davidann, J. and Surgita, Y. eds., *Trans-Pacific relations: America, Europe, and Asia in the 20th century*, Praeger Publishers, Westport, CT, 2003

Johnson, C., *Blowback: the costs and consequences of American empire*, Time Warner, London, 2000

Jones, G., *Multinationals and global capitalism*, Oxford University Press, Oxford, 2005

Jones, M., *Conflict and confrontation in South East Asia 1961–65: Britain, the United States and the creation of Malaysia*, Cambridge University Press, Cambridge, 2002

Julien, F., trs Lloyd, J., *The propensity of things: towards a history of efficacy in China*, The MIT Press, Cambridge, MA, 1995

Kagan, R., *Dangerous nation: America's foreign policy from its earliest days to the dawn of the 20th century*, Vintage Books, New York, 2006

Kagan, R., *The return of history and the end of dreams*, Atlantic Books, London, 2008

Kagan, R., *The world America made*, Vintage Books, New York, 2013

Kagarlistky, B. (trs Clarke, R.), 'Ukraine: a country that might have been', *Links International Journal of Socialist Renewal*, 12 June 2014. Available at: http://links.org.au/node/3911

Kanet, R. E., *Russian foreign policy in the 21st century*, Palgrave Macmillan, Basingstoke, 2010

Kanimori, T, and Xhao, Z., *The Renminbi exchange rate revaluation: theory, practice and lessons from Japan*, Asian Development Bank Institute, Tokyo, 2006

Kaplan, R. D., 'How we would fight China', *The Atlantic*, 295:5 (June 2005), 49–64

Kaplan, R. D., *Asia's cauldron: the South China Sea and the end of a stable Pacific*, Random House, New York, 2014

Karnow, S., *In our image: America's empire in the Philippines*, Ballantine Books, New York, 1989

Katsiaficas, G. *Asia's unknown uprisings vol.2: people power in the Philippines, Burma, Tibet, China, Taiwan, Bangladesh, Nepal, Thailand and Indonesia, 1947–2009*, Thomson Shore, Dexter, MI, 2013

Keck, Z., 'Russia as a US-China battleground state', *The Diplomat*, 20 November 2013. Available at: http://thediplomat.com/2013/11/russia-as-a-u-s-china-battleground-state-3/

Kellogg, P., 'Contours of a multipolar century', *Rethinking Marxism*, 27:4 (2015), 558–70

Keohane, R. and Nye, J., *Power and interdependence: world politics in transition*, Little, Brown & Co., Boston, MA, 1989

Khoo, N., *Collateral damage: Sino-Soviet rivalry and the termination of the Sino-Vietnamese alliance*, Columbia University Press, New York, 2011

Kiernan, B., *The Pol Pot regime: race, power and genocide in Cambodia under the Khmer Rouge, 1975–79*, Yale University Press, New Haven, CT, 2002

Kissinger, H., *On China*, Penguin, New York, 2011

Kissinger, H., *World order*, Penguin, New York, 2014

Klare, M. T., *Beyond the 'Vietnam syndrome': US interventionism in the 1980s*, Institute for Policy Studies, Washington, DC, 1982

Koirala, K. R., 'Nepal and its neighbors', *The Diplomat*, May 2016. Available at: http://thediplomat.com/2016/04/nepal-and-its-neighbors/

Kolko, G., *Anatomy of a war: the United States, Vietnam and the modern historical experience*, The New Press, New York, 1985

Kolko, G., *Confronting the Third World: US foreign policy 1945–80*, Pantheon, New York, 1988

Kolko, G., *The politics of war: the world and United States foreign policy, 1943–45*, Pantheon, New York, 1990

Kolko, G., *Century of war: politics, conflicts and society since 1945*, The New Press, New York, 1994

Krepinevich, A. F., *Why AirSea Battle*, Centre for Strategic and Budgetary Assessments, Washington, DC, 19 February 2010

Kupchan, C. A., *No one's world: the West, the rising rest and the coming global turn*, Oxford University Press, New York, 2012

Lau, E., *Southeast Asia and the Cold War*, Routledge, Hoboken, NJ, 2012

Lawrance, A., *China's foreign relations since 1949*, Routledge, Abingdon, 1975 (reissued 2005)

Lee, R. B. and Patterson, W., *Korean-American relations 1866–1997*, State University of New York Press, Albany, 1999

Leffler, M. and Legro, J. eds, *To lead the world: American strategy after the Bush Doctrine*, Oxford University Press, New York, 2008

Lewis, J. and Xue, L. T., *China builds the bomb*, Stanford University Press, Stanford, 1991

Lin, J. Y. F., *Demystifying the Chinese economy*, Cambridge University Press, Cambridge, 2012

Lin, J. Y. F., 'From flying geese to leading dragons: new opportunities and strategies for structural transformation in developing countries', *Global Policy*, 3:4 (2012), 397–409

Lindemann, B. A., *Cross-Straits relations and international organisations*, Springer VS, Wiesbaden, 2012

Lipcsy, P., 'Japan's Asian Monetary Fund proposal', *Stanford Journal of East Asian Affairs*, 3:1 (spring 2003), 93–104

Lo, C. K., *China's policy towards territorial disputes: the case of the South China Sea islands*, Routledge, Oxford, 1989

Luthi, L. M., *The Sino-Soviet split: Cold War in the Communist world*, Princeton University Press, Princeton, NJ, 2008

McCarthy, Major C. J., 'Anti-Access/Area Denial: the evolution of modern warfare', *luce.nt*, US Naval War College Student Journal, 2010. Available at: https://www.usnwc.edu/Lucent/OpenPdf.aspx?id=95

McCormack, G., *Client state: Japan in the American embrace*, Verso, London, 2007

McCormack, G., 'The end of the Postwar? The Abe government, Okinawa, and Yonaguni Island', *The Asia-Pacific Journal*, 12:49 (2014), 1–20

MacKinnon, A., *Rising eagle, falling dragon*, Campaign for Nuclear Disarmament, London, 2013

McKinnon, R. I and Ohno, K., *Dollar and Yen, resolving economic conflict between the United States and Japan*, The MIT Press, Cambridge, MA, 1997

McMahon, R. J., *Colonialism and Cold War: the United States and the struggle for Indonesian independence, 1945–49*, Cornell University Press, Ithaca, NY, 1971

Madan, T., 'Indian Prime Minister Modi's foreign policy: the first 100 days', Brookings Institute, 29 August 2014. Available at: https://www.brookings.edu/opinions/indian-prime-minister-modis-foreign-policy/

Maddison, A., *The world economy, Vols 1 and 2*, OECD, Paris, 2006

Maddison, A., *Chinese economic performance in the long run*, OECD, Paris, 2007

Maddison, A., *The contours of the world economy, 1–2030 AD, essays in macro-economic history*, Oxford University Press, Oxford, 2007

Mahan, A. T., *The influence of sea power upon history, 1660–1783*, Little, Brown & Co., Boston, MA, 1890

Malraux, A., trs. Chevalier, H. M., *The human condition*, Vintage, London, 1933 (reissued 1990)

Mann, J., *The China fantasy. How our leaders explain away Chinese repression*, Viking Books, New York, 2007

Marsden, P., *Afghanistan: Aid, armies and empires*, I.B.Tauris, London, 2009

Marx, K., *The revolutions of 1848*, Verso, London, 2010

Maxwell, N., 'Sino-Indian border dispute reconsidered', *Economic and Political Weekly*, 34:15 (April 1999), 10–16

Mazza, M., 'Taiwan's crucial role in the US pivot to Asia', *American Enterprise Institute*, 9 July 2013. Available at: http://www.aei.org/publication/taiwans-crucial-role-in-the-us-pivot-to-asia/

Mearsheimer, J. J., *The tragedy of great power politics*, W.W. Norton & Co., New York, 2001

Mearsheimer, J. J., 'Why China's rise will not be peaceful', 17 September 2004. Available at: http://mearsheimer.uchicago.edu/pdfs/A0034b.pdf

Mearsheimer, J. J., 'China's unpeaceful rise', *Current History*, 105:690 (April 2006), 160–2

Menshikov, S., 'Russian capitalism today', *Monthly Review*, 51:3 (July-August 1999), 81–100

Milanovic, B., *The haves and the have-nots*, Basic Books, New York, 2011

Milward, A. S., *The reconstruction of Western Europe, 1945–51*, University of California Press, Berkeley, 1984

Ming, Z. and Williamson, P. J., *Dragons at your door: how Chinese cost innovation is disrupting global competition*, Harvard Business School Press, Boston, MA, 2007

Mitter, R., *China's war with Japan, 1937–1945: the struggle for survival*, Allen Lane, London, 2013

Mohan, C. R., *Crossing the Rubicon: The shaping of India's new foreign policy*, Viking (India), New Delhi, 2003

Mohan, C. R., 'India's new role in the Indian Ocean', *India Seminar*, 617 (January 2011). Available at: http://www.india-seminar.com/2011/617/617_c_raja_mohan.htm

Morgenthau, H. J., *Politics among nations: The struggle for power and peace*, McGraw-Hill, New York, 1948

Myoe, M. A, 'Myanmar's China policy since 2011: determinants and directions', *Journal of Current Southeast Asian Affairs*, 34:2 (2015), 21–54

Nathan, A. J. and Scobell, A., *China's search for security*, Columbia University Press, New York, 2012

Navarro, P., *The coming China wars: Where they will be fought, how they can be won*, Financial Times Press, Upper Saddle River, NJ, 2008

Navarro, P., *Crouching tiger: What China's militarism means for the world*, Prometheus Books, Amherst, NY, 2015

Nazemroaya, M. D., *The globalisation of NATO*, Clarity Press Inc., Atlanta, GA, 2012

Nolan, P., 'Imperial archipelagos', *New Left Review*, 80 (March–April 2013), 77–95

Nye, J. S., *Is the American century over?* Polity Press, Cambridge, 2015

Nye, J. S., 'Only China can contain China', *Huffington Post*, 12 March 2015. Available at: http://www.huffingtonpost.com/joseph-nye/china-contain-china_b_6845588.html

Ohno, T., *The Toyota production system: beyond large-scale production*, Productivity Press, New York, 1988

Oudenaren, J. van, *Détente in Europe: The Soviet Union and the West since 1953*, Duke University Press, Durham, NC, and London, 1991

Pant, H. V. and Joshi, Y, *The US pivot and Indian foreign policy: Asia's evolving balance of power*, Palgrave Macmillan, Basingstoke, 2016

Pantsov, A. V., *Mao: the real story*, Simon & Schuster, New York, 2012

Pantsov, A. V. and Levine, S. I., *Deng Xiaoping: a revolutionary life*, Oxford University Press, Oxford, 2015

Pettis, M., *Avoiding the fall: China's economic restructuring*, Carnegie Endowment for International Peace, Washington, DC, 2013

Pongsudhirak, T., 'An unaligned alliance: Thailand-US relations in the early 21st century', *Asian Politics & Policy*, 8:1 (January 2016), 63–74

Radchenko, S., *Two suns in the heavens: The Sino-Soviet struggle for supremacy, 1962–1967*, Woodrow Wilson Centre Press, Washington, DC and Stanford, CA, 2009

Rask, C. and Wong, C., 'Status quo revisited: the evolving ties between China and Myanmar', *Knowledge@Wharton*, 20 December 2013. Available at: http://knowledge.wharton.upenn.edu/article/status-quo-revisited-evolving-ties-china-myanmar/

Rogin, J., 'Did Obama bring down Hatoyama?', *Foreign Policy*, 2 June 2010. Available at: http://foreignpolicy.com/2010/06/02/did-obama-bring-down-hatoyama/

Rosenbluth, F. M. and Thies, M. F., *Japan transformed: political change and economic restructuring*, Princeton University Press, Princeton, NJ, 2010

Ross, J., *Yī pán dà qí? Zhōngguó xīn mìngyùn jiěxī* (The great game of Go: new perspectives on China's future), Jiangsu Phoenix, Beijing, 2016

Ross, J., *Key trends in globalisation, 2009–2016*. Available at: http://ablog.typepad.com/

Sachs, J. D., 'TPP is too flawed for a simple "yes" vote', *Boston Globe*, 8 November 2015

Sakwa, R., *Putin: Russia's choice*, 2nd edition, Routledge, Abingdon, 2008

Sargent, D. J., *A superpower transformed: the remaking of American foreign relations in the 1970s*, Oxford University Press, Oxford, 2015

Schaffer, T. C., *India and the United States in the 21st century: reinventing partnership*, The CSIS Press, Washington, DC, 2009

Schendal, W. van, *A history of Bangladesh*, Cambridge University Press, Cambridge, New Delhi and New York, 2009

Shepard, W., *Ghost cities of China*, Zed Press, London, 2015

Shin, G., *One alliance, two lenses: US-Korea relations in a new era*, Stanford University Press, 2010

Short, P., *Pol Pot: the history of a nightmare*, Hodder & Stoughton, London, 2005

Simon, W. S. and Goh, E. eds, *China, the United States, and South-East Asia: contending perspectives on politics, security, and economics*, Routledge, Abingdon, 2008

Skidmore, M. and Wilson, T. eds, *Dictatorship, disorder and decline in Myanmar*, Australian National University Press, Canberra, 2008

Smith, D., *The dragon and the elephant. China, India and the new world order*, Profile Books, London, 2008

Snow, E., *Red star over China: the rise of the Red Army*, Victor Gollancz, London, 1937

Starr, S. F. ed., *Xinjiang: China's Muslim borderland*, M.E. Sharpe Inc., New York, 2004

Steinberg, J. and O'Hanlon, M. E., *Strategic reassurance and resolve: US-China relations in the 21st century*, Princeton University Press, Princeton, NJ, 2014

Steinmo, S., *The evolution of modern states: Sweden, Japan and the United States*, Cambridge University Press, New York, 2010

Stiglitz, J., *Globalisation and its discontents*, Penguin, London, 2002

Stone, I. F., *The hidden history of the Korean War: America's first Vietnam*, Monthly Review Press, New York, 1952

Taggart Murphy, R., *The real price of Japanese money*, Weidenfeld & Nicolson, London, 1996

Thompson, J. A., *A sense of power: the roots of America's global role*, Cornell University Press, Ithaca, NY, 2015

Tol, J. van, Gunzinger, M., Krepinevich, A. F. and Thomas, J., *AirSea Battle: A point-of-departure operational concept*, Centre for Strategic and Budgetary Assessments, Washington, DC, 18 May 2010

Torri, M., 'The "Modi wave": Behind the results of the 2014 general elections in India', *The International Spectator*, 50:2 (June 2015), 56–74

Trenin, D., *From Greater Europe to Greater Asia: the Sino-Russian Entente*, Carnegie Moscow Centre, Moscow, 2015

Tyner, J. A., *Iraq, terror and the Philippines will to war*, Rowman & Littlefield, Lanham, MD, 2005

Valverde, K.-L. C., *Transnationalising Viet Nam: community, culture, and politics in the diaspora*, Temple University Press, Philadelphia, PA, 2012

Vogel, E. F. ed., *Living with China. US-China relations in the 21st century*, W.W. Norton & Co., New York, 1997

Vogel, E. F., *Deng Xiaoping and the transformation of China*, The Belknap Press of Harvard University Press, Cambridge, MA, 2011

Vu, M. K., *The dynamics of economic growth: policy insights from comparative analyses in Asia*, Edward Elgar, Cheltenham, 2013

Wallerstein, E., *The decline of American power*, The New Press, New York, 2003

Waltz, K., *Theory of international politics*, Waveland Press, Long Grove, IL, 2010 (reissued)

Wang, C. H., 'The Party and its success story', *New Left Review*, 91 (January–February 2015), 5–37

Wei, C. X. G., *China-Taiwan relations in a global context: Taiwan's foreign policy and relations*, Routledge, Abingdon, 2012

Wei, L., *China in the United Nations*, World Century Publishing, Hackensack, NJ, 2014

Weller Taylor, K., *The birth of Vietnam*, University of California Press, Oakland, 1983

White, H., *The China choice: why we should share power*, Oxford University Press, Oxford, 2013

Williams, A. W., *The tragedy of American diplomacy*, W.W. Norton & Sons, New York, 1959

Woodward, S. L., *Balkan tragedy: chaos and dissolution after the Cold War*, Brookings Institution, Washington, DC, 1995

World Bank, *China 2030: building a modern, harmonious, and creative society*, World Bank, Washington, DC, 2013

Xi Jinping, *On the governance of China*, Foreign Language Press, Beijing, 2014

Xi Jinping, 'Towards a community of common destiny and a new future for Asia', 28 March Speech at Boao Forum for Asia, 29 March 2015. Available at: http://news.xinhuanet.com/english/2015-03/29/c_134106145.htm

Yan Xuetong, 'China's new foreign policy: not conflict but convergence of interests', *New Perspectives Quarterly*, 31:2 (2014), 46–8

Yoshihara, T. and Holmes, J. R., *Red star over the Pacific: China's rise and challenge to US maritime strategy*, Naval Institute Press, Annapolis, MD, 2013

Young, M. B., *The Vietnam wars 1945–1990*, HarperCollins, New York, 1991

Young, W. K., *Transforming Korean politics: democracy, reform and culture*, Routledge, London and New York, 2015

Zhang, J. and Zhu, T., 'Re-estimating China's under-estimated consumption', *Social Science Research Network*, 7 September 2013. Available at: https://ssrn.com/abstract=2330698

Zheng, B. J., *China's peaceful rise, speeches of Zheng Bijian*, Brookings Institution Press, Washington, DC, 2005

Index